Impact of TRIPS in India

Impact of TRIPS in India

An Access to Medicines Perspective

Prabodh Malhotra

palgrave
macmillan

First published 2010 by
PALGRAVE MACMILLAN

Palgrave Macmillan in the UK is an imprint of Macmillan Publishers Limited, registered in England, company number 785998, of Houndmills, Basingstoke, Hampshire RG21 6XS.

Palgrave Macmillan in the US is a division of St Martin's Press LLC, 175 Fifth Avenue, New York, NY 10010.

Palgrave Macmillan is the global academic imprint of the above companies and has companies and representatives throughout the world.

Palgrave® and Macmillan® are registered trademarks in the United States, the United Kingdom, Europe and other countries.

ISBN-13: 978–0–230–27278–1 hardback

This book is printed on paper suitable for recycling and made from fully managed and sustained forest sources. Logging, pulping and manufacturing processes are expected to conform to the environmental regulations of the country of origin.

A catalogue record for this book is available from the British Library.

Library of Congress Cataloging-in-Publication Data
Malhotra, Prabodh, 1951–
Impact of TRIPS in India : an access to medicines perspective / Prabodh Malhotra.
p. ; cm.
Includes bibliographical references.
ISBN 978–0–230–27278–1 (hardback)
1. Pharmaceutical industry—India. 2. Pharmaceutical policy—India. 3. Health services accessibility—India. 4. Agreement on Trade-Related Aspects of Intellectual Property Rights (1994) I. Title.
[DNLM: 1. Agreement on Trade-Related Aspects of Intellectual Property Rights (1994) 2. Drug Industry—India. 3. Health Services Accessibility—India. 4. International Cooperation—India. 5. Patents as Topic—legislation & jurisprudence—India. QV 736]
HD9672.I52M35 2010
338.4′761510954—dc22 2010027535

10 9 8 7 6 5 4 3 2 1
19 18 17 16 15 14 13 12 11 10

Printed and bound in Great Britain by
CPI Antony Rowe, Chippenham and Eastbourne

Dedicated to my late parents
Krishna Vati and Sham Lal Malhotra

Contents

Part III Global Perspective

List of Tables

List of Figures

List of Boxes

Abbreviations

ABS	Australian Bureau of Statistics
AIDS	Acquired Immunodeficiency Syndrome
ANVISA	Agência Nacional de Vigilância Sanitária (National Health Surveillance Agency Brazil)
AYUSH	Ayurveda, Yoga & Naturopathy, Unani, Siddha, Homoeopathy
BCG	Boston Consulting Group
BDMA	Bulk Drug Manufacturers Association
CBO	Congressional Budget Office
CDRI	Central Drug Research Institute
CDSCO	Central Drugs Standard Control Organization
CMH	Commission on Macroeconomics and Health
CRAM	Contract Research & Manufacturing
CSIR	Council for Scientific and Industrial Research
DCGI	Drugs Controller General of India
DGCIS	Directorate General of Commercial Intelligence and Statistics
DPCO	Drug Price Control Order
EFPIA	European Federation of Pharmaceutical Industry and Associations
EGA	European Generic Medicines Association
EMEA	European Medicines Agency
EPL	Effective Patent Life
FDA	Food and Drug Administration
FICCI	Federation of Indian Chambers of Commerce and Industry
GATS	General Agreement on Trade in Services
GATT	General Agreement on Trade and Tariffs
GOI	Government of India
HIV	Human Immunodeficiency Virus
IBEF	India Brand Equity Foundation
ICRIER	Indian Council for Research and International Economic Relations
IDMA	Indian Drug Manufacturers Association

IFPMA	International Federation of Pharmaceutical Manufacturers Associations
IMF	International Monetary Fund
IP	Intellectual Property
IPO	Indian Patent Office
IPRs	Intellectual Property Rights
IRDA	Insurance Regulatory and Development Authority
ISM	Indian System of Medicines
MHRA	Medicines and Healthcare products Regulatory Agency
MNCs	Multinational Companies
NIH	National Institutes of Health
NLEM	National List of Essential Medicines
NGO	Non Government Organisation
NPPA	National Pharmaceutical Pricing Authority
OECD	Organisation for Economic Co-operation and Development
OPPI	Organisation of Pharmaceutical Producers of India
PBS	Pharmaceutical Benefits Scheme
Pharma	Pharmaceutical(s)
PhRMA	Pharmaceutical Research and Manufacturers of America
PPP	Public–Private Partnerships
RBI	Reserve Bank of India
TB	Tuberculosis
TGA	Therapeutic Goods Administration
TRIPS	Trade Related Aspects of Intellectual Property Rights
UNCTAD	United Nations Conference on Trade and Development
UNCTC	United Nations Centre on Transnational Corporations
UNDP	United Nations Development Programme
US	United States of America
USPTO	United States Patent and Trademark Office
WHO	World Health Organization
WIPO	World Intellectual Property Organization
WTO	World Trade Organization

Foreword

I read this book with great interest both as an academic and in the perspective of a policy practitioner in the emerging economy of India. As a senior policy adviser in Government of India at a time when Arthur Dunkell's draft was being intensely debated in the then GATT, and Indian society was deeply divided on the desirability of the TRIPS proposal, with one group of stakeholders railed against another and the politics of consumer interest in drug prices was pitted against the interests of a group of pharmaceuticals producers in India (and the multinationals present in the country), there was much confusion of perceptions in policy circles about the right course of action for India. Many of the issues concerning the industry as well as the perceived interests of consumers were not properly understood, with very little guidance available then from received academic wisdom.

The book provides a thorough historical perspective on intellectual property rights in the global context and outlines the environment in which the GATT operated and played its roles and transformed into the present WTO, the role of the TRIPS agreement in general and its relevance in respect of the pharmaceutical industry, patents, innovations, and their attendant aspects. It traces the development of India's pharmaceuticals industry with the government's political mandate for providing low-cost drugs and formulations as well as the overall development policy imperatives for a strong domestic industry, and benchmarks it for other developing countries also. It also provides a very good review of the experience of the present group of developed countries with respect to intellectual property regimes in a dynamic world and how they dealt with these issues in the pre-WTO regimes; and the list of cases examined include those of USA, Switzerland, Germany, Japan, and other SE Asian countries in the *Pax Britannica* world and beyond through the GATT years. This provides a very thorough background in which the entire analysis of this book is nuanced.

The book gives a very competent statement of India's intellectual property regime for the pharmaceuticals industry and how it has aided its development during the drug price control regime that started in the 1970s subsequent to the British legacy. But it makes the very important distinction between drug price control, TRIPS, and their consequences on the Indian pharmaceuticals industry on one hand, and access to medicines by the masses in the context of widespread poverty and lack of healthcare infrastructure, on the other. It considers various alternatives to the extant TRIPS regime of the WTO as suggested in the literature. It goes on to suggest a model of IndiaHealth programme that merits serious consideration by policy makers.

This book should have been written sooner, but the thorough research that has gone into it, perhaps it could not have been possible earlier. Now that it is available the book should be read by academic researchers, policy makers in Government, and inter-governmental agencies and the civil society at large for a good grounding on the subject.

Shovan Ray
Professor
Indira Gandhi Institute of Development Research
Mumbai, India
10 February 2010

Acknowledgements

Writing this book has been a long and difficult journey full of ups and downs. The word 'thanks' falls well short of the level of gratitude I would like to express to those who helped me get through the difficult times during this journey. The loss of my father in 2007 and my own subsequent serious health problems were but two major setbacks. At times I felt very low and wanted to just walk away. I am glad that some people had more faith in me than I did.

First and foremost, I would like to thank Professor Bhajan Grewal for his professional advice and intellectual support. I am also grateful to Professor Peter Sheehan for his unparalleled patience and encouragement throughout my academic journey. I would like to thank Dr Bruce Rasmussen and Dr Kim Sweeny for clarifying my frequent queries. I am indebted to Professor Sardar Naz Islam for his guidance with publishing this book. I would like to acknowledge the friendship and encouragement of my colleagues Dr Dexin Yang, Dr Sudath Arummapperuma, and Dr Tri Lam. I also feel indebted to Dr Hans Lofgren of Deakin University for sharing his research material with me.

This book has been completed with the direct and indirect help of many people. It would be impossible to thank every one of them. However, I would like to express my gratitude to my guru Pandit Chintaman Datar for regularly ringing me up at around 4.30 am and encourage me to continue. My sincere thanks to Dr Anand Kulkarni and his family, Jitendra Bhatia, Ravish Goyal, and Reinhard Schenk for their support. I would also like to thank Dr Prem Phakey for his comments on earlier drafts. My special thanks to Mrs Usha Phakey and Mrs Pande for their motherly role in my life.

I would like to express my sincere appreciation to Mr Ammu Menon of Coimbatore and Mr Rajesh Solanki of New Delhi and many friends around the world for their help with the data collection. Thank you everyone. I would also like to acknowledge Officials at the Directorate General of Commercial Intelligence and Statistics, Kolkata, for their help with the exports data. I am indebted to anonymous reviewers whose comments helped me improve the clarity of expressions in building the arguments. I am also grateful to the following organisations for giving permissions to reproduce Tables in this book:

- Department of Health and Ageing, Government of Australia;
- Publishers of Indian Journal of Medical Ethics; and
- Population Reference Bureau.

I would like to thank my late mother Krishna, who shares her name with the Lord, for her blessings from heaven. I would also like to express my gratitude to my late father, who unfortunately passed away before this book was published. I would like to dedicate this book to my beloved parents.

Writing this book was like climbing a mountain and I would not have been able to climb it without the support of my family. To my wife Gabriela (Neelam), I say thank you for putting bread and butter on the table every day. To our children Sikander (Mintu) and his wife Sam, Vidhi and her partner Adam, Shekhar and Danny, I would like to acknowledge their support for this book.

Finally, coming from a small village in India, I always dreamt but never expected to reach this level of academia and publish with Palgrave Macmillan. I didn't think I had the ability to complete this journey. I firmly believe God's mercy helped me at every step in reaching this destination. Thank You for guiding me in the right direction.

1
Introduction

1.1 Introduction and background

The controversies regarding the inclusion of intellectual property in the World Trade Organization (WTO) talks are well documented in the literature, in particular, on the agreement on Trade-Related Aspects of Intellectual Property Rights (TRIPS). A number of experts have studied the impact of implementing the TRIPS agreement in India (see for example Galpalli 2004; Lanjouw 1998; Scherer and Watal 2001). However, the impact of TRIPS in India is most comprehensively covered by Chaudhuri (2005). While the global media has drawn attention of governments, public health activists, and non government organisations (NGOs), a significant number of articles covering specific aspects of the impact have also been published in academic journals. Notwithstanding the great contributions made by the distinguished authors and experts in the field, none of the studies examines the issues in the post-TRIPS setting, as all the studies were undertaken pre-implementation and/or relied on pre-TRIPS data.

In the wake of the level of attention the TRIPS agreement has drawn internationally, it was considered rather important to undertake a post-implementation analysis and support or dispel the apprehensions associated with the agreement. While it would be too early to ascertain the full impact of the implementation, this book examines the impact using the most recent data and determines the changes in drug prices and market behaviour. In other words, this book attempts to understand and explain scientifically the most likely impact of TRIPS on access to medicines.

The term *access to medicines* is indeed a multi-dimensional term. According to Gray and Matsebula (2003), improving access to essential medicines requires improvement in four components of healthcare provision: namely, (1) ensuring rational selection (of drugs), (2) providing sustainable financing, (3) ensuring efficient systems for distribution, and (4) maintaining affordable drug prices. While the model developed in Chapter 8 considers all four areas noted in the Gray and Matsebula study, this book regards the absence of sustainable financing as the principal hindrance to access to medicines. This approach is consistent with the literature on affordability of drugs. For example, the World Bank (2002) points out that nearly 25 per cent of the poor people in India do not even seek healthcare because of the costs. Thus, the primary focus of this book remains on how to improve access to medicines by reducing costs of drugs to increase affordability. In Chapter 8, we also undertake sensitivity analysis of the proposed model to consider the long-term sustainability of financing such a programme from the public purse.

Since India's independence in 1947, its pharmaceutical industry has passed through several crucial phases of development. Until the early 1970s, India's patent regime provided patents for products as well as processes in pharmaceuticals. Multinational companies (MNCs) held all the patents on drugs and pharmaceuticals and dominated the Indian healthcare market. India's domestic pharmaceutical industry was almost non-existent and the local manufacturing of medicines was negligible. India was a net importer of drugs and pharmaceuticals, and the result was that drug prices in India were among the highest in the world. The vast majority of the Indian population lived below the poverty line, and access to medicines was limited to 15–20 per cent of the total population (Bhagat 1982).

In the 1970s, India introduced an array of protectionist measures including drug price controls and controls over foreign exchange. As a part of these measures, Patents Act 1970 was introduced abolishing pharmaceutical product patents but allowing process patents for seven years from the filing date. This change meant that every drug was virtually generic and hence could be legally copied for sale. The new landscape provided Indian firms opportunities to enhance their reverse engineering skills and develop new manufacturing processes. In other words, India followed a model allowing the manufacture of copies of drugs patented elsewhere. Over the next three decades, the domestic firms proliferated making India almost self-sufficient in medicines. The drug prices in India dropped to be one of the lowest in the world and access to medicines increased to around 35 per cent of the population. Even at these low prices, access to medicines remained beyond the reach of two-thirds of India's population.

During the period of protectionist framework, India also became a net exporter of pharmaceuticals. India's drugs were initially exported to developing countries and the former Eastern Bloc countries. India supplied the poor countries with low-cost imitations of patented drugs as well as off-patent generics. India's exports increased drug availability as well as reduced drug prices in the developing countries. More recently, highly regulated markets such as the US and European countries have also become the destination of India's exports of off-patent generics. Thus, Indian firms have played a major role in significant price reductions after patent expiry in the overseas markets.

In 1991, India began introducing policies of economic liberalisation and industrial reforms. As a part of this policy shift, India joined the WTO when it was established in 1994 and as such was obliged to sign the TRIPS agreement. While developed countries implemented the agreement virtually spontaneously, developing countries were given until 2000, and countries such as India, which previously did not provide product patents, were given until 2005 to implement a TRIPS compliant patent regime. Unless the WTO grants further extensions, the least developed countries (LDCs) have until 2016 to introduce the required changes.

The TRIPS agreement set out minimum standards for intellectual property protection across all member states. This standard is significantly higher than what the developing nations previously had. For example, TRIPS provides patents for 20 years. Before TRIPS, the protection in the US was 17 years and in the EU was 15 years. The extension of the protection term is more significant in the developing member states. For the developing countries, including India, which previously did not provide product patents, the new regime has effectively raised the protection term from 0 years to 20 years in these countries.

1.2 Key issues and key questions

With the implementation of the TRIPS agreement since 2005, India has re-introduced product patents in pharmaceuticals for 20 years. In simple terms, this change means that patented products can no longer be copied for sale in the domestic market or for exports. But holistically seen, the new regime has wider implications for the domestic pharmaceutical industry, its exports, drug prices, and access to medicines within and outside India.

The new industrial landscape severely restricts the competitive environment that existed in India over the last 30 years. This change also creates monopolies for patent holders which almost entirely are MNCs. Many questions arise in the wake of these changes: How would the change affect availability and prices of patented drugs introduced in India? With the sizeable domestic industry that India now has, is the market likely to return to the pre-1970 MNCs domination?

Indian pharmaceutical industry is now faced with unprecedented challenges within its own territory and outside. The industry is undergoing a transformational process and trying new business models. Is the overall number of domestic firms likely to shrink? Are the small local firms likely to survive in the long run? What role would they play in the future provision of India's healthcare? Business models of domestic firms could determine what drugs are manufactured in India, where these drugs are marketed, and at what price? All these factors play a vital role in providing access to medicines.

There are general apprehensions that drug prices in India and also in other developing countries will rise significantly due to the regime change. Any rise in drug prices is going to further restrict access to medicines. Patented medicines are likely to be priced significantly high when launched in India. Thus, only a small share of the population would have access to those medicines. How can the entire Indian population gain access to and benefit from the latest drugs?

Specifically, this book addresses the following seven questions:

1. How does the regime change impact on India's pharmaceutical exports, particularly exports of the low-cost imitations of patented drugs to the poor countries?
2. What is the effect of TRIPS on foreign direct investment (FDI) into the Indian pharmaceutical industry?
3. How is the business model of domestic firms changing after TRIPS?
4. What impact does the regime change have on the innovative activities within the Indian pharmaceutical industry?
5. How effective have the price controls in India been in providing access to medicines until now and what form of price controls is India likely to have in future?
6. How can India extend access to medicines to its entire population?
7. Is the TRIPS agreement fair to the developing countries?

The TRIPS compliant regime does not affect India's exports of off-patent drugs. However, it is necessary to analyse India's exports of low-cost imitations of patented drugs to poor countries, where drug prices and affordability are a major issue. This is because most of the health expenditure is generally met by the households' out-of-pocket spending and medicine costs constitute 60–70 per cent of the total health expenditure (WHO 2004b). With its low-cost exports, India has played a crucial role in expanding access to medicines in these countries. Thus, any constraints on India's ability to export low-cost imitation drugs would adversely affect access to medicines in the poor countries.

Are the innovative activities likely to increase due to the regime change? What role are the MNCs and the Indian contract-research firms likely to play in the development of new drugs in India? Is the surge in local innovation likely to help India discover and develop drugs to meet its own unmet needs? Large MNCs show little interest in developing new drugs for tropical diseases, because the potential for high returns is absent. Thus, if domestic firms could develop new drugs for tropical diseases, this would increase access to medicines in the poor world.

Is India's pharmaceutical sector likely to attract more FDI as a result of TRIPS compliant regime? How does the FDI in the pharmaceutical sector compare with other sectors within the Indian economy? A significant increase in FDI could substantially change the landscape of India's pharmaceutical industry. On the one hand, an increase in the number of players could intensify the market competition, lower the drug prices, and thereby improve the access to medicines. On the other hand, if the FDI is instead targeted at takeovers of domestic firms, it could shift the market dynamics in favour of MNCs and India could, in the long run, revert back to pre-1970 situation with rising drug prices, further restricting the access to medicines.

1.3 Organisation of the book

This book is divided into three parts. Part I comprising Chapters 2 and 3 examines the influence of global forces on the availability and affordability of new drugs at a broader level. Chapter 2 considers the negotiations transforming the GATT (General Agreement on Tariffs and Trade) into the WTO and the signing of the concluding agreements. In particular, it examines the role of TRIPS in the pharmaceutical industry. Chapter 3 examines global pharmaceutical industry and investigates its influence on the process and the costs of bringing new drugs to the market.

Part II consists of Chapters 4–8 and pertains to issues directly related to India. Chapter 4 traces the development of India's pharmaceutical industry and examines the underpinning factors. Chapter 5 considers

India's patent regime and its significance in the development of its pharmaceutical industry. Chapter 6 assesses India's regulatory environment with an emphasis on drug price controls and considers policy options for India. Chapter 7 discusses health insurance in India and its implications. Chapter 8 examines India's public health expenditure and develops an equity-driven model for providing healthcare, including access to medicines, to India's entire population. The model proposed for India is based on the Australian healthcare model and modified to incorporate India's particular demographic characteristics.

Part III in Chapters 9, 10, and 11 presents final discussions from the global perspective. Chapter 9 questions the appropriateness of TRIPS for the developing countries and examines the costs and benefits of implementing TRIPS. Chapter 10 considers alternative models for financing the development of and patenting new drugs. Chapter 11 summarises the main findings of the book.

Part I

Influence of Global Forces on Access to Medicines

2
The WTO and the TRIPS Agreement

2.1 Introduction

The Uruguay Round of Multilateral Trade Negotiations concluded in 1994 with the signing of around 60 agreements, annexes, decisions, and understandings including the umbrella agreement that established the World Trade Organization (WTO 2010). Besides establishing a framework for dispute settlement and trade policy reviews, the agreements covered the following major areas. The General Agreement on Tariffs and Trade (GATT) that existed since 1947 was brought under the WTO. The Agreement on Trade-Related Investment Measures (TRIMs) and the General Agreement on Trade in Services (GATS) were signed as a part of the deal to establish the WTO. The Agreement on Trade-Related Aspects of Intellectual Property Rights (TRIPS) became a foundation block for the WTO (Maskus 2000b). The TRIPS agreement sets minimum standards for intellectual property protection in all member countries. In recent years, regional and bilateral agreements on investment, free trade, and other disciplines have forced developing countries to raise protection standards for intellectual property beyond what is required under TRIPS. These higher protection standards, known in the literature as TRIPS-plus conditions, restrict access to medicines and jeopardise public health in developing countries (Malhotra and Grewal 2008). The Intergovernmental Working Group on Public Health, Innovation and Intellectual Property calls for ensuring that bilateral trade agreements do not incorporate TRIPS-plus provisions that reduce access to medicines (WHO 2006a).

With its mission to facilitate boundless global market environment for international trade, the WTO is one of the most important international economic institutions today. This multilateral body is charged with establishing and enforcing the legal framework for free flow of goods and services across nations. The WTO also provides a forum for negotiations for further liberalisation of trade, and for considering additional multilateral disciplines covering other trade-related aspects.

The WTO varies significantly from the GATT on a number of accounts. For example, the GATT dealt with trade only, whereas the WTO relates to services as well as trade. Second, a significant difference between the GATT and the WTO is that intellectual property was never a part of the former. Observers like Dunkley (2001) argue that:

> ...the TRIPS agreement was unnecessary as most of its functions have, for up to a century, been fulfilled by...conventions such as the Paris Convention...Rome Convention...and the UN-based World Intellectual Property Organization (WIPO).
>
> (Dunkley 2001, p. 69)

The WIPO is responsible for promoting intellectual property (IP) and administers 23 international treaties on IP matters. The WIPO has a membership of 180 countries. Yet it is perceived as a 'toothless tiger'. In particular, developed countries were 'dissatisfied with the implementation of the IPRs through the WIPO as it did not have an effective enforcement system' (Zutshi 1998, p. 41). In contrast, the WTO is significantly more powerful with an enforcement mechanism, a Dispute Settlement Body (DSB) and an Appellate Body.

Third, the WTO is an organisation while the GATT was a treaty and as such, the role of the WTO is much more extensive and rigid than the flexibilities the GATT provided. The GATT permitted the member countries to select disciplines based on national interests and opt out of unsuitable agreements. In contrast, the WTO is a wholly integrated package binding member countries to all WTO agreements. There is no option of selecting agreements on the basis of suitability or national interests. This is particularly notable because the TRIPS agreement forces member states to adopt standards of intellectual property rights disregarding (and often inconsistent with) their income level or level of development. Members do not have the liberty to opt out of such agreements. Many experts are apprehensive that national governments would, to a certain extent, have little control over specific disciplines. For example, Hoekman (2002) suggests that 'the adoption of specific multilateral rules may affect detrimentally the ability of governments to regulate domestic activities and deal with market failures' (p. 4).

Fourth, the actual functioning of the two entities is significantly different. Under the WTO Rules and Procedures Governing the Settlement of Disputes, a defendant member no longer has the ability to block the adoption of a WTO panel report (Hertz 1997). This is a considerable departure from the old policy. Under the GATT:

> ... when a ruling went against a country, the country could block the adoption of the panel decision by denying the needed consensus. Smaller nations were often left fuming when the United States used this tactic to delay unfavourable decisions indefinitely.
>
> (Drohan 1996, p. A12)

Dispute settlement under the GATT was a time-consuming process that often did not resolve the problems. By comparison, the WTO dispute resolution process follows a strict timetable for consultations, panel investigations, as well as for appeals. Moreover, the WTO decisions are enforceable. Under the GATT, investigations went on endlessly and decisions-delivered often gathered dust while parties continued to argue (Drohan 1996).

The large countries may not be able to technically block a WTO decision, but they certainly influence it. Large MNCs, certain trade associations, and some governments use bullying tactics to pressurise international organisations to achieve a favourable outcome (Reichmann 1998). The WTO acknowledges that while 'the private sector, non-governmental organizations (NGOs) and other lobbying groups do not participate in WTO activities except in special events such as seminars and symposiums', they can [and they do] 'exert their influence on WTO decisions through their governments' (WTO 2006a, p. 9). In its attempt to dislodge myths about the running of the WTO, its Web site emphasises that 'the WTO does not dictate to governments to adopt or drop certain policies. In fact, it's the governments who dictate to the WTO' (WTO 2006a, p. 2). The question, which begs to be asked here is, which governments dictate to this powerful institution. It certainly would not be the developing country governments.

Before we examine the TRIPS agreement and its impact on the pharmaceutical industry, we consider the correlation between patents and innovation, which is the basic premise for the agreement.

2.2 Patents and innovation

A patent is a property right granted by a sovereign state to the inventor of a novel, non-obvious, and useful invention (Lehman 2003). Patents grant monopoly rights to inventors for disclosing their invention to the public domain. While rewarding inventors with monopoly rights encourages innovation, patents may also hinder further technical progress by preventing others from making a similar invention due to the risk of infringement. Economists and inventors have been divided over the issue of rewarding inventors with patent protection and this issue has been controversial for a very long time. The controversy gained new heights between 1850 and 1875, when the critics of patent protection demanded a complete abolition of the patent system. Indeed, for a while, it looked as if the abolitionist movement was going to win (Machlup & Penrose 1950).

A brief review of the intellectual property rights in the historical context provides a recap of the issues involved in the controversy. According to Government of Australia (2008), intellectual property refers to property of mind or intellect, which in business term means ownership of proprietary knowledge. Claims of ownership of intellectual property, as such, appear to have begun with the identifiable markings of goods around 6000 years ago (Ruston 1955). But there is no evidence to suggest that others were prohibited from copying the originals. According to Dongre (1982), sale of knowledge was considered a bad thing and as such prohibited in ancient India. Similarly, the notion of human ownership of ideas or their expressions was also absent from the Chinese, Islamic, Jewish, and Christian civilisations of the pre-modern world (Hesse 2002).

The IPRs in a formal sense first emerged with the enactment of what later became known as the Venetian Statute of 1474 designed to establish ownership of knowledge and promote innovation (Nard & Morriss 2006). The Venetian Statute was not concerned with the inventor receiving specific benefits. Before IPRs were formalised in Europe, the rulers utilised [letters of] grants for the exclusive exploitation of innovative and previously unknown practices (David 1993). Britain issued its first patent in 1559 to Jacobus on the basis that 'the innovator should receive certain benefits and rights relative to his invention' (May & Sell 2006, p. 80).

In the US, each state operated under its own patent rules until the late 1700s. The Philadelphia convention in 1787 was the first attempt to have a federal patent law. The proposed national patent and copyright provisions at the convention became the basis for the Patent Act in 1790, which along with the Venetian Statute of 1474 and the British Statute of Monopolies of 1624 are considered to be the three main pillars of the intellectual property development around the world (Nard & Morriss 2006). Patent laws were introduced in Austria (1810), Russia (1812), Prussia (1815), Belgium and the Netherlands (1817),

Spain (1820), Bavaria (1825), Portugal (1837), and in Saxonia (1843) (Machlup & Penrose 1950). In Germany, the 1877 Statute created a federal patent system. The patent fees in Germany were deliberately set high to eliminate claims for frivolous inventions (Khan 2002). The current Indian Patents Act denies patents for frivolous inventions, but faces challenges from pharmaceutical MNCs for doing so.

Inventors are also divided over patent protection. The first group of inventors preferred to protect their inventions. For example, the Wright brothers had secured patents in aviation. Similarly, James Watt had patented his invention of steam engine. This approach could be considered what Hofstede (2001) calls *individualist* for being protective of its knowledge and preventing others from using it. The inventor deserves to be rewarded for his genius under this concept. However, as Ashton (1964) notes that the problem with this concept is that it blocks further progress, as it did in steam technology by preventing others from constructing new types of steam engines. The industrial revolution did not really take off until Watt's patent expired in 1785.

The second group of inventors had a different approach. Benjamin Franklin for example refused to patent his famous stove. He argued that 'as we enjoy great advantages from the invention of others, we should be glad of an opportunity to serve others by any invention of ours, and this we should do freely and generously' (cited in Cole 2001, p. 84). Henry Ford, the father of the auto assembly line, was another critic of patents who withdrew all patents to allow unrestricted access to all Ford inventions (Flink 1990). This approach could be considered what Hofstede calls *collectivist* for sharing their knowledge with all. This approach is more considerate of the society as a whole at the expense of an individual reward. The inventor has no formal rights but gets wider acceptance and recognition by the society.

The debate on the protection of intellectual property has gained fresh momentum in the wake of the TRIPS agreement that clearly favours the *individualist* approach. Experts remain as divided on this issue today as they were more than a hundred years ago (Hope 2003) as the following two sub-sections reveal.

2.2.1 The case for protection of intellectual property rights

A large body of literature advocates strong protection of intellectual property rights to encourage innovation. For example, Solow (1957) and Dennison (1979) argue that the technical progress leading to economic growth would not have taken place without the protection of IPRs (cited in Cole 2001). North (1968) also supports this argument and suggests that the lack of systematic protection of property rights until recent times was the main reason for the slow technological progress and innovation. North holds that the development of systematic incentives through protection of IPRs increased private returns and encouraged technological innovation.

A study was conducted recently to find out how the absence of patent protection would affect innovations (i.e. delayed or not introduced at all). Mansfield (1986) randomly selected 100 large firms across 12 industries in the US (chemical, pharmaceutical, office equipment, petroleum, machinery, fabricated metal products, electrical equipment, motor vehicle, instruments, primary metals, rubber, and textiles) and sent them a questionnaire. He also interviewed 25 senior executives from these firms and combined them with responses from individual firms to estimate industry-wide results.

According to Mansfield, around two-thirds of the new pharmaceutical products would not have been introduced without patent protection. However, this share was 30 per cent in the chemical industry and declines further in the petroleum, machinery, and fabricated metal products industries. 'Patent protection was not essential for the development or introduction of any of their inventions' in the office equipment, motor vehicle, rubber, and textile industries (Mansfield 1986, p. 174).

The mission of the Pharmaceutical Research and Manufacturers of America (PhRMA) noted in its (2007) Annual Report suggests that strong intellectual property incentives and abolition of price controls are the necessary keys to encourage the discovery of new drugs. The PhRMA (2002) argues that the developing countries should have the same level of protection as the developed countries, because stronger patents will stimulate more research efforts to discover new drugs needed in developing countries. This argument lacks the support of empirical evidence, however. India had a stringent regime for 60 years before the introduction of Patents Act 1970 with little investment or innovation in its pharmaceutical industry.

Lehman (2003) suggests that developing countries would benefit from new medicines for tropical diseases by introducing stringent patents regime, because it would lead to the development of pharmaceutical markets. But this argument appears suspect, as it ignores the fact that stronger patents would also mean a market with higher drug prices, making the drugs inaccessible to the people in the developing countries. As Mayne (2002) points out, stronger patents in poor countries will not change the basic market reality and that reality is the lack of purchasing power. Developing countries already have large markets in terms of patients. What these countries do not have are neither the medicines to treat the tropical diseases nor the capacity to pay for the available medicines. When Lehman speaks of the 'development of a market', he also speaks of a monopoly market, in which the patent holder would be free to charge monopoly prices.

To his credit, Lehman also suggests that consumers in all countries should share the burden of drug development 'equitably by paying for medicine at a price level consistent with their means' (p. 14). It is not clear, however, what this equity would mean in a country like India? As will be discussed in later chapters, two-thirds of Indians do not currently have access to medicines even at the world's lowest drug prices that exist in India today. Under the stronger (post 2005) protection and *sharing the burden of drug development* as Lehman suggests, drug prices would rise significantly and access to medicines would be restricted even further. If the pricing level was consistent with the means of the poor as Lehman also suggests, the prices would have to fall instead of rising. Accordingly, the argument for introducing stringent patent regimes in the developing world remains less than convincing.

Khan (2002) suggests that the industrial supremacy of the US is a testimony to its treatment of inventors and inducements held out for innovative activity. The US has one of the most successful patents systems in the world with more than 6 million patents granted since the system was established in 1790, notes Khan. The US introduces 70 per cent of the new drugs worldwide, and this is because the US has the world's strongest intellectual property regime (PhRMA 2007). However, as noted below, Europe provides stronger protection for pharmaceutical patents than the US, yet, the share of new drugs discovered in Europe has declined over the last decade. In 1992, six out of ten the top-selling drugs originated in Europe compared with just two of the top ten products introduced in 2002 (Verheugen 2005).

The basic protection under TRIPS is the same in the US and the European countries. The US provides five years of data exclusivity compared with up to ten years in Europe. This means that the generic manufacturers cannot rely on the data submitted by the originator company during that period. The US provides for the so-called 'Bolar provision' to enable the generic manufacturers to test and prepare the bio-equivalency of patented drugs. Thus, the generic version would be ready for launch upon patent expiry. By comparison, a number of European countries do not provide Bolar provisions, which delays the entry of generics. In fact, according to Nigel Stoate, a London-based solicitor specialising in intellectual property, the EU negotiators were seeking to have the Bolar provisions abolished as a pre-condition for Hungary, Poland, Slovakia, and Slovenia to join the EU (Stoate 2001/2002). The originators enjoy the extended monopoly in the EU countries. Finally, under the US law, pharmacists are permitted to provide generic substitutions for patented drugs. This is not the case in many European countries. Consequently, the sale of originator products by prescriptions would be higher in Europe than in the US as the 2006 sales shows. According to the European Generic Medicines Association (2007), generics constituted 10 per cent or less of the sales by volume in a number of countries, including Italy, Ireland, Greece, Finland, Portugal, and Switzerland. By comparison, the generics share in the US accounted for almost 60 per cent in 2005 (PhRMA 2007).

The comparison of patent protection between the US and EU suggests that stronger patent regime may not necessarily attract investors to invest into the pharmaceutical research and development (R&D). Other factors, such as the size of the US market, lack of price controls, and availability of public funding for research through National Institutes of Health (NIH) also appear to influence the investor decisions (see Chapter 3 for details). There could be no disagreement that the development of new drugs requires large funds and patents provide incentives for investors to invest into pharmaceutical R&D. However, patents are not the only way to spur innovation as the opponents of protection claim.

2.2.2 The case against protection of intellectual property rights for medicines

A significant number of experts remain unconvinced about the need for stronger IPRs to increase innovation. They question the role patents have played in technological progress or economic growth. Ashton (1964) for example argues that discovery and development would have occurred even without the framework of patenting, because competitiveness and pursuit of new knowledge are also major drivers of innovation. Mokyr (1990) also argues that a patent system may have been a stimulus to invention, but it certainly was not a necessary factor. He believes that contribution of patents to innovation is grossly overstated.

Professor Davis (1994) of Cleveland State University argues that from an economist's point of view, patents are an embarrassment to the idea of a free-market. He opines that patents are essentially a form of subsidy insofar as the government grants the patentee the opportunity to charge a monopoly price for its product. The difference between the monopoly price and free-market price is, effectively, a subsidy to the patent holders. The government, instead of paying the patent holder directly, authorises the patentee to collect the premium from consumers, but the end effect remains the same, suggests Davis.

Hayek (1988) holds that a slavish application of the concept of intellectual property has done a great deal to foster the growth of monopoly. He questions the award of monopoly as the most appropriate and effective form of rewarding investors for investments in scientific research. In a world of scarce resources, free marketing optimises resource allocation increasing efficiency. Granting patent rights to create monopolies seems contradictory to the concept of free marketing. Referring to intellectual property rights, Cole (2001), suggests that:

> ... since these rights do not arise from the scarcity of the appropriated subject matter; ... rather, their sole purpose is to create scarcity, thereby generating the monopoly rents for holders of such rights. In such case the law does not protect property over the scarce good, since the law itself created the scarcity ... and in case of patents and copyrights, the scarcity arises only after the property right is defined. (pp. 80–1)

Thomas Jefferson, the third President of the US, was explicitly against protection of patents when he had said: 'Knowledge is like a candle – as it lights another candle, light of the original candle is not diminished' (cited in Stiglitz 2006, p. 108). Similarly, Posner (2002), a distinguished judge on the U.S. Court of Appeals for the Seventh Circuit, also holds that the use of intellectual property by one person does not reduce the value of its use by another. Knowledge grows when shared and it stops growing when locked away. Monopolising knowledge is considered impediment to free marketing and economic growth. Perhaps that is why the strongest claim against the concept of patenting came from *The Economist* (1851). 'No possible good can ever come out of patent law, however admirably it may be framed' (cited in Singleton 2006).

Former Vice President of the World Bank and Nobel laureate Stiglitz (2002b) believes pharmaceutical patents cause unnecessarily hardship to the poor in the developing countries. Market competition would force businesses to innovate in any case, he argues. In order to secure an edge over competitors, entrepreneurial firms would invest into innovative products and develop efficient processes to manufacture them regardless of the level of protection provided.

Scientists do not seem to be concerned about patent protection. They generally hold that patents at best could be considered a bonus, because basic research is not dependent on patents. Basic research goes on regardless. It goes on because science is looking for new knowledge. Thomas Alva Edison, the holder of 1000 patents, believed that '[A patent] is simply an invitation to a lawsuit.... [I have] lost all faith in patents, judges and everything else relating to patents' (cited in Melethil 2005, p. E723). Melethil (2005) sums up the concept of patenting as 'scientists invent, lawyers patent' (p. E723).

The controversy over patenting presents a real dilemma. Arguments of the proponents as well as the opponents of patents have some degree of merit and claims of neither side can be dismissed entirely. On the one hand, patents seem to provide incentives for investments into R&D. On the other hand, patents create monopolies, which is contrary to the concept of free and competitive markets. Machlup, one of the leading economists of the twentieth century, acknowledges the validity of arguments on both sides. In his famous review of the patent system, he states:

> If we did not have a patent system, it would be irresponsible, on the basis of the present knowledge of its economic consequences, to recommend instituting one. But since we have had a patent system for a long time, it would be irresponsible, on the basis of present knowledge, to recommend abolishing it. The last statement refers to a country such as the United States of America – that's not a small country and not a predominantly non-industrial country, where different ways of argument might well suggest another conclusion.
>
> (Machlup 1958, p. 80)

While the controversy over patents in general continues, patents in pharmaceuticals in particular have more significance than in the other industries. For example, the patents in the music industry may raise the cost of entertainment. People can choose to forego the expensive form of entertainment and its effect would be minimal. The same cannot be said, however, about the pharmaceutical industry. If a patented medicine is so expensive that most patients cannot afford to buy it, this could mean the difference between life and death for patients. If a large number of people have to go without medicines because of high prices, health outcomes would suffer and patents would become a national problem, particularly in the developing world. Thus, the impact of the

TRIPS agreement on the pharmaceutical industry and healthcare should be kept in perspective.

2.3 The TRIPS agreement

The TRIPS agreement requires all members of the WTO to provide a set of minimum standards for protection of intellectual property, including patent protection for pharmaceuticals (WTO 1994). This obligation has resulted in substantial amendments to IP regimes of more than 140 countries, including the US (Jorge 2004). Prior to TRIPS, the level of protection varied significantly across different countries. Developing countries generally allowed so-called 'weak' protection comprising process patents but not product patents. Developed nations had relatively stronger IP regimes including pharmaceutical product patents. The TRIPS agreement has revolutionised the international intellectual property law (Reichman 2000), raising the standards of protection in areas such as copyrights, trademarks, and patents.

As members of the WTO, developed countries were required to introduce the TRIPS requirements from 1995, whereas the developing countries were given until 2000 to implement the same. Developing countries, such as India that had previously disallowed product patents in pharmaceuticals, were granted additional five years to change the patent regime. Consequently, India became TRIPS compliant from 1 January 2005. The least developed countries (LDCs) have until 2016 to introduce TRIPS compliant regimes.

A number of experts have stressed the significance of TRIPS, especially for the developing countries. For example, Shiva (2004) describes the TRIPS agreement as 'the most far-reaching determinant of human rights to food, health, livelihood and creativity in the context of globalisation' (p. 665). According to Correa (2006), the most crucial impact of TRIPS, as far as the developing countries are concerned, is the mandating of the implementation of IPRs, notably patents for pharmaceutical products. In the editorial of the special issue of the *Journal of International Economic Law* devoted to TRIPS, Professor Frederick Abbott (1998) writes that:

> ...the most critical policy issue to be addressed at the international level with respect to the international intellectual property system of laws and institutions is how it can best be constructed and implemented to facilitate economic growth and social welfare in the developing and newly industrialising countries.
>
> (Abbott 1998, p. 498)

2.3.1 The role of TRIPS in the pharmaceutical industry

While the TRIPS agreement covers copyrights, trademarks, and patents, we focus only on patents, because of their applicability to the pharmaceutical industry. Article 1 of TRIPS provides that 'members may, but shall not be obliged to, implement in their law more extensive protection that is required by this agreement, provided that such protection does not contravene the provisions of this agreement' (*Agreement on Trade-Related Aspects of Intellectual Property Rights (TRIPS)* 1994). A consequence of this provision has been that a large number of regional and bilateral agreements have introduced even stronger IPRs than the TRIPS agreement stipulates (these 'TRIPS-Plus' provisions are considered later in the chapter).

In all, the TRIPS agreement has 73 Articles that can be divided into three major components. The first component (Articles 1 to 40) sets out the aims and objectives, and the standards of IPRs. The second component (Article 41 to 61) deals with enforcement mechanisms. The final component (Articles 62 to 73) deals with specific mechanisms, such as the transitional arrangements, technical cooperation, technology transfers, and the institutional arrangements for monitoring and review, which are devoted to addressing the special needs of developing countries (UNDP 2003, p. 203). The major points relevant to pharmaceutical patents are as follows:

'Patents shall be available for any inventions, whether *products* or *processes*, in *all* fields of technology, provided that they are new, involve an inventive step and are capable of industrial application ... and whether the products are imported or locally produced' (Article 27). *Products* and *all* are relevant here, because patents on pharmaceutical and food products had previously been excluded in many countries. Developing countries, such as India, had provided process patents, but not product patents. Thus, the previous regime allowed reverse engineering to re-manufacture a patented product by a different process. The first part of Article 27 effectively prevents the use of reverse engineering.

The second part of the Article refers to equal treatment of local and imported products for patenting purposes. The implications of this part would be that companies would simply import patented products from their home countries (presumed developed). This would constitute working of the patent in the host country (presumed developing). Forcing importers of patented products to manufacture locally would be deemed a contravention of the provisions of Article 27. Patent regimes in countries like Brazil and India with fairly developed pharmaceutical industries provide for compulsory licensing in case of non-working patents. But when the patented products are being imported, such provisions cannot be invoked to grant compulsory licences. The absence of competition results in consumers paying monopoly prices. The domestic players also lose out on participating in the manufacture of new products.

The term of protection must be a minimum of 20 years from the filing date (Article 33). Previously, the patent term in many countries was shorter and significantly shorter in developing countries. India, for example, disallowed product patents but provided protection for processes for seven years from the filing date or five years from the date of grant whichever was shorter. Thus, the new protection term is a significant change in the developing countries. Comparatively, the term extension in developed countries is relatively small (from 17 years to 20 years in the US for example).

A patent confers on the patentee the exclusive rights, to prevent third parties not having owner's consent from the acts of: making, using, offering for sale, selling, or importing the patented product; and in case of subject matter of a patent being a process, to prevent third parties not having owner's consent from engaging in any of the activities noted above for the purpose of obtaining the patented product by that process (Article 28).

The intent of this article, which is to exclude others from engaging in the manufacture of the patented product, has been criticised by some for not considering the potential benefits of participation of others in technology advancements. For example, Somaya (2000) examines the ideology behind the patent systems in four leading countries: namely, the US, the UK, Germany, and Japan. He concludes that while authorities in the US and the UK support the exclusivity of property rights of patentees, the Japanese and the Germans authorities view inventions more as a public good and less as a private good. According to Somaya, the emphasis of the official approach in Japan and Germany is more on the dissemination of technology and less on its exclusivity, as patents are viewed more as a means to reward inventions and less as a right to exclude others from using it (cited in Drahos & Braithwaite 2002). The fact remains that in spite of these important differences among the developed countries, the TRIPS agreement is positioned closer to or identical with the ideology of the US and the UK.

2.3.2 Flexibilities under TRIPS

The TRIPS agreement provides flexibilities viewed as 'limited exceptions to the exclusive rights conferred by a patent, provided that such exceptions do not unreasonably conflict with a normal exploitation of the patent and do not unreasonably prejudice the legitimate interests of the patent owner, taking into account the interests of third parties' (Article 30). The rationale of these provisions is to provide low-cost alternatives to originator medicines. In national emergencies and under other circumstances that render their use necessary, the flexibilities such as compulsory licences and parallel imports can be used without the consent of the right holder.

The conditions, under which the provisions of flexibilities could be used, remained controversial however, until resolved at the Doha Ministerial Conference in 2001. The Declaration on the TRIPS Agreement and Public Health (generally known as the Doha Declaration) states that:

> ...the TRIPS Agreement does not and should not prevent members from taking measures to protect public health (and).... We affirm that the Agreement can and should be interpreted and implemented in a manner supportive of WTO members' right to protect public health and, in particular, to promote access to medicines for all.
>
> (Paragraph 4)

and

> ...each provision of the TRIPS Agreement shall be read in the light of the object and purpose of the Agreement as expressed, in particular, in its objectives and principles.
>
> (Paragraph 5(a))

The Doha Declaration also affirms each member's right to determine its own grounds to make use of the flexibilities. The Declaration also allows members freedom to define what constitutes a national emergency. Useful as they are for countries with a reasonably developed pharmaceutical industry, these flexibilities are no great help for a large number of the LDCs that have no pharmaceutical industry or insufficient manufacturing capacity to meet their health needs. That this latter group of countries could not make use of these flexibilities is recognised by the Declaration in stating that:

> ...members with insufficient or no manufacturing capacities in the pharmaceutical sector could face difficulties in making effective use of compulsory licensing under the TRIPS Agreement. We instruct the

> Council for TRIPS to find an expeditious solution to this problem and to report to the General Council before the end of 2002.
>
> (Paragraph 6)

The Decision of the WTO made on 30 August 2003 is now known as Article 31*bis*. Under this Article, *any least-developed country* is eligible to import low-cost generics from a source other than the originator. The process of such import is significantly complex and highly time-consuming. Klein's (2003) description is perhaps most befitting the plight of the poor countries to overcome the complexity of these provisions when she writes that 'countries wanting to import cheap generics must jump through multiple hoops to prove they are truly in need, unable to afford patented drugs and incapable of producing the medicines domestically' (p. 12). However, the fear of retaliation as well as the complexity of the process to import have kept the poor nations away from making use of these provisions. After almost four years of sustained effort, Rwanda became the first country in May 2008 to import generic versions of an on-patent medicine under Article 31*bis*.

2.3.2.1 Compulsory licensing

A compulsory licence refers to 'an authorisation given by the government for the use by a third party, without the consent of the right-owner of a patent or other intellectual property right' (Correa 2002a, p. 48). While TRIPS does not use the term 'compulsory licensing', Article 31 refers to 'other use without authorization of the right holder' instead. Compulsory licences can be granted under the circumstances determined by members themselves. However, certain conditions for such use of a patent are stipulated.

The proposed user must have 'made efforts to obtain a voluntary licence from the right holder on reasonable commercial terms and conditions and that such efforts have not been successful *within a reasonable period of time*' (Clause b). This omission of spelling out what a reasonable period of time could cause unnecessary delays as well disputes. The Indian experience shows that some MNCs did not respond at all to requests by domestic manufacturers for a voluntary licence or they deliberately dragged on for years (see for example Chaudhuri 2005). Specificity of maximum period time would have eliminated any eventuality of such problems.

'The right holder shall be paid adequate remuneration in the circumstances of each case, taking into account the economic value of the authorization' (Clause h). The term *adequate* is not defined in the TRIPS agreement. This omission is also likely to cause contradictions and disputes. This is because different regimes place different values on what constitutes adequate. Under the previous patent regime, India had a ceiling of 4 per cent on royalties paid to the patentee under compulsory licensing. By comparison, these royalties were capped at 40 per cent in the UK, while there was no maximum limit on royalties in the US (Koshy 1995).

2.3.2.2 Parallel imports

Parallel imports, or parallel trade, refer to arbitrage of movement of genuine originator products from a low-priced country to a high-priced country without the consent of the right holder. The principle of parallel imports was extensively developed in the framework for European integration (Correa 2002a). To avoid market fragmentation, the European Court of Justice later extended this principle to the entire common market. According to Scherer and Watal (2001), certain conditions have to exist for parallel trade to occur. There must be underlying monopoly power and/or market imperfections. The originator company exploits the patent through a strategy of price discrimination, suggest Scherer and Watal. In other words, both countries have the same product sold at different prices. The term 'parallel imports' must not be mistaken for importing low-cost generics. It explicitly refers to moving commercial quantities of originator products to take advantage of a price difference.

The question is whether moving a patented product to another country constitutes an infringement of the rights of the holder. The TRIPS agreement is silent on it and states 'nothing in this Agreement shall be used to address the issue of the exhaustion of intellectual property rights' (Article 6). Correa (2002a) however suggests that this silence in the Article is recognition of the 'possibility of legally admitting parallel imports, based on the principle of exhaustion of rights' (p. 43). Parallel imports are justified applying the doctrine of exhaustion to intellectual property. Experts argue that unless explicitly notified, the sale of a patented product gives the purchaser 'all the normal rights of an owner, including the right to resell' (Cornish 1989, p. 200). Under the US law, the doctrine of exhaustion is known as the 'first sale doctrine' (Yusuf & Moncayo von Hase 1992).

The Doha Declaration addresses the issue of parallel imports to a certain extent, but does not explicitly define the *exhaustion of rights*. Again the Doha Declaration grants members the freedom to customise their regime to suit their national circumstances. The Declaration states that:

> ...the effect of the provisions in the TRIPS Agreement that are relevant to the exhaustion of intellectual property rights is to leave each member free to establish its own regime for such exhaustion without challenge, subject to the MFN and national treatment provisions of Articles 3 and 4.
>
> (Paragraph 5(d))

Parallel imports do not affect the manufacturer's overall global sale by volume. However, they do reduce the global revenue of the company. This is because the company sells more products in the low-priced country and arbitrageur capitalises on the price difference by moving them for sale in a high-priced country. Parallel imports of pharmaceuticals are common within the EU countries. Brand medicines sold in Portugal and Spain are often moved for resale in France, Germany, or the UK. In 2006, parallel imports constituted 15.2 per cent of sales in Denmark, 14.7 per cent in the UK, 13.3 per cent in Sweden, and 10.4 per cent in the Netherlands. In other EU-countries, the share of parallel trade was less than 10 per cent of sales. The European Federation of Pharmaceutical Industry and Associations (EFPIA) (2008) estimates the size of parallel trade in Europe at €4.3 billion in 2006.

2.3.2.3 Other flexibilities

Other flexibilities available under TRIPS include use of the patented drug for the purpose of experimental research, and for the so-called Bolar exemption. The use for the former allows inventing around and improvement on the patented product. The latter allows testing of generics to establish the bio-equivalency to a patented product in order to obtain marketing approval. This facilitates timely launch of generics on patent expiry. While the US, Canada, and Australia have incorporated these exemptions into their framework, other countries had doubts whether such exemption would be consistent with the TRIPS obligations. The consistency of the 'Bolar exemption' with TRIPS was examined by the Dispute Settlement Body (DSB) in a case between Canada and the European countries. In 1998, the European communities and their members requested the WTO to examine the application of Bolar provisions in the Canadian Patent Act with regard to Canada's obligations under TRIPS. In 2000, the DSB panel concluded that Canada's law was consistent with TRIPS in allowing the development and submission of information on bio-equivalency in order to obtain marketing approval for patented products without the consent of right holder. However, Canada's practice of allowing the manufacture and stockpiling of generics during the last six months immediately prior to the patent term was not consistent with the TRIPS obligations (WTO 2000). While this ruling makes it clear that the Bolar exemption is, in fact, consistent with TRIPS, only a handful of developing countries, such as Argentina, Israel, and Thailand have included them in their regimes (Correa 2002a).

The US and other industrialised countries attempted to limit the use of flexibilities by specifying the diseases and the circumstances, under which the flexibilities could be used. The primary reason for imposing these limitations is profit-driven and 'from the prospective of public health, limiting access programs and TRIPS flexibilities to particular diseases would be quite dangerous and unnecessary' (Outterson 2008, p. 321). If a country dares to make use of the flexibilities provided under TRIPS, it gets into trouble, particularly with the US. The case of South Africa versus the 'big pharma' is well-documented in the literature. More recently, Brazil and Thailand faced significant resistance from the US in their attempts to issue compulsory licences in order to address their public health needs.

When the US and the European countries could not get their way in TRIPS, they switched to new tactics. They introduced TRIPS-plus provisions into regional and bilateral agreements on trade, investment, and intellectual property. Malhotra and Grewal (2008) examine 15 bilateral and regional agreements involving the US or the EU and developing countries. These agreements leave little or no room for developing countries to make use of the flexibilities provided under TRIPS. For example, their analysis of the US–Sri Lanka agreement on intellectual property shows the veracity of the US intent to ensure the poor countries are deprived of the opportunity to intervene if and when the need arises.

2.3.3 Protection of submitted data

This issue involves protection of test data for establishing efficacy and safety of a product submitted to relevant authorities for obtaining marketing approval. The generation of such data requires extensive testing of medicines on thousands of subjects over several years at substantial costs. Manufacturers of originator products submit these data to seek marketing approvals. A large number of countries, developing and developed alike, allow generics manufacturers to submit data proving bio-equivalence to the originator product for granting marketing approval for follow-up products. For example, before 1984, the United

States Food and Drug Administration (USFDA) did not allow generic manufacturers applications for marketing approvals to rely on the test and other data submitted for a new drug application by originator companies (Baker 2008). The Patent Term Restoration Act (1984) or more popularly known as the Hatch-Waxman Act permits testing of medicines to determine the bio-equivalency of a generic drug to a patented product. A submission of an *Abbreviated* New Drug Application (ANDA) along with the proof of bio-equivalency calls upon authorities to rely on the originator data submitted for safety and efficacy under this Act (Clements 2007–08).

Two different terminologies are used for the protection of the submitted data; namely, data protection and data exclusivity. *Data protection* relates to unrestricted reliance by authorities on the submitted data for subsequent product approvals. These data however must not be disclosed to third party users. *Data exclusivity* refers to confidentiality of the regulatory file submitted to regulatory authorities for a specific period (Morag-Sela et al. 2004). Data exclusivity prohibits authorities from relying on the originator data for the approval of subsequent products. This form of exclusivity effectively delays the development and market approval of generics. In the absence of provisions for reliance on the originator data, generic manufacturers would have to conduct their own clinical trials to establish the safety and efficacy. The repeat of such trials is not only unnecessary and expensive; it takes a few years to complete. Drahos et al. (2004) doubt if ethical standards committees would approve a repeat of such studies putting patients at risk to provide data that are already known. For doing so would contravene the basic international standards of human research ethics. The US filed a case against Argentina in the WTO alleging many aspects of Argentinean patent system, including the approval of non-patented drugs by relying on data submitted by originators, violated TRIPS. In Argentina, the domestic pharmaceutical industry accounts for around half the pharmaceutical sales; hence, despite being listed each year on USTR's 'Priority watch' under Special 301, Argentina has not changed its approval process (Shadlen 2009).

The US provides data exclusivity for a period of five years. The EU's pharmaceutical legislation introduced comprehensive reforms in 2004. Since then, the EU provides data exclusivity for 8 + 2 + 1 years meaning the following. Generic manufacturers may apply for market approvals eight years after an originator product first enters the market. But the actual market entry of generics will only be allowed after ten years of the launch of the originator product. If new therapeutic indications (new uses) on the originator products are authorised, data exclusivity may be extended by another year (EurActiv 2005). Less developed countries prefer data protection as compared to data exclusivity. New economies within the EU, such as Poland and Hungary, have requested a 15-year transition period for introducing data exclusivity.

While the TRIPS agreement does not explicitly mention the word *data exclusivity*, the Agreement is also vague in defining its position on the protection of the submitted data. Article 39.3 of TRIPS states that:

> ....Members, when requiring...the submission of undisclosed test or other data, the origination of which involves a considerable effort, shall protect such data against unfair commercial use. In addition, Members shall protect such data against disclosure, except where necessary to protect the public, or unless steps are taken to ensure that the data are protected against unfair commercial use.
>
> (Article 39.3)

The Article is not clear in its intentions on at least two accounts. First, the Article does not spell out how the data are to be protected. It leaves open to questioning that if the authorities can rely on the data to approve subsequent products without disclosing the data to third parties. Second, a definition of 'unfair commercial use' is not provided in the TRIPS agreement. These ambiguities in the Article have resulted in controversial interpretations by different parties with vested interests. Originator companies and their representative associations such as the PhRMA argue that the provisions of the Article refer to data exclusivity. They contend that under Article 39.3, the authorities cannot rely on the submitted data for subsequent approval during the patent term. Developing countries supported by public health advocates, NGOs, and civic society groups argue that TRIPS obligations amount to data protection and not to data exclusivity. After an intense public debate however, India is preparing to modify its Patents Act to provide data exclusivity for five years counted from the first market approval granted anywhere in the world. A significant number of poor countries also provide data exclusivity under obligations of their bilateral and/or regional agreements.

2.3.4 Other Articles of importance

A number of Articles are of particular interest with regard to our later discussions. Article 7 states the objectives of the TRIPS agreement as:

> ....The protection and enforcement of intellectual property right should contribute to the promotion of technological innovation and to the transfer and dissemination of technology, to the mutual advantage of producers and uses of technological knowledge and in a manner conducive to social and economic welfare, and to balance of rights and obligations. (p. 323)

Article 8 states the principles of the Agreement. It states that:

> ....Members may, in formulating or amending their laws and regulations, adopt measures necessary to protect public health and nutrition, and to promote the public interest in sectors of vital importance to their socio-economic and technological development, provided that such measures are consistent with the provisions of this Agreement. (p. 323)

These two Articles are fundamental to the development of the TRIPS agreement and provide developing countries what Correa (2002b) calls sufficient manoeuvrability, as these countries may amend their regimes to incorporate their unique requirements for economic and technological development and to meet their public health needs. The objectives of the TRIPS agreement are clearly stated to contribute to the mutual advantage of *producers and users...conducive to social and economic welfare, and to balance of rights and obligations*. In accordance with Article 8, members may *adopt measures necessary to protect public health and nutrition*.

The TRIPS agreement obliges member countries to:

> ...provide for criminal procedure and penalties to applied at least in cases of wilful trademark counterfeiting or copyright piracy on a commercial scale. Remedies available shall include imprisonment and/or monetary fines sufficient to provide a deterrent, consistently with the level of penalties applied for crimes of corresponding gravity...Members may provide for criminal procedures and penalties to be applied in other cases of infringement of intellectual property rights, in particular where they are committed wilfully and on a commercial scale.
>
> (Article 61)

Although the TRIPS agreement mentions the need for balancing the rights and obligations of producers and users, the Agreement clearly favours the producers. It mandates member countries to introduce criminal procedures to protect the interests of the patent holders. But the Agreement has no provisions to deter the patent holders from abusing their intellectual property rights. It does not balance the rights and obligations of producers and users of knowledge. As Zutshi (1998) notes 'consistency is not a virtue practiced by nations, particularly in trade negotiations' (p. 44).

Under the provisions of Article 71, the TRIPS agreement is to be reviewed every two years starting from 1 January 2005. At the next opportunity, leading developing countries like India, China, and Brazil should include the following for the agenda. The European Commission (2008)[1] has identified the problem of excessive patenting by drug companies as one issue for such a review. We suggest that the criminal procedures and penalties under provisions of Article 61 of TRIPS should also be applied to excessive patenting. In any case, developing countries should consider introducing similar provisions to hold the top officials of companies accountable for excessive patenting. This type of deterrent would be a *measure necessary to protect public health*. The suggested measure is by no means anti-innovation but needs to be seen in the right context to appreciate its intentions.

2.4 Conclusions

The TRIPS agreement stipulates minimum standards for protection of intellectual property, which is considerably higher than the protection previously provided in developing countries. A large number of developing countries previously did not provide product patents for pharmaceuticals. The Doha Declaration on TRIPS and Public Health reaffirms member states' rights to protect public health. It emphasises the flexibilities built into the TRIPS agreement available to members, should the need arise. Members are free to determine their own grounds to make use of the flexibilities, such as compulsory licensing and parallel imports. Least developed countries with no or insufficient capacity to manufacture pharmaceuticals to meet their own public health needs can import low-cost generics during the protection period. However, the fear of retaliation and the complexity of the process to import keep poor countries away from using these provisions.

The stated objectives of IPRs under the TRIPS agreement include *mutual advantage of producers and users* and *to a balance of rights and obligations*. Yet, the Agreement clearly favours the drug producers. The Agreement obliges members to provide for criminal proceedings with penalties of imprisonment and/or fines for commercial infringers of copyrights and other intellectual property rights. The Agreement calls for punishing (small) firms/individuals inflicting a monetary damage to the right holder. The Agreement would indeed be balancing the *rights and obligations of producers and users* if it also called for the same kind of treatment for companies for excessive patenting (such as filing up to 1300 patents on a single medicine). This level of patenting of 'anything and everything' denies access to medicines and has a realistic potential for loss of life. This issue needs to be addressed in the next review of TRIPS. Independent of TRIPS, developing countries need to consider amending their regimes to introduce provisions similar to those of Article 61 of TRIPS and fill this gap.

3
The Global Pharmaceutical Industry and Developing New Drugs

3.1 Introduction

The pharmaceutical industry is highly capital-intensive and research-intensive. Firms in this industry depend significantly on the pipeline of new drugs, which secure patents with a potential for high returns and profits on best selling drugs can be substantial. With its extensive R&D of new drugs, the pharmaceutical industry has contributed significantly to improving the length and quality of life (Schweitzer 1997). The pharmaceutical research is a high risk/high reward environment, in which, large MNCs dominate the industry (OECD 2001). Thus, priority-setting by large MNCs determines the direction of pharmaceutical research.

Despite the significant risk of failures in the R&D, the pharmaceutical industry is very profitable. In fact, the pharmaceutical industry has been the most profitable of all industries since at least 1960. According to a recent study by the Organisation for Economic Co-operation and Development (OECD) for the 1960–91 period, the return on equity in the pharmaceutical industry was the highest at 18.4 per cent for the largest 500 industrial companies. This return was more than 50 per cent higher than the corresponding returns in the second ranked telecom sector at 11.9 per cent (OECD 2001). Another study finds that the 'profits on assets of the nine largest pharmaceutical companies were 4½ times greater in 2003, than the average profits for the Fortune 500 companies' (Mayne 2005, p. 26). Yet, the industry seems least interested in developing drugs for diseases prevalent in poor countries.

The pharmaceuticals industry sits firmly at the interface of globalisation and healthcare. Firms in this industry are increasingly either becoming global or are competing with global firms for markets, for capital investment, and for skilled workforce. As a part of their globalising strategies, large MNCs are shifting some of the functions to low-cost countries saving in costs and tapping into local labour markets. Lacetera (2001) suggests that it is not uncommon for large firms to 'granting stock options and [even] seats on the board of directors, as means to "hold" scientists within the organization for long periods' (p. 45). Small firms struggle to secure venture finance for R&D projects, and also lose out on the skilled workers in high demand, because small firms simply cannot match the remuneration and the perks offered by the MNCs let alone beat them. The globalisation process has opened up traditionally protected markets, in which, MNCs are benefiting at the expense of small domestic firms with virtually no or little gains for the consumers.

3.2 The industry structure

The global pharmaceutical industry predominantly has a two-tier structure. First, a small number of large MNCs primarily based in the US, Europe, and Japan dominate the industry. Within this group, the US dominance is noticeable from the fact that of the top 15 companies by pharmaceutical sales, around half have their headquarters in the US alone (OECD 2008). The largest 100 MNCs known as the 'big pharma' manufacture and supply nearly 80 per cent of the world's drugs (OECD 2001). These companies, also known as the originator companies for their lead role in developing new drugs, hold most of the pharmaceuticals patents. According to Franz Humer, the Chairman and CEO of F. Hoffman-La Roche, the level of market concentration has significantly increased in the last two decades. The collective market share of the world's top ten companies in the pharmaceutical industry has doubled from 25 per cent in 1985 to 50 per cent in 2005 (Humer 2005). In 2006 also, the top ten companies accounted for around half of the global sales (OECD 2008). According to Dukes (2006), this group of companies plays:

> ...only a minor role in most developing countries, especially those at the middle and lower levels of development, where it has confined itself very largely to the sale of its products through local agents to relatively affluent urban populations (p. 11).

The second group consists of a large number of small to medium enterprises (SMEs) located in developed countries but also in developing countries like Brazil, China, India, Israel, and South Africa. This group of companies is classified as generics manufacturers, because generally they do not engage in innovative activities, particularly in basic research.

These companies supply off-patent products competing against the MNCs after patent expiry on their innovator product. Some of the SMEs engage in a subservient role to the 'big pharma' in contract research and manufacturing known in the literature as the CRAM activities. The contract research firms provide a valuable link in the R&D chain but undertake only a part of the research process. These firms lack the resources to fully develop new drugs and market them on their own. Other second tier firms are the manufacturers of intermediates such as bulk drugs also known as active pharmaceutical ingredients (APIs). Bulk drugs or APIs are the basic ingredients to produce formulations that is ready-to-consume-medicines such as capsules, tablets, injectibles, and syrups.

3.2.1 Pharmaceutical sales, companies, and profits

The global pharmaceutical sales increased from US$356 billion in 2000 to cross the half a trillion dollar mark for the first time in 2004. In 2006, the sales reached $643 billion and the companies based in the US accounted for $253 billion, Europe (including the UK) $226 billion, Japan $61 billion, and the rest of the world $103 billion (Medicines Australia 2008). The world pharmaceutical market grew at around 9.5 per cent in 2001 and 2002, peaked at 16.4 per cent in 2003, before declining to 12.5 per cent in 2004, and further declining to below 8 per cent in 2005 and 2006.

The EFPIA (2008) estimates that in 2006, the US pharmaceutical industry accounted for almost 40 per cent of the global sales. With this share, the US industry now leads the global pharmaceutical landscape, a role traditionally the European pharmaceutical industry had played. The corresponding share of whole of Europe combined constituted 35.2 per cent, followed by Japan at 9.5 per cent, and the rest of the world (ROW) at 16 per cent. By comparison, India's contribution was around 1.3 per cent by value and around 8 per cent by volume (Nanda & Khan 2005).

Ever since the discovery of Tagamet, the first blockbuster[1] in 1976, there has been a significant shift in the industry's marketing and growth strategy. The 'blockbusters are the backbone of large originator company strategies aimed at recouping R&D investments' (European Commission 2008, p. 33). 'Delivering a blockbuster drug is the Holy Grail for any pharmaceutical company' (Gassmann et al. 2008, p. ix). This is because blockbusters are the most profitable products yielding six times their average R&D investments and 55 per cent of all new drugs' quasi-rents (Scherer 2007). While the global pharmaceutical sales increased by around 80 per cent from 2000 to 2006, the increase in the number

Table 3.1 Blockbuster drugs and sales (2000–06)

Year/ Category	Total pharmaceutical sales ($ billion)	Blockbuster share (%)	Blockbuster sales ($ billion)	No. of blockbusters	Average blockbuster sales ($ billion)
1	2	3	4 = (2*3%)	5	6 = (4/5)
2000	358	23	82.3	46	1.79
2001	386	24	92.6	51	1.82
2002	421	30	126.3	58	2.18
2003	490	29	142.1	70	2.03
2004	545	31	169	87	1.94
2005	601	36	216.4	94	2.30
2006	643	36	231.5	105	2.20

Source: Based on Scrip News (2005c, p. 13), OECD (2008, p. 11), Scott (2006), and Cutler (2007).

of blockbuster drugs during the same period was more significant (see Table 3.1). Blockbusters increased by from 46 in 2000 to 87 in 2004 to 105 in 2006 and their share of total pharmaceutical sales increased from 23 per cent of to 36 per cent, which suggests that pharmaceutical sales have progressively become more blockbuster oriented and more concentrated than at the beginning of the study. Table 3.1 shows that the average blockbuster sales have increased from $1.79 billion in 2000 to $2.20 billion in 2006. In four of the seven years studied, the average has been over $2 billion. This once again confirms that the industry is becoming more blockbuster oriented.

According to Gassmann et al. (2008), 24 companies accounted for marketing the 58 blockbuster drugs in 2002. In 2003, Lipitor became the first 'super blockbuster' or mega blockbuster by annual sales exceeding $10 billion and its sales further increased to more than $13 billion in 2006. In its annual review (2007), Pfizer notes 8 blockbusters (Lipitor, Norvasc, Celebrex, Lyrica, Viagra, Xalatan/Xalacom, Zyrtec/Zyrtec D, and Detrol/Detrol LA) totalling sales of $25.9 billion. The Pfizer review also shows another 5 drugs (Camptosar, Zyvox, Chantix/Champix, Geodon/Zeldox, and Genotropin) with sales of between $843 million and $969 million, which could possibly become blockbusters in 2008/2009 (Pfizer 2007).

While blockbuster drugs boost company's global sales, these drugs also increase company dependency on such products. For example, Lipitor sales constituted 30 per cent of Pfizer's and Risperdal accounted for 35 per cent of Johnson & Johnson's global sales in 2007 (European

Commission 2008). These sales often continue to occur or even rise during the patent period. However, the patent expiry on such a product is likely to have implications for the company. If the company is not ready with a replacement drug, before the patent expires, its revenues as well as its market capitalisation could suffer significantly. In Lipitor's case, Pfizer has been trying to keep competitors out of the market for as long as possible. Ranbaxy, an Indian generics manufacturer, and Pfizer have been in litigation with regard to the Lipitor patent in a number of countries. The Lipitor patent is due to expire in 2011/2012 in the US and most of the other developed countries. Torcetrapib, a cholesterol drug, was being developed to replace Lipitor upon patent expiry (Bloomberg 2006). In 2006, Pfizer abandoned further testing of Torcetrapib for safety reasons. The scale of the significance of this drug can be appreciated from the fact that after Pfizer announced the halt of clinical testing of Torcetrapib, the company's market value fell by $21 billion overnight and 10,000 job cuts followed (Cutler 2007).

Over the last two decades, mergers and acquisitions (M&A) have significantly reduced the number of companies at the top of the pharmaceutical industry. Danzon et al. (2007) study the M&A activity of 383 pharmaceutical /biotechnology firms for the 1988–2001 period. They find that large firms merged because of expected excess capacity due to expiry on patents and gaps in a firm's product pipeline. The SMEs primarily used mergers as an exit strategy in response to financial problems. Danzon et al. estimate the effects of mergers using a propensity score to control for selection based on observed characteristics. Controlling for merger propensity, they conclude that merged large firms experience a positive change in enterprise value, sales, and R&D output. But these firms record slower growth in operating profit compared with firms that did not merge. The foregoing authors also conclude that mergers may be a response to a problem, but they are certainly not a solution.

In 1983 for example, Pfizer ranked 6 with sales of less than $2 billion. However, by 2003, with sales of nearly $40 billion Pfizer had become the world leader. In the process of growth, Pfizer acquired a number of companies including Warner & Lambert for $90 billion in 2000 (Deloitte Recap 2009) and Pharmacia for $60 billion in 2003 (Frank & Hensley 2002). The significance of the latter acquisition is that Lipitor actually belonged to Pharmacia, which has now become the flagship drug for the acquirer. Pfizer's gigantic size can be appreciated from its market capitalisation that now competes directly with the economic size of some of the nations. Pfizer ranks 17 ahead of Sweden (19) and well ahead of Singapore (39) (Blech 2006). In January 2009, Pfizer was negotiating to take over Wyeth for $68 billion. This acquisition, if completed, would place Pfizer at almost an unchallengeable position. Wyeth has been among the top ten companies since early 2000s.

Similarly, Novartis reached the top ten companies in 2003 by taking over Ciba-Geigy as well as Sandoz that ranked in top ten in 1983 and 1993. Glaxo merged with SmithKline Beecham to form GlaxoSmithKline (GSK). Likewise, the emergence of Bristol-Myers Squib (BMS) can also be attributed to mergers and acquisitions. On the one hand, mergers and acquisitions reduce the number of competitors in the market. On the other hand, they boost sales as well as the market share of the new entity increasing company's market power and profits.

The pharmaceutical industry is the most profitable industry as noted in the introduction. The profitability in the pharmaceutical sector is highlighted by operating margin of most of the top 20 companies. In 2004, Pfizer ranked first with more than $21 billion operating profit and a net income of over $11 billion. Had Pfizer not merged, collective profits of the individual companies (Pfizer, Warner Lambert, and Pharmacia) would have been even higher (Danzon et al. 2007). In 2004, Merck & Co had close to 60 per cent operating profit margin followed by Pfizer at 40.96 per cent, Takeda at 35.38 per cent, and Amgen at 31.73 per cent.

3.2.2 Major pharmaceutical markets, pharmaceutical spending, and generics

The global pharmaceutical market has registered significant growth over the last few decades. From 1970 to 2002, the global market grew at an average of 11.1 per cent annually but has slowed down to a rate between 5 per cent and 8 per cent since (Gassmann et al. 2008). In the last 20 years, the market dynamics have shifted the global pharmaceutical sales. The top six markets now are the US followed by Japan, Germany, France, the UK, and Italy. In 2007, nine OECD countries accounted for around 80 per cent of the global sales of pharmaceuticals (OECD 2008). The US share as a percentage of the global sales increased from 28 per cent in 1987 to almost 44 per cent in 2004. The corresponding share of the European and Japanese markets declined from over 40 per cent to around 30 per cent and from more than 21 per cent to 11 per cent, respectively (EFPIA 2006; Lewis et al. 2005). When these shares are measured against the shares of global production of pharmaceuticals (noted earlier), the US remains a net importer of pharmaceuticals, while the EU is a net exporter.

Higher growth rate in smaller markets is likely to drive global sales over the next decade. For example, China recorded the highest annual growth (28 per cent) in 2004, while Australia (24 per cent), Brazil, and the UK (21 per cent) also grew significantly (Mathew & Torreblanca 2005). By comparison, the US and Japan both had 8 per cent growth. But in absolute terms, the total of even this moderate growth in both markets added more than the collective sales of Australia, South Korea, Brazil, and India. In 2007, the pharmaceutical market in Asia grew at 13.1 per cent, in Europe at 6.7 per cent, and in the US at 4.2 per cent (EFPIA 2008). This growth rate if continued in Asia is likely to enlarge the Asian markets significantly. However, in the wake of the financial meltdown in 2008, the Asian growth rate is likely to slow down, while the true nature of growth remains unpredictable.

One of the major reasons for such a huge size of the US pharmaceutical market is its pharmaceutical expenditure per capita. According to The Economist (2005b), the US spent $728 per capita on pharmaceuticals accounting for 12.9 per cent of the total health expenditure in 2003. Sager and Socolar (2006) estimate the US health expenditure per capita in 2006 to be at $7256. If the pharmaceutical expenditure as a share of the health expenditure remained constant at 12.9 per cent in 2006, it would translate into $936 being spent on drugs for each person living in the US. All OECD countries spent less than $500 on pharmaceuticals per capita in 2003, except France and Canada, which spent $606 and $507, respectively. Pharmaceutical expenditure as a share of total health expenditure in the US was 12.9 per cent that is lower than the OECD average (17.5 per cent). However, this share is particularly high in the former Eastern Bloc countries, for example Hungary (27.6 per cent), Slovak Republic (38.5 per cent), Poland (30.3 per cent), but also South Korea (28.8 per cent).

Two specific characteristics set the US pharmaceutical market apart from the rest of the world. Firstly, most of the new drugs are launched in the US first. According to IMS data, 65 per cent of sales of new drugs marketed since 2002 are generated in the US compared with 24 per cent in the EU (cited in EFPIA 2008, p. 5). Secondly, new drugs are patented and the US has the world's highest drugs prices for patented drugs. The European markets are generally governed by drug price controls and universal health programmes. In contrast, the US does not control drugs prices and provides only limited healthcare programmes such as Medicaid and Medicare covering specific segments of the population.

This factor pushes the pharmaceutical spending per capita upwards in the US.

3.2.2.1 *Role of generics*

Governments are increasingly faced with rising healthcare costs and containing which have become an essential part of future public policy debates. The problem of rising healthcare costs is acknowledged even by industry leaders. For example, Richard Clark, President and CEO of Merck, is also the Chairman of the PhRMA. In the *Annual Report* (2008) of the PhRMA his message as the chairman reads:

> .... rapidly growing health costs globally are creating even greater pressures on utilization and payment and reimbursement systems. The pressure to control overall health care costs is real even though pharmaceutical costs are being targeted by critics well beyond their actual contribution to rising healthcare costs.
>
> (PhRMA 2008a, p. 2)

The US is also facing the healthcare issue. According to Professor Frederic Scherer of Harvard University (2007), 'healthcare in the United States continues to be a pressing public policy issue' because the healthcare expenditures 'surpassed the $1.5 trillion mark in 2002, comprising a record 14.9 per cent of gross domestic product' (GDP) (p. 267). Dr Phillip Brown, former editor of the Scrip Magazine (2004), estimates that the US federal and state authorities spend around 7.5 per cent of the GDP on healthcare. This means that almost half of the health expenditure comes from private sources such as insurance companies but also including out-of-pocket expenditure of almost 50 million uninsured Americans, who mostly rely on low-cost generics. Because 'the uninsured find many drugs too expensive' and 'if current cost trends continue, Americans are likely to lose their tolerance for paying substantially more than Canadians do for the same brand-name drugs' (Cutler 2007, p. 1292).

It is well known in the literature that the generics entry in the US market coincides with drops in prices significantly below the price charged for the originator product. The drop in price is gradual and dependent on the number of generics entering the market. First generic entrant in the US generally gets six months' market exclusivity. Thus, there is little incentive for a significant drop in price. However, when more generics enter the market, the price declines rapidly. According to the Generic Handbook (2007), 'the average retail price for a generic prescription in

2005 was $29.82 or 29.3 per cent of the $101.71 branded drug average' (p. 21). When the patent of Ciprofloxacin expired for example, generics entry forced a price drop of over 90 per cent in the US (Kamath 2004). If the price of generics did not drop significantly as it currently does, the total health expenditure in the US would rise substantially. In that case, the pharmaceutical spending per capita would be much higher than the current level.

Generics in the US are low priced relative to other countries and generics constitute a significant share of the US market. The share of generics by volume increased from 51 per cent in 2000 to 67 per cent in 2007 in the US (PhRMA 2008b). The PhRMA deliberately uses the word *sales* (instead of volume) to exaggerate the share of generics. The word *sales* is usually associated with the dollar value, which in the case of PhRMA's description of share of generics is misleading. To put into the right perspective, in the 12 months to June 2005, generics accounted for 60 per cent of total prescriptions in the US but constituted just 12 per cent of the total *sales*. In dollar value, this share represented $21.5 billion of the $179 billion pharmacy sales for the period (Genepharm 2005).

Globally, generics accounted for 14 per cent of the sales value in 2007 (OECD 2008). In Australia, the generics share was estimated at 17.9 per cent of the Pharmaceutical Benefits Scheme (PBS) expenditure (Sweeny 2008). Across European countries, the share of generics by sales varies significantly from a low of just 6.4 per cent (Spain) to as high as 45.6 per cent in Slovakia (EFPIA 2008). Generally, countries with a well-developed pharmaceutical industry tend to have lower share of generics, for example Switzerland and France at 11.6 per cent and 8.7 per cent, respectively. These countries have policies in place to support the innovative industry and discourage the use of generics. Countries with relatively less developed industry tend to have high share of generics (e.g. Slovakia). However, some exceptions to this rule can be observed. The EFPIA study shows that share of generics in the UK and Germany is 23.8 per cent and 30.5, respectively, and we know that both countries have one of the most advanced pharmaceutical industries.

The European Commission (2008) suggests that in the EU, generics first enter the market at a price on average 25 per cent lower than the originator price. Two years later, the generics price falls on average to 40 per cent below the originator price. Generics typically capture around 30 per cent of the volume sold at the end of the first year and 45 per cent after two years.

By comparison, generics in Australia are technically priced at the same level as the originator price even after patent expiry. If a generic product enters at a lower price than the originator, the government simply reduces the base price of the originator. Consumers wishing to purchase the originator product pay a brand premium. Thus, there are no real incentives to offer low prices on generics in countries with healthcare programmes such as Australia's PBS. However, Government of Australia (2007b) and Lofgren (2007) suggest that recent policy initiatives have been aimed at reducing the price paid for generics. In 2005, Australia introduced a mandatory discount pricing of 12.5 per cent on the launch of the first alternative brand of an already PBS-listed drug; however, with substantial incentives offered to pharmacists, around 40 per cent of prescriptions are dispensed with a brand premium, even when a generic alternative is available (Lofgren 2007).

Under the changes initiated in 2007, PBS-listed items would be divided into Formulary 1 (F1) and Formulary 2 (F2). Medicines, for which only a single brand is listed on the PBS (mainly patented drugs) or have just one supplier, would be placed under F1. Medicines with multi-brands would come under F2 category, which is further divided into two sub-groups. Category F2A would list medicines with low price competition. Commencing on 1 August 2008, prices for medicines under F2A will be annually reduced by 2 per cent for three years. This is in addition to the 12.5 per cent discount for the first alternative brand noted above. From August 2007, suppliers listing of a new brand must also agree to disclose the actual market price as a pre-condition to listing. Category F2T would list medicines where price competition is high. Medicines listed under F2T will be subject to a one off mandatory price reduction of 25 per cent. The 12.5 per cent discounted price will also apply where relevant. Price reductions for medicines listed under F2T flow on to all brands, strengths and forms of all medicines to which that medicine is interchangeable (Government of Australia 2007b).

Sweeny (2008) studies the impact of price changes in Australia after patent expiry of 103 medicines from August 1991 to July 2005. Different medicines had different patent expiry dates. During Sweeny's study, a total of 112 patents expired on medicines. He uses 'the Commonwealth price to pharmacist divided by the manufacturer's pack size because it provides the clearest picture of trends in prices' (Sweeny 2008, p. 112). Of all the medicines studied, only 46 (or 41 per cent) attracted competing brands for at least one of the forms of the medicines. Sweeny also finds that 17 of the medicines registered either price increases, or no changes or insignificant decreases in price despite the competing brands being present in the market. For example, patent on Aciclovir expired in September in 1995. Under an arrangement with GSK, the originator, Arrow Pharmaceuticals and Alphapharm had their products listed prior to the patent expiry but they did not drop the price. The first and second decrease in price of mere 3 per cent each time occurred in August 1999 and February 2003, possibly following the market entry of Douglas Pharmaceuticals, Genepharm, and Hexal Australia.

3.3 Developing new drugs

According to the European Commission (2008), the life cycle of a new medicine consists of three distinct stages. Stage 1 involves from research and development to market launch. Stage 2 is the period between market launch and patent expiry. Stage 3 is the period following the loss of market exclusivity, when generics can enter the market. Stage 3 has in part been considered above. Stage 2 is the core topic of this book and discussed throughout the book. Stage 1 is discussed hereunder.

It is well established that the drug development process involves significant investments, technical know-how, and it takes several years to complete the process. In recent years, investments into pharmaceutical R&D have grown much faster in the US than in the EU suggesting a shift in the R&D base. The EFPIA (2008) notes that between 1990 and 2007, the R&D investments increased by 330 per cent in the EU compared with 520 per cent increase in the US. While the EU has been a traditional leader in pharmaceutical innovative activities, the recent shift in investment has implications for the EU as well as for the Japanese industry as the following study shows.

A recent study examines new chemical or biological entities developed over a 20-year period in the leading regions. The EFPIA (2008) study divides the period into four five-year sub-periods. In the first sub-period (1988–92), the EU introduced 97 new entities (drugs) followed by Japan with 63. The US ranked third with 52 entities and the rest of the world (ROW) could manage just 5 new entities. In the second sub-period (1993–97), the EU still led with 90 followed by the US with 66. The Japanese contribution declined to 61 with ROW at 6. In the third sub-period (1998–2002), the US (77) overtook Europe (68), Japan (29), and the ROW (4). In the final sub-period (2003–07), the US (66) remained the leader, followed by Europe (48), Japan (15), and the ROW also with 15 new drugs. In the final sub-period, productivity in all regions declined, except the ROW, where the output more than tripled over the previous sub-period. At the same time, the Japanese output declined significantly.

The US is appreciated as the leading pharmaceutical market, especially for the sale of new drugs because the US allows high drug prices. The US is tolerated as the lead manufacturer of pharmaceuticals, while this trend might not last long as this function is shifting[2] to low-cost countries. However, shifting the R&D base to the US has become a worrisome factor for the Europeans. A recent study by Gambardella et al. (2000) for the European Commission notes:

> .... In particular, the observed concentration of research and innovation in the USA is worrying because Europe risks to be relegated into the fringe of the industry, surviving and even thriving through imitation, generics, marketing, but giving up a large share of the value added and becoming dependent on the USA for the development of new products. (p. 66)

Historically, the Europeans, Germany, Switzerland, and the United Kingdom in particular, have been the leaders in the development of new drugs. While the EU's stringent patent regime supports innovation, the US offers incentives such as research funding through the National Institutes of Health (NIH) that attracts investors to the US. Should there be a change in the pharmaceutical pricing principles in the US, which is likely following President Obama's recent election, the attractiveness to shift the R&D base to the US might decline. According to Professor Cutler of Harvard University, high drug prices that the US has and the differences in drug prices that currently exist between the US and other major markets especially Canada are not sustainable in the long run (Cutler 2007). Currently, high prices in the US offer to yield high returns on R&D investments. This incentive is likely to be affected by any changes to the drug pricing mechanism.

3.3.1 The process of drug development

The process of developing drugs involves a number of stages at which candidates (also labelled substances, compounds, or molecules) are tested for safety and efficacy. The drug development begins with the screening of around 10,000 candidates and the number of candidates progressively declines during the testing phases eventually transforming just one of those candidates to a marketable product.

After a successful pre-clinical testing (conducted first on small then on large animals), a manufacturer must first file an investigational new drug application with the Food and Drug Administration (FDA) in order to undertake the human trials. However, the initiation of human trials can, and often does, occur first outside the US (DiMasi et al. 2003). The US Congressional Budget Office (CBO) (1998) defines the three phases of human trials as follows. Phase-I tests the candidate on fewer than 100 healthy volunteers to determine safe dosage level and toxicity. Phase-II tests the new drug on 50 to 200 patients with the disease the drug is expected to combat. This phase determines the safety and efficacy. Phase-III tests the drug on thousands of people to see whether the benefits are statistically significant and to uncover any side-effects. The USFDA usually requires two controlled Phase-III trials before approving a new drug. There are also Phase-IV studies that involve post-marketing surveillance looking for adverse drug reactions (ADRs) that may not have been picked up during controlled trials. In case of high incidence of ADRs, the new drug may be withdrawn from the market as it was in the case of Vioxx.

During the development process, a large percentage of candidates drop out at the pre-clinical stage; nevertheless, this percentage has progressively declined in recent years. With the introduction of new technologies, development processes have become more efficient than before. Wilding (2002) studies the improvement in drug development and notes that the percentage of dropouts at the pre-clincial stage has declined from 70 per cent in 1997 to 53 per cent in 2001. The share of dropout candidates in Phase-I is around 10 per cent or less but significantly higher in Phase-II (15 per cent–27 per cent). This is because Phase-II by design is the first trial to test the efficacy of the drug. By the time, Phase-III trials begin, the efficacy has almost certainly been established. The share of drugs dropped in Phase-III is between 5 per cent and 10 per cent and at Pre-registration stage is less than 5 per cent. The late dropouts have implications for the costs of unsuccessful drugs. The later a candidate drops out, the higher the costs that the company would have to write off.

3.3.2 Development time

The literature appears to be dominated by the industry view that it takes 10–12 years to develop a new drug. This view is often extended and emphasised through regular studies and seminars sponsored by the pharmaceutical industry. The PhRMA supported by its European counterpart namely the EFPIA and other organisations representing innovator firms justifies the high price of originator product on the basis that it takes so long and it costs so much to bring a new drug to the market. The same reasons are also given to justify raising the protection of intellectual property in poor countries.

According to Pfizer (1999), the drug development time has increased from 8.8 years in the 1964–69 period to 11.0 years in the 1970s to 13.2 years in the 1980s as well as in the 1990s (cited in Gassmann et al. 2004). DiMasi (2001) suggests the development time to be even longer in recent years than the Pfizer estimates. His estimates for the 1960s and 1970s are similar to those of Pfizer, but increase to 14.2 years for the 1980s and 1990s. The implications of long development period are that the effective patent life (EPL) of the product gets reduced. Patents are taken out at the early stages of the development process. Thus, the clock for patent expiry starts ticking with the filing of the patent application. It is a race against time – the quicker a product can be developed and marketed, the longer the effective patent life or the exclusive market period a product has. What the foregoing studies suggest is that the EPL or the market period of a patented product has declined by 5.4 (14.2–8.8) years over the 30 years since the 1960s.

Other experts do not agree with the Pfizer/DiMasi view. In contrast, they claim that the drug development time has either remained the same or has in fact declined significantly in recent years. A US government agency; namely, the Congressional Budget Office (CBO) (1998) finds that the total development time remained 8.2 years for new drugs developed and approved between 1984 and 1995. The CBO concludes that for drugs approved in 1994 and 1995, the approval time was shorter but was offset by the longer clinical testing phase; thus, the total development did not change much. Lloyd (2002) studies the development time of drugs developed over a 15-year period, which he divides into three sub-periods. In the first sub-period (1986–90), he suggests that the drug development time was 109 months (9.1 years), which declined to 96 months (eight years) in the second sub-period (1991–95) and further declined to 71 months (5.11 years) in the final (1996–2000) sub-period. Lloyd explicitly notes that there was:

> ... compelling evidence that R&D times have indeed shortened considerably over the past 15 years and this improvement has occurred across all phases of development. In fact, the reduction in time taken to conduct Phase II and Phase III trials in particular is rather impressive. So it would appear that while the industry (if) not doing drug development any better, it is at least doing it quicker.
>
> (Lloyd 2002, p. 73)

The PhRMA's own industry profile (2004) also suggests that the drug development time (clinical and approval phases) has declined by around two years from the 1980s to 2000s.

The decline in drug development time is amplified by the significant reduction in drug approval time in recent years at the FDA. For example, *Parexel's Bio/Pharmaceutical R&D Statistical Sourcebook 2007/2008* shows that the approval time for new drugs in the US is as follows (Mathieu 2007). During the 1990–92 period, a total of 64 drugs were approved by the FDA. Of these, 19 new drugs were approved in 1990, 30 drugs in 1991, and 25 drugs in 1992. Of these, the approval time on 12/19, 13/30, and 12/25 was more than two years. In fact, it took many years to approve some drugs. Searle's Daypro (122.5 months), Wyeth-Ayerst's Lodine (97.1 months), Wyeth-Ayerst's ISMO (96.1 months), Abbott's Prosom (84.2 months), R.W. Johnson's Vascor (84.0 months), and SmithKlineBeecham's Ralafen (70.5 months) are some of the examples. Just 11 of the 64 (or 17.2 per cent) drugs were approved within 12 months during the 1990–92 period. In contrast, 18 new drugs were approved in each year in 2005 and 2006. From the 36 approvals, 22 or 61.1 per cent of the new drugs were approved within a year. According to CBO (1998), it took 2.9 years on average to grant a new drug approval between 1984 and 1995. The recent statistics show a significant improvement in the approval time effectively increasing the exclusive market period for a new product.

The approval time at the FDA improved significantly after the user pay fees were introduced under the Prescription Drug User Fee Act (PDUFA) of 1992. Under the Act, the FDA could employ more staff to accelerate the approval process. According to the CBO (1998), all new drug applications have to be approved within 180 days, except where agreed upon with the applicant. This change since the early 1990s has reduced the approval time significantly. The industry lobbied strongly for the Act directly and through studies at the Center for the Study of Drug Development at Tufts University. According to Austrom and Howard (1994), the industry wants to bring new drugs to the market faster because delay in launch costs $1 million each day in lost sales. However, a major drawback of this Act is that it places the FDA in a compromising position on the strictness of the approval process.

3.3.3 Development costs

Drug development is an expensive function of the pharmaceutical industry. Broadly, the development costs can be divided into four components. While the pre-clinical component incurs significant costs

(27 per cent), clinical trials Phases I to III (48 per cent) are the most expensive component constituting almost half of the development costs. Phase III alone accounts for more than half of the costs of clinical trials. As noted earlier, this phase involves testing the new drug on thousands of people compared to the tests on relatively small populations under Phase I and Phase II. This phase is basically the final phase before obtaining marketing approval that cost around 6 per cent. The post marketing surveillance (Phase-IV) and uncategorised expenditure account for the rest of the development costs (EFPIA 2008).

In dollar terms, the drug developments' costs would vary for different types of drugs. For example, costs of developing a drug to treat a chronic disease would be substantially higher than the costs to develop a drug for short-term diseases. Drugs for chronic disease require longer testing periods to determine the efficacy level incurring additional costs. However, the drug development costs also vary significantly between authors representing opposing views. On the one hand, the industry representing innovator pharmaceutical firms and the studies it sponsors come up with one set of figures surpassing $1 billion in 2007. On the other hand, industry experts estimate the costs of a new drug to be no more than $100 million. Hereunder we examine why the development costs are so different.

Hansen (1979) estimates the costs of developing a new drug at $54 million in the 1970s. In the early 1980s, these costs were estimated at between $70 million and 90 million rising to $125 million in 1986 (Wiggins 1987 as cited in Gambardella 1995). DiMasi (1991) estimates the development costs at $231 million in 1990. DiMasi et al. (2003) estimate the costs of bringing a new drug to the market at $802 million that have grown to more than $1.3 billion in 2007 (DiMasi & Grabowski 2007). While all these estimates include the costs of dropout candidates, other studies question this $ figure (see for example Collier 2009; Dukes 2006; Goozner 2004, details later in the chapter). Moreover, DiMasi, Hansen, and Grabowski acknowledge that in recent years, the widespread use of new technologies, such as combinatorial chemistry techniques and high-throughput screening, may have made the discovery process more cost-efficient than before.

While the contribution of the foregoing studies is duly acknowledged, a number of issues affecting the development costs need to be considered. Studies in foregoing paragraph are predominantly based at the Center for the Study of Drug Development at the Tufts University in Boston or they are based on previous studies undertaken at the Center. According to Graham Dukes, an international lawyer and Professor

Emeritus at the University of Groningen, this 'Center was from the start financed primarily by the research-based industry and saw it as its mission to undertake policy studies that could support the industry case on various contentious issues' (Dukes 2006, p. 239). Studies at this Center would have a natural bias towards the research-based industry. In their attempt to expel any doubts of bias in their study, DiMasi et al. (2003) explicitly note that 'the authors did not receive any external funding to conduct this study' (p. 183). But it is well established that the Center is financed by the industry. The DiMasi and Grabowski (2007) study published in the *Managerial and Decision Economics* does not make any reference to any funding. Instead, the editorial of the journal by Vernon and Manning (2007) reads that this issue is 'devoted to the industrial organization and political economy of the pharmaceutical industry' and that 'we also thank Pfizer Inc for financial support'.

We now examine how the costs are deliberately distorted to please the industry. First, the cost estimates are based on *confidential* data that may be inflated anyway. In any case, such data cannot be independently verified leaving ample room for distortion. Second, DiMasi (1991), DiMasi et al. (2003), and DiMasi and Grabowski (2007) calculate the actual outlay for a new drug as follows. Of the total development costs claimed in the 1991 study, the actual outlay was estimated at $114 million (49.4 per cent), $403 million (50.2 per cent) in 2003, and $452 million (34.3 per cent) in 2007 including the costs of dropout candidates. The authors then *time-adjust* these costs to derive capitalised costs, which the economists call opportunity costs. According to Goozner (2004), the opportunity cost assumes:

> ...that the money invested in research and development today, which won't have a payoff for many years down the road, could have been spent on other things or turned back to shareholders as additional profit. (p. 237)

Goozner suggests that it was misleading to include the opportunity costs in the calculation of drug development costs. In the pharmaceutical industry, the R&D investments yield the highest returns in any industry. To suggest that the investors could have invested elsewhere instead is an absurd proposition. Why would investors invest elsewhere expecting a lower rate of return? To inflate the perhaps already exaggerated outlay through their *confidential* questionnaire undermines the integrity of research.

Few other facts not considered (or deliberately overlooked) in the DiMasi and DiMasi et al. studies estimating the costs are as follows. The companies reap significant benefits in tax on R&D investments bringing down the actual costs. Public Citizen (2001) critically analyses the DiMasi studies and also estimates the costs using data on development costs supplied by the industry. After accounting for tax benefits, Public Citizen estimates the costs of a new drug at between $57 million and $71 million in the 1990s including the costs of dropouts. Dr Marcia Angell, former editor-in-chief of the *New England Journal of Medicine* points out that the DiMasi estimates were based on a deliberately selected sample of expensive drugs making no allowance for tax rebates to boost the costs. She suggests 'that the real cost per drug is well under $100 million' and 'were it anywhere near the claimed $802 million, the industry would not be so secretive about the data' (Angell 2004, p. 46).

Another fact distorted in the DiMasi studies is the contribution of publicly funded research undertaken at academic and other health institutes. According to Scherer (2000), the NIH provides considerable financial and technical support to the pharmaceutical research. DiMasi et al. (2003) mention in passing that some new compounds investigated by pharmaceutical firms did in fact originate in government or academic institutions undermining the role these institutions play in research.

In contrast, the NIH (2000) studies the development of 5 drugs (Zantac, Zovirax, Capoten, Vasotec, and Prozac) with sales of more than $1 billion in 1995 and finds that 55 per cent of the research was undertaken at the NIH and another 30 per cent at the foreign academic institutes (cited in Public Citizen 2001). Only 15 per cent of the research was carried out by the industry. The NIH conclusion usurps all industry claims. The NIH finds that:

> ...public researchers often tackle the riskiest and most costly research, which is basic research, making it easier for industry to profit. The NIH report discovered that only 14 per cent of the drug industry's total R&D spending went to basic research, while 38 per cent went to applied research and 48 per cent was spent on product development.
>
> (cited in Public Citizen 2001, p. 10)

The pharmaceutical industry is the most R&D-intensive among industries (DiMasi et al. 2003). According to the annual report of the PhRMA (2008a), the industry spent around 16.5 per cent of its global revenue on R&D in 2007. In dollar terms, the industry expenditure was $58.8 billion. In absolute terms, the R&D expenditure has more than doubled since 1993 when it was $27.3 billion. According to Mathieu (2007), after the industry itself, the NIH is the largest source for funding medical research. In 2007, through its total of 28 institutes, the NIH is estimated to have spent around $29 billion on supporting and conducting research.

Since the 1980s, the size of the pipeline has enlarged significantly. The top ten companies by pipeline had on average 60–70 new drugs in the development phases in 1985. Ciba-Geigy ranked at the top with 81 new drugs in the pipeline. In 2005, Sanofi-Aventis had 215 drugs in the development phase. This increase has mostly been the result of mergers and acquisitions in the industry as noted earlier in the chapter. Ironically however, while the size of the drug pipelines and investments in R&D have increased due to mergers, overall innovation is decreasing (Cruddas and Gannon 2009).

3.3.3.1 Pharmaceutical marketing

The pharmaceutical industry emphasises its R&D expenditure at every opportunity to justify the high prices and patent protection for new drugs. What the industry does not appear to be happy to disclose is that it spends significantly more on marketing than it does on R&D. The OECD (2001) *Report on Competition and Regulation Issues in the Pharmaceutical Industry* suggests that the industry's marketing expenditure is around double that of its R&D expenditure. On the one hand, pharmaceutical firms are notorious for their perks and freebies to influence physicians to prescribe their medicines (Kassirer 2005). In his book titled *Inventing Disease and Pushing Pills,* Blech (2006), highlights the antisocial behaviour of the industry. Blech suggests that 'for every single doctor the pharmaceutical industry is spending 8000 to 13,000 Euros a year on marketing' (p. 16). He also suggests that GSK alone employs an army of 17,000 pharmaceutical advisers in the US and Europe.

Firms in this industry engage in unethical practices to promote the products they want to sell. In 2005, the Canadian Pharmaceutical Industry Association introduced rules to place on probation, suspend, or even expel companies not meeting its marketing standards (Scrip News 2005a). In Canada, companies can also be fined for breaching its code of conduct Can$10,000 for the first offence, Can$15,000 for the second, and Can$25,000 for the third breach with any additional violations rising to Can$50,000. According to Scrip News (2005a), AstraZeneca was placed on probation for series of breaches of the code. On the other hand, the industry is not forthcoming with all the facts when marketing new products. Harvey (2005) suggests that the industry distorts the promotion process through selectively promoting the benefits of the latest and most expensive drugs and withholding information about the side effects, contradictions, and opportunity costs.

3.3.4 Direction of pharmaceutical research

This is the most critical part of drug research directly affecting access to medicines in the poor countries. Priority-setting by decision makers, primarily at large MNCs, determines the direction of pharmaceutical research. At present, there is a 10/90 research gap. This term refers to the fact that only 10 per cent of the biomedical research funding is targeted to the diseases accounting for 90 per cent of the global disease burden (Barry 2003). This gap was first identified by Global Forum for Health Research (1999). Implications of this gap are 'the vast divisions in the health status of the relatively high – and low income groups within a society' (Commission on Macroeconomics and Health 2001, p. 22). Mortality rate among children in the poorest quintile, in developing countries such as Bolivia, Turkey, and India, is significantly higher than those in the richest quintile. Murray and Lopez (1996) study the global burden of disease and project the possible causes of deaths to year 2020. In their study, they represent the base-, optimistic-, and pessimistic view of the top ten causes of deaths worldwide to year 2020. Tuberculosis appears on all three lists suggesting that this disease is certainly one of biggest killers of humans. Despite the large number of people dying and projected to die over the next two decades, large MNCs do not appear interested to commit research funding in this direction. This is because tuberculosis is common in poor countries but almost non-existent in the developed world.

Global Forum for Health Research (2004) estimates that the private pharmaceutical industry now accounts for 42 per cent of all health research spending. Public funding of high income and transition economies (47 per cent), public funding of low- and middle-income economies (3 per cent), and NGOs account for the rest of the funding. Yet, there appears to be no change in the direction of pharmaceutical research. According to Labonte and Schrecker (2006), 'public funding agencies in many industrialized countries are linking priorities to the anticipation of commercial returns' (p. 25). One would expect the pharmaceutical industry in the developing countries to set priorities towards meeting the needs of the poor. However, the Indian pharmaceutical industry is also focused on developing products to serve the wealthy markets of the developed world, simply because the poor lack the purchasing power. Priority-setters in the pharmaceutical research appear to have forgotten the advice from one of the founding fathers of the pharmaceutical industry. In the often cited visionary quotation, George W. Merck says, 'Medicine is for people. It is not for the profits. The profits follow, and if we have remembered that, they have never failed to appear' (see for example, Dr Reddy's 2004; Hawthorne 2003).

The governments in the poor countries need to develop and introduce equitable healthcare programmes that include access to medicines. Programmes of such type are more important in the poor countries, where medicines constitute a significantly large share of health expenditure relative to developed countries. The model for India in Chapter 8 is an example other countries could replicate. This model has been developed taking into account India's health and industry requirements. Under the model, India's entire population would have access to medicines, which would encourage research-based companies to invest into drugs for the diseases of the poor.

3.4 Conclusions

The global pharmaceutical industry is dominated by large MNCs primarily based in the US, Europe, and Japan. These companies hold most of the pharmaceutical patents worldwide. Through mergers and acquisitions, the MNCs are progressively getting larger and typically have much larger new product pipelines than ever before. The industry concentration has reached such an extent, where the top ten companies account for around half the global pharmaceutical sales.

In particular, the US dominates global pharmaceutical industry in its capacity as being both the largest manufacturer and the largest consumer of pharmaceuticals. The recent shift of R&D from Europe to the US is a disturbing development for the Europeans who until recently were the leaders in pharmaceutical innovation. Japanese output in drug development has also declined over the last 10–15 years, while the rest of the world has increased its share of new drugs.

The pharmaceutical research is expensive involving a process spanning over several years. However, the industry's own claims regarding R&D costs and the time required for developing new drugs appear to be gross exaggerations. The methodology used in the studies on which these claims are based has been widely criticised for inflating the costs. The real costs of bringing a new drug to the market are likely to be significantly lower than the figures suggested by the industry and the industry-sponsored research.

The pharmaceutical industry spends significantly more on marketing than it does on R&D. If ethical standards were effectively enforced, the methods pharmaceutical firms employ to promote new and expensive drugs would breach these standards in most countries. It is common knowledge that firms in this industry often provide perks to physicians in return for prescribing their medicines.

Private firms in the pharmaceutical industry account for less than half of the R&D expenditure. Governments, NGOs, and other agencies provide the rest of the funding. Large pharmaceutical MNCs are focusing on developing the blockbuster drugs that are considered to be the backbone of the MNCs for recouping their R&D investments. In recent years however, even the public institutes have become more focused on research with a potential for great returns. The 10/90 research gap is widely accepted but continues, because the poor lack adequate resources to pay a price that the industry expects. Governments in developing countries need to consider new models to provide equitable healthcare, including access to medicines that would encourage research-based companies to develop medicines for the diseases of the poor.

Part II

Access to Medicines in India

4

Development of India's Pharmaceutical Industry

4.1 Introduction and background

The development of India's pharmaceutical industry has played a significant role in boosting the availability and affordability of pharmaceuticals. With significantly lower manufacturing costs relative to those in developed countries, Indian companies were able to lower the drug prices and increase access to medicines in India as well as in other low- and middle-income countries (LMICs). A number of policies introduced in the 1970s (discussed later in the chapter) underpinned this growth from a virtually non-existent pharmaceutical industry to becoming the world's largest producer of generics.

India's large pharmaceuticals industry now plays a vital role in the country's economy employing around 500,000 directly and 1.9 million indirectly (OPPI 2003). In broad terms, the total industry output accounts for 1.3 per cent of the world market by value and around 8 per cent by volume (Nanda & Khan 2005). The difference in market share by value and by volume suggests that the Indian pharmaceutical products are priced low relative to the other products in the global market. Recognising the economic significance of this industry, the Government of India, in August 2008, established the Department of Pharmaceuticals under the Ministry of Chemicals and Fertilizers. Previously, this responsibility rested with the Department of Chemicals and Petrochemicals.

India's introduction of economic reforms in 1991 laid the foundation for industrial de-licensing in a range of industries including pharmaceuticals. Subsequently, the annual growth rate in the pharmaceutical industry increased to around 25 per cent for two years and since then, the industry has been growing at around 15 per cent annually.

India's pharmaceutical industry is expected to maintain its rate of growth at more than 10 per cent per annum over the next few years compared with the estimated growth for the pharmaceutical industries of the US at 5–6 per cent and of Europe at 3–4 per cent (Cygnus 2007).

The total industrial product of India's pharmaceutical industry increased from US$12 billion in 2005–06 to around US$19 billion in 2007–08 with exports also increasing from US$3.8 billion to US$7.2 billion in the respective years (GOI 2006a, 2009). These figures suggest that the domestic market also improved from US$8.2 billion ($12 billion–$3.8 billion) in 2005–06 to US$11.8 billion ($19 billion–$7.2 billion) in 2007–08. This is a significant increase from US$333 million in domestic sales in 1970 (Pradhan 1983). The significance of the increased industry output is that it helped India become almost self-sufficient in formulations and reduce dependency on previously imported bulk drugs. India now manufactures around 350 (around 70 per cent) of the bulk drugs used in the domestic production of formulations (Pharmaceutical & Drug Manufacturers 2005a; Swain et al. 2002). It is imperative that the industry product and the growth be kept in its true perspective. The industry product is measured in monetary value, which in India's case is known to be low relative to other countries. A major drawback with the value data is that they club together the expensive medicines with the low-cost drugs distorting the data on access to medicines. The data on volume sales would provide more accurate data on access to medicines in terms of the number of patients served.

4.2 Growth of the India pharmaceutical industry

The number of firms in India's pharmaceutical industry grew from 2257 in 1969–70 to around 23,000 units in 2004 (see Table 4.1), although

Table 4.1 Estimates of manufacturing units 1969–70 to 2004

Period	Year	No. of units	Growth %
1	1969–70	2,257	
2	1979–80	5,156	128.4
3	1989–90	16,000	210.3
4	1999–00	20,053	25.3
5	2004	23,000	14.7

Source: Compiled from Galpalli (2004); Pharmaceutical & Drug Manufacturers (2005b); and Pradhan (1983).

estimates of exact number varies from 5700 (Essentialdrugs 2004; The Expert Committee 2003) to 10,000 (OPPI 2006) and to 23,000 (Galpalli 2004). A number of official documents refer to 20,000 pharmaceutical manufacturers (GOI 2002c, 2006c; WHO 2004b); hence, we use this number as a point of reference in this book.

While the decadal growth in manufacturing units from 1970 to 1980 was substantial, the subsequent decade registered the highest growth of over 210 per cent. The principal reason for this growth was a range of industrial policies introduced in the 1970s. These policies restricted the movement of foreign exchange and placed special conditions on firms with more than 40 per cent foreign equity. At the same time, by abolishing product patents and granting only process patents, the Patents Act 1970 broke the monopoly of the patent holders. The MNCs held 99 per cent of the drugs and pharmaceutical patents in India between 1947 and 1957 (Aggarwal 2004). Given the low innovative skills of the domestic industry in the pre-1970 period, it would be safe to assume that the MNCs' domination in patents would not have diminished before the introduction of Patents Act 1970.

In 1970, the pharmaceutical MNCs dominated the Indian market, in which, the domestic firms had only 15 per cent share. Following India's introduction of restrictive measures, the number of MNCs in India declined from 63 in the 1970s to 32 in 2004 (Chaudhuri 2005). The new industrial landscape created opportunities for domestic firms to acquire innovative skills in order to develop new processes to manufacture patented drugs. The share of indigenous manufacturers increased to 50 per cent in 1982 and by 2000, they accounted for more than three quarters of the Indian market (Shah 2003). Today, India and Japan are the only major markets where MNCs do not dominate.

In 2004, the top ten pharmaceutical MNCs (GSK, Pfizer, Abbott, Aventis, Novartis, Wyeth, Merck, AstraZeneca, Janssen Cilag, and Infar India) collectively accounted for less than 19 per cent of India's pharmaceutical market (Novartis 2004). In the same year, the share of top ten domestic firms (Cipla, Ranbaxy, Nicolas Piramal, Sun Pharma, Dr Reddy's, Zydus Cadila, Aristo Pharma, Alken, Lupin, and Wockhardt) was more than 30 per cent. However, these figures are measured in monetary value, which often marginalises the role small pharmaceutical firms play in providing low-cost medicines.

4.2.1 The significance of the small pharmaceutical firms

Under the policies introduced in the 1970s, government subsidies encouraged the development of small manufacturing units resulting in a high market fragmentation. In 2005, around 8000 manufacturing units belonging to the small-scale[1] industry (SSI) category accounted for around 50 per cent of the market by volume and 29 per cent by value (GOI 2007e). This is a significant increase on the 15 per cent share by value held by the 2179 SSI units in 1980–81 (Pradhan 1983). This comparison demonstrates the importance of the small pharmaceutical firms at the low end of the market. When we consider the substantial rise in India's market size over the last three decades noted earlier in this chapter, the contribution of the small manufacturers becomes even more significant.

Access to medicines in India has increased from 15–20 per cent of the population in 1980–81 (Bhagat 1982) to 35 per cent in 2001 (WHO 2004b). Absolute numbers show the following change. India had a population of 683 million in 1981, of which 15–20 per cent means that the number of Indians with access to medicines was around 102–136 million. In 2001, India' population had reached 1029 million and at 35 per cent, 360 million Indians had access to medicines. This means that an additional 224–258 million people had gained access to medicines between 1981 and 2001.

Several studies suggest that small-scale firms have significantly contributed to extend access to medicines in India, as the brand-generics manufactured by the large pharma companies are significantly more expensive than the generic-generics manufactured by the small firms. Medico Friends Circle (2006) reported that Aventis charged Rs. 95 for a tablet of Levofloxacin when the same drug was offered by a domestic manufacturer for only Rs. 7. Another study found that the wholesale price of a generic-generic ten tablet strip of Nimesulide 100 mg was as low as Rs. 1.20 compared with the retail price of Rs. 38.61 charged for Nise by Dr Reddy's Labs (DRL) (cited in Gupta 2004).

Das et al. (2007) examined the wholesale prices of 20 drugs and suggested significant mark-ups charged by the big brand firms relative to the small manufacturers. They reported that the largest difference between highest and lowest price was for Amlodipine – a difference of more than 881 per cent. Amtas, the *most sold* brand was manufactured by Intas, one of the leading Indian firms with a price more than 318 per cent higher than the lowest priced product in the same category. The DRL was charging over 580 per cent more for Omez than the lowest priced product in that category. They noted that except JB Chemicals and Aristo, all large firms including Nicholas Piramal (NPML), Ranbaxy, USV, Wyeth, and GSK had priced their products significantly higher than the lowest priced products in their respective categories.

The drugs in the above studies were all off-patent generics. The *most sold* brands at higher pricing levels suggest significant marketing power that the large manufacturers exert relative to small firms. This market power in the drug industry is characterised by strong promotional competition rather than price competition (Bhagat 1982; Medico Friends Circle 2006). Blech (2006) suggests that pharmaceutical companies offer a range of perks to influence the doctors in return for prescribing their brand names. In contrast, cost-effective generics are rarely promoted (Harvey 2005). Minwalla (2003) believes that if generic[2] names were used in prescribing instead of brand names, it could limit the influence of marketing power of the pharmaceutical companies. In India, generic prescribing was first recommended by the Hathi Committee in 1975 and also considered by the Sen Committee (2005). The drug industry remains opposed to the concept and generic prescribing remains unimplemented (Scrip News 2005b). The drug industry claims that generic prescribing would shift the choice of medicines from doctors to chemists, which would be inappropriate for consumer interests (Roy & Madhiwala 2003). We believe however that generic prescribing in India could further increase access to medicines, because generic prescriptions would give the patients freedom to choose low-cost products over more expensive brands prescribed by the doctors, arguably under the influence of the manufacturers. However, the switch to generic prescribing policy would require adequate regulatory safeguards to ensure that generic drugs are bio-equivalent with the originator drugs (McLachlan et al. 2007).

4.3 Exports and imports

Indian pharmaceutical industry started from a low manufacturing base with exports of drugs and pharmaceuticals constituting less than 3 per cent of the industry product from 1970 to 1980 (Bhagat 1982). In subsequent years, exports grew significantly and in 2007–08, accounted for over a third of the industry product (GOI 2009). In the late 1980s, India turned from a net importer of pharmaceuticals to a net exporter, with its products now selling in more than 170 countries (Aggarwal 2004). In absolute terms, India's trade surplus in pharmaceuticals has increased from €370 million (~$520 million) in 1997–98 to €2 billion (~$2.8 billion) in 2007–08 (Perlitz 2008).

Two recent factors have contributed to improving the drug quality and boosting the India pharma exports. First, following the report of the Expert Committee (2003) on drug regulatory issues and spurious drugs, the Indian Government introduced new measures to raise manufacturing standards in the pharmaceutical industry. Under Schedule M of the Drugs and Cosmetics Act 1940, Good Manufacturing Practices (GMP) developed by the World Health Organization (WHO) were made mandatory for all pharma manufacturing units from 1 July 2005 (GOI 2007e).

Second, a significant number of manufacturing units have obtained in recent years compliance certification by the national authorities for exports to those specific markets. The standards in many countries are significantly higher than the WHO–GMP and the number of Indian manufacturers meeting these standards is increasing. For example, India has 84 units approved by the USFDA, which is the largest number of manufacturing units approved by the agency outside the US. Other countries with significant number of FDA approved units are Italy (60), Spain (25), and China (22) (FICCI 2005). A significant number of India pharma units are also approved by other regulatory authorities such as the MHRA (the UK), TGA (Australia), and ANVISA (Brazil). The significance of these certifications is a compliance guarantee for quality assurance providing an impetus for its pharma exports to highly regulated markets.

The initial focus of the domestic industry was on exports to the developing countries, erstwhile Soviet Union, and Commonwealth of Independent States (CIS). After the introduction of the Drug Price Competition and Patent Term Restoration Act of 1984, commonly known as the Hatch-Waxman Act in the US, generics did not have to undergo extensive clinical trials for sale in the US (Bower & Sulej 2007). Instead, generic producers had to prove bio-equivalence to the originator drug to gain market approval. Since the mid-1990s, India has been increasingly exporting pharmaceutical products to the highly regulated markets including the US.

In 2005–06, the top ten destinations made up around 43 per cent of the India's total pharmaceutical exports, in which the regulated markets dominated (GOI 2007e). The US was the largest destination for India's pharmaceutical exports. Five out of the top ten destinations were OECD countries collectively accounting for almost two-thirds of the value for top ten destinations. The significance of exports to the highly regulated market is that the domestic industry feels confident and is capable of producing drugs that meet the world's highest standards.

From 1980–81 to 1992–93, India's pharmaceutical exports fluctuated considerably, but have been relatively steady since 1993–94 (Chaudhuri 2005). In absolute terms, the exports increased from Rs. 464 million in

Table 4.2 Exports of India's pharmaceutical industry (Rs. Million) (1999–00 to 2006–07)

Year	Total	Change %
1999–00	72,302	21.33
2000–01	87,575	21.12
2001–02	98,347	12.30
2002–03	128,379	30.54
2003–04	152,132	18.50
2004–05	178,578	17.38
2005–06	215,790	20.84
2006–07	249,420	15.58

Source: Compiled from Government of India, various years, Annual reports, Department of Chemicals and Petrochemicals, Ministry of Chemicals, and Fertilizers, New Delhi.

1980–81 to Rs. 72,302 million in 1999–00 and to Rs. 249,420 million in 2006–07. Over the 27 years study period, the exports averaged positive annual growth of 27.3 per cent compared with the average growth in the industry product at 15.41 per cent during a similar period. Consequently, the exports component of the industry product has been continuously rising. Table 4.2 shows India's pharmaceutical exports growth from 1999–00.

In 2004, the government established Pharmexcil, a high level body to assist the pharmaceutical industry to explore the export potential by organising networking opportunities in India and abroad (GOI 2005d). Patents on a number of lucrative drugs with annual sales of over $100 billion are due to expire by 2012, which means that one-sixth of global sales or one-fourth of the US sales will disappear for large MNCs (The Wharton School 2008). This change will provide Indian generic manufacturers ample opportunities to boost exports.

4.3.1 TRIPS, India's pharmaceutical exports, and access to medicines

Two questions are addressed in this sub-section. First, how do India's exports increase access to medicines? Second, how are India's pharmaceutical exports likely to be affected in the wake of apprehensions that the implementation of TRIPS would put an end to its low-cost exports to poor countries?

First, the case of antiretrovirals (ARVs) used in HIV/AIDS treatment illustrates the contribution made by India's pharmaceutical industry to significantly reduce the price and extend access to medicines. The case, in which 39 pharma MNCs instituted legal proceedings against South Africa for allowing the sale of cheaper versions of ARVs, is well documented in the literature and in the media the world over. In the wake of widespread global demonstrations, the pharma companies withdrew the case. In 2001, Cipla, an Indian manufacturer offered to supply a generic version of ARVs at $800 per patient-a-year compared with the price between $10,000 and $15,000 charged by the MNCs for the same supply (Weissman 2007). The Cipla offer was later revised down to $350 per patient-a-year to supply the ARVs to South Africa (Global-Challenges 2008). Cipla is now the world's largest manufacturer of ARVs by volume and at $150 per patient for a year's supply of ARVs, around 40 per cent of the HIV/AIDS patients worldwide undergoing the ARV therapy take Cipla drugs (Wikipedia 2008). Other Indian companies such as Ranbaxy have also joined in supplying low-cost HIV/AIDS drugs to extend access to medicines in poor countries. A number of NGOs, including the Clinton Foundation, Global Fund to Fight AIDS, Tuberculosis and Malaria, and the UNAIDS programme significantly depend on the low-cost supplies from India.

The Indian pharmaceutical Industry also contributed to increasing access to medicines in the developed countries. The core business of India's pharmaceutical exports to the highly regulated markets has been the off-patent generics and the level of competition after patent expiry has resulted in significant reductions of the originator price. For example, after the patent on Ciprofloxacin expired in the US, 11 generic versions were launched in the market. The intense competition led to a 97 per cent drop from the price the originator had charged (Kamath 2004). The DRL, one of the Indian firms to launch the generic version of Ciprofloxacin, claimed that 'even at the price, we made 50 per cent profit' (cited in Mukreja 2004). By 2005, the DRL version of Ciprofloxacin had captured around 17 per cent share of the US market (Dr Reddy's 2005). The DRL has 50 Drug Master Files (DMFs)[3] in Canada, 128 in the US, and 71 with the European agency (Dr Reddy's 2008). Collectively, India accounted for 25 per cent of the Abbreviated New Drug Applications (ANDA[4]s) and over 25 per cent of the DMFs filed in the US in 2007 and 2008, which is 'the largest share in registration granted in the world including the USA' (GOI 2009, p. 8).

Thus, we conclude that the Indian pharmaceutical industry has contributed, and continues to contribute, significantly to lowering drugs prices in the importing countries. Leading Indian firms draw significant proportion of their sales revenues from overseas markets. Ranbaxy,

DRL, and Cipla, respectively generate around 70 per cent, 60 per cent, and 50 per cent of their sales revenues in overseas markets. Other firms including Sun Pharma, Torrent, Wockhardt, Nicholas Piramal, Lupin, and Zydus Cadila collect a substantial share of their sales revenues from overseas. With its products selling at low prices, India's pharmaceutical industry is contributing to extend access to medicines in more than 170 countries.

Now we return to the second question; namely, the likely impact of TRIPS on India's pharmaceutical exports. Two distinct groups of countries import pharmaceuticals from India. The first group consists of the highly regulated markets of the US and other developed countries with stringent patent regimes. Implementing TRIPS will not affect India's ability to continue to export to this group of countries, because only off-patent products are exported to these markets and the export of such products remains unaffected under TRIPS, as the legal restrictions in these countries did not allow the import of imitated versions of patented drugs.

The second group consists of low- and middle-income countries (LMICs) with relatively lax patent regimes. This group of countries has been the main importers of India's supply of generic versions of on-patent drugs. To determine the impact TRIPS might have on India's drug exports to this group of countries, we use two sources: namely, IndianData.com provides data on items exported and GOI (2007b) provides destination for each drug exported. Malhotra (2008) analyses every single drug exported from 2000–01 to 2002–03 for patent expiry in South Africa. The purpose of this examination was to assess which exports might be affected after 2005.

As India did not provide product patents pre-2005, exports data were examined for patent expiry at the destination country. South Africa was chosen as a country of reference for patent expiry, because it has the largest number of people living with HIV/AIDS and where access to medicines is a major issue. India is the largest supplier of low-cost ARVs used in the treatment of HIV/AIDS.

Each drug was separately checked for the date of patent expiry with reference to the first year of inquiry being 2000. For example, if a drug was found to be patented in South Africa until 2000 or beyond, the whole item[5] was regarded as patent protected and was included in the calculation. If however, the patent expired in 2000, this item was included only for one year (i.e. 2000–01), and similarly for the other years.[6] Of the 309 items India exported during the study period, a total of 26 drugs (grouped under 14 items – see total-1 Table 4.3) were patent

Table 4.3 Drugs and pharmaceuticals with patent expiry in 2000 or beyond

Original item no.	Product	Export value (US$ million)		
		2000–01	2001–02	2002–03
43	Captopril (1994), Lisinopril (1999), Enalapril (1999) Ramipril (2001), Perindopril (2001), Benzepril (2002) – formulations thereof in tablets, etc.	$0.9767	$2.0792	$2.1802
48	Cefixime and its salts (2000)	$1.2236		
56	Cetirazine – formulations thereof (2002)	$0.5851	$0.6107	$0.5041
95	Famotidine – formulations thereof in tablets, etc. (2000)	$0.4690		
98	Fluticasone – formulations thereof in tablets, capsules, etc. (2001)	n/a	$0.0290	
145	Lansoprazole – formulations thereof in tablets, etc. (2005)	$0.3771	$0.5935	$0.4615
150	Lomefloxacin (2004)	$0.0580	$0.0647	$0.3452
151	Loratadine – formulations thereof (2001)	$0.7121	$1.0176	
186	Norfloxacine – Frmltns thereof in Caps etc. (2002)	$5.7380	$2.2532	$2.2319
187	Ofloxacin (2001)	$0.0359	$0.1409	
211	Other Carcino – Chemotherapeutic Drugs (e.g. Cyclophosphamide, chlorambucil, paclitaxel (2013), tamoxiphen, etc.)	$0.9364	$1.3763	$1.4316
256	Roxythromycin (2000), Azithromycin (2008) Clarithromycin (2005 Taisho and 2013 AstraZenecca) in capsules, injections, etc.	$3.0088	$2.4282	$3.8423
258	Simvastatin (2001); Lovastatin (2000); Atrovastatin (2007)	$0.2691	$1.9269	$4.3967
309	Zidovudine – formulations thereof (2006)	$0.0640	$0.3348	$0.8683
Total – 1		$14.4538	$12.855	$16.2618
	No data available on patent expiry on the following items			
55	Cephaloridine	$0.4023	$0.9936	$0.1500
87	Dxamtasne Tblts etc incl. Eye/Ear Drops etc.	$2.9199	$2.8304	$2.4342
272	Syntocinone Injection	$0.0407	$0.0018	$0.0355
Total – 2		$3.3629	$3.8258	$2.6197
Grand total		$17.8167	$16.6808	$18.8815

Source: Malhotra (2008, Table 4).

protected in 2000 or beyond in South Africa. Data on patent expiry on three items were not available. These items are listed separately in the table, but considered as patent protected in the grand total. Patents on 6 of these drugs had expired before 2000, and were due to expire on another 4 drugs in 2000, 6 drugs in 2001, and 3 drugs in 2002. Accordingly, these drugs were included in our examination only for that part of the period when they were under patent, but excluded from calculations for the subsequent period. The remaining 7 drugs had patent protection beyond 2002.

Table 4.3 shows the export value of the items under patent protection in South Africa during the study period. The numbers in the first column correspond to the item numbers in the original table (available from Indiandata.com). The exports data from GOI (2007b) show that India exported 249 drugs grouped into 309 items under the category of drugs and pharmaceuticals during the period of inquiry. A significant number of items had more than 3–4 drugs grouped together under the same item number. The main findings of the study are summarised below.

The total value of exports affected by the new regime would be $17.18 million for the year 2000–01. For the years 2001–02 and 2002–03, this value would be $16.68 million and $18.88 million, respectively. In order to translate these values into relative terms, we consider India's total pharmaceutical exports, which stood at $1.95 billion, $2.18 billion, and $2.65 billion for 2000–01, 2001–02, and 2002–03, respectively. Thus, India's exports of imitations of patented drugs as a share of its total pharmaceutical exports that could be affected by the new regime would amount to 0.91 per cent, 0.77 per cent, and 0.71 per cent for the respective years.

Based on the data examined, it can be concluded that in relative terms, the impact of TRIPS on India's exports is likely to be quite small. In fact, only around 1 per cent of India's pharmaceutical exports may be in jeopardy due to TRIPS. However, the overall impact of TRIPS on potential exports and patient welfare is likely to be considerably greater than simply the value of exports lost. This difference arises due to two reasons. First, India's drug prices are among the lowest in the world. So, the dollar value is likely to under-represent significantly the scale of populations that would be denied access to medicines after the regime change. Second, the implementation of TRIPS has closed all future opportunities for India's domestic industry to develop new processes and provide cheaper alternatives to expensive innovator drugs. This loss would adversely affect access to medicines to the poor in India and other LMICs.

4.3.2 Imports

Initially, India was heavily dependent on imports from Germany, France, Switzerland, and the UK. Now India's imports are primarily confined to bulk drugs, which until recently came mainly from European countries (Roumeliotis 2006). The Chinese accession to the WTO in 2001 changed the global landscape for bulk drugs providing Indian manufacturers with a wider choice of suppliers. India's pharmaceutical imports from China now rank ahead of any other country. In 2005–06, the top ten countries accounted for over 81 per cent of India's total pharmaceutical imports. While the developed countries dominated the list of top ten suppliers of Indian imports, China alone contributed to around 42 per cent of the total of the top ten suppliers of pharmaceutical products to India (GOI 2007e).

India's drugs imports have also increased significantly in recent years. These imports grew from Rs. 1125 million in 1980–81 to Rs. 44,272 million in 2005–06. The growth in pharmaceutical imports has not been stable throughout the period. At 75.7 per cent, the highest annual growth was recorded in 1995–96 after the signing of the WTO agreements. The lowest imports growth was in 1990–91, when a negative figure of 7.4 per cent was recorded.

Though generally discouraged by Indian policy makers, the pharmaceutical imports have played a significant role in the development of the Indian pharmaceutical industry. Before the industry began to manufacture bulk drugs domestically, imported bulk drugs were used to manufacture formulations for the domestic and overseas markets. India still imports around 30 per cent of the bulk drugs used in the manufacture of formulations. This means that even today, the total Indian demand for bulk drugs could not be met without the contribution of the imports. Since the Indian law now treats the foreign companies at par with the Indian firms and the special conditions forcing the MNCs to manufacture in India now abolished, imports are likely to increase in the future. Imports are also likely to play significant role in the availability of patented medicines in India. The pharma MNCs holding most of the patents worldwide are unlikely to manufacture the patented drugs in India, because the MNCs tend to import these drugs from the parent company rather than produce them in a developing country (Phadke 2000).

4.4 Foreign direct investment

This section examines foreign direct investment (FDI) in the Indian pharmaceutical industry with a view to determine the importance of

IPRs in attracting the FDI. The significance of this examination is to assess if implementing TRIPS is likely to increase FDI into India's pharmaceutical sector.

Before examining the FDI data, it may help to know that under the policies introduced in the 1970s, foreign equity in the pharmaceutical industry was reduced to 40 per cent or less. Companies with more than 40 per cent foreign equity were treated as Foreign Exchange Regulation Act (FERA)[7] companies and as such, were subject to special conditions (RBI 2005). Following the economic reforms introduced in 1991, foreign equity in the pharmaceutical industry was progressively raised to 100 per cent (GOI 2002d) and the Indian law now treats foreign companies at par with domestic companies (Smith 2000).

The discussion in this section questions the assertion made in a number of studies that a positive correlation existed between strong IPRs and high levels of investment, particularly in pharmaceutical industry (for example, Lippoldt 2006; Mansfield 1995; Maskus 2000a; Seyoum 1996). Their assertion is based on the basic premise that theft or unauthorised use of intellectual property was a perceived threat to global investors. The degree of this threat depended on the stage of development of the industry and other characteristics, such as manufacturing and R&D capabilities, infrastructure, and skilled labour in the host country (Nunnenkamp & Spatz 2003). A recent survey of the knowledge-intensive industries including pharmaceutical industry suggests that around 35 per cent of global investors consider IPRs as a challenge to India's future competitiveness (A T Kearney 2004). The findings of the same survey could also be interpreted, however, to suggest that around two-thirds of global investors did not consider IPRs was an issue in India.

In the light of this contradiction, a systematic examination was conducted of FDI in India's pharmaceutical industry over a period of 25 years (1975–2000).[8] This investigation is based on the five-yearly FDI data from Shah (2003) for the study period. Using the average exchange rate (based on IMF database) for each five-year period, the data are converted from Indian Rupees to US dollars, because the US$ is the standard format used for FDI the world over. Using the CPI index (World Bank database), the data were then converted from current value to constant 2000 value providing a common denominator for the data in different five-year blocks. The results are then used to assess whether or not the implementation of TRIPS would impact the level of FDI in India in general and in the pharmaceutical industry in particular.

In constant value, the level of FDI into the pharma sector was the highest in the 1975–80 period (see Table 4.4). The level of investment in Period 1 was higher by all measures than the sum of Period 2 and

Table 4.4 FDI into the Indian pharmaceutical sector in Rs. million (1975–2000)

No.	Period	Rs. (current)	Rs. (constant 2000)	US$[9] (current)	US$ (constant 2000)
1	1975–80	3,050	20,333.33	$364	$1,016.76
2	1980–85	1,200	5,333.333	$120	$218.18
3	1985–90	2,000	5,952.381	$140	$210.21
4	1990–95	5,300	10,037.88	$198	$243.84
5	1995–00	15,200	18,357.49	$390	$420.26

Source: Author calculations based on Shah (2003), slide 16, IMF database, and the World Bank database.

Period 3. In constant Rupees terms, the investments in Period 5 were close to but lower than the level of Period 1. The final period relates to time when India had already signed the WTO agreements including the TRIPS agreement. In contrast, Period 1 followed the introduction of restrictive measures in India, during which, the investments (US$ constant) constituted around 93 per cent of the total sum of the rest of the study periods.

The highest investments in the Indian pharmaceutical industry relate to the five-year block, following the introduction of the Patents Act 1970 and the FERA 1973. The investments significantly declined following the introduction of Drug Price Control Order 1979 (discussed in Chapter 6). Table 4.4 shows that foreign investments continued in the pharmaceutical industry even after product patents were abolished in India. A number of other countries had a similar experience, where FDI rose after a weak patent regime was introduced. For example, after Turkey abolished patenting of pharmaceutical processes and products in 1961, the level of FDI increased significantly (Seyoum 1996). Also in Brazil, the level of FDI in the pharmaceutical industry increased substantially after the country abolished product patents (UNCTC 1993). In contrast, Nigeria's introduction of stringent protection of IPRs did not translate into FDI increase (Aderibigbe 1990; Adikibi 1988).

These findings suggest that FDI is not necessarily based on IPRs alone. Other factors also play a significant role in investment decisions. For example, availability of human resources or more specifically skilled labour is a crucial determinant of FDI (Schneider & Frey 1985). In India's case, its human capital is arguably one of its biggest strengths of comparative advantage and a significant pull factor in attracting FDI (Palit & Nawani 2007). While the low-cost human capital was also available in the 1980s, there is no explanation for the significant drop in FDI in the 1980–85 period, other than perhaps a delayed reaction by the foreign investors to India's weakened patent regime. India's introduction of good manufacturing practices (GMP) and the approval of a large number of manufacturing units by the FDA and other regulatory in recent years have significantly improved India's reputational value at the international level. Other factors such as low manufacturing and R&D costs, a large of pool of highly skilled English speaking workforce, a market of 300 million middle class, and a proven record of economic growth are significant considerations boosting the investor confidence.

After economic reforms were introduced in 1991, progressive increase in the FDI pushed the pharmaceutical sector into the top ten sectors attracting FDI. A study of top ten sectors by FDI for the 15-year period (1991–2005) suggests that the drugs and pharmaceutical sector attracted US$936 million compared with $1.8 billion invested in the chemical sector and more than $4.2 billion invested in the electrical equipment sector during the study period (GOI 2006i). Of all investments made into the pharmaceutical sector during 1991–2005 period, more than 38 per cent were made in 2004 alone, which could possibly be in anticipation of the TRIPS compliant regime from 2005 (Chadha 2006).

A T Kearney (2004, 2005, 2007) study top ten countries by investor confidence for the 2003–07 period.[10] They find that China retained the top spot for investments throughout the entire period. India's ranking improved significantly from sixth in 2003 to third in 2004, which was ahead of Germany, France, and Australia. In 2005 and 2007, India ranked second ahead of the US, and the UK. The *World Investment Report* also suggests India ranked second behind China with the US being third in outlook for investments (UNCTAD 2007). Both studies suggest that India has significantly gained investor confidence over the last few years.

Investments into manufacturing or into R&D are made through acquiring an existing facility or developing a new facility from scratch known as green-field investments. In 2004, India and China together accounted for around half of all green-field and expansion projects in developing countries (UNCTAD 2005). In the pharmaceutical industry, a number of MNCs have recently invested into R&D facilities in India. AstraZeneca started a large R&D facility for research on tuberculosis in Bangalore (Bengaluru) in 2003 that was later expanded to include pharmaceutical development. Pfizer started clinical research in India back in 1995 and expanded to include a biometrics unit in 1998 along with formulation development in 2004. By June 2005, Eli Lilly, Sanofi-Aventis, Novartis, and GlaxoSmithKline had started clinical research units and Novartis and GlaxoSmithKline had biometrics centres in India (Mukherjee 2005).

What impact is the FDI into the pharmaceutical sector likely to have on access to medicines? Our conclusion is that unlike exports, FDI is not expected to significantly increase access to medicines. There is no doubt that if the new FDI goes into new facilities to develop and/or manufacture medicines for the domestic market, the drug supply would increase. However, this would not necessarily increase the affordability of medicines. This is because if the new investment goes into acquisition of an existing firm or facility, there would be no net increase in the supply of drugs on the market. Furthermore, new investments are unlikely to be made into the development of new drugs for tropical diseases prevalent in India and other LMICs.

4.5 Emerging business models in the pharmaceutical sector

The emerging business models hold the key to the future of India's pharmaceutical industry. The recent changes, such as the new investment policies and the reintroduction of product patents, have changed the industrial landscape in India, and the pharmaceutical industry stands at critical crossroads – looking back at one path stemming from its traditional strategies, and looking ahead at another path characterised by emerging business models (Heinen & Perry 2006). The industry, as a whole, is going through an unprecedented transformation through mergers and acquisitions, strategic alliances, and outsourcing of major functions such as research and development, manufacturing, and marketing. The outlook for the future is that this process of consolidation is likely to stabilise the market environment with greater concentration of market power and with fewer competitors in the pharmaceutical market (Madanmohan & Krishnan 2003).

The increased global interdependency, advances in information and technology, and the falling costs of telecommunication and global travel have changed significantly the way businesses operated. These changes have also affected the operations of the large MNCs, as summed up in the following statement:

> ...Globalization has resulted in increasing fragmentation of production networks of multinational enterprises. Several functions, which used to be performed in one location, are now getting dispersed over multiple countries for maximising benefits offered by specific features of different locations.
>
> (Palit & Nawani 2007, p. 4)

The return of 'big pharma' companies, such as Merck & Co, after 20 years to India indicates the beginning of a new dawn in the Indian pharmaceutical market. A significant number of MNCs have set up their manufacturing and/or R&D operations in India. Under mounting pressure of rising costs, global pharmaceutical companies are increasingly seeking alliances with their competitors. Even core competencies, such as R&D and clinical trials, are now being outsourced to specialist firms in low-cost economies, including India (Chataway et al. 2007). For example, in 2005 alone, there were 39 co-development and co-marketing deals as well as 129 licensing agreements signed worldwide (Scrip 2006). The emerging forces of globalisation have led a large number of Indian pharmaceutical companies to form alliances with other domestic or foreign enterprises. The DRL describes the new industrial landscape as a place of:

> ...networks of innovative alliances – between boutique R&D companies and pharmaceutical players, between different pharma companies, between pharma players and clinical research organisations – many of which are mediated by third party risk capital of venture capital enterprises.
>
> (Dr Reddy's 2005, p. 3)

The changing business models in the pharmaceutical industry represent only a fraction of the changes taking place across the business sphere India wide. In a broader economic context, the Indian industry in general referred to as India Inc in the media, has been revising its business models. Using the strong economic growth in the domestic market as a stable platform, Indian companies are rapidly launching themselves in the overseas markets. For example, between 2003 and 2006, India Inc acquired 307 overseas firms worth more than US$20 billion (Aiyer 2006) and Indian investors invested close to $40 billion in the four years to 2007–08 (RBI 2008). These investments suggest that the Indian businesses are increasingly becoming global thinkers indicating a significant shift in the mindset of Indian entrepreneurs, including the pharmaceutical industry.

Studying the impact of TRIPS on domestic pharmaceutical companies in the Latin-American markets of Argentina, Brazil, and Mexico, Shadlen (2009) finds that

> ...some pharmaceutical firms have adapted to the new environment and changed their business models to operate in a world of patent

> protection, and plenty of others have simply ceased operations, most countries' generic pharmaceutical industries retain the capacities to join coalitions of resistance to the new IP arrangements. (p. 8)

Similarly, the Indian domestic pharmaceutical companies have adopted a range of models to fit into the new industrial landscape. While a dozen or so leading Indian companies have embarked upon drug discovery with a view to fully integrate into the global pharmaceutical industry, their business models vary significantly. On the one hand, Ranbaxy and DRL are pursuing a competitive model with aggressive marketing and patent challenges to the MNCs in a number of large markets including the US. Both companies have had success in securing six-months exclusive market access as a first generic supplier to the US market after patent expiry. Both companies have also entered into alliances with MNCs and signed lucrative deals as a result of these challenges. However, this is a high risk business model with high rewards for successful challenges. For example, Ranbaxy spent US$25 million in 2004 and US$30 million in 2005 on fighting patent litigations (Bisserbe 2006).

In a recent study, Bower and Sulej (2007) suggest that the business models of the internationally successful Indian pharmaceutical companies are significantly different from those of the biotech firms in the US and Europe. They suggest that the Indian business model made more financial sense and provided more stability than that of their EU and US counterparts. The Indian firms follow a 3-step strategy for steadily increasing their cash generative capability. The first step is to make generics for the home market to become financially secure. Then target the generics markets in the US and Europe to provide a financial boost through increased sales revenue. The final step is to develop in-house capability in drug discovery and development. In contrast, the Western biotech firms start with an initial discovery capability, attract finance and complementary expertise through strategic alliances with pharmaceutical companies, venture capital and public equity finance, and become profitable at a much later stage (Bower & Sulej 2007).

The base of the model adopted by Indian firms is what Prahalad describes as the 'fortune at the bottom of the pyramid' with some of the most effective sales occurring at the lowest threshold of consumer markets (Prahalad 2005). However, in the rapidly changing industrial landscape, different Indian firms are likely to adopt different business models. Ernst & Young describe five different models for India's drug manufacturers (cited in FICCI 2005).

Model-I represents the fully integrated companies with capability to undertake drug development, manufacturing, and marketing. A number of leading Indian firms pursue this strategy. For example, DRL is fully integrated company with subsidiaries in the US, the UK, Germany, Brazil, Russia, New Zealand, Turkey, and Mexico, and joint ventures in Australia, China, and South Africa (DRL Web site). Companies such as Ranbaxy and DRL have now enhanced their capabilities to conduct original research. Biocon, a leading Indian biotech firm, launched BIOMAb EGFR for cancer in 2006. This is the first indigenously developed medicine in India (Mazumdar-Shaw 2007).

Model-II describes companies with their own facilities to reverse engineer and manufacture, and market off-patent generics. This model is less capital intensive relative to Model-I, because it does not require investments for developing new drugs. The primary business of companies pursuing this model remains the manufacture and export of generics. A large number of domestic firms pursue this strategy and serve the local, regional, and overseas markets.

Model-III describes the typical contract research organisations (CROs) specialising in undertaking R&D functions on contract from other firms. The services of a typical CRO include providing pre-clinical leads and conducting clinical trials. These contracts could take different forms, such as licensing deals with milestone payments or royalties upon successful development of a drug. Anticipating significant growth in contract research, a number of Indian companies have floated separate entities dedicated to R&D. For example, Biocon's Syngene for pre-clinical discoveries and Clinigene for clinical trials, DRL's Aurigene Discovery Technologies and Sun Pharma's Sun Pharma Advanced Research Company (SPARC) are separate business entities dedicated to contract research (Kamath 2007).

Recently, Ranbaxy and GSK signed a co-development agreement under specific conditions. GSK will provide Ranbaxy the leads on compounds to screen them for optimisation and conduct pre-clinical tests and GSK will take care of the human trials. The two firms will co-promote the product in India while GSK will retain exclusivity in the developed markets. Other major contracts include AstraZeneca and Torrent, Biocon owned Syngene with BMS, Dyax Corp with Glenmark, and Johnson & Johnson with The Chatterjee Group (TCG) (company Web sites). An industry report on India's leading 100 pharmaceutical companies indicates that 57 companies are engaged in drug discovery, 41 companies in contract manufacturing, 22 companies in clinical trials, and 26 companies in contract research (Cygnus 2005).

However, these figures suggest that some of the companies pursue mixed strategies and engage in all or many of the above activities.

The primary objective for outsourcing research to low-cost countries is to reduce the costs of developing new drugs. In India, costs of drug discovery and development, and clinical trials are about a third and a fifth, respectively, of those in the Western countries (FICCI 2005). The KPMG (2006b) estimate those costs in India to be about one-eighth and one-tenth of the Western levels. This is primarily because after the US, India has the second largest English speaking highly skilled workforce employable at low costs relative to those in the Western countries. For example, a pharmacist with PhD costs $15,000 p.a. compared with $100,000 in the US (Bower & Sulej 2007).

Shifting drug development to India also has a number of other reasons. India has a large pool of patients with a diverse range of diseases. India's regulatory framework with regard to clinical trials is significantly less complex than the frameworks in the US and other developed markets (Heinen & Perry 2006). Under the current framework, drugs developed in India are free of price controls for the life of the patent (GOI 2005a). The Indian law also provides a 150 per cent weighted tax deduction on in-house R&D expenditure (GOI 2002d).

Model-IV describes companies undertaking contract manufacturing. With the governments worldwide trying to contain the escalating healthcare costs, the pharma industry is forced to reduce the R&D and manufacturing costs. It is not surprising that an increasing number of MNCs are outsourcing drug manufacturing to India, because the manufacturing costs are significantly lower in India than in the US/EU (KPMG 2006a). Some of the recent agreements include manufacturing intermediate for Nexium (esomeprazole) (Dishman Pharma/AstraZencea); intermediates for protonix (pantoprazole) (Cadila Healthcare/Altana); and Ranitidine API (Shasun Chemicals/GSK).

This model has significant advantages for both parties. The contract manufacturers are focused on manufacturing and not concerned with the product sales or market fluctuations. The overseas partners could neutralise the low-cost advantage Indian firms have developed and compete in the US and European markets against other Indian firms. This could intensify the competition and lower the prices increasing access to medicines in the respective markets in the short term. In the long term however, this intensification could also drive Indian firms out of those markets and reduce access to medicines.

Two factors hamper small companies from tapping into the lucrative contract manufacture business. First, small companies are likely to have the capability but not the capacity to contract manufacturing large volumes for the big pharma companies. Second, it is unlikely that the small manufacturing units would have compliance certification from the regulatory authorities, such as the FDA (the US), TGA (Australia), or MHRA (the UK), hindering manufactured products from being exported.

Model-V represents companies forming alliances for co-marketing products in new markets. These collaborations are designed to help manufacturers with promising product lines but lacking distribution and marketing strengths to launch products in the global market (Mathew 2006). In 2006, Ranbaxy acquired a 10 per cent stake in the Hyderabad-based Zenotech Labs to launch the latter's injectible oncology products under its own label in the international markets.

Leading Indian companies are becoming MNCs themselves with acquisitions of overseas firms incorporating global marketing opportunities into their business model. Table 4.5 below shows a selection of overseas acquisitions by Indian firms. It should be noted that the main focus of all the acquisitions has been generics expansion into

Table 4.5 Selected foreign acquisitions by India pharma

Year	Acquirer	Target	Country	Transaction value US$ million
1995	Ranbaxy	Ohm Labs	United States	n.a.
1997	Sun Pharma	Caraco	United States	7.5
1998	Wockhardt	Wallis	United Kingdom	9
2000	Ranbaxy	Basics	Germany	8
2000	Ranbaxy	Veratide	Germany	5
2001	Zydus Cadila	German Remedies	Germany	n.a.
2002	Ranbaxy	Signature	United States	n.a.
2002	Unichem	Niche Generics	United Kingdom	5
2002	Dr Reddy's	BMS	United Kingdom	16
2003	Wockhardt	CP Pharma	United Kingdom	20
2003	Zydus Cadila	Alpharma	France	6.6
2003	Sun	Caraco	United States	42
2004	Ranbaxy	RPG Aventis	France	84
2004	Glenmark	Lab Klinger	Brazil	5
2004	Dr Reddy's	Trigenesis	United States	11
2004	Jubilant Organosys	PSI group	Belgium	16
2005	Dishman	Synprotec	United Kingdom	n.a.
2005	Malladi	Novus	United States	19m Euro

Table 4.5 (Continued)

Year	Acquirer	Target	Country	Transaction value US$ million
2005	Matrix	22% of Docpharma	Belgium	217m Euro
2005	Torrent	Heumann Pharma	Germany	n.a.
2005	Strides Acrolab	NA	Poland	8
2005	Strides Acrolab	>50% of Beltapharma Spa	Italy	1.9
2005	Sun	Valeant	Hungary	n.a.
2006	Dr Reddy's	Betapharm	Germany	$570

Source: Compiled from various company reports; Kaul (2004); Kamath and Krishnan (2004); Taylor (2005) and FierceBiotech (2006).

wealthy markets. While the size of the Indian acquisitions is relatively small compared with that of the big pharma companies, it provides the Indian companies a foothold into the wealthy markets. The acquired firms have established sales revenue, experience in the local markets, and infrastructure for marketing the acquirer's products.

There is yet another business model emerging in the Indian pharma industry and may become quite important in the wake of the TRIPS agreement. As noted above, under the TRIPS agreement, the LDCs have till 2016 to implement the agreement meaning that the reverse engineering model can be continued to manufacture and export cheaper versions of patented drugs out of these 49 countries (Chadha 2006). Consequently, Indian pharma companies may shift their manufacturing bases from India to LDCs (Mueller 2007b). Sun Pharma, one of the leading Indian firms recently inaugurated its manufacturing facility in Bangladesh. Another Indian company, the Ahmedabad-based Cadila Pharma was expected to set up its manufacturing plant in Ethiopia in 2007 (Babu 2007). This model provides significant advantages at least till 2016 over the current regulatory environment in India.

4.6 Conclusions

India's pharmaceutical industry developed initially under the protection of the anti-competitive government policies introduced in the 1970s, and subsequently continued its rapid growth even after the introduction of industrial de-licensing as a part of the economic reforms in 1991. Today, the Indian pharmaceutical industry has grown into a globally competitive indigenous industry that is increasingly integrating into the global industry through not only imports and exports, but also via FDI, outsourcing, and contracting arrangements with overseas partners. While overseas MNCs once dominated the Indian pharmaceutical market, they now account for about a quarter of the domestic market. Leading domestic firms generate significant share of their revenues in overseas markets. A large number of small manufacturers account for around half of the domestic supply by volume.

A net importer of pharmaceuticals until the late 1980s, India is now a net exporter of pharmaceuticals. The economic liberalisation and the reforms to industrial policies introduced since 1991 provided a boost to India's exports of pharmaceuticals. The highly regulated markets, including the US, are the top ten destinations for India pharmaceutical exports. India's drug exports have contributed significantly to increase access to medicines in LMICs and industrialised markets. However, despite having arguably the world's lowest drug prices, around two-thirds of India's population remains without access to medicines.

The FDI in the pharmaceutical industry is not only influenced by the protection of IPRs. Other factors, including R&D and manufacturing costs, availability and costs of skilled labour, exports potential, and compliance certification for quality also play a significant role in investment decisions. While the pharmaceutical sector has become one of the top ten industries to attract foreign investments in recent years, it is unlikely that foreign investments would lead to developing medicines for tropical diseases.

In the wake of the recent changes to the industrial landscape, India pharmaceutical firms have adopted a mixture of new business models. Leading Indian pharmaceutical companies are expanding through overseas acquisitions and exports now constitute a significant share of their annual sales revenue. Other firms are opting for alliances and contract manufacturing roles. There are indications that some Indian firms may relocate their manufacturing operations to the LDCs to take advantage of the delayed implementation of TRIPS in those countries. The survival of small manufacturers could be jeopardised by the changing dynamics in the market, which would be counterproductive from the access to medicines perspective. With the abolition of highly protective measures that once favoured the domestic Indian pharmaceutical industry, the new industrial landscape foreshadows significant challenges for the indigenous players.

5
TRIPS and the Indian Patents Regime

5.1 Introduction

India's patent regime is fairly young relative to that of the developed world. Colonial India first introduced patents protection in 1856 compared to Venice in 1474 and Germany in 1484. Since then, India's patent regime has undergone a number of reforms to reflect the government policy on the industrial framework. The first Act relevant to the modern pharmaceutical industry was the Indian Patents and Designs Act 1911. This Act provided patents for pharmaceutical *products* and *all known* and *possible processes* for 16 years extendable by another ten years if the patent had not generated sufficient returns for the patent holder (Lalitha 2002).

Before World War I, India had less than a dozen indigenous companies. The Patents and Designs Act 1911 restricted growth of the indigenous industry by denying them opportunities to manufacture new drugs. By granting patents on all *known* and *possible processes* to manufacture the drug, this Act denied further innovation around the patented drug that is common to the pharmaceutical industry. For example in recent years, Eli Lilly, a large MNC, took out 56 patents in the US on the known processes to manufacture Cefaclor. Ranbaxy, a leading Indian firm successfully developed a non-infringing process to manufacture the same drug and licensed the process back to Eli Lilly for a substantial remuneration (Rangnekar 2005). A series of 50:50 joint ventures followed in the wake of Eli Lilly's recognition of Ranbaxy's superior research capabilities (Lanjouw 1998). These types of opportunities for follow-up innovation were denied under the Patents and Designs Act 1911.

The most significant change to shape the indigenous pharmaceutical industry model was the introduction of the Patents Act 1970 (the 1970

Act), which abolished product patents for drugs and pharmaceuticals (also food and agricultural products), and recognised only a single process actually used in the manufacture. The 1970 Act (enacted April 1972) limited protection to seven years from date of filing or five years from date of grant whichever was shorter (GOI 1972). This Act effectively meant that every drug was potentially generic allowing firms to manufacture new drugs immediately after a patent was granted. Indian firms developed skills to copy new drugs by 'reverse engineering' and reproduce the same drug using a different manufacturing process.

5.2 Impact of regime change on pharmaceutical industry

The rapid growth of the domestic pharmaceutical industry attracted a large number of new entrants resulting in increased industry competitiveness and lowered drug prices. With a large pool of English speaking low-cost manpower skilled in engineering and chemistry in India, the elimination of product patents provided ample opportunity for capacity building in pharmaceutical innovation and increasing efficiency. Low manufacturing costs made it possible to significantly reduce the prices of copies of on-patent drugs not only in India but also in other countries with weak patent regimes. The Indian pharmaceutical industry enhanced institutional capabilities to manufacture processes for simple antibiotics to complex drugs used in treating HIV/AIDS, cancer, and cardiovascular diseases.

Following the introduction of Hatch-Waxman Act 1984 in the US and similar provisions elsewhere, the generic manufacturers could submit an abbreviated new drug application (ANDA) with the proof of bioequivalence to the originator drug. This change in the US law saved generic manufacturers significant costs of conducting their own tests and created opportunities for early introduction of generics. On the one hand, Indian manufacturers began entering the markets of developed countries with generic versions of blockbuster drugs at very low prices (Lanjouw 1998). The industry began to realise the enormous potential and shifted its focus from manufacturing reverse-engineered copies of patented drugs to producing generics for off-patent drugs for exports to lucrative markets such as the US (Malhotra 2008).

On the other hand, India was supplying low-cost imitations of on-patent drugs to a large number of poor countries. The significance of India's pharmaceutical industry in lowering the drug prices and increasing access to medicines in both developed and developing countries became particularly evident in the supply of antiretrovirals (ARVs) used for treatment of HIV/AIDS (Narrain 2005). Indian firms supply 84 per cent of the AIDS drugs used by Médecins Sans Frontières (MSF) to treat thousands of patients across 30 countries (Mueller 2007a) (see Chapter 4 for details).

As a signatory to the WTO agreements signed in 1994, India was obliged to change its patent regime by 1 January 2005. India adopted a three step approach to make this change. In accordance with the conditions set out for the Transitional Arrangements in the TRIPS agreement, India introduced the (first) Patents (Amendment) Act 1999 to provide a mailbox for filing product patent applications. While the actual processing of these applications did not begin until after the introduction of product patents in 2005, the mailbox was designed to establish the filing dates for patent applications. Under the (first) Amendment, companies applying for product patents through the mailbox could also apply for Exclusive Marketing Rights (EMRs) for a period of up to five years or till the date of grant or rejection of the patent application – whichever was shorter. The TRIPS agreement provides that EMRs be granted if a patent for the drug was obtained in a WTO member state after 1995 (when TRIPS came into effect), and marketing approval for the drug was also obtained in that country (Article 70.9). The EMRs practically had the same effect as a patent driving existing generics out of the market and supplying the drug under monopoly prices. See the case of Glivec for example in Box 5.1.

Box 5.1 Exclusive Marketing Rights (EMRs) in India

India grants first EMRs

Novartis became the first company to obtain EMRs in India. Under Patent application No. 1602/Mas/98, Novartis filed a patent application for Glivec (imatinib mesylate) with the Indian authorities on 17 July 1998. Glivec is used to treat Chronic Myeloid Leukaemia (CML) and was launched in India in 2002. In November 2003, the company was granted EMRs for five years for Glivec and a notification was published in the Gazette of India on 13 December 2003.

The cost of Glivec at Rs. 1,20,000 per month compared with the price of generic versions of the same drug already in the market at around Rs. 10,000 per month (Jatania 2004). After EMRs were granted, Novartis obtained an injunction from the Madras

High Court barring domestic firms including Ranbaxy, Cipla, and Sun Pharma from producing and marketing the generic versions of Glivec.

The grant of EMRs to Novartis was challenged by a number of parties including NATCO, an Indian manufacturer of the generic version, the Indian Pharmaceutical Alliance (IPA) representing leading domestic firms including Ranbaxy, and the Indian Drug Manufacturers' Association (IDMA). The challengers argued that the patent on the active pharmaceutical ingredient (API) imatinib mesylate was filed before the deadline of 1 January 1995; namely in the US on 28 April 1994 and in Canada on 1 April 1993 (Narula 2004). It was argued that Glivec was a modified form of an existing compound; therefore the subject matter was neither patentable in India nor eligible for EMRs.

The Mumbai-based Cancer Patients' Aid Association (CPAA) also filed a writ petition in the Supreme Court of India challenging the grant of EMRs to Novartis. It was argued that the absence of low-cost generics would effectively mean denying the Right to Life enshrined in the Article 21 of the Indian Constitution. The government is responsible to its people and, hence, must maintain control over the prices of life-saving drugs, suggested the CPAA. After considering the arguments of various parties, the Controller on 25 January 2006 rejected the patent application and terminated the EMRs granted to Novartis (GOI 2006g). Novartis appealed against the termination and was awaiting the outcome.

Source: Based on authors cited in the Box.

The grant and revocation of EMRs for Glivec raise the following questions. First, the domestic firms were locked out of the market as a result of EMRs granted to Novartis for more than two years. Consequently, the domestic firms incurred loss of potential sales and income. Currently, there is no provision to automatically compensate the barred generic manufacturers for loss of their potential sales/income. Were the generic manufacturers to take collective action, who would be responsible for compensating the domestic companies? Would it be Novartis as the beneficiary of the EMRs, or the Indian State as the administrator of the framework and granter of the EMRs?

Second, the drug price in this case was raised 10–12 times of pre-EMRs scenario forcing patients and their families into unnecessary hardship. Healthcare costs are one of the major reasons for household indebtedness often resulting in sale of family assets (GOI 2006d). If the monopoly price of Glivec charged under the EMRs led to the sale of such assets, who would be responsible for compensating the families and restoring the rightful ownership of the sold family assets? Under the provisions for drug price controls, India collects the over-charged amount from the pharmaceutical companies and places these amounts in a special account. India could consider introducing a similar framework to collect the difference between the lowest priced generic and the price actually charged by the right holder, and distribute the amount among the rightful stakeholders. This method may not deter all frivolous claims, but it would provide a framework to reclaim the over-charged price. Provision of such a framework would be expected to avoid or at least minimise recurrence of Glivec-like situations under grant of patents.

The (second) Patents (Amendment) Act (2002) introduced changes to patentable subject matter, extended the term of protection to 20 years, and changed conditions for compulsory licensing. This amendment also shifted the onus to the alleged infringer in patent infringement disputes. Under the previous regime, the alleger (patent holder) had to prove the infringement by the alleged party. Under the new Act, the alleged infringer has to provide burden of proof, which is a significant departure from the doctrine of 'presumption of innocence'. Under fear of prosecution, the domestic companies could stop engaging in innovative activities that may involve the risk of potential patent litigation. The first and second amendments laid the ground work to introduce the final amendment.

The third and final amendment to the Patents Act 1970 was delayed, because the Indian Parliament got dissolved in early 2004 in preparation for general elections. Initially, the coalition partners in the new government under Prime Minister Manmohan Singh could not agree on the terms of reference for the final Bill. Consequently, a President's Ordinance was issued in December 2004 to ensure India met the deadline of 1 January 2005. After reaching consensus, in March 2005, the (third) Patents (Amendment) Act (2005) was passed through both Houses of the Indian Parliament (Bill No. 32-C of 2005).

The Patents (Amendment) Act 2005 introduced product and process patents for food, pharmaceuticals, and drugs. The Patents Act, as it stands now, has the following implications. The domestic industry's previous practice of reverse engineering and manufacturing of imitations of patented products has been disallowed. Consequently, the absence of market competition is likely to raise the drug prices and restrict access to medicines. The extension of patent term from 7 years to 20 years will significantly delay the entry of generics. The so-called 'Bolar provisions' under the current Act allow generic manufacturers to conduct necessary tests and prepare for the drug launch. However, the actual launching of generic versions of a patented drug cannot take place until the patent expires.

5.3 The post TRIPS patents regime

The major differences between the pre- and post-TRIPS Patents Act are summarised in Table 5.1. Other main points covered by the amendments are considered below.

The new regime provides patents for any invention granted under the Act. Patentable inventions must involve an inventive step defined as '*a feature of an invention that involves technical advance as compared to the existing knowledge, or having economic significance, or both*' (Section 2 (1)(ja)). The expression '*economic significance*' in the new law is neither a classical patentability criterion nor does it have anything to do with inventions (Ram 2006). Under this principle, the Patents Controller assesses the economic significance of an invention based on the data furnished by the patent applicant. This practice places a question mark on the application of the principle itself. This is because there is no evaluation of the application based on the input of any independent data. The data supplied by the applicant itself are likely to have a bias favouring the application that is likely to influence the Controller's decision.

The following subject matter is not patentable under the new regime:

> .... The mere discovery of a new form of a known substance which does not result in the enhancement of the known efficacy of the substance or the mere discovery of any new property of new use for a known substance or of the mere use of a known process, machine or apparatus unless such known process results in a new product or employs at least one new reactant.
>
> (Section 3(d))

The provisions of Section 3(d) have the following implications. A new use or a new form of a known substance as such would not be patentable. It is not uncommon for pharmaceutical companies to find

Table 5.1 Major differences in the pre- and post-TRIPS Patents Act

Category	**Pre-TRIPS**		**Post-TRIPS**	
	Patents Act 1970	**Implications**	**Recent amendments**	**Implications**
Product patents	No	Able to reverse engineer and reproduce	Yes	*Reverse engineering disallowed*
Process patents	Patent granted on a single process actually used for manufacturing	Easy to follow up with a new process	Multiple processes patentable	*Difficult to develop a non-infringing process*
Patent term	Seven years from date of filing or five years from date of grant whichever is shorter	Relatively short term	20 years from date of filing	*Relatively long term for monopoly rights*
Pre grant opposition	Yes	Allows the opportunity to object before patent granted	Yes	*Allows the opportunity to object before patent granted*
Post grant opposition	No	N/A	Yes, within 12 months of grant of a patent any person can submit/lodge a claim disputing/objecting the patent	*Allows the opportunity to raise concerns after patent has been granted*
Compulsory licensing (CL)	After three years of grant of patent	Practically unrestricted applicability	After three years of grant of patent under specific conditions	*Only for domestic market supply*
Exports under CL	Unrestricted	For domestic or exports	Under Section 92A (1) conforming to 30 August Decision of the WTO	*Only under specific conditions including labelling to prevent re-export*

Data protection	N/A	N/A	Yes, against unfair commercial use. No data exclusivity	*Possible disputes with delays to introducing generics*
Patent infringement disputes	*Onus on the patentee to prove the infringement*	*No or few disputes*	*Onus on the alleged infringer to prove non-infringement*	*Escalation of disputes. Small domestic firms likely to shy away from innovation*

Source: Compiled from on GOI (1972, 1999, 2002b, 2005c).

new uses or new forms of existing drugs and seek patent extensions on the basis of these discoveries in a number of countries including Australia, but such extension is not a TRIPS requirement. For example, the first patent on Zidovudine, an antiretroviral, was filed in 1964. Counting 20 years from date of *first* filing, the patent should have expired in 1984. Yet, the patent on the drug in a large number of countries, including the US, is technically still valid (Shah as cited in Hiddleston 2007). This is because the patent holders keep finding new ways to extend the patent term. According to IMS (2004), patent on the combination of Zidovudine, Lamivudine, and Indinavir in most countries, including Australia, is due to expire in 2016 or later. In the US, the patent on Merck's Crixivan (combination of the three drugs) is due to expire in 2021 with a possibility of further extension (IMS Health 2004). The Orange Book of the Food and Drug Administration (FDA) shows that there is no patent on Zidovudine as such. Patents on Lamivudine and Indinavir are due to expire in 2011 and 2012, respectively (FDA 2008). Yet, the manoeuvrability permitted under the US law allows companies to add around ten years of patent rights on a combination of the three drugs. This is because countries such as the US and Australia grant patent extensions for new uses (indications) of existing drugs. This type of perpetuation of patents would not be possible under the Indian law.

The process of seeking patent extensions based on such manoeuvrability is known as ever-greening in the literature (House of Commons Health Committee 2005). Section 3(d) of India's Patents Act is designed to prevent ever-greening. But there are practical difficulties in implementing the provisions of this clause. For example, Section 3(d) requires evidence of enhancement of known efficacy of the substance. Proving the difference in efficacy at the time of filing a patent application is not practical. Patents are usually filed at the early stages of drug discovery. The efficacy of a drug is established during clinical trials. The process of clinical trials (on human subjects) follows the pre-clinical testing (on animals). It takes several years for the entire process of clinical trials to establish efficacy.

Under the TRIPS agreement, member countries are required 'to make patents available for any inventions, whether products or processes, in all fields of technology without discrimination, subject to the normal tests of novelty, inventiveness and industrial applicability' (Article 27.1). What constitutes an invention is however not defined in TRIPS. India does not provide patents for 'the mere discovery of any new property of new use for a known substance or of the mere use of a known process' (Section 3(d)). India views these discoveries frivolous and denies patents. Novartis, a Swiss MNC, alleges that this denial by India contravenes the TRIPS agreement.

A number of studies support the Indian view. In the early part of the twentieth century, a committee was established by the UK Government to examine issues related to patent-protected medicines. The findings of the Select Committee on Patent Medicines (1914) included:

- that the [patented] remedies are of a widely differing characters, comprising (a) genuine scientific preparations; (b) unobjectionable remedies for simple ailments; and (c) many secret remedies making grossly exaggerated claims of efficacy;
- that this last-mentioned class (c) of [patented] remedies contains none which spring from therapeutical or medical knowledge, but that they are put upon the market by ignorant persons, and in many cases by cunning swindlers who exploit for their own profit the apparently invincible credulity of the public; and
- that this [practice] constitutes a grave and widespread public evil... (House of Commons Health Committee 2005, p. 7)

The above findings suggest that even at that time, firms in the pharmaceutical industry did not hesitate from trying to obtain patents on frivolous claims. While the firms and the industry have changed significantly since then, the will to exploit the consumer to the maximum has only intensified. The House of Commons Health Committee (2005) concludes that when the patent on a product expires, the originating company is deemed to have been rewarded for risks of innovation. Yet, originators keep inventing new ways to extend periods of exclusivity.

Almost 100 years after the first inquiry in the UK, the industry is better equipped and more aggressive than ever to test the regulatory framework and extend the monopoly rights well beyond the intention of the law. For example, the European Commission recently launched an investigation into the pharmaceutical industry, because the Commission had information indicating that the industry competition may be restricted or distorted. The preliminary report suggests that the innovator companies use 'a tool-box of instruments aimed at ensuring continued revenue streams for their medicines' (European Commission 2008, p. 401). In some cases, up to 1300 patents were filed for a single drug as a strategy to keep competitors out of the market, notes the Commission. Strategies such as these make a mockery of the spirit of rewarding innovators for disclosing their innovations to public. In the name of promoting innovation, this blatant abuse of the system is, in fact, harming the future innovation. In light of the reports of the House of Commons Health Committee and the European Commission, the Indian law appears to be rightfully proactive in preventing the frivolous claims.

Novartis filed a writ challenging the Section 3(d) of the Patents Act in the Madras High Court[1] in 2005. The challenge was widely viewed as a test case between the MNCs and India. The writ attracted worldwide condemnation of the company action by health activists, NGOs, and a significant number of countries including Norway and Germany. More than 420,000 people worldwide, including Nobel Laureate Archbishop Desmond Tutu and the former Swiss president and health minister Ruth Dreifuss, signed a petition calling upon Novartis to drop the case (Bidwai 2007). In February 2007, the European Parliament in a written declaration called upon Novartis to 'withdraw its complaint in order to guarantee continued access to affordable generic medicines for all' (European Parliament 2007, p. 2). Mueller (2007a), a legal expert, opines that Section 3(d) of India's Patents Act 'does not necessarily impose stricter requirements than are used elsewhere' (p. 543), negating the Novartis writ. Basheer (2008), a renowned expert on intellectual property also suggests that every country needs to calibrate the pharmaceutical patent protection in accordance with its own national circumstances and Section 3(d) is, in many ways, an example of that calibration by India (cited in Kumar 2008). In August 2007, the Madras High Court rejected the Novartis legal challenge. The Court held that the arguments put forward by Novartis would limit competition and reduce access to medicines, especially for the poor who cannot afford the expensive drugs for cancer and other diseases. Novartis has now lodged an appeal with the Supreme Court of India.

5.4 Provisions to oppose patents

The patent applications can be opposed before or after the patent is granted. India first introduced provisions for pre-grant opposition to pending patent applications under the Patents and Designs Act 1911. These provisions were carried forward into the Patents Act 1970 and have also been retained in the 2005 amendments. After a patent application has been published and the patent has not yet been granted, *any person* can submit an application opposing the grant of such patent. Along with Brazil and Jordan, India remains one of few countries to have pre-grant opposition provisions (Mueller 2007b).

Under the President's Ordinance in 2004, India also introduced provisions for post-grant opposition and retained these provisions under the 2005 amendments. The post-grant opposition must be filed within 12 months of the grant of patent. The post-grant opposition applications would be heard by a three-person Opposition Board that must not include the original patent examiner. Should the patent be revoked, the patent holder may appeal to the Appellate Board.

At this stage of development of India's pharmaceutical industry, the industry lacks patent literacy.[2] Pre- and post-grant oppositions to patents provide opportunities for the domestic firms and other stakeholders to file counter claims. Pre-grant opposition has an advantage over the post-grant opposition. Leading experts agree that pre-grant opposition is better because it provides an opportunity to stop the patent before it is granted. For example, Drahos (2008) suggests that:

> ... a guiding principle for the developing countries should be prevention rather than cure; i.e. it is much better to find ways to prevent pharmaceutical patents of doubtful validity from getting onto the patent register, rather than trying to remove them through costly litigation. (p. 168)

Once the patent is granted and the product is launched in the market, the price is going to be considerably high under monopoly rights. Under post-grant opposition, the patients continue paying high prices while the case is waiting to be heard. The submission of pre-grant objections eliminates that possibility and shortens the period of monopoly prices even where companies may have obtained exclusive marketing rights pending their patent applications. Pre-grant opposition was instrumental in the rejection of patent application and revocation of the exclusive marketing rights granted to Novartis for Glivec (noted earlier in Box 5.1).

Inserting the words '*any person*' in the opposition to grant of patents has provided opportunities for other stakeholders, such as NGOs and health activists, to lodge their objections with the Indian Patent Office. For example, the pre-grant opposition by the Positive Women's Network and the Indian Network for People Living with HIV/AIDS resulted in the rejection of the patent application filed by the German MNC Boehringer Ingelheim for Nevirapine syrup, used in the treatment of children living with HIV/AIDS. The opposition argued that the syrup formulation of Nevirapine was a new form of a known drug first invented in 1989, and thus older than the 1995 cut-off date that India's Patents Act considers eligible for patenting (MSF 2008). In another case, a pre-grant opposition has also been filed against a patent application by GlaxoSmithKline (GSK) for its fixed dose combination of two AIDS drugs: namely, Zidovudine and Lamivudine or AZT/3TC (Combivir). This submission is based on a different technicality. Under the Indian law, a combination of known drugs is not an invention and hence should not be granted a patent, argue the citizen groups[3] opposing the patent application (IP-Watch 2006). Isn't it strange that Cipla, an Indian company, challenged GSK's patent on Combivir in the UK on the basis of 'lack of novelty' and won the case in 2004, yet the application for Combivir remains in the mailbox in India (Gehl Sampath 2006)?

In March 2006, Roche was successful in beating off the opposition and becoming the first company to obtain a product patent under India's new regime for Pegasys, which is used for treating hepatitis C (Jyothi-Datta 2006). Wockhardt, an Indian drugmaker, has lodged a post-grant opposition challenging the Pegasys patent (Jyothi-Datta 2007). In December 2007, Pfizer obtained a patent on Maraviroc, first patent in India on an anti-AIDS drug. A number of NGOs, such as Lawyers Collective, were also considering a post-grant opposition to the Maraviroc patent (Managing Intellectual Property 2007).

5.4.1 Rising litigations

With the implementation of the new regime, patent litigations have emerged in India in growing numbers. In the short history of product patents in India, the number of litigations has been rising, as patent applications from the mailbox are progressively published. The Indian situation is not uncommon, because 'with any new legislation, changes in terminology will likely result in uncertainty and litigation' (McEwan 2005, p. 62). In the initial stages of a new regime, litigations are a part of the evolutionary process. Litigants on both sides do everything in their power to set a precedent to favour their interests.

In India's case, the originator companies and the generics manufacturers are testing how different provisions of the Patents Act are interpreted. The originator companies are trying to impose their own interpretations of TRIPS in order to raise the protection level to that of developed countries. The interests of the generic manufacturers lay in keeping the protection level to the minimum. If litigations focused on outcomes to provide certainties to encourage innovation, the litigations could be considered beneficial in the long run. But in recent years, originator litigants have become more focused on blocking the development of a new competing product rather than protecting an invention of their own (European Commission 2008). This development is counter-productive.

Dr Hamied, Chairman of Cipla, warns that 'the new patent legislation will certainly lead to numerous litigations. It will herald an era of monopoly in vital and life-saving drugs in general that would be detrimental to the interest of the consumer' (cited in Cipla 2005, p. 9). The US experience shows that the launch of the first blockbuster drug Tagamet in 1976 changed the mindset of the industry, leading to a sharp increase in patent litigations in the US. The number of lawyers per thousand population in the US, which had remained fairly stable between 1900 and 1970, tripled between 1970 and 1998 due to a boom in litigations (Caplow et al. 2006), lending further indirect evidence to the argument advanced by Dr Hamied. India already has a significant backlog of cases before the courts and does not need further increase in the number of cases. An expert estimates that India has over 38 million cases pending in courts and at current rates it would take nearly 320 years to dispose them (Debroy cited in GOI 2007d). An escalation of the patent litigations would only add to the existing pile. Even if the patent-related cases were given priority because of public health issues, further delays would occur to the cases in the queue to be heard.

India's Patents Act is still evolving and the country should consider including some measures to lessen the number of litigations. Perhaps consideration should be given towards introducing a clause similar to that in Australia, where Section 26C of the Therapeutic Goods Act 1989 (as amended following the signing of the Free Trade Agreement (FTA) between Australia and the US) provides for the imposition of penalties of up to A$10 million for unnecessarily delaying the entry of generics in the market with frivolous claims. The aim of the amendment was to ensure that legal 'proceedings are not otherwise vexatious or unreasonably pursued' (Section 26C(4)(c)).

Introduction of a similar clause in the Indian legislation should have prevented the filing of several patents, including those filed by Novartis for Glivec and by Boehringer Ingelheim for Nevirapine. Both companies knew that the drugs they were trying to patent were registered elsewhere pre-1995 and would not qualify for a patent in India. Under the proposed clause, GSK would also be unlikely to apply for a patent on Combivir knowingly that *a substance obtained by a mere admixture resulting only in the aggregation of the properties of the components thereof or a process for producing such substance* would not be patentable in India (Patents Act 1970, Chapter 2, Section 3). In a recent case, the High Court in Gujarat in Cadila Pharmaceuticals Limited v. Instacare Laboratories Pvt Ltd. (2001(21) PTC 472 (Guj)) held that 'development of a combination medicine by a pharmaceutical company does not amount to patentable invention' (Embassy of the United States 2008). Moreover, the UK court's ruling against the GSK would be a discouraging factor in lodging a patent application if India introduced a deterrent clause.

5.4.1.1 Companies already engaged in copying a product now under patent

Until 2005, Indian pharmaceutical companies reverse engineered patented products and produced imitations thereof. This was possible because India did not provide patents for pharmaceutical products as noted earlier. Under the regime introduced since 2005, copying a patented product and reverse engineering is disallowed. Prior to 2005, a large number of Indian firms were manufacturing drugs, for which patent applications have been filed under the new regime. Before the new regime was introduced, there was uncertainty in these manufacturers' ability to continue in the post-2005 scenario. However, according to the new regime, these manufacturers may continue to manufacture imitations of the patented product under conditions noted below.

A large number of the foreign patent applications in the mailbox are expected to be for products the Indian companies had been copying under the pre-TRIPS regime. Under India's new patent regime, companies that had made significant investments and were already engaged in producing and marketing of copied versions of patented drugs prior to 2005 may continue without the fear of being prosecuted (Section 11A (7)). Nevertheless, the patent holders shall be entitled to receive a 'reasonable royalty' from the (Indian) enterprises. Up to year 2000, the number of new drugs approved was almost static, except for 1996 and 1997 when it slightly increased (see Figure 5.1). A significant rise in the

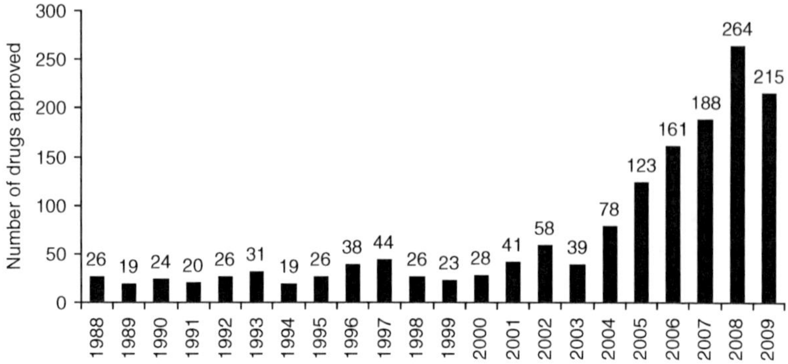

Figure 5.1 New drugs approved in India (1988–2009)
Source: Compiled from GOI (2010) and Tamilnadu Pharmaceutical Sciences Welfare Trust (2008).

number of new drug approvals can be observed from 2000 and a further rise from 2004 onwards.

Domestic companies took advantage of the transition period and launched as many products as possible before the 1 January 2005 deadline. By some estimates, there are over 12,000 patent applications submitted via the mailbox (NISTADS 2005). More than 80 per cent of these applications belong to foreign MNCs (Ram 2006). In the absence of firm data, drug approvals since 2005 could be used as a guide for possible drugs with patent applications pending (see Figure 5.1). A further examination of the drugs approved since 2004–05 suggests that most of the approvals were for combination drugs rather than new drugs with therapeutical breakthroughs. It may be noted that in India, marketing approvals and granting patents are functions of different authorities that operate totally independent of each other. In contrast, the FDA generally does not grant approvals for drugs that are likely to contravene a US patent.

5.4.1.2 *Compulsory licensing*

Compulsory licensing refers to a practice when a government allows someone else to produce the patented product or process without the consent of the patent owner (WTO 2006b). The TRIPS agreement does not use the term 'compulsory licensing', but refers to 'use without authorization of the right holder' (Article 31). Under the TRIPS agreement, compulsory licensing is one of the flexibilities and an important instrument for governments to provide patented drugs at lower prices and increase access to affordable healthcare (Abbott 2005). Under Article 31, reaffirmed by the Doha Declaration on TRIPS and Public Health, member states are free to determine the grounds for granting compulsory licences. India considered its TRIPS obligations and the requirements of its pharmaceutical industry in developing the grounds for compulsory licensing. Mueller (2007b) opines that India has 'the world's most elaborate compulsory licensing scheme' (p. 504). The provisions for compulsory licensing in the Indian Patents Act are representatives of India's interests and suitable to its industry needs. Moreover, these provisions are well within the guidelines for flexibilities provided under the TRIPS agreement.

5.4.1.3 Granting compulsory licences

Any time after the expiration of three years from the date of the grant of a patent, *any person* interested may make application to the Controller for grant of compulsory licence. The Controller must grant compulsory licences within six months where the applicant has made efforts to obtain a licence from the patentee on reasonable terms and conditions without any success. According to Mueller (2007b), certain provisions of the Indian act are so vague that 'virtually any refusal of a patentee to [voluntarily] licence could be deemed prejudicial to some form of trade in India' and result in the government granting a compulsory licence (p. 590).

With respect to granting compulsory licences under the new regime, two issues need to be considered. First, observers such as Ram (2006) argue that adding six months to grant the compulsory licence unnecessarily extends the waiting period from three years to three and a half years before the product can be supplied to the market. The waiting period could be shortened by allowing applications for compulsory licences before the three years period expires. This would allow the processing of applications within the three years. Alternatively, reducing the six months period to grant the licence to a 30-day period would expedite the product to the market.

Second, the expressions 'reasonable terms and conditions', used in connection with voluntary licensing, are not defined in the Patents Act. This omission leaves the terms open to different interpretations, creating uncertainties. As the following example illustrates, in the past, this ambiguity has caused significant delays for compulsory licensing (Chaudhuri 2005, p. 94).

The Neo-Pharma Industries, an Indian firm sought licence from Parke-Davis to manufacture one of its patented drugs. The Indian subsidiary and the US-based parent company took more than two years to decide, as to who would negotiate with the interested party. When the negotiations eventually began, the parent company did not formally refuse, but just sat over the proposal. The government finally granted a compulsory licence to Neo-Pharma but the licence was stayed on a court order obtained by Parke-Davis. This example illustrates how the omission of specificity in the Act could unintentionally contribute to significant delays in the granting of compulsory licences, effectively defeating the purpose of compulsory licensing.

By comparison, Canada simplified its procedure for compulsory licensing as far back as 1969 by placing the time limit of two months for the patent holders to file counter claims. This change enabled authorities to grant over 613 licences between 1969 and 1992 compared with just 22 compulsory licences granted between 1923 and 1969 when the country did not have a time limit in place (Chaudhuri 2005). Similarly, Norway has a limit of 30 days for the patent holder to respond.

It is clear from these examples that India should consider a similar time limit to increase the efficiency and certainty in the industry. Under ordinary circumstances, India would not be expected to issue a compulsory licence before 2009/2010. This is because the first product patent under the new regime was not granted until 2006. And only after the expiry of three years time period can India begin the process to grant compulsory licences.

Under specific circumstances, the government may issue compulsory licences anytime after granting a patent. In cases of national emergency, extreme urgency, public non-commercial use including public health crisis, compulsory licence can be issued immediately after a patent has been granted. Under the TRIPS agreement, compulsory licensing is designed 'predominantly for supply of the domestic market' (Article 31 (f)). However, the Indian Patents Act also provides for compulsory licensing for the purpose of exporting patented pharmaceutical products to least developed countries (LDCs) – countries with no or insufficient pharmaceutical manufacturing capacity. These provisions correspond to the Waiver Decision of 30 August 2003 of the WTO (later adopted as Article 31*bis* of the TRIPS agreement) allowing countries with no or insufficient pharmaceutical manufacturing capacity to import patented drugs from a low-cost supplier. A number of countries including Canada and the EU have also enacted similar provisions for exports of generic versions of patented drugs in accordance with the WTO decision.

However, the process to issue a compulsory licence for exports is extremely complex. For example, India may grant a compulsory licence, if the importing country has issued compulsory licence for that product, provided that the product is patented in that country and/or the importing country has, by notification or otherwise, allowed importation of the patented product from India (Abbott 2003). Despite the provisions built into India's Patents Act, frequent use of these provisions to issue compulsory licences is unlikely at least in the foreseeable future. There are two reasons for this. First, the process to import medicines under the Waiver Decision of the WTO is highly complex and time-consuming. Second, the fear of retaliatory measures by the first world nations prevents the third world nations from using these provisions. This perhaps explains why Rwanda, in May 2008, became the first country to use the provisions of the Waiver Decision and import the imitations of AZT+3TC+NVP for HIV/AIDS patients from Canada. The whole process was so cumbersome that it took four years of sustained effort to achieve this single use of the WTO decision. Moreover, Apotex, the Canadian manufacturer involved in the process has indicated its reluctance to use the process again (Elliott 2008).

The words *any person interested* in the Indian Patent Act[4] allow the filing of applications for compulsory licences by any of the stakeholders. While the domestic firms may apply for compulsory licensing to enter the market, the inclusion of *any person* allows other stakeholders such as health activists and NGOs to also make applications for compulsory licensing to increase access to medicines. For example, Singh (2008) suggests that the Cancer Patients Aids Association (CPAA) is seeking compulsory licensing for around 20 cancer drugs patented by large drug MNCs including Roche, Pfizer, AstraZeneca, GSK, and Novartis. Singh notes that Roche charges Rs. 130,000 and Rs. 100,000 for an injection of Herceptin and Mabthera, respectively. The main reason for the CPAA making these applications is that these drugs are priced too high for most Indians to afford.

5.4.1.4 Response of domestic firms

Domestic firms in the industry have reacted differently to the new patent regime. On the one side are some firms prepared to take significant risks and test the new regime, while on the other side, some firms adopt a rather safer approach. In January 2008, Cipla, a leading Indian drug company and a known opponent of the TRIPS regime, launched Erlocip, an imitation of Taraceva, on which Roche was granted a patent in India in 2007. Taraceva is used to treat lung cancer, and Cipla has lodged a post-grant opposition. Roche's appeal for an injunction to stop Cipla from manufacturing was rejected by the Delhi High Court in

March 2008, citing public interest and the significant price difference between the two brands of the same drug as the reasons (Cipla 2008). Taraceva is priced at Rs. 4800 a tablet compared with Rs. 1600 for Erlocip. In the wake of the High Court ruling, Ranbaxy, DRL, and Sun Pharma may also adopt the same path as Cipla.

Encouraged by the Delhi High Court ruling, Cipla launched an imitation of Roche's anti-infection drug Valcyte in September 2008. Valcyte is priced at more than Rs. 1000 a tablet compared with Rs. 245 for Cipla's Valcept (Mathew 2008). Roche holds a valid patent in India for Valcyte and has initiated legal proceedings against Cipla for infringement of patent and trademark. A number of companies including Ranbaxy and Cipla as well as the Delhi Network of Positive People (DNP+) living with AIDS have filed post-grant opposition against the patent that is yet to be heard.

Other companies have adopted different approach to the new industrial landscape. Natco, a Hydrabad-based small firm, has applied for a compulsory licence for Taraceva. The company already manufactures the drug and sells it in Nepal at Rs. 1400 a tablet. Nepal is among the least developed countries (LDCs) and as such not obliged to comply with TRIPS till 2016. From the limited data available since the implementation of the new regime, it would appear that large Indian companies with capabilities to manufacture patented products are prepared to take the large MNCs head on while smaller firms appear to adopt a risk avert approach.

The Cipla approach to enter the market with Erlocip and Valcept offers considerable price reductions relative to the patented products. The Delhi High Court decision not to issue an injunction against Cipla is likely to encourage other large Indian companies to follow the same path. The High Court decision would be disappointing for the patent holder, but the decision reflects the flexibilities within the framework of the Indian law. In view of public interest, the intention of the decision clearly is to keep drug prices at a level closer to that of income of vast majority of Indians.

5.4.1.5 Appeals against the Indian Patent Office decisions

Until recently, appeals against the decisions of the Indian Patent Office could be filed at the High Courts. This appeals process was recently changed and there are two reasons for it. First, as noted earlier, the courts have a significant backlog of cases to be heard. Lodging an appeal with the courts would unnecessarily delay the hearing. Second, patent litigations require specialised skills for examination of the matter put before the court. Under the recent amendments to the Patents Act, an Intellectual Property Appellate Board (IPAB) has been established to hear appeals against the decisions, directions, or orders made by the Indian Controller of Patents. The IPAB became operational on 2 April 2007 and pending appeals in the High Courts were transferred to the Appellate Board (MedIndia 2007). The establishment of the IPAB is expected to expedite the appeals process, and the decisions made by the IPAB would be rendered as final. Except for writ petitions on 'patent illegality', 'miscarriage of justice', or 'a question of law that merits attention', no further direct review of the Appellate Board decisions will be available through the Indian court system (Mueller 2007b). The non-availability of 'further review' of the IPAB decisions could be considered a good thing eliminating the lengthy delays under the previously available 'almost endless' appeals process. The fact that the IPAB decisions will be final brings certainty in the industry.

5.5 Uncertainties and ambiguities

In the wake of such a major change as implementing the TRIPS compliant regime in India, some uncertainties and ambiguities would be expected and they are part of the evolutionary process. Different interest groups have different interpretations of the provisions introduced in the recent amendments to the Indian Patents Act. The following areas remained contentious between different stakeholders including different sections of the government that have difference of opinions:

- If it would be TRIPS compatible to limit the grant of patent for pharmaceutical substance to new chemical entity or to new medical entity involving one or more inventive steps (examination of Section 3(d));
- If it would be TRIPS compatible to exclude micro-organisms from patenting;
- What steps should be taken with regard to data protection in the context of Article 39.3 of TRIPS Agreement; and
- Whether data protection can be offered under the existing legal provisions or an appropriate new dispensation is required.

Two separate committees were established to examine the above issues. A Technical Expert Group on Patent Law Issues under the Chair of Dr Mashelkar, India's chief scientist at the time, examined the issues 1 and 2. In the interest of the pharmaceutical industry in general and more specifically, in the wake of Novartis' challenge, the investigation of the first issue was very significant. This group submitted its final report in December 2006, but subsequently withdrew the report due to alleged plagiarism and the issues remain unresolved.

The issue of *data protection* versus *data exclusivity* has also been a bone of contention between those who support a stringent patent regime and those who prefer minimum protection. This debates hinges on protecting undisclosed test or other data submitted by the first applicant (originator) to the regulatory authorities to obtain marketing approval for pharmaceutical or agricultural chemical products. The generation of such data takes several years and incurs considerable costs. If the subsequent applicants (generic manufacturers) can provide bio-equivalence to the originator drug, no further test data are required (Sauer & Sauer 2007). Under *data protection*, the authorities can, without disclosing it to third parties, rely on the originator data saving the subsequent applicants' significant costs. *Data exclusivity* refers to confidentiality of the regulatory file submitted to regulatory authorities for a specific period (Morag-Sela et al. 2004). Under *data exclusivity*, the reliance on the originator data is prohibited during the period of exclusivity forcing subsequent applicants to conduct their own tests and effectively barring the generics entry until the exclusivity period expires. This debate is a consequence of the ambiguities of the TRIPS agreement stating that:

> .... Members, when requiring, as a condition of approving the marketing of pharmaceutical or of agricultural chemical products which utilize new chemical entities, the submission of undisclosed test or other data, the origination of which involves a considerable effort, shall protect such data against unfair commercial use. In addition, Members shall protect such data against disclosure, except where necessary to protect the public, or unless steps are taken to ensure that the data are protected against unfair commercial use.
>
> (Article 39.3)

The terms *unfair commercial use, considerable effort* and *disclosure* are not described in the TRIPS agreement, and hence, have been interpreted differently by different interest groups. Furthermore, the TRIPS agreement does not mention how long this protection be provided for or how this protection be carried out. An independent study finds that Article 39.3 does not create property rights, nor a right to prevent others from relying on the data for the marketing approval of the same product by a third party, or from using the data except where unfair (dishonest) commercial practices are involved (Commission on Intellectual Property Rights Innovation and Public Health 2006).

The International Federation of Pharmaceutical Manufacturers and Associations suggests that data exclusivity is an intellectual property right that should not be confused with the protection provided by other rights, especially patents (IFPMA 2004). There are significant differences between the rights under data exclusivity and under patents. While data exclusivity does not prevent other firms from conducting their own trials, the prohibitive costs effectively stop generic manufacturers from doing so. Unlike patents, data exclusivity is automatic (similar to copyrights), does not incur additional costs or renewal fees, and has no provisions for exceptions such as compulsory licensing (Clift 2007). Yet, the data exclusivity creates a patent-like barrier on the drugs outside the patent protection and prevents generics entry for the entire period of exclusivity (So 2004). For example, Taxol was derived from natural extracts; hence, could not be patented. The US National Cancer Institute discovered Taxol in 1962 and licensed it to Bristol-Myers-Squibb (BMS) for commercial development in 1991. BMS kept generics out of the market through data exclusivity (Pugatch 2004).

Internationally, the debate on the interpretation of Article 39.3 has divided the world into two distinct groups: namely, the developed countries with advanced research capabilities and the developing countries with less developed pharmaceutical industries. The former group of countries views the provisions of Article 39.3 as mandating data exclusivity. The interpretation of the latter group of countries in contrast appears to be along the lines of data protection. The developed countries led by the US have, through other means, such as bilateral or regional agreements and the use of Special 301, forced a significant number of poor countries to adopt data exclusivity potentially jeopardising healthcare in those countries (Malhotra & Grewal 2008; Timmermans 2007) (see Chapter 2 for more details). The promotion of data exclusivity appears to be, in part, large MNCs' attempt to nullify or minimise the benefits of early introduction of generics gained under the Hatch-Waxman Act 1984.

In India, the pharmaceutical MNCs, some research-oriented Indian firms, such as Nicholas Piramal, and the Planning Commission of India favour data exclusivity. Most Indian firms, Ministry of Health and Family Welfare and other sections of the government as well as the NGOs such as Oxfam and MSF argue that TRIPS obliged India to provide data protection against unfair commercial use and not to data exclusivity. The difference of opinions remained and the issue was handed over to an Inter-Ministerial Consultative Committee (IMCC) under the chair of Mrs Reddy, Secretary, Department of Chemicals and Petrochemicals.

The IMCC used a consultative approach to gain the views of concerned departments, field experts, industry delegations, NGOs, and other stakeholders and submitted its report in May 2007. The report suggests that under Article 39.3, the regulatory authorities are free to rely upon the data submitted by first applicant to grant marketing approvals to subsequent applicants without disclosing the data to them. However, the report finds that the current Indian law does not meet the minimum requirements of the TRIPS agreement for data protection. The report makes recommendations in three key areas: namely, pharmaceuticals, traditional medicines, and agrochemicals. Nevertheless, we only consider the recommendations relevant to the pharmaceutical industry in this book.

The IMCC recommended a two-step approach to data protection. The first step relates to *data protection* during a transitional period not specifically defined in years or with a fixed date. The transitional period would end once the Central Drug Authority (CDA), an autonomous body under the Ministry of Health and Family Welfare, is established. During the transition period, India should adopt the 'trade secret' form of protection and take appropriate steps to safeguard non-disclosure of undisclosed data. However, the generics may be approved by relying on the data submitted by originators.

In the second step, the IMCC recommended a five-year *data exclusivity* under the following conditions. First, the data exclusivity would be provided only to post-1995 molecules and only to those not yet introduced in India. This exclusivity would be provided to undisclosed data and not extended to data already published or publicly available. The data exclusivity for patented drugs should under no circumstances extend beyond the 20-year period of patent protection in India.

Second, the marketing approval becomes invalid if the product is not launched within six months of its grant and if not marketed for 12 consecutive months anytime thereafter. Under these circumstances, the authorities can grant marketing approvals to subsequent applicants by relying on the original data, even though the data exclusivity period may not have expired.

Third, the period of data exclusivity may be counted from the date of the first marketing approval anywhere in the world, if the originator applies for marketing approval in India within 24 months of that date. Generics producers may apply for marketing approval with the express consent of the originator within the above-stated 24-month period or without the originator's authorisation after this period. However, should the generics applicant apply within this 24-month period for tentative marketing approval, the application would become final on the day after the expiry of the 24-month period, provided the originator does not apply for a marketing approval within this period. In case, the originator applies within this period, the tentative approval will not become final until after the expiry of the five-years data exclusivity period counted from the date of the first launch anywhere.

Fourth, in accordance with the provisions of the Patents Act, compulsory licensing would override the data protection, so that data protection does not jeopardise the spirit of compulsory licensing. Finally, activities under the 'Bolar provision' would be exempted from data protection. Under the Bolar provisions, companies undertake drug testing to prepare for a market launch after the protection period expires.

The IMCC recommendations, if implemented, would force the originator companies to launch their products in the Indian market with a shorter lag than in the past. In the 1970s and 1980s, the drug lag in India measured against the first approval granted by the USFDA has in some cases been more than 12 years (Keayla 1996). Most of the new drugs post-1970 were introduced by the domestic manufacturers rather than the originator companies. Under the IMCC recommendations, Indian companies would use the Bolar provisions to prepare for the timely launch of generics in the post data protection period. Unlike a significant number of countries under contractual obligations disallowing them to use compulsory licensing, India would be able to override data exclusivity when granting compulsory licensing. This provision is important for India being the leading supplier of generics and low-cost imitations of patented drugs to the developing world.

5.5.1 Access to medicines and the new patent regime

How does the new patent regime impact on access to medicines? Considering the similarities between the post-2005 and pre-1970 patent regimes, it could be assumed that the impact would be to push drug prices higher. There is one significant difference between pre-1970 and post-2005 situation, however. In the pre-1970 period, India's domestic pharmaceutical industry was virtually non-existent, compared to the world class industry of the post-2005 period. Yet, this difference may not be sufficient reason to rule out the widely held apprehension that in the post-TRIPS world drug availability and drug prices are likely to put medicines beyond the reach of the poor people, as witnessed in the following comment:

> .... If I were a hapless citizen of India, I would hope for the TRIPS system in the WTO to collapse; and for the development of some alternative form of rewarding innovations in medicines that matter to me, my family and my country.
>
> (Srinivasan 2008, p. 68)

The TRIPS compliant regime has been in force in India for four years now. During this short period, India has had a number of drugs introduced such as Glivec, where the originator has priced the drug significantly beyond the affordability of common Indians. The pre-1970 domestic industry was not developed sufficiently to offer alternatives and India was paying the highest drugs prices. The post-2005 domestic industry however is in a strong position to manufacture and supply low-cost generics. The case of Cipla to produce copies of Taraceva[5] shows the preparedness of domestic companies to play their role in lowering the drug prices. The Delhi High Court decision not to grant injunction against Cipla demonstrates that the courts are ready to back up the domestic industry in its attempt to increase access to medicines. Under its international obligations, India has implemented the TRIPS agreement, which, appears to be a hindrance to the access to medicines. India needs to devise new strategies for broadening the access to healthcare, including medicines, for its entire population without infringing or abandoning the TRIPS agreement. These issues are also the focus of our discussion in Chapter 8.

5.6 Pharmaceutical innovation

The object of this section is to assess the impact of TRIPS on the level of innovation in the Indian pharmaceutical industry. We use two methods to measure the level of innovation; namely, the number of new drugs developed and the number of patents filed. First, an examination of the number of new drugs developed in India shows the extent of innovation in the pharmaceutical industry under both the pre-1970 (strong) and post-1970 (weak) patent regimes.

Second, an empirical study by the National Institute of Science Technology and Development Studies (NISTADS) shows the number of patents filed between 1990 and 2002. The significance of this period is that it relates to the years before and after India's signing of the WTO agreements. The findings suggest that the innovation level increased significantly after India signed the WTO agreements.

These results appear to confirm Basheer's hypothesis about innovation. A professor in Intellectual Property Law at the National University of Juridical Sciences at Kolkata, Basheer (2008) suggests that most countries need to imitate first, before developing capabilities to innovate and strong IP regimes stand in the way of permitting imitation on the way to subsequent innovation (cited in Kumar 2008). India's stringent pre-1970 patent regime did not help its pharmaceutical industry to develop or enhance its innovative skills. The industry developed under the post-1970 weak patent regime.

Chaturvedi (2005) studies new drugs developed in India under both the pre-1970 and the post-1970 regime. She concludes that just 4 drugs were developed between 1921 and 1972 compared with 12 drugs developed from 1978 to 1997. Her findings are significant on two accounts. First, the number of drugs developed in India may be small relative to those developed in the wealthy nations. It demonstrates nevertheless the capabilities of the Indian scientists. With the minimum resources that the research institutes had before the economic reforms of 1991, developing new drugs was indeed a remarkable achievement.

Second, even after abolition of product patents under Patents Act 1970, development of new drugs remained in progress. Not only the domestic institutes, but a large MNC also contributed to developing new drugs during that period. Ciba Geigy (now part of Novartis) developed two new drugs (Sintamil and Tinazolin) in 1978. However, most of the new drugs were developed at the Central Drugs Research Institute (CDRI) that was now involved in developing Bulaquin (antimalarial), Picroliv (liver, kidney), and CDRI-99/373 (antiosteoprosis) (CDRI 2008).

The involvement of private enterprises in drug development remained limited during the period of weak patents. Following the economic reforms in 1991, particularly since India's accession to the WTO, innovative activities in the private sector have increased. A small number of leading Indian firms have in recent years embarked on discovering new molecules in the pursuit of developing new drugs (see Table 5.2). Leading Indian firms have significantly increased their R&D expenditure and embarked upon drug discovery. The R&D spending of the top five Indian pharmaceutical companies crossed US$500 million in 2006 (Mazumdar-Shaw 2007). The total sales revenue of the top five companies for the year was less than $5 billion taking their R&D spending to over 10 per cent of sales. This is a significant increase from less than 2 per cent hitherto the Industry spent on R&D. By comparison, leading MNCs

Table 5.2 Development of drugs by select Indian firms (2006–07)

Company	No. of molecules in pipeline	Phase I	Phase II	Phase III
DRL	9	2	3	1
Ranbaxy	10		2	
Glenmark	6	2	2	
Nicholas Piramal	6		3	
Wockhardt	5	2	1	
Zydus Cadila	4	2	1	

Source: Compiled from the companies' Web sites.

spend around 14–15 per cent of sales on R&D. The Australian pharmaceutical industry's expenditure on R&D remains around 3 per cent of sales (Sweeny 2002). Since 2005, the R&D expenditure in the Indian industry in general and in the pharmaceutical sector in particular has increased significantly. The Department of Scientific and Industrial Research (DSIR) in India annually publishes a list of firms with in-house R&D capabilities and their R&D expenditure. According to the 2007–08 annual report of the DSIR, over 40 pharmaceutical companies spent more than Rs. 50 million each (GOI 2008a).

The NISTADS (2005) examines India's innovative activities by patents filed between 1990 and 2002. The examination divides the period into three sub-periods: 1990–94, 1995–98, and 1999–2002 and finds that India's patent filings in India and in the US have significantly increased in recent years, in the chemical and pharmaceutical sectors in particular. The NISTADS study divides India's patent applications into the following categories: 1) India Owned Patents (IOP) such as domestic firms, institutions, universities; 2) Foreign Owned Patents (FOP) refer to patent filings by Indian subsidiaries of foreign companies; and 3) Unassigned referring to non-institutional Indian individuals.

India's patent applications filed with the United States Patent and Trademark Office (USPTO) were as follows. From the first to the final sub-period, the IOPs increased from 48 to 125 to 523, respectively. While the filings from first to second sub-period more than doubled, they more than quadrupled between the second and final sub-period. During the same periods, the FOPs' increase was relatively moderate rising from 54 to 61 to 161. The increase in the Unassigned patents from 23 to 34 to 50 was even less significant than the increase in the FOPs.

A sector-wise breakdown of India's patents filed with the USPTO provides more details of innovative activities across major industries. The

IOPs filed by chemical industry increased from 24 to 42 to 166 in the three sub-periods, while pharmaceutical industry increased from just 9 to 48 to 227. Another noteworthy change in the IOPs was in the biotechnology sector that increased from 0 to 7 to 46 in the three sub-periods. In contrast, the FOPs in the chemical sector increased from 10 to 6 to 22 and in the pharmaceutical sector, declined from 29 to 14 in the second sub-period before rising back to 30 in the final sub-period. The main increase in the FOPs was in the electronics and miscellaneous sectors. The Unassigned patents did not register significant changes in any particular sector.

The patent activity at the Indian Patent Office (IPO) was different to that filed with the USPTO. At the IPO, the number of FOPs was significantly greater than the IOPs. However, the overall FOPs progressively declined in the sub-periods following India's signing of the WTO agreements. The number of FOPs declined from 6533 (1990–94) to 5004 (1995–98) to 4348 (1999–2002). The progressive decline in the number of FOPs at the IPO is ironic, because after India signed the TRIPS agreement in 1994, India was obliged to strengthen its patent regime. Yet, the number of FOP filings in India progressively declined.

The IOP activity progressively increased from 1247 to 1594 to 2046 in the three sub-periods. The increase in the IOPs is suggestive of industry's anticipation of the then upcoming regime change. The increase could be, in part, attributed to the industrial and economic reforms introduced in 1991. The Unassigned patents at the IPO fluctuated from 617 to 742 to 473 in the three sub-periods.

A sector-wise composition of the patents filed at the IPO suggests that the decline in the FOP activity is more significant in sectors marked as chemicals, machinery, and miscellaneous sectors than other sectors. The decline in the FOP applications needs to be understood in the right context however. Foreign MNCs account for over 80 per cent of the estimated 12,000 applications for product patents in the mailbox (NISTADS 2005; Ram 2006). The patent applications for pharmaceutical products filed before 2005 were lodged into the mailbox. Thus, those applications would not show as FOPs, because they only became active after 2005 when the processing of the applications first began.

The IOPs filed with the IPO increased in the chemical sectors from 419 to 492 to 668, while the pharmaceutical sector increased from 221 to 305 to 547 filings. Other noteworthy increase was from 32 to 38 to 60 in IOPs in biotechnology. These figures show progressive increases in these sectors. Nevertheless, the level of increase in the IOPs filed in India is considerably lower than the IOPs filed in the US. The Unassigned category also shows substantial increase from 24 to 35 to 70 in the pharmaceutical sector.

Malhotra (2008) analyses strengths and weaknesses of India's research capabilities and finds that India's innovative activity is highly concentrated in the pharmaceutical and chemical sectors. The Council of Scientific and Industrial Research (CSIR) alone accounted for most of India's patent activity. This is because, with 84 of nation's premier research institutes under its ambit, the CSIR has the largest network of institutes in the country. The concentration is demonstrated by the fact that from 1990 to 2002, only 8 institutes, including the CSIR, filed more than 10 patent applications, and collectively accounted for 80 per cent of the IOP activity at the USPTO. This level of concentration indicates that apart from the CSIR, only a handful of industry players are engaged in research that is globally competitive. The analysis further shows that companies such as Dabur and Panacea have more patent applications in the US than in India suggesting the focus of their research is on serving the US market rather than India.

India's leading players in pharmaceuticals are investing significantly into basic research, changing their business model from reverse engineers to innovators. With the gradual rise in patent literacy, more domestic firms are likely to join the basic research that would enhance India's global competitiveness. While it is too early to reach definitive conclusions on how much of this rise in the level of innovation directly resulted from implementing TRIPS, these activities are likely to continue increasing further the level of innovation in coming years.

5.6.1 The role of government in innovation

The Indian government offers various support measures to encourage the industry to undertake R&D. For example, drugs developed indigenously are free from any price control. The incentives also include 150 per cent weighted tax deductions on in-house R&D expenditure in the pharmaceutical industry, including expenses on clinical trials. The government also provides limited funding under the Pharmaceutical Research and Development Support Fund (PRDSF) to boost research on diseases like malaria, and tuberculosis, although the total budget for the PRDSF, which consists of interest generated on the deposit of Rs. 1500 million (~US$36 million), is miniscule by global standards (GOI 2005a). The Indian Council of Medical Research (ICMR) has also set up Medical Innovation Fund with cash rewards for innovative ideas (Alexander 2007). Small in monetary terms (by comparison, Pfizer alone has a R&D budget of $7 billion), these rewards are a symbolic gesture to acknowledge the origin of innovation.

The government is considering a new law; namely, the India Innovation Act and Innovation Zones to boost innovative activities. Similar to the Special Economic Zones, the concept of Innovation zones is aimed at bringing together different stakeholders in the innovation chain and offer significant incentives for investors. The India Innovation Act is likely to be modelled along the lines of the 'America Competes Act', which focuses on the following three key areas to maintain and improve innovation in the US in the twenty first century: increasing research investment; strengthening education opportunities in science, technology, engineering, and mathematics from elementary through graduate school; and developing an innovation infrastructure (FICCI 2007).

The current rates of high economic growth and the development of its pharmaceutical industry now place India in a strong position to take a lead to address the 10/90 gap noted in Chapter 3. India needs to introduce programmes with significant incentives to attract investment and establish mechanisms such as the public–private partnerships (PPP) to develop drugs for diseases specific to the developing countries.

5.7 Conclusions

Under the Indian Patents and Designs Act 1911, product patents were granted for pharmaceuticals. The Patents Act 1970 repealed the product patents and granted patents for a single process actually used in manufacturing the drug. This change allowed the reverse engineering model that played a central role in the development of domestic pharmaceutical industry.

As a member of the WTO, India was obliged to implement the TRIPS agreement and the Patents Act 1970 was amended accordingly. However, ambiguities in the Act remain regarding patentable subject matter, plants organisms, and data protection. In the overall scheme of things, these ambiguities could be considered as an integral part of the evolutionary process. These ambiguities are not unique to India. Developing – and developed member states remain divided on the interpretation of the terms used in the TRIPS agreement.

Section 3(d) of the Patents Act is designed to prevent ever-greening of patents. India regards claims, such as new uses or new forms of existing substance, as frivolous and does not grant patents for such claims. A large number of studies support India's position. Large MNCs allege that this Section contravenes the TRIPS agreement. Novartis has challenged the validity of this contentious Section in the Indian Courts. Hundreds of thousands of people across the world have signed petitions against the Novartis challenge. Norway and the European Commission have appealed to Novartis to drop the case. The Supreme Court is yet to hear the case. A Novartis win would severely restrict access to low-cost medicines.

Under the new regime, India has granted product patents on a small number of drugs. However, domestic companies have also launched imitations of a number of patented products. The courts have so far refused to grant injunctions to stop the domestic manufacturers. This was primarily because the price difference between the originator product and the copy has been too great to ignore. India should consider introducing provisions to deter patent applications with frivolous claims in order to keep drug prices low and minimise patent litigations.

The innovative activities in India have increased substantially over the last decade and India is increasingly becoming a significant player in filing patent applications in the US. However, apart from the public institutes under the ambit of the CSIR, only a small number of pharmaceutical companies are engaged in patent filings in the US. This suggests that innovative activities of a limited number of Indian firms are globally competitive. The data on patent filings also suggest that the Indian innovative activities are more focused on serving the rich markets of the developed world than providing low-cost medicines for the poor in the developing countries.

6 Price Controls and Drug Affordability in India: Policy Options

6.1 Introduction

Earlier work (Goddard et al. 2006) served to emphasise the significance of drug price controls that are an important policy instrument, because health systems cannot rely entirely on market mechanisms for healthcare delivery. Price controls are a method of regulating drug prices for achieving health policy goals (Gray & Matsebula 2003). The governments use interventions from the supply side by controlling drug prices and/or from the demand side by restricting reimbursements and by raising patient co-payments (Cai & Salmon 2005). From the manufacturers' perspective, price controls restrict free market activity, limit profits, and restrict return on investment.

All developed countries, including the US, and most of the developing countries, have some degree of control over drug prices. Ballance et al. (1992) study drug price controls in different countries and find the following. A group of developed countries including Austria, Belgium, Finland, France, Italy, Norway, and Sweden as well as developing countries such as China, Egypt, India, Mexico, Pakistan, and Thailand have substantial price controls over drugs prices. Limited price controls exist in countries including Australia, Canada, Germany, Japan, the US, and the UK and also in Argentina, Brazil, Indonesia, Uruguay, and Venezuela. A small number of countries such as Chile, Hong Kong, Kenya, Malaysia, Sri Lanka, and Taiwan had no price controls.

It should be noted from the outset that the TRIPS agreement, the implementation of which is the primary focus of this book, is not concerned with price controls. In other words, drug price controls do not constitute a contravention of the agreement. The TRIPS agreement is concerned with the protection of intellectual property rights, and not with full range of market regulations.

6.2 Drug price controls in India

India's drug price controls have evolved over a long period of time. India had one of the highest drug prices in the world in the 1960s when the vast majority of Indians lived below the poverty line (Lall 1974). The 1962 border conflict with China became a turning point signalling India's shift towards price controls. Since then, the price control framework has gone through substantial changes. The scope and level of Drug Price Control Orders (DPCO) have been progressively reduced since 1979. The milestone changes to the framework are considered below. Table 6.1 shows the evolution of price controls in India. The DPCO currently in force was pronounced in 1995.

Table 6.1 Drug price controls in India at a glance

Year	Framework	Level of control	Approx. market share (%)
Pre-1970	1963: Defence of India Act. 1966: Essential Commodities Act.	Formulations only: 1963: Drug prices frozen; 1966: Drug Prices (Display and Control) Order	Not known
DPCO 1970	Essential Commodities Act.	Almost all Bulk drugs and their formulations	Indirectly, the entire market
DPCO 1979	Drug Policy – 1977	347 Bulk drugs and their formulations	80%
DPCO 1987	Drug Policy – 1986	142 Bulk drugs and their formulations	60%
DPCO 1995	Drug Policy – 1994	74 Bulk drugs and their formulations	>40% at the time of implementation, but now accounts for around 25%
DPCO 2004*	Pharmaceutical Policy – 2002	38 Bulk drugs and their formulations	>20%

Note: * proposed but not yet enacted.
Source: Compiled from Drug Policy – 1977 (GOI 1977); Drug Policy – 1986 (GOI 1986); Drug Policy – 1994 (GOI 1994); Pharmaceutical Policy – 2002 (GOI 2002d); and other documents from Government of India.

6.2.1 DPCO – 1995

India's formulations market uses around 600[1] drugs, of which 74 or around 12 per cent are currently under price control. Drugs for price control are selected on the basis of criteria that have changed significantly over the last 30 years. Essentiality is no longer a criterion. Under the 1995 rules, the drugs listed on the Schedule[2] would be based on 1990 market value of the drug and the following criteria would apply regarding the sales revenue and market share of manufacturers, and number of manufacturers in that segment of the submarket.

For a bulk drug with a turnover of Rs. 40 million or over:

- the number of producers of such a drug must be less than five;
- the number of formulation manufacturers who use this drug must be less than ten; and
- the leader of such formulations' retail market has a share of 40 per cent or over.

For a bulk drug with a turnover of less than Rs. 40 million:

- the bulk drug turnover must be over Rs. 10 million; and
- the leader of such formulations' retail market has a share of at least 90 per cent (GOI 1995, Section 7).

The changes to the selection criteria for placing drugs under price control have the following implications. First, the criteria for inclusion or exclusion of a drug lack transparency and appear irrational. These criteria are based on the market data of 1990 that are static. In contrast, a basis as dynamic as market environment would require continuous monitoring of market data and accordingly amend the list of drugs under price control. However, such is not the case under the current DPCO. Consequently, some truly life-saving and essential drugs have been excluded while some dubious drugs have fallen under price control (Narrain 2004). Thus, manufacturers could charge high prices for essential drugs and the prices could vary significantly between companies as the following study demonstrates.

Das et al. (2007) observed significant price variations between different brand products for the same drug. The highest price difference noted was 881 per cent (Rs. 4.81 v. Rs. 0.49) for Amlodipine 5mg, an anti-hypertensive drug but also used to treat angina. Amlodipine is on the Essential Drug List 1996 as well as on the National List of Essential

Medicines (NLEM) 2003, but is not under price control. If the drug were price controlled, the price differences were likely to be minimum.

Second, there is no provision for updating, adding new drugs to, or deleting old ones from the list. Over 300 new drugs have been discovered since the implementation of the DPCO – 1995, yet no new drugs have been added to the list. The WHO Model List of Essential Drugs is updated every two years. If the Indian list were based on current market environment, the list would be updated annually.

Third, India's healthcare needs are constantly changing. Until recently, India's disease burden primarily consisted of the tropical diseases. However, the recent spread of HIV/AIDS and the emergence of lifestyle diseases such as cancer and cardiovascular diseases have significantly added to India's disease burden. The current framework ignores these ground realities.

6.2.2 Pre-1970 Price controls

Under the Defence of India Rules, prices for all formulation were frozen in 1963. This prevented the industry from raising drug prices in case of excessive demand following the war with China. In 1966, the government issued the first Drug Prices (Display and Control) Order under the Essential Commodities Act[3] 1955. Under this Order, manufacturers had to obtain government approval before increasing prices on formulations with mark-ups of up to 150 per cent over ex-factory costs. Foreign MNCs generally had a higher mark-up and thus remained mostly unaffected by the price control measures. Of all the applications filed for price increases under this Order, MNCs accounted for just 6 per cent, but held around 68 per cent market share (Chaudhuri 2005). Large MNCs benefited from this provision at the expense of small domestic producers, who had priced their products at the low end of the market. From consumers' perspective, the 1963 price freeze was better than the 1966 price controls, because the former applied to all formulations without any qualification.

6.2.3 DPCO – 1970

The DPCO or the Order – 1970 formed a part of India's policy shift towards increased controls and protectionism. Under this Order, almost all bulk drugs were brought under the Essential Commodities Act, which gave the government the power to fix a ceiling price for essential[4] bulk drugs. Return on capital was the consideration for fixing the ceiling prices for bulk drugs, while cost-based pricing determined the retail prices of formulations. The controls were also applied to mark-ups and overall profits.

It is argued that the cost-based approach used for formulations, which to a large extent remains unchanged to date, has a number of flaws. First, determining actual costs as opposed to claimed costs is a problem, because authorities could not independently ascertain the costs of new drugs, except for the costs submitted by manufacturers.

Second, the cost-based approach indirectly encourages imports over locally manufactured products. For the imported products, the landed cost is used as the basis for calculating the market price, which leaves loopholes for transfer pricing.[5] For example, Pfizer charged US$9000 per kg for a material available from Italy at US$125 per kg; Sandoz imported at US$60,000 an item available from Germany at US$23,000 (Lanjouw 1998, p. 12). The practice of transfer pricing is not confined to a country or a company. The MNCs including Glaxo, Parke-Davis, Merck Sharp & Dohme, and Wyeth frequently engaged in transfer pricing. Recently, an out of court settlement with the US authorities of a litigation involving transfer pricing cost the UK-based GSK over US$4 billion in 2006 (mX 2006). The implications for consumers are high drug prices through inflated costs claimed.

6.2.4 DPCO – 1979

Following the protectionist policies introduced in the early 1970s, the government constituted a high-level committee to find ways to make India self-sufficient in manufacturing drugs and formulations. The Hathi Committee Report (HCR) submitted in 1975 is considered to be the most comprehensive study on India's pharma industry. The HCR made a number of important recommendations including wholesale nationalisation of the drug industry; developing a list of essential drugs; controlling drugs prices based on essentiality; establishing a National Drug Authority; and mandatory use of generic names for all single-ingredient products. High level of influence of the pharmaceutical industry in New Delhi ensured that most of the recommendations of the HCR remained unimplemented. However, the HCR became the basis for the new framework. Essentiality became a criterion for placing drugs under price control and the number of such drugs declined to 347. The Drug Policy – 1977 and the Patents Act 1970 (discussed in previous chapter) laid the foundation stone for India's domestic pharma industry, which eventually brought down the drug prices, and made the country self-sufficient in pharmaceuticals.

6.2.5 DPCO – 1987

In the mid-1980s, India began introducing measures towards industrial liberalisation. The Drug Policy – 1986 titled 'Measures for Rationalization, Quality Control and Growth of Drugs and Pharmaceuticals Industry in India' was the first clear indication of India's strategic shift from protectionist regulatory framework to adopting a more liberal approach. Under the DPCO – 1987, the number of drugs under price control was reduced from 347 to 142. In value terms, the collective market share of drugs under price control reduced from 80 per cent to 60 per cent. Thus, it would be safe to assume that the 205 drugs taken off the list were low priced, or had low sales or both.

While the drug price controls played an important part in achieving the low prices, the enforceability and the effect of stand-alone price controls remained questionable. There was no dedicated agency to practically oversee the market activity and enforce price controls. The monitoring of the prices was left to the State Drug Controllers, for whom, this was not among their primary tasks. The enforcement and prosecution required a body at the central level.

In 1999, the National Pharmaceutical Pricing Authority (NPPA) was established. The express functions of the NPPA include the implementation and enforcement 'of the provisions of the Drugs (Prices Control) Order in accordance with the powers delegated to it' (GOI 2003a). Here 'in accordance with the powers delegated to it' becomes important for two reasons. First, with just 75-staff, the NPPA is significantly understaffed for effective policing (The Sen Committee 2005). It mainly relies on State Drug Controllers and other sections of the government. Second, if a case of over-pricing of a drug is brought to the NPPA's attention, it can only serve the offending company notices to deposit the overcharged amount. The companies usually ignore the notice or go to court and obtain a stay order. The NPPA on average recovers Rs. 150 million annually from drug companies, most of which remains in litigation and there is uncertainty about its quantum and final recovery (GOI 2005a). With the inadequate powers and the lack of sufficient staff, currently delegated to the authority, the NPPA is far from being effective.

6.2.6 DPCO – 2004 (proposed but not yet enacted)

Under the Pharmaceutical Policy – 2002, the DPCO – 2004 was planned, which would have reduced the number of drugs under price control from 74 to 38. However, following a legal action by citizen groups, drugs earmarked for price-decontrol from 2004, could not be set free, and the status quo remains (GOI 2005a). Responding to a petition jointly filed by the citizen groups,[6] the Supreme Court of India (India's apex court) made an order on 10 March 2003, directing the Union Government to ensure that essential and life-saving drugs did not fall out of price control and to review the drugs that were essential and life saving in nature (Narrain 2004).

6.3 Continuing search for alternatives

Different sections of the Indian Government have different views on the scope of drug price controls. The Ministry of Health and Family Welfare, and the Ministry of Chemicals and Petro-Chemicals, would prefer to bring all 354 essential drugs under price control. The Prime Minister's Office and the Planning Commission would rather seek alternatives to the expansion of price control.

Several committees have been constituted to examine drug prices and related issues. While all such committees, including the National Manufacturing Competitiveness Council (NMCC), the National Commission on Macroeconomics and Health, and the Standing Committee on Chemicals and Fertilizers have made valuable contributions to the debate, work of the following committees is considered particularly relevant to drug price controls.

First, a committee constituted by the Director General, Health Services reviewed the National Essential Drugs List (NEDL) 1996 and compiled the National List of Essential Medicines (NLEM) 2003. The committee chaired by Dr S.D. Seth followed the general principles of the WHO on essential drugs and identified as such 'that satisfy the priority healthcare needs of the population' (The Seth Committee 2004, p. iii). Other terms of reference included India's disease burden; safety and efficacy; comparative cost-effectiveness; and infrastructure for delivery. The NLEM 2003 contains 354 drugs compared with 286 in the NEDL 1996. Both numbers are in stark contrast with just 74 drugs under price control since 1995. From the 354 drugs (NLEM 2003), only 15 or less than 5 per cent are currently price controlled, which demonstrates the parameters of the framework not keeping pace with the dynamics of public health.

Second, Minister of Chemicals and Fertilizers in 2004 constituted a committee under the Chairmanship of G.S. Sandhu. The terms of reference given to the Sandhu Committee were to review the span of price control in light of Supreme Court orders. The Sandhu Committee used a consultative process involving the industry, NGOs, health activists, and field experts.

The Sandhu Committee found the current framework to be 'not very effective' and recommended two types of monitoring: namely, intensive monitoring and normal monitoring (cited in The Sen Committee 2005, p. 80). The intensive monitoring would cover all 339[7] drugs in the NLEM 2003 basket currently not price controlled. Drugs in this category would be rigorously watched and a ceiling of 10–15 per cent annual increase applied. Price increases beyond that would be deemed as over-charging and the extra amount would be recovered from the company. Normal monitoring would imply the continuation of the current practices of the watchdog and would apply to drugs outside the NLEM basket.

For consumers, the net benefits of the Sandhu Committee's recommendations remain doubtful. First, to place 339 drugs under intensive monitoring would not be possible with the staff levels and limited powers, which the NPPA currently has. Second, if annual increases of 10–15 per cent were permitted, the price would more than double every few years (at 10 per cent in eight years and at 15 per cent in five years), which would be detrimental to consumer interests and drug affordability. In comparison, France caps drug price rises at annual CPI level, which would be significantly lower than 10–15 per cent. In New Zealand, drug prices are negotiated every five years, and remain fixed for the term.

The Sandhu Committee also recommended: mandatory price negotiations at launch of patented drugs, greater coverage of health insurance, special programmes for people living below the poverty line, and reducing of taxes and levies on essential drugs. For government procurement of drugs, it recommended replicating the open-tender approach already adopted by the Rajasthan Model of Medicare Societies that saves patients over 50 per cent on the market prices.

Third, the Sen Committee was constituted by the Prime Minister's Office 'to explore options other than price control for achieving the objectives of making life-saving drugs at reasonable prices'. The Committee under the Chairmanship of Proneb Sen, Principal Advisor, Planning Commission, met with all stakeholders including the industry, international agencies, health professionals, NGOs, and academics. While the industry suggested that 'price regulations are not necessary for drugs and that competition should be able to provide the necessary discipline', the Sen Committee opined that 'the pharmaceutical industry by its very nature is non-competitive, and requires active public intervention to ensure competitive outcomes' (The Sen Committee 2005, p. 19). In its report submitted in September 2005, the Sen Committee re-emphasised that price controls were an essential instrument to curb the market behaviour and made the following principal recommendations. Price controls should:

- apply only to formulations and not to bulk drugs or any upstream products;
- not be based on the turnover, but on essentiality of the drug;
- take into considerations the effect of control on the entire therapeutic class; and
- be replaced with price ceilings, within which the companies would be free to position themselves and the ceilings to rise in accordance with the Wholesale Price Index (WPI) for manufactured goods.

The Sen Committee recommended reference pricing to replace the cost-based pricing on the following guiding principles. For existing essential drugs, the price quoted in the bulk procurement by government or other agencies would become the reference price. For new drugs, it would be based on the average price of the top three selling products by value in the therapeutic category, and if less than three brands in the market, the average of all existing medicines would be taken. If no reference found domestically, then the lowest price anywhere in the world would be the reference price. The companies would be free to approach the *Price Negotiations Committee* to review the ceiling price on the basis of superior therapeutic cost-effectiveness. All patented drugs and their formulations would be subject to mandatory price negotiations before the market approval would be granted.

Following the submission of the various committees' reports, the Department of Chemicals and Petrochemicals put out a draft of the Pharmaceutical Policy – 2006 (Part A), which would become a blue print for future directions. Part B, that is the new price control framework, would be released after finalisation of Part A. The policy draft (Part A) contains a number of provisions relevant to drug prices including mandatory price negotiations of patented medicines before marketing approval and capping of trade margins.

6.3.1 Trade margins

As a part of its terms of reference, the Sandhu Committee examined trade margins and found that there were no limits on trade margins on non-scheduled drugs. The 'government was concerned over the exploitation of consumers by retailers and pharmaceutical companies that were charging up to 1000–2000 times margin from the customers',

Ram Vilas Paswan, Minister for Chemicals and Fertilizers (cited in The Tribune 2004). The average margins were around 500 per cent on the generics; however, anecdotal evidence pointed to margins of over 200,000 per cent in certain cases (GOI 2005f). The Sandhu Committee recommended that the trade margins for wholesaler and retailer be capped as follows:

- 8 per cent and 16 per cent, respectively, on scheduled drugs;
- 10 per cent and 20 per cent, respectively, on non-scheduled brands; and
- 15 per cent and 35 per cent, respectively, on generics (The Sen Committee 2005, Appendix).

A number of countries place limits on trade margins. The following studies show how the above recommendations compare with other countries. Sakthivel (2005) suggests that in the US, wholesaler and retailer margins are around 2 per cent and around 15 per cent, respectively. By comparison, corresponding margins in Spain are 12.4 per cent and 43.7 per cent. In Australia, trade margins depend on a formula negotiated within the context of five-yearly Community Pharmacy Agreements between the Commonwealth Government and the Pharmacy Guild (last one in 2006). Since then, wholesaler margin has been 7 per cent of the price-to-pharmacist (PTP). Retailer margins depend on the dispensed price and vary from around 15–16 per cent on ready[8] items of up to $180 to less than 5 per cent on items of over $1000 (Sweeny 2008).

Under the current price control framework in India, the consumer does not necessarily pay a low price for generics. The significantly high margins, common on generics as noted above, means that the dispensing retailer is the highest beneficiary in India, and not the consumer. The exorbitant margins of thousand per cent and more make even the generics unaffordable for the poor masses of India. With the level of poverty prevalent in India, the Sandhu Committee recommendations for trade margins are more in line with what India needs.

6.4 Market behaviour

We assess the market behaviour for drug prices by two different examinations. First, during recent negotiations with the government regarding the scope of price controls, 11 domestic pharmaceutical companies voluntarily agreed to reduce prices on selected formulations. We examine the claimed prices of these drugs against the actual prices in the market. Second, we examine the changes in prices of 405 drugs in the 2005–08 period that demonstrate the post-TRIPS price movement.

6.4.1 Price reductions under the voluntary agreement

As a part of the agreement reached between pharmaceutical companies and the government, 11 companies agreed to reduce the prices of 886 formulations by 1 October 2006 (GOI 2006h). The agreed prices of these 886 items were checked against the prices published in 2007–08 editions of CIMS, Drug Today, IDR Pharmacy Compendium. While the government's own assessment indicated that as at 14 May 2007, only 295 or a third of the agreed items had their prices reduced (GOI 2007a), our own item by item examination of the list revealed the following.

The 886 items included a pregnancy test card, 7 Ayurvedic medicines, at least 31 forms of iron, vitamins, or other nutritional supplements. Notwithstanding the positive role the foregoing items play in healthcare, it is argued that these items could not be viewed as (allopathic) formulations. It was found that from the 886 items, only 134 or 15.1 per cent were listed in CIMS[9] (July–October 2007), Drug Today (October–December 2007), or IDR (November 2007–January 2008). Our findings are summarised in Table 6.2 below, which shows that out of the 134 items listed, 103 items had a price higher than the agreed price while 16 items had a lower price (full details in Appendix A). The Table also shows that the prices on 9 items were lower than or equal to the agreed price in at least one reference book but higher in the other(s). Only 6 items were found to have the correct prices in all three reference books.

The significance of items listed in the reference books would be that these items would be available in substantial parts of India, while the unlisted items may be targeted at niche markets in certain region(s) with low sales. A recent study concluded that from the medicines listed in CIMS, less than a third were available in urban and even less in rural West Bengal (Das et al. 2007). If less than a third of medicines listed in CIMS were available in West Bengal, which is considered to be one of the more progressive states, it can be safely assumed that in the less developed states such as Bihar, Orissa, and Uttar Pradesh,[10] the number of medicines available would be even less. The 752 items not listed in any of the reference books would have insignificant sales, which would render the voluntary agreement trivial. It is highly unlikely for

Table 6.2 Summary examination of claimed price reductions (2008)

S.no	Manufacturer	No. of items priced				No. of Items	Claimed no. of items with	%age of items
		High	Low	Mixed	Equal	Referenced	Prices reduced	Referenced
1	Alembic	12			1	13	109	11.93
2	Alkem Laboratories	9		6		15	22	68.18
3	Cadila Healthcare	17	4	3		24	391	6.14
4	Cipla	37			1	38	49	77.55
5	Emcure Pharmaceuticals	8				8	10	80.00
6	Lupin	7			4	11	68	16.18
7	Medley Pharmaceuticals	3	5			8	30	26.67
8	Nicholas Piramal	2				2	18	11.11
9	Ranbaxy Laboratories		4			4	72	5.56
10	Unichem Laboratories					0	16	0.00
11	Wockhardt	8	3			11	101	10.89
	Total	103	16	9	6	134	886	15.12

Source: Author.

the doctors anywhere to prescribe medicines that are not listed in the reference books. Consequently, this price reduction agreement would have minimum impact on the sales revenue of the companies involved. The implications for the consumer are that despite the widely publicised price reductions, most of these drugs continue to be sold at higher prices. The benefits of these claimed price reductions to the consumer would be limited.

6.4.2 Examining changes to drug prices (2005–08)

This examination studies the drug prices for 405 formulations for the period 2005–08. This study was initially based on the research of prices of 152 formulations for the period 1994–2004 by Sakthivel (2005). The significance of this period is that India signed the TRIPS agreement in 1994 and the Sakthivel study was considered to reflect the market behaviour in the lead up to the implementation of the agreement in 2005. While the contribution of the foregoing study is gratefully acknowledged, the Sakthivel[11] study considered the brands, but did not consider strengths, forms, quantity, or packs of the formulations. The omission of these parameters does not make any allowance for a follow-up study. To illustrate the point, Sakthivel listed price changes on two amoxicillin formulations: namely, Novaclox and Novamox. Yet, we found and considered 13 different versions (7 for Novaclox, and 6 for Novamox) packed in different forms, strengths, and quantities. This lack of specificity by Sakthivel (2005) made it difficult to compare the price changes of the formulations in the pre- and post-TRIPS period.

This examination compares prices of formulations listed in Drug Today (January–March 2005) with CIMS (July–October 2007), Drug Today (October–December 2007), and IDR (November 2007–January 2008). The 405 items were selected from the 10 leading therapeutic groups (see Appendix B for details). Table 6.3 provides an overview of the main findings of the two studies.

Over 70 per cent items during 1994–2004 and over 31 per cent during 2005–08 had a price increase. The difference in the level of increase is significant. During the first study period, 11 items (7.24 per cent of 152) or 10.3 per cent of 107 items had more than 10 per cent increase. During the second period of study of 83 items (20.44 per cent of 405) or 64.84 per cent of 128 had a double-digit increase, of which 57 items (14.03 per cent of 405) or 44.53 per cent of 128 drugs registered a price increase of 20–70 per cent. Notwithstanding the lesser number of items, the first study did not find increases of more than 18.19 per cent over a ten-year period. The post-2005 increases are substantial considering the shortness

Table 6.3 Price changes during two study periods

Period	Studied items	Price unchanged	Price reduced	Price increased	Lowest increase	Highest increase
Sakthivel study						
1994–2004	152	19 (12.5%)	26 (17.1%)	107 (70.4%)	0.18% on Crotorax-HC	18.19% on Urografin
Our study						
2005–08	405	214 (52.71%)	64 (15.76%)	128 (31.28%)	0.08% on Zimalgin	107.4% Fluracil

Source: Author estimates.

of the study period. All therapeutic groups, except the HIV/AIDS group had price increases over the study period. In the HIV/AIDS group, prices either reduced or remained unchanged. While pharma companies themselves provide prices to publishers of these books, it could be argued that the reference books used in our study do not represent the actual market prices, which is possible. However, the prices movement determined by our study of these books could not be disputed.

Of the 405 formulations studied, 149 were under the current price control (DPC – 1995) and 231 were on the National List of Essential Medicines (NLEM 2003). From the formulations that had prices increased from 2005 to 2008, 71 were listed in the NLEM and 25 were under the DPCO – 1995. While the increases on most items, which are under price control, were found to be minimal, the price increases for items outside price control were significant including those on the essential medicines list. Had essentiality been a criterion under the current price control mechanism, all formulations listed on the NLEM would have been considered for price control. The likely result in the market would have been minimum price increases for all items listed on the NLEM.

While the NIPER (2006) report suggests that TRIPS is unlikely to have an effect on drug prices in the times to come, our analysis clearly demonstrates that prices have indeed risen, from which, the following conclusions can be drawn. The current price control framework does not deliver affordable medicines, which the government-appointed experts consider essential. In the lead up to the implementation of the TRIPS agreement in 2005, there were apprehensions among citizen groups and other stakeholders that after 2005, drug prices would rise substantially in India, which would further erode the drug affordability. Our analysis of post-2005 price changes confirms those fears.

Against the backdrop of the above discussions, India needs to explore other options. Until now, the Indian approach to healthcare has been patchy and incomplete. The past policies provided a framework that underpinned the growth of the domestic pharma industry and brought down the drug prices. Yet, around two-thirds of India's population remain without access to medicine, which is in stark contrast with India's recent economic growth. Under the Indian Constitution, the State is charged with the responsibility to 'regard the raising of the level of nutrition and the standard of living of its people and the improvement of public health as among its primary duties' (Article 47). With India's future policy directions in disarray, its policy makers need to consider healthcare options that are equitable, affordable, and implementable. India could learn from other countries' experiences and see how they make the essential drugs affordable to the poor as well as keep the industry growing.

6.5 Price control models

Developed countries generally provide fully integrated programmes that employ drug price controls on the one hand and deliver equitable healthcare on the other. Under these programmes, products listed on the formulary are subsidised by the government, and this listing is considered the key to manufacturers' success in these markets. The process for listing is rigorous and involves both manufacturers and the authorities agreeing to specific pricing conditions. The price control framework has two components: namely, negotiating the drug price (supply side), and controlling the demand to influence the quantity sold. Governments in different countries employ a range of instruments to achieve their policy objectives. The principal instruments are considered hereunder.

Introducing a new drug into these markets is usually a two-stage process: namely, seeking marketing approval and listing on the formulary for reimbursement. The focus of this discussion is on the latter. Generally, an application for listing a new drug on the formulary requires the manufacturer to supply the data on safety, efficacy, and in many cases also on the cost-effectiveness of the drug relative to comparator. These data enable the government to evaluate the drug and assess its price. One of the most commonly used methods for the drug assessment is reference pricing.

Reference pricing and pharmacoeconomic analysis are used to establish the true value of the benefits of a new drug (Harvey et al. 2004). Reference pricing allows price comparisons against existing drugs within the same molecular/ therapeutic group or against a basket of countries where the (proposed) drug is already marketed. Under the molecular comparison, the proposed drug is compared for costs against existing drugs and/or therapies to treat the same condition. Reference pricing is commonly used for follow-up generics, which must not be more expensive than the innovator drugs in the market. Reference pricing helps minimise the pharmaceutical costs because the lowest priced brand becomes the benchmark for others within the same therapeutic group (Sweeny 2008). Reference pricing is not suitable for more effective drugs relative to the existing ones.

Reference pricing highlights the price interdependency, which results from the use of third country prices for the calculation of permissible domestic prices (WHO/WTO 2001). The drawback of reference pricing is that pricing level in the reference country could affect the price acceptability in the domestic negotiations. With the increased use of prices as a reference in other countries, the market separability is disappearing and the countries are merging into larger markets with similar price levels.

In 1993, Australia pioneered the pharmacoeconomic (cost-effectiveness analysis) criterion for the drug price assessment. The pharmacoeconomic criterion measures 'value for money' on the basis of the evidence of a new drug's likely cost and clinical effectiveness relative to the existing treatment alternatives. The cost-effectiveness analysis (CEA) seeks to maximise health gains within the budget constraints (Goddard et al. 2006). The CEA has gained wider acceptance in the process of price determination in a number of countries including the UK, Germany, and New Zealand. Some other price control models are as follows.

The UK model is based on controlling the overall profits and return on capital but does not fix the drug prices. The pricing of branded prescription medicines is indirectly controlled through the Pharmaceutical Price Regulation Scheme (PPRS), under which prices are negotiated every five–six years between the government and the pharma industry. The last PPRS was negotiated in 2005. The PPRS determines the prices of all brand medicines primarily sold to the National Health Service (NHS) and the hospitals. Under the measures introduced in 2000 and in 2005, certain (branded and unbranded) generics sold to community pharmacies and dispensing doctors under the 'Maximum Price Scheme' place a ceiling on the prices of these generics (Department of Health 2005). In the UK, all prescription medicines are reimbursed except those on the negative list. India has, in the past, tried to control drug prices by limiting profits. This approach has a limited applicability, because, under this policy, the manufacturers would exploit the flexibility and raise the drug prices to the highest level possible without exceeding the overall profitability.

In New Zealand, the Pharmac determines the drug price and the level of subsidy for reimbursement and lists the drugs on the Pharmaceutical Schedule. Under certain conditions, the manufacturer cannot set the price higher than the subsidy. The Pharmaceutical Schedule includes certain over-the-counter, patented, and off-patent products. The Pharmac calls for tenders for the exclusive supply of a sole brand in a chemical listed for a fixed period. The manufacturer has exclusive and guaranteed product sales in exchange for an agreed price. The agency also negotiates the listing of a drug in exchange for lowering the price and subsidy of another (Braee 2001).

The tendering process is already used in a number of Indian states such as Karnataka, Maharashtra, Tamil Nadu (Tamil Nadu Drug Corporation), and Rajasthan for purchase of medicines. This approach could provide significant advantages for India if the tendering process was centralised to purchase the medicines at the national level rather than by individual states, because the central government would have much larger negotiating power. While the New Zealand approach helps the state negotiate low prices on a particular brand, it effectively locks out competitors from the market for the duration of the contract, which reduces choice for prescribers and consumers.

In Canada, the Patented Medicine Prices Review Board (PMPRB) sets the 'factory gate' prices, at which the manufacturers sell the patented medicine to wholesalers, hospitals, and pharmacies. The Board has no jurisdiction over the wholesaler, or retail prices. The prices for generics as well as over-the-counter (OTC) drugs are also outside the control of the PMPRB. While each province and territory has its own drug insurance plans that vary in cost-sharing arrangements and drugs reimbursed, all plans encourage the use of generics (Sketris et al. 2003). The price of a new (patented) drug is governed by existing drugs within the same therapeutic group available in Canada. For innovative drugs, the median price in France, Germany, Italy, Sweden, Switzerland, the UK, and the US is used to determine the maximum price for the proposed drug (Government of Canada 2008).

The Canadian system seems to be working reasonably well for patented medicines, and these cost significantly less in Canada than in the US. It is evident from the US patients' purchase of their prescription medicines across the border. As Canada does not exercise any control over the price of the generics, these are generally higher priced than the US. The overall Canadian approach would not suit India's situation, where the generics account for over 90 per cent of the market. Besides, the state-by-state healthcare approach would increase the gap that already exists in health outcomes between states in India.

In 2004, Germany established the Institute for Quality and Efficiency (IQWiG) to provide the benefits evaluation and cost-benefits assessment for pricing, and level of reimbursement for innovative drugs (Graf von der Schulenburg 2007). The healthcare reforms introduced in 2007 allow the apex body of health insurance funds to stipulate the maximum reimbursement price for patented drugs based on the cost-benefit assessment (Verband der Forschender Arzeneimittelhersteller 2007). Germany also calls for mandatory prescription of the most cost-effective drug within the therapeutic group. Introduced in Germany since 1993, the physician drug budgets also reinforced the cost-effective analysis approach. Under this policy, individual physicians could still prescribe drugs of their choice subject to not exceeding their drug budgets (Schreyoegg & Busse 2005). The mandatory prescription of most cost-effective drugs would help India reduce the use of less effective drugs and increase the use of low-cost generics. An approach such as the IQWiG would help analyse a new drug for efficiency and its 'value for money'.

In Australia, before applying to the Department of Health and Ageing for a listing on the PBS, the product must be approved for marketing by the Therapeutic Goods Administration (TGA) and registered on the Australian Register of Therapeutic Goods (ARTG). As at 17 June 2008, there were 11,364 medicines on the ARTG (TGA, 2008, pers. comm.[12] 17 June).

The listing of a product on the PBS is a rigorous process that evaluates safety and efficacy, assesses the proposed drug for value, considers cost of proposed drug against the products already listed, and/or compares the price in other countries. There are two main bodies involved in the process: namely, the Pharmaceutical Benefits Advisory Committee (PBAC) and the Pharmaceutical Benefits Pricing Authority (PBPA).

The PBAC considers the effectiveness and cost of a proposed benefit compared to alternative therapies, and provides advice to the PBPA regarding the findings of alternatives on their cost-effectiveness. The PBPA uses a number of criteria including PBAC comments on clinical and cost-effectiveness, and reference pricing in the same therapeutic group and/or the price of the drug in other countries. The final process includes negotiations between the government and the manufacturer to agree a mutually acceptable price, and 'this is where the government uses its monopsonistic purchasing strength to achieve lower prices relative to those paid in international markets' (Duckett 2004, p. 60). The manufacturer can argue on a cost-effectiveness basis that their medicine is superior to the comparator justifying a price premium (higher price), or on a cost-minimisation basis, which means that the proposed medicine is equivalent to the comparator but priced lower (Sweeny 2008).

These price control models provide an overview of instruments that have been successfully used in different countries. Some of the committees appointed by the Indian Government have considered some of these instruments. For example, the recommendations of the Sen Committee included reference pricing, and cost-effectiveness analysis. India could consider these models to develop its own price control framework that would be more effective, than the current system, in providing essential drugs at affordable prices.

6.6 Conclusions

Over the last 30 years, the price control framework, in conjunction with other regulatory measures, ultimately lowered the drug prices in India. However, India's experience shows that controlling drug prices alone is not sufficient to provide an affordable healthcare to all. Indian policy makers could learn from other countries and consider the options presented to develop a strategy or set of strategies to negotiate and maintain low drug prices. There is a need to streamline the hierarchical nature of the regulatory structure, recognise drug pricing, and affordability as inseparable and interdependent in providing healthcare. This recognition would need to form the basis of the new policy.

The committees appointed by different departments reached different conclusions on the level of control, that is price control/price monitoring or formulations/bulk drugs. Nevertheless, the committees unanimously agreed that essentiality should be the primary basis for drug selection criteria. The implicit conclusion reached is that the changes to the selection criteria introduced under the DCPO – 1995 was a mistake that has resulted in unnecessarily high prices on essential drugs.

The enforcement agency, namely the NPPA, does not have adequate manpower to effectively undertake the tasks the NPPA is assigned to perform. The current rules do not provide the NPPA adequate powers for effective enforcement. The authorities have had limited success in recovering from the companies the over-charged amounts. The recovery process is cumbersome and when taken into account the recovery time and costs, the net gains to the society are questionable.

7
Health Insurance in India

7.1 Introduction

Health insurance is defined as 'any mechanism which covers the risks of payment for health care at the time of its requirement' (Ellis et al. 2000, p. 207). Most of the industrialised nations, except the US, and a small number of developing countries, provide health insurance programmes to cover most of their populations for substantial share of their health expenditure including pharmaceuticals. In the US, the public health insurance (Medicaid, Medicare, and Military combined) covered only 27 per cent of the population in 2006 (DeNavas-Walt et al. 2007). The debate for universal healthcare and increased price controls in the US has gained momentum in recent years. However, experts such as Santerre and Vernon (2006) oppose the introduction of drug price controls in the US and argue that such a move would result in much higher costs than benefits to the society.

In Australia, the Pharmaceutical Benefits Scheme (PBS) provides subsidised medicines and the Medicare programme covers for visits to the doctors and hospitalisation at public institutions. The downside of relying purely on universal health insurance is that public hospitals in Australia have waiting periods of several months or years for non-emergency procedures. People with private health insurance can access private or public healthcare facilities without waiting.

7.2 The Indian approach to health insurance

In contrast to the developed world, most developing countries including India do not have universal health insurance programmes. Until recently, the lack of appropriate framework in India barred private investors from participating in the insurance sector, which remains underdeveloped. The life insurance industry was nationalised in 1956 and 176 companies were merged to form the Life Insurance Corporation of India. The nationalisation of the entire general insurance business followed in 1972. The General Insurance Business (Nationalisation) Act, 1972 (GIBNA), was enacted to nationalise and takeover the shares of 55 Indian insurance companies and the undertakings of 52 insurers carrying on general insurance business (General Insurance Corporation of India 2008). Lack of competition meant that there was no pressure on the state-owned enterprises to promote insurance. The sector became so inefficient that the overall insurance penetration remained at just 6 per cent (Nagendranath & Chari 2002). In recent years, in the Annual Reports of the all four state-owned insurers; namely, National Insurance, New India Assurance, Oriental Insurance, and United Insurance, which account for most of India's insurance sector, health insurance did not get a mention. The life insurance plays a dominant role in India, in which, the Life Insurance Corporation (LIC), another state-owned enterprise, is the largest insurer.

The absence of universal health insurance in India created a vacuum, which different groups tried to fill. The approach has been fragmented with employment-based private groups, public sector employees, and community-based insurance groups providing the health cover for specific segments of the population. In 1948, the Employees State Insurance Corporation (ESIC) launched the Employees State Insurance Scheme (ESIS), which provided medical benefits. This scheme was started as a compulsory social security benefit scheme for workers in the formal sector (Ellis et al. 2000). The scheme covered non-seasonal factories using power with 10 or more employees or non-power using non-seasonal firms employing 20 or more (Gupta & Trivedi 2005). A major difficulty of this scheme is that small firms, which employ fewer workers than the stipulated minimum limit, cannot be covered under the ESIS. According to IAMR (2003), the ESIS covered 8 million or just 2 per cent of India's 411.5-million-strong workforce (cited in Gupta & Trivedi 2005). The scheme is based on premiums through payroll tax of 4.75 per cent on the employer and 1.75 per cent on the employee, and substantially funded by the respective state governments. The scheme provides healthcare through dedicated dispensaries and hospitals.

The Central Government Health Scheme (CGHS) was started in 1954. The CGHS is designed to provide healthcare to the current and former Central Government employees and their families. Similar to the ESIS, the CGHS also has dedicated dispensaries, most of which are allopathic.

The CGHS is criticised because 'the large central bureaucracy in India definitely belongs to the middle-income and high-income categories, they are likely to make above-average use of health services' (Ellis et al. 2000, p. 210). The CGHS has long waiting lists and requires significant out-of-pocket costs for treatment. Despite being mostly funded by the Central Government, the out-of-pocket upfront costs discourage low-paid employees from using the CGHS scheme. The ESIS and CGHS collectively cover around 3 per cent of the population including employees and their families (Garg 2000).

Other schemes for the employees of various Ministries and Departments also provide health cover. Railways Health Services, Defence Medical Services, and Ex-Servicemen Contributory Health Scheme collectively provide health benefits to around 15 million Indians. Ministry of Textiles offers health cover for workers in the textile sector. The health package for handloom weavers is non-contributory but restricted to treating TB, Asthma, and inflammation of alimentary system and the maximum annual benefit is Rs. 1500 (US$38) per weaver. This scheme covers around 4 per cent of the 6.5 million weavers. Health package insurance for handicraft artisans, in collaboration with United India Insurance provides reimbursements of up to Rs. 15,000 for hospitalisation. While the state-owned health schemes, such as the ESIS and CGHS, have been widely criticised for their performance, the Railways Health Services have become a benchmark of their own. The railways provision of high quality healthcare is ensured through 'high degree of accountability, mainly because of very alert labour unions, and well-informed and aware employee population' (Gupta & Trivedi 2005, p. 4135). The public health insurance schemes and government-sponsored programmes, such as for the handloom weavers, amount to around 85 million or less than 10 per cent of India's population (ibid.). No equity-based programmes provide health cover for those, who work in the unorganised sector or are out of work.

Some community-based health insurance schemes as well as NGO-run schemes also operate in parts of India, which cover only small amount of people. Rag-picker's scheme in Pune (Maharashtra) recognises the importance of the role these poor people play in cleaning up the city. In conjunction with the New India Assurance, the Municipal Corporation provides reimbursements of up to Rs. 5000 for hospitalisation. The State of Karnatka, in conjunction with Karuna Trust, which is an NGO, and National Insurance, provides health cover for families living below the poverty line (BPL). A premium of Rs. 30 for BPL and Rs. 60 for non-BPL families is payable. Students Health Home in West

Bengal cover around 1.6 million students, for which, the state government provides an grants-in-aid on direct medical expenses of up to 50 per cent (Acharya & Ranson 2005).

Health insurance for the poor has gained momentum in India in recent years (Ahuja & Narang 2005). In 2003, the Vajpayee government launched a Universal Health Insurance (UHI), specifically designed for the poor, which did not bring the desired results however. Under the programme, the government agencies, such as the United India Insurance Company, and the New India Assurance Company, would implement the policy. The insurance premium was considered nominal. An individual would pay Rs. 1.00 a day (Rs. 365 a year), while a family of up to five (including the first three children) would pay Rs. 1.50 a day (Rs. 548 a year), and a family of seven (including the first three children and dependent parents) would pay Rs. 2 a day (Rs. 730 a year) (The New India Assurance Company 2008). For the BPL families, the government would contribute Rs. 100 to the annual premium. Under the policy, New India would reimburse expenses of hospitalisation up to Rs. 30,000 (~US$750) and a limit of Rs. 15,000 (~US$375) would apply to a single disease.

The UHI programme remained a non-starter and the uptake of the policy was negligible. The lack of awareness of the programme among the target population was considered to be the main reason. The following factors also contributed to the failure of the programme. First, under the programme, the benefits were confined to the hospitalisation and that only at specified public hospitals, when the private healthcare sector, such as local doctors account for 82 of healthcare delivery (Acharya & Ranson 2005). Second, the programme provided for reimbursement of expenses, which meant that the poor would have to pay for treatment first and seek reimbursement later. For practical reasons, it would not be possible for the poor, the BPL families in particular, to raise funds for treatment. Third, against the high costs of treating diseases such as cancer or cardiovascular diseases, the extent of total benefit and the limit on a single illness were set significantly low. A monthly supply of imatinib mesylate for chronic myeloid leukaemia marketed by Novartis as Glivec costs Rs. 120,000. Even the generic versions cost between Rs. 10,000 and 12,000 a month.

The Singh government recently launched its own health insurance programme for the BPL poor. The new policy known as the Rashtriya Swasthya Bima Yojana (RSBY) facilitates direct billing the authorities (that is no paying first and seeking reimbursement later), and the premium in full for the BPL families would be paid by the government.[1]

The RSBY was supposed to become operational on 1 April 2008 in Delhi and Haryana, and the programme was expected to be rolled out in the other states over the coming years. According to Mr P Chidambaram, the then Finance Minister, 'There would be no paucity of funds for the scheme, which would benefit over 30 million people' (OneIndia 2007). The beneficiaries will be issued Smart Cards, which will facilitate cash-less transaction up to Rs. 30,000 so that the poor would not have to pay anything for medical treatment. This programme has a sunset clause of 2012.

Under the RSBY programme, pre-existing illnesses would be covered and the transportation costs up to Rs. 1000 would also be covered. The only one-off cost, the poor would have to pay, would be Rs. 25, the cost of Smart Card. However, the details of the policy do not indicate if the new programme caters for visits to private doctors or if it covers the treatment by Ayurvedic, Yoga, Unani, Siddha, and Homoeopathic (AYUSH) practitioners that are dominant in rural India. The RSBY is specially designed for BPL families and it is too early to comment on the impact of the RSBY on the health of the poor or how the BPL segment may respond to the latest call of the government to enrol into this programme. With the sunset clause in 2012, the programme appears more like an attempt to provide a quick-fix rather than a long-term commitment that is required to address the nation's healthcare problem.

7.2.1 Private health insurance in India

In contrast to employment-based compulsory health insurance or universal healthcare, private health insurance is voluntary and purely based on affordability. The more comprehensive benefits are sought, the higher the premium has to be paid. The private health insurance uptake in the developed world is significantly higher relative to developing countries. Recent studies concluded that 69 per cent Canadians had private insurance for partial or full coverage of prescription medicine, while 19 per cent were publicly insured. Around 12 per cent of Canadians, who were likely to have the least education and lowest incomes, had no insurance for prescription drugs (Harten & Ballantyne 2004). In the US, in 2006, the employment-based or directly purchased private health cover accounted for 67 per cent of the population, while 47 million or almost 16 per cent of the population did not have any health insurance (DeNavas-Walt et al. 2007). Around 45 per cent of Australians have private health insurance. The Australian government encourages uptake of private health insurance by providing a 30 per cent tax rebate on the cost of the insurance.

The significance of third party payers such as private health insurers increases substantially in developing countries, where medical costs, including drugs are met by out-of-pocket household expenditure. For example, Malaysia does not provide universal health insurance programmes or drug price controls. A recent study found that around 15 per cent of the Malaysian population had private health insurance, where the drug prices were too high relative to the average income (Ibrahim & Bahri 2003). The foregoing study suggests that Malaysians would benefit from lower drug prices if price controls were introduced.

In India, the concept of private health insurance is a recent phenomenon. Under the reforms initiated in the insurance sector since 1999, foreign equity of up to 26 per cent is permitted. Among the 24 private companies that have been granted licences under the new policy, there are 9 general insurers including a standalone health insurance company (IRDA 2008). The entrance of domestic conglomerates, such as the Birla group and the Ambani group (Reliance Health), demonstrates the emerging economic significance of the health insurance. Despite the private health insurance registering a growth of 30 per cent in 2005–06 in India, it still amounted to less than 1 per cent of the population having private health insurance (IRDA 2007). However, the market size of private health would be limited to the middle class of 300 million Indians because of the costs. In the wake of the low health insurance incidence, the drug prices, which form the bulk of the healthcare costs in India, become more significant.

The General Insurance Corporation (GIC), through the major four state-owned enterprises (noted earlier in the chapter), launched the Mediclaim health insurance scheme back in 1987. Mediclaim provided only hospital cover and domiciliary expenses for groups and individuals. The number of people covered under Mediclaim increased to around 1.3 million in 1993–94 (Ellis et al. 2000), which was a fraction of India's large population. The reasons for low penetration were lack of promotion, high premiums, and no cover for the out-patient (non-hospitalised) care, which account for most of India's healthcare delivery. The absence of competition made the Indian insurance sector inefficient.

Mahal (2000) studies the administrative costs as a percentage of total expenditure of health insurance programmes. He finds India's health insurance system in the public sector (5.0–14.6 per cent) to be significantly less efficient relative to the US (2.1 per cent Medicare) and Chile (1.8 per cent). In the private sector, India (20.0 per cent) is less efficient than Chile (18.5 per cent) and the US (5.5 per cent), when the cost range is taken at the lower end. The US (40.0 per cent) is less efficient than India (32.0 per cent) when the cost range is taken at the higher end in the private sector. The recent introduction of competition in the insurance sector, which was absent under public sector monopoly prior to the regulatory changes, may increase efficiency in the health insurance sector.

The inefficient insurance sector had the following implications for Indian consumers. This means that the costs to provide health insurance in India were higher than in the US and Chile. Consequently, these high costs would have been passed on to the consumers. With the increasing number of new entrants in the insurance sector in recent years, competition is expected to intensify, which is likely to increase the efficiency and lower the costs.

While opening-up of the insurance sector to foreign investors is widely viewed as a positive step, the increase in the private insurance may have hidden costs to the poor. The poor may suffer longer delays at public institutions because resources are likely to be diverted to privately insured patients (Garg 2000). Experts suggest a number of steps to safeguards the interests of the poor (Ferreiro 2000). The privately insured should not be subsidised at a public facility. 'Those who prove to have the payment capacity to buy a private health insurance should pay the full rate (real cost of delivery, including investment provisions) of the health care given by a public provider' (ibid., p. 81). It could also be argued that the privately insured are more likely to seek treatment at private facilities, which would free more resources for the poor at the public institutions. This would mean that a rise in private health insurers would indirectly contribute to improved access to healthcare including access to medicines for the poor.

Most of the public and private health insurance programmes, except the Defence Medical Services, and Ex-Servicemen Contributory Health Scheme, which provide cashless healthcare, are based on reimbursement of the expenses occurred. This feature alone makes the provision of healthcare cumbersome and inefficient. Whether it is ESIS, CGHS, or Mediclaim, the requirement to reimburse rather than paying the provider directly causes unnecessary financial hardships to the poor, and discourages the sick from seeking treatment.

7.3 Patient co-payments

Generally, the healthcare programmes in most of the countries in the OECD[2] including Australia are funded by the government through some form of universal healthcare. The government subsidy accounts for the bulk of the drug costs, and patient/insurance co-payments cover the remainder. On the one hand, the co-payments are considered necessary to prevent and/or minimise the abuse and wastage of medicine. On the other hand, these payments place a substantial burden on the society and deny access to medicine to the poorer sections. A study of the Canadian market concludes that while shifting costs to patients reduces public expenditure (and discourages wastage), it also decreases patients' use of essential and discretionary medications resulting in poor health outcomes (Harten & Ballantyne 2004).

High patient co-payments also deny access to medicines. In Australia, around 23 per cent of prescriptions for general patients are not filled, because of the high patient co-payments (Blendon et al. 2002). Among the concession card holders, this share is only 2 per cent. The Blendon et al. study demonstrates that the general patient co-payments in Australia are set too high, because the co-payments do not consider the range of income levels within the general patients category. It is a 'one size fits all' approach. A more comprehensive framework that considers progressive co-payments for different income levels similar to the Income Tax payments would be more appropriate for Australia. We argue that the co-payments' gap between concession card holders and the general patients is so large (see details below) that it discourages families at the lower end of the general patient category from purchasing the prescribed medicines. Another category set closer to the concession co-payments, say at 150 per cent of the concession co-payments, that is A$8.10 at the 2010 level, could encourage this patients group to buy the medicines. The increase in PBS costs would be offset by gains in rise in living standard, reduction in time off-work, and increased productivity.

The PBS has been operating successfully since 1948. Initially, all medication on the PBS were provided free of cost. In 1960, for general patients, a co-payment of A$0.50 was introduced that increased over time reaching A$33.30 in 2010. For concession card holders,[3] a co-payment of A$2.50 was introduced in 1990, which has since increased to A$5.40 (2010). The amount of co-payment is annually adjusted in accordance with the consumer price index (CPI).

Where there are two or more brands of the same drug listed on the PBS, the government subsidy is limited to the cost of the lowest priced medicine in the same therapeutic group. If the patient opts for the more expensive brand, the difference (brand premium) is paid by the patient in addition to the co-payment. The payment of brand premium does not count towards the Safety Net threshold. The Safety Net threshold is

Table 7.1 PBS Safety Net thresholds from 1 January 2010

Category	PBS Safety Net threshold	PBS Safety Net contribution
General patients	A$1281.30	A$5.40
Concession card holders	A$324.00	Free

Source: Government of Australia (2010).

designed to help families or individuals with chronic illnesses that need a lot of medicine. Once the total of patient co-payments has reached the threshold limit in a calendar year, the medicines become less expensive for the remainder of the year for general patients as well as concession card holders. Table 7.1 provides details of Safety Net threshold and patient contributions in 2010 that annually change on 1 January in accordance with the CPI index.

The PBS programme in Australia has been successfully covering the entire population for most of the drugs over half a century. Over this period of time, Australia has developed a system to determine what drugs should be approved and at what price. The online availability of the information increases transparency of the process that helps the manufacturers, healthcare providers, as well as consumers.

Under Australia's fully integrated provision of healthcare, the Medicare levy is an indirect payment for healthcare, and the out-of-pocket patient co-payments directly contribute towards medicine costs. While Medicare provides access to basic healthcare needs such as visits to the local doctor, the PBS subsidises the medicines and keeps the out-of-pocket payments at a reasonable level.

By comparison, India's attempts have been directed to control drug prices, and thereby extend healthcare affordability. The drug prices in India have not been low relative to other factors in the healthcare delivery. The drug share of total healthcare costs is five to six time higher in India than in the OECD countries. The out-of-pocket private health expenditure, when compared with the patient co-payments in Australia, is also many times higher in India. The public health programmes served only specific employee groups or certain regions, and the share of private health insurance in India is insignificant.

There exists a large gap between India's provision of healthcare and those who need to access it. No attempts were made to develop a fully integrated programme that co-ordinates and meets the entire healthcare needs of the Indian society. A healthcare programme similar to that of Australia could fill the gap that currently exists in India's provision of healthcare for all. Development of such a programme is the focus of the next chapter.

7.4 Conclusions

In India, health insurance is a fairly new and does not form part of the mainstream insurance business that is dominated by life insurance. Health insurance forms a part of employment-based cover provided in selected manufacturing and service industries. Some localised groups and NGOs also provide limited health insurance programmes for specific population or work groups. However, all these programmes provide cover that is considered insufficient in cases of injury or serious illness.

In recent years, successive Indian governments have attempted to roll out health insurance programmes for the poor. However, the implementation and uptake of these programmes have remained a real challenge. Consequently, millions of poor are denied access to medicines.

Until recently, the insurance sector was closed to private investors. The lack of competition made the insurance sector, the public insurance sector in particular, significantly inefficient. Recent changes to investment guidelines provide for limited private investments and would be expected to raise the efficiency level in the sector.

The concept of private health insurance is very new to Indian consumers. The participation of Indian conglomerates in private health suggests high growth and rapid development of the sector. Nevertheless, in the wake of the prevalence of poverty in India, private health insurance would be expected to remain beyond the reach of more than 70 per cent of the population.

India's drug prices are low relative to those in other countries in absolute terms, but not low in relative terms. If the drug expenditure in India, as a share of total health expenditure, were to attain the level closer to that of most of the OECD countries, drug prices in India would need to fall significantly in absolute terms, which is highly unlikely. Consequently, India needs to develop a fully integrated and equitable programme to provide access to healthcare, including medicines, to its entire population.

8
Broadening Access to Medicines and Healthcare in India

8.1 Introduction

There is a significant part of the Indian community that contributes to the economic activity such as rickshaw-pullers but hardly gets a mention in the literature. This group of people is too rich to belong to the BPL families and too poor to belong to the middle-class Indians. The 300 million strong middle-class (M-class) Indians are the primary target for marketers and often acknowledged in the global media. The around 350[1] million estimated poor, who live below the poverty line of $1-a-day (BPL1), have drawn worldwide attention because of their significant size in contrast to India's economic success in recent years. In between the M-class and the BPL1, there are around 450 million Indians, who live on around US$2-a-day (BPL2). The population in the BPL2 group and lower end of middle class group mostly get into irrecoverable debts in health crisis. India's healthcare would be incomplete without addressing the needs of all three segments of the community.

A significant factor for long-term planning in healthcare is that Indians are now living substantially longer than a century ago and the population has slowly begun to age. The ageing factor plays a vital role in healthcare planning because the aged people are the major recipients of healthcare delivery. For example, in 2004, people aged 65 years and over accounted for 13 per cent of the Australian population (Australian Bureau of Statistics 2006) and yet, pensioners and other concession cardholders accounted for almost 80 per cent of the drug expenditure (Duckett 2004). In India, share of the aged as a percentage of the total population has increased from 6.5 per cent in 1981 to 7.4 per cent in 2001 (GOI 2006b, 2006e). The current share of the aged is estimated to be around 8 per cent that is expected to grow to 9 per cent by

2016 (GOI 2006b). Similar to the rest of India's population, more than 70 per cent of the aged live in the rural and less than 30 per cent in the urban areas (GOI 2006j).

It is ironic that while the population has begun to age in India, the public health expenditure has declined. As a share of the aggregate expenditure on social services, medical, and public health expenditure averaged 16.0 per cent during the 1990–95 period but declined to 11.9 per cent in the 2001–06 years (RBI 2007). India's public health expenditure as a percentage of the gross domestic product (GDP) increased significantly from just 0.22 per cent in 1950–51 to 1.05 per cent as a share of the GDP in 1985–86 (GOI 2006f). Since around mid-1990s, this expenditure has been below or around 0.9 per cent of the GDP. By comparison, the public health expenditure in most of the OECD countries averages around 5 per cent of the GDP (WHO 2006b).

In India, the states account for approximately two thirds of the total public health expenditure and the Union Government contributes around one-third (Economic Research Foundation 2006). Raymus (2007) studies India's public health spending as a share of total expenditure from 1981 to 2005. He finds that the Union Government increased the share of public health expenditure from 0.22 per cent to 0.83 per cent during the study period. However, this increase was offset by a higher rate of decrease in the share of the States. Thus, consumers in a large number of states suffered a net loss in public health expenditure.

The low level of public health expenditure on the one hand leads to poor health outcomes (by the poor not seeking healthcare) and lower productivity. On the other hand, it forces the out-of-pocket household spending on healthcare to increase. In 2004–05, households in most of India's states accounted for more than 75–80 per cent of total healthcare expenditure (GOI 2005e). The household spending on healthcare was highest in Nagaland (91.7 per cent), while this share was more than 80 per cent in 11 states including Bihar, Uttar Pradesh, and Madhya Pradesh that are among the most populated states.

While the number of BPL poor in India has declined from 54.88 per cent of the total population in 1973–74 to 26.1 per cent in 2001 (GOI 2003b), the vast majority of India's population remain without access to medicine. A WHO report on the World Medicine Situation estimates that between 649 million and 811 million Indians were without access to medicine (WHO 2004b) and the principal reason for this is the lack of affordability under the current system of healthcare.

The policies of the successive Indian governments have focused, as noted in earlier chapters, on developing domestic pharmaceutical industry, but little attention was paid to increasing access to medicine. These policies were primarily aimed at making the country self-sufficient in drugs and medical equipment (GOI 1952, Chapter 32). While price controls and other policy measures indirectly increased the share of population with access to medicine from 15–20 per cent in 1980 (Bhagat 1982) to around 35 per cent in more recent years (Nanda 2006; WHO 2004b), access to medicines as such has never been the explicit focus of the government policies.

India's Second Five-Year Plan proclaimed that, in conjunction with the Constitution of India and the Directive Principles of State Policy, the Parliament had accepted a socialist pattern of society as the guiding objective of the Plan (GOI 1957) (Chapter 19, Clause 13). In subsequent years, the socialist principles were applied to the development policies of industries including the drugs and pharmaceutical industry. In the 1980s, India began the process of economic reforms that became more pronounced in 1991. These reforms progressively liberalised the economy with pro-industry measures, such as de-licensing and relaxed controls, but did little to increase access to medicines to the poor.

Similar to India's past policies, the National Pharmaceutical Policy – 2006, which is currently under discussion, also contemplates different methods of price controls or price monitoring attempts to keep drug prices low. In the wake of the implementation of the TRIPS agreement since 2005, a recent report of the Planning Commission notes that 'provisions of compulsory licensing and parallel imports under the patent regime will keep prices of patented medicines within the common man's reach' (GOI 2007e, p. 13). These provisions could make drugs available in India but would not place them within common man's reach.

In the wake of India's recent status as a rising economic power, introduction of social policies for lifting the health status of the poor would be timely and essential for the long-term economic development. This would be necessary because several studies have reported a direct correlation between the health of its people and economic growth of a nation (see for example, Abegunde & Stanciole 2006; Misra et al. 2003). Even India's First Five-Year Plan acknowledged that 'in terms of resources for economic development, nothing can be considered of higher importance than the health of the people' (GOI 1952, Chapter 32, Clause 1). According to the World Development Report (2006), when the traditional model of relying on the public hospitals works badly, especially for the poor and excluded groups, an equity-based health system should be considered (World Bank 2006).

Against this background, this chapter proposes an equity-based, integrated healthcare programme for a broader access to medicines and healthcare to India's entire population. The IndiaHealth model is based on the Australian experience, but has been modified to incorporate the India's specific features, such as demographics, income levels, and affordability issues. The proposed IndiaHealth model recognises that as India's population could increase to reach 2 billion by 2050, the proportion of the high users of healthcare, that is the population of over 65 years of age, would also increase significantly from the current level. This demographic change would require substantial additional resources devoted to healthcare. The IndiaHealth model also acknowledges the very high incidence of poverty in India noted in the introduction. Recognition is also given to the pressing healthcare needs of people with disabilities. Based on the total numbers of people in the various income groups and age groups, different levels of out-of-pocket co-payments are proposed. The total costs of implementing the proposed model are calculated, including separate estimates for the public sector and for out-of-pocket private costs. The costs of the proposed IndiaHealth model are also checked against the commitment of India's current government to increase public expenditure on healthcare.

8.2 Providing access to medicines in India

The proposed model is based on the principle of government–patients sharing the burden of healthcare, with the government accounting for a larger share. The patient co-payment on medicines would be income-tested to ensure affordability. Two particular groups of the population, namely those with mental and psychological disabilities and those living below the poverty line (of $1 per day), would not be required to contribute towards the cost of medicines. The rest of the population would make co-payments to share the burden with government. The total impact of this proposal on the public budget would be around 1.6 per cent of the GDP for 2010. This level of public spending on healthcare is consistent with the commitments made by the current government under the Common Minimum Programme.

Under the proposed model, IndiaHealth cards would be issued as a device to identify different population groups and their entitlements. Sensitivity tests show that it would be possible to adjust the government–patient balance of the financial cost, if necessary. It should be noted from the outset that the proposed model does not call for the discontinuation of free distribution of drugs through public pharmacies, community pharmacies, or drug banks. However, under the proposed model, patient co-payments would apply to outpatient prescriptions. A thorough and careful consideration of the operational dimensions and complexities associated with the proposed model would be a pre-requisite to the success of the model.

It is also important to note at this point that although the model presented below is about healthcare financing, this does not imply that financing of drugs alone will fix all the problems of access to medicines in India. Other aspects of healthcare delivery system will also need to be improved. These include: treatment of outpatients by rural medical practitioners (RMPs) who are not always formally qualified and act more as local drug vendors; and difficulties in identifying the poor so that benefits of the new model are not wrongly appropriated by the non-poor. These aspects would also need to be addressed in complementary reforms to service delivery to make effective and sustainable improvements in the access to medicines to India's entire population.

8.2.1 Developing the IndiaHealth model

The following methodology was applied to develop the proposed model. Healthcare models adopted by Australia, Canada, Germany, New Zealand, and the United Kingdom were considered (noted in chapter 6) and the Australian and New Zealand models shortlisted. However, after more careful considerations, the New Zealand model was also ruled out for designing a model for India's provision of healthcare.

In New Zealand, the government puts out the tenders, to which the manufacturers respond. Under this model, all firms other than the successful bidder are effectively locked out of the market. Unsuccessful bidders could market their products but without listing for reimbursement, their product sales would be negligible. If such a model were used in India, a single supplier to the entire Indian market could possibly achieve economies of scale and undercut the price significantly. But it would also create a monopoly for the duration of the contract, which may not be particularly helpful to the domestic pharma industry. India has over 8000 small domestic manufacturers, who do not have the capacity to serve the entire market. Under the proposed model, survival of firms would predominantly depend on listing their products on the formulary. Excluding the small manufacturers could effectively send them out of business, which would not be in India's interests.

The Australian model was considered to be more appropriate for India with a significant number of firms to meet its healthcare needs. The

Australian model provides opportunities for the small manufacturers to list their products, especially in the off-patent generics category. In an open market, small manufacturers generally price their products significantly lower than the big brand names creating a competitive environment. Thus, the small manufacturers would use the cost-minimisation approach noted under the Australian model. A successful listing of a small manufacturer's product would force other firms to lower their prices reducing the overall healthcare costs.

8.2.2 The proposed model

Under the proposed model, a new organisation called MedicineIndia would be responsible for sourcing adequate supply of the required medicines at appropriate prices. MedicineIndia would primarily be guided by the principles contained in *Equitable access to essential medicines: a framework for collective action* (WHO 2004a). Other WHO documents for the rationale for the proposed model include:

- *Effective medicines regulation: ensuring safety, efficacy, and quality* (2003a);
- *How to develop and implement a national drug policy* (2003b);
- *Promoting rational use of medicines: core components* (2002a); and
- *The selection of essential medicines* (2002b).

The structure of MedicineIndia would have three subordinate authorities; namely, the National Pharmaceutical Pricing Authority (NPPA), the National Pharmaceutical Evaluation Authority (NPEA), and the National Drug Authority (NDA). Each of the authorities would perform specific tasks to achieve the overall objectives of MedicineIndia.

The primary responsibility of the NPPA would be to assess and negotiate the drug price based on the data submitted by the manufacturer. The drug evaluation process would be based on the principles of pharmacoeconomics,[2] which compares the net benefits to the net costs at a given price (Henry et al. 2001). In other words, the NPPA assessment would measure the cost-effectiveness of the proposed drug. The current office of the NPPA is responsible for determining and revising the prices for drugs listed under price control. Thus, it would be easy for the current NPPA to take on the new responsibilities under MedicineIndia.

The NPEA would be a new establishment consisting of experts with technical knowledge and experience in drugs. The role of the NPEA would be to provide an independent advice on pharmaceutical evaluations based on technical assessment of the proposed drug. The independence of this body would remove any bias in the drug evaluation process. In the long run, the NPEA would set up an institute similar to the IQWiG (Institut für Qualität und Wirtschaftlichkeit im Gesundheitswesen) in Germany providing information on effectiveness, quality, and efficiency of drugs, non-drug interventions, and raising public awareness on health (INHATA 2008).

If the price determined by the NPPA was considered too low and/or evidence could be provided to prove superior therapeutic effectiveness to warrant a higher price, the manufacturers could approach the *Price Negotiations Committee,* which would function similar to an appellate body. In accordance with the suggestions of the Sen Committee (2005), a price negotiating committee would be established comprising the Chairman of MedicineIndia and outside experts drawn from other government departments, the Indian Council of Medical Research (ICMR), health professionals, pharmacologists, and civil society organisations (The Sen Committee 2005).

The National Drug Authority (NDA) would be the sole body responsible for establishing and maintaining quality standards and granting market approvals. Currently, the Drug Controller General of India (DCGI) is responsible for the approval of licences of specific categories of drugs, such as blood and blood products, while the Central Drug Standards Control Organisation (CDCSO) grants approvals for the rest of the drugs. Both offices carry out similar functions causing confusion and making the system inefficient. The office of the DCGI and the CDCSO would merge to form the NDA. The central body would integrate both offices into a single authority increasing efficiency. The idea of an authority similar to the USFDA was first conceived by the Hathi Committee 30 years ago and reiterated in the Drug Policy 1986 and again by the Mashlekar Committee (2003), GOI (2005a), and the Sen Committee (2005).

8.2.3 Implementing the IndiaHealth model

This sub-section outlines the practical details associated with the implementation of the proposed model for delivery of healthcare and access to medicines. In the Sixth Five-Year Plan (1980–85), India adopted the policy of 'Health for all by 2000 AD' enunciated in the Alma Ata

Declaration in 1977 (GOI 1980, Chapter 22, paragraph 16). This has been the objective for a long time. The proposal here is designed to make its achievement more likely.

8.2.3.1 IndiaHealth cards

IndiaHealth cards would be issued to all Indians regardless of their social and economic status or place of residence. All IndiaHealth cardholders would be entitled to seek treatment at the public hospitals as well as from authorised allopathic doctors and practitioners of traditional Indian systems of medicine. The authorised Rural Medical Practitioners (RMPs), practitioners of all systems of medicine, except yoga,[3] would be issued with a prescriber number printed on the prescription together with the prescriber's name and address.

The prescription would be presentable at authorised pharmacies and dispensing doctors/practitioners. The patients would be responsible for co-payments where applicable and the government would contribute towards the rest of the medicine costs. The retailers would be issued with a dispenser number, which would be used to request reimbursements. The correct verification of the prescriber details on the prescription would be the basis for authorisation for reimbursement to the dispensing agency. The validation of the qualifications would be the key to authorising doctors, RMPs, practitioners of traditional medicines, and pharmacists. The Indian Government recently initiated pilot programmes to formally train and validate the qualifications of practitioners of traditional medicines in order to bring them into mainstream healthcare providers (GOI 2008b). This process is just a beginning of the long-term strategy required to recognise the significance of the services provided by the RMPs, and practitioners of traditional medicines in India's overall provision of healthcare.

The IndiaHealth cardholder entitlements would be income tested and the patient co-payments would vary accordingly. For estimation of the patient co-payments, the Australian healthcare experience provides a good guide. Australia has a two-tier system of co-payments. In 2010, the patient co-payments were fixed at A$5.40 for the concession[4] cardholders (e.g. pensioners, low-income earners) and up to A$33.30 for general patients. Some critics argue that the general patient co-payments in Australia are set too high. For example, a recent study of Australian healthcare has suggested that around 23 per cent of prescriptions are not filled, because of the high patient co-payments (Blendon et al. 2002).

In respect of income, the Indian population may be divided into the following broad categories:

1. the poor living below the poverty line of $1-a-day (BPL1);
2. the population with an income of around $2-a-day (BPL2);
3. the lower middle class (M1); and
4. the upper middle class (M2).

Based on these population groups, the proposed model would adopt a four-tier co-payment programme (see Box 8.1). Learning from the Australian experience, the level of co-payment has been set sufficiently low to encourage people to use the prescribed medicines. The poor living below the poverty line (BPL1) would make no co-payments at all, while the population in the next income level (BPL2) would contribute Rs. 10 per prescription. The co-payment for the people in the lower and upper middle class would be set at Rs. 25 and Rs. 50, respectively. In Australia, patient co-payments are CPI[5] indexed annually. The co-payments in India would remain fixed for the first three years, and would be WPI[6] indexed annually thereafter.

These four income groups have been further divided into the following eight categories. This division was considered necessary to accommodate the significant diversity in income levels that exists among the Indian population. Each category would be issued with clearly identifiable colour-coded IndiaHealth cards. Cardholders would have entitlements specific to each population group (see Table 8.1).

As reliable data are not available for the accurate number of people in each category and their true financial status, the 1999–2000 income tax brackets are used as a guide for the above segmentation of the population. It should be understood from the outset that the income

Box 8.1 Different levels of patient co-payments

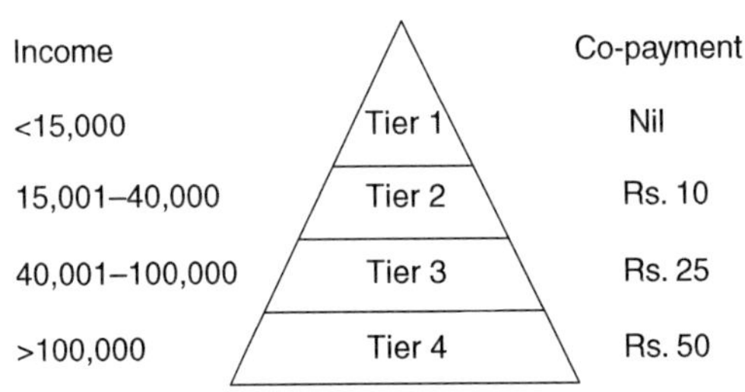

Source: Author.

Table 8.1 Entitlements of IndiaHealth cards at a glance

S. No	Income p.a. (Rs.)	Category	Colour	Co-payment per prescription (Rs.)	SafetyNet Threshold (Rs.)	Co-payment per prescription (post SafetyNet) (Rs.)
1	None	S-Card	Brown	Nil	n.a.	Nil
2	<15, 000	B1-Card	Red	Nil	n.a.	Nil
3	15,001–40,000	B2-Card	Yellow	10	500	Nil
4	15,001–40,000	A1-Card	White/Yellow	10	500	Nil
5	40,001–100,000	A2-Card	White/Purple	25	1125	10
6	40,001–100,000	M1-Card	Purple	25	1125	10
7	>100, 000	A3-Card	White/Green	50	2000	25
8	>100, 000	M2-Card	Green	50	2000	25

Source: Author.

brackets represent different levels of income that exist in India. Those brackets are not necessarily the true reflection of the number of people in the income range. The segmentation identifies each population group, its income range, the type of IndiaHealth card, and the number of estimated cards. Because the proposed model considers different income levels and different age groups separately, we needed to make certain assumptions about the population of the aged[7] within different income groups. Thus, we have made the following assumptions across all income groups. First, the aged population is a constant share at around 5 per cent. This assumption is consistent with the United Nations' (2005b) study on population for 2005. The number of cards in the aged group is based on the assumption that each card in this group would list two adults over the age of 65 years.

Second, the average Indian family consists of five members across all income groups. This is consistent with the recent GOI (2006j) study. The population, except the population group over the age of 65 years, in each group is divided by five to obtain the number of cards for that group. The number of cards for the aged group assumes two adult members per card.

Third, the Indian middle class is estimated at 300 million. This population size is consistent with a study by Knowledge@Wharton (2008), of which, the aged group (at 5 per cent) would account for 15 million or 7.5 million families of aged couples. From these 7.5 million middle-class aged families, 2.5 million families would possibly qualify for each of the A1-Card, A2-Card, and A3-Cards. Different types of IndiaHealth cards, each population group, and its entitlements would be as follows. Figure 8.1 shows an illustration of the IndiaHealth card.

8.2.3.2 S-Card

The S-Card would be issued to persons with special physical or psychological needs such as handicapped. No income test would be required for this population group. This group makes no co-payments on prescriptions. The total number of people in this category is estimated to be 40 million.[8] The number of S-Cards would correspond to the population in the category, because only the individual cardholder would be listed for entitlements.

8.2.3.3 B1-Card

The B1-Card would be issued to the people (BPL1 category) with an annual income of less than Rs. 15,000 (~$375). This population group is considered to be living below the poverty line of $1-a-day (BPL1). No tax

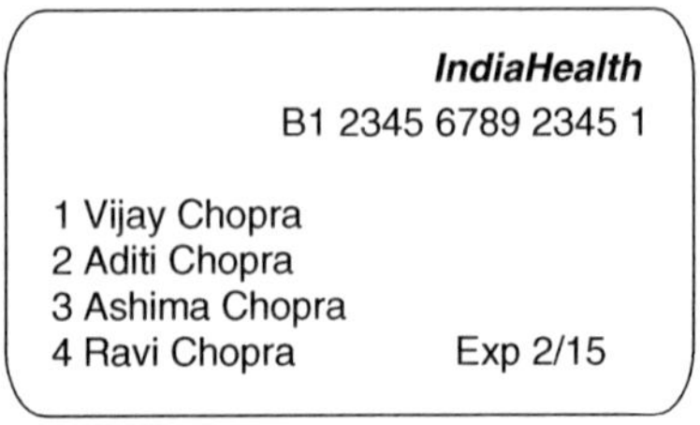

Figure 8.1 The proposed IndiaHealth card
Source: Author.

returns were recorded for this category for 1999–2000. An estimated 350 million Indians belong to this category. At 5 per cent of 350 million, 17.5 million elderly population would be issued with 8.75 million B1-Cards (Aged). At 5 members per family, 66.5 million B1-Cards would be issued to the remaining 332.5 million population in this income group. Thus, the total number of B1-Cards would be 86.5 million (8.75 + 66.5 + 11.25 from B2-Card (Aged)). Holders of B1-Cards would make no co-payments towards prescriptions.

8.2.3.4 B2-Card

The B2-Card would be issued to the people (BPL2 category) with an annual income of Rs. 15,001 (~$375)–Rs. 40,000 (~$1000). This group is considered to be living below $2-a-day (BPL2). In 1999–2000, this group accounted for 12.98 per cent of the total number of individual tax returns filed (GOI 2003c, pp. 176–7). However, the tax returns indicate only the number of people at the higher end of the income range in this group. No tax returns would be recorded for people close to the lower end of the scale. The total size of this group is estimated to be 450 million. At 5 per cent of 450 million, 22.5 million elderly population would be issued with 11.25 million B1-Cards (Aged). This is because the Aged in this group are considered to have income level closer to that of BPL1. Thus, the total number of B2-Cards would be 85.5 million (remainder of (450–22.5)/5). Holders of B2-Cards would make a co-payment of Rs. 10 per prescription.

8.2.3.5 A1-Card

The A1-Cards would be issued to middle-class retirees with an annual income of between Rs. 15,001 (~$375)–Rs. 40,000 (~$1000). The number of cards in this group is estimated to be 2.5 million. Holders of A1-Cards would make a co-payment of Rs. 10 per prescription.

8.2.3.6 A2-Card

The A2-Cards would be issued to middle-class retirees with an annual income of between Rs. 40,001 (~$1000)–Rs. 100,000 (~$2500). The number of cards in this group is estimated to be 2.5 million. Holders of A2-Cards would make a co-payment of Rs. 25 per prescription.

8.2.3.7 A3-Card

The A3-Cards would be issued to middle-class retirees with an annual income of above Rs. 100,000 (~$2500). The number of cards in this group is estimated to be 2.5 million. Holders of A3-Cards would make a co-payment of Rs. 50 per prescription.

8.2.3.8 M1-Card

The population in the lower middle class with an annual income of Rs. 40,001 (~$1000)–Rs. 100,000 (~$2500) would be entitled to M1-Cards. This group of people accounted for around two-thirds of the total number of individual tax returns in 1999–2000. From the 285 million middle-class population (300 million–15 million aged), two-thirds or 190 million is estimated to belong to M1 category. Allowing 5 members per family, the total number of cards would be 38 million (190 million/5). Holders of M1-Cards would make a co-payment of Rs. 25 per prescription.

8.2.3.9 M2-Card

The M2-Cards would be issued to the higher middle-class people with annual income of over Rs. 100,000 (~$2500). This group constituted over 20 per cent of the overall number of tax returns. The total size of this group is estimated at 95 million (285 million–190 million in preceding category). At 5 members per family, 19 million M2-Cards would be issued. Holders of M2-Cards would make a co-payment of Rs. 50 per prescription.

The distinction between different types of cards is important for estimating the total contribution of patient co-payments. This is because the non-contributory (the B1-Cards and S-Cards) would make no co-payments and the number of people covered under specific cards would also vary. For example, the S-Card would list a single individual with special needs. The A-Cards for the aged category would entitle the listed individuals or couples to IndiaHealth services. All other cards, except S-Card and A-Cards, list the entire family, that is the parents and their dependent/unmarried children.

8.2.3.10 Safety Net threshold

The Safety Net threshold is a safeguard to keep medicines affordable by limiting out-of-pocket co-payments for cardholders who need a large number of medicines. Under the Safety Net, after a cardholder reaches the prescribed Safety Net threshold, all subsequent medicines on the formulary are provided at a concession for the remainder of the year.[9] In 2010, under the Australian model, the Safety Net threshold is reached after co-payments of A$324 (60 prescriptions @ A$5.40 each) in a calendar year for the concession cardholders and A$1264.90 (38 prescriptions @ A$33.30 each) for general patients (Government of Australia 2010). If a more expensive brand medicine is purchased or prescribed than the medicine listed on the formulary, the additional premium would not count towards the Safety Net threshold. The high number of prescriptions for Safety Net for the elderly and other concession cardholders alludes to the fact that the population in the aged group need more medicines than the younger people.

The Safety Net in Australia has a *20-day Rule*. Under this Rule, repeats of specific medicines listed[10] must not be dispensed within 20 days of the previous supply, except when explicitly authorised by the prescribing doctor. The cost of a medicine repeated within 20 days may not count towards the safety net threshold (Government of Australia 2007a). If the Safety Net is already reached, a repeat supply of the same medicine within 20-days may incur pre-Safety Net co-payment. This rule is designed to prevent any abuse of the system, such as stocking up of medicine at a concession. India could consider a similar rule with the same objectives.

The proposed model considers different income levels in India and proposes a three-tier Safety Net threshold. Under the proposed model, the Safety Net threshold would be reached after 50 prescriptions in a 12-month period for B2-Cards and A1-Cards. Holders of these cards would get all subsequent medicines free of cost for the remainder of the year, which means that the most these families would spend on medicines would be Rs. 500 in a 12-month period.

After 45 prescriptions, holders of M1-Cards and A2-Cards would pay Rs. 10 for all subsequent medicines for the rest of the year. After 40 prescriptions, holders of M2-Cards and A3-Cards would pay Rs. 25 for all subsequent medicines for the rest of the year. Holders of B1-Cards or S-Cards holders are exempt from any co-payments; thus, the Safety Net would not apply.

In India's case, the Safety Net is expected to maximise the poor's access to medicines, who carry the largest disease burden. In addition, sufferers of chronic diseases and serious illnesses such as cancer, for which the cost of medicines is significantly high, would benefit from lower co-payments after reaching the Safety Net threshold. Patient co-payments for all those on the IndiaHealth card count towards the Safety Net threshold. Larger families would also benefit from the Safety Net. They would benefit because the more family members on the card, the more likelihood of them getting sick and faster the family would reach the Safety Net threshold.

While married children may be living in the same household, they would need to apply for their own IndiaHealth card. The separate cards would prevent exploitation of the system and reaching the Safety Net prematurely. It is because all persons listed on each card would be counted as one family and the total amount of co-payments made for each card would be counted towards Safety Net threshold. While the S-Cardholders would have the same entitlements as the BPL1 group, people with special needs would not be issued with B1-Cards. This is because the S-Card would apply to a single individual, as opposed to the B1-Cards being for the entire family.

8.2.4 Comparing out-of-pocket expenditure

This subsection intends to examine the out-of-pocket (OOP) expenditure under the proposed model. First, the OOP expenditure under the current model is established. Then these data are used vis-a-vis the proposed model. Under the current model, the total out-of-pocket household expenditure is estimated as follows. According to a health survey conducted in 2005–06, the monthly per capita household health expenditure was Rs. 44 in rural and Rs. 71 in urban area, of which 64 per cent (Rs. 28.16) and 56 per cent (Rs. 39.76), respectively accounted for medicines (GOI 2007c). Based on these data and the rural–urban (70:30) composition of India's 1140[11] million population, the Indian average of household expenditure on medicines was derived (see Table 8.2). In 2005–06, a family of five spent Rs. 3126 on health, of which Rs. 1898.40 was spent on medicine.

Using the data from Table 8.2, expenditure on medicines, the out-of-pocket private expenditure, and government expenditure is calculated for the same year under the proposed model. In order to compare the out-of-pocket expenditure under the current model and under the proposed model, expenditure after reaching Safety Net has to be estimated. The Australian experience provides a useful guide for estimates on post-Safety Net medicine expenditure. Sweeny (2008) suggests that concessional and general patients constitute 25 per cent and 75 per cent of the Australian population, respectively. He notes that for the year

Table 8.2 Calculating current health and medicine expenditure (Rs.) in 2005–06

Category	Population (million)	Monthly health expenditure		Monthly medicine expenditure	
		Per capita (Rs.)	Total Rs. (million)	Per capita (Rs.)	Total Rs. (million)
Rural	798	44	35,112	28.16	22,471.68
Urban	342	71	24,282	39.76	13,597.92
Total (India)	1140		59,394		36,069.6
Based on the above data		**Yearly health expenditure**		**Yearly medicine expenditure**	
Rural			421,344		269,660.16
Urban			291,384		163,175.04
Total (India)			712,728		432,835.2
Per person		625.2		379.68	
Per family of five		3126		1898.4	

Source: Author estimates based on GOI (2007c, 200f).

2006–07, the post-Safety Net accounted for 11.66 per cent of the total expenditure on PBS medicines for general patients and over 21 per cent for concession cardholders.

The IndiaHealth model is based on the premise that those who can afford should pay more, and those who cannot should pay less. Population groups at the lower end of the income scale (B1-Cards) as well as holders of S-Cards do not make any co-payments at all towards the cost of the medicines. The provisions of the Safety Net would not apply to these two categories. For holders B2-Cards or A1-Cards, the maximum out-of-pocket contribution would be limited to reaching the Safety Net. All subsequent medicines would be supplied free of cost for the rest of the year to these two categories. Holders of cards in the remaining four categories (A2, M1, A3, and M2) upon reaching the Safety Net would be entitled to medicines at a concessional rate thereafter. For these four categories, another 10 per cent was added to the total in order to estimate the post-Safety Net out-of-pocket expenditure. For most of the Indian population, the out-of-pocket expenditure declines significantly under the proposed model (see Table 8.3).

All categories, except A3-cards and M2-cards, would be better off under the proposed model. The holders of the B1-cards as well as holders of S1-Cards would be best off. Population groups in B2 and A1 categories would be significantly better off and save annually Rs. 1398 (1898–500) per family. For holders of A2-cards and M1-cards, the out-of-pocket annual expenditure on medicines would also fall to around two-thirds from the current level. Holders of A3-cards and M2-cards or around 9 per cent of the total population would pay 15.8 per cent more than the current level. At a high income level, an increase in the expenditure on medicine is considered justifiable.

In absolute terms, the national average household (of five members) expenditure on drugs would decrease from the current level of Rs. 1898 to Rs. 598.[12] After deducting the number of non-contributory cards (B1-Cards and S1-Cards), the average annual drug expenditure of a contributory household would be around Rs. 943.[13] This would still amount to substantial savings on the current level. The contribution of third parties, such as private insurance, charities, and NGOs is not considered for reasons discussed later in this chapter.

Table 8.3 also shows the composition of total out-of-pocket co-payments and government contributions towards the drug expenditure under the proposed model. Based on GOI (2007c), the total out-of-pocket expenditure on medicines for 2005–06 is estimated to be Rs. 432,835 million. Currently, this expenditure is met entirely by

Table 8.3 Annual expenditure on medicines under current and proposed models

S. No.	Category	Estimated population (million)	Estimated no. of cards (million)	Total drug expenditure, India (Rs. million)	Total out-of-pocket co-payments (Rs. million)	Government contribution (Rs. million)	Average out-of-pocket co-payments per family (Rs.)	Average out-of-pocket drug expenditure per family (Rs.)
1	2	3	4	(current) 5	(proposed) 6	(proposed) 7 = (5 – 6)	(proposed) 8	(current) 9
1	S-Card	40	40.00	15,187.2	0	15,187.2	0	1898.4
2	B1-Card	350	86.50*	132,888	0	132,888	0	1898.4
3	B2-Card	450	85.50**	170,856	42,750	128,106	500	1898.4
4	A1-Card	5	2.50	1,898.4	1,250	648.4	500	1898.4
5	A2-Card	5	2.50	1,898.4	3,093.75	0	1238	1898.4
6	M1-Card	190	38.00	72,139.2	47,025	25,114.2	1238	1898.4
7	A3-Card	5	2.50	1,898.4	5,500	0	2200	1898.4
8	M2-Card	95	19.00	36,069.6	41,800	0	2200	1898.4
	Total (India)	1140	236.50	432,835	141,419	291,416	598	1898.4
				100%	32.67	67.33		

Note: *Includes 8.75 million aged with B1-Cards and 11.25 million aged with B2-Cards.
**Excludes 11.25 million Aged from this group.
Source: Author estimates based on GOI (2007c, 200f).

out-of-pocket household expenses. The Table shows that under the proposed model, the annual household expenditure on medicines would decline to Rs. 141,419 million or around a third of the current level. The share of the government would account for around 67 per cent of the total expenditure on medicines.

While the share of patient co-payments would decline to around 33 per cent of India's total drug expenditure, this share would still be twice the share of that of the Australian population towards the cost of medicines. For the financial year July 2005–June 2006, Australians filled out 168,322,615 prescriptions at a cost of over A$6.5 billion, from which the government spending accounted for A$5.4 billion. The patient contribution of A$1.1 billion constituted less than 17 per cent of Australia's total expenditure on medicines for the year (Government of Australia 2006). However, the proposed model significantly reduces the household share of the expenditure on medicines from the current level. Public contribution as a share of India's total expenditure on medicines would increase significantly to offset the reduction in household expenditure.

The proposed model provides a complete healthcare package, which would be a significant departure from the past policies. The past policies focused on controlling prices of allopathic medicines rather than providing healthcare. The past policies contributed to the development of India pharma but lacked a cohesive vision for the entire healthcare industry. The traditional systems of medicine were not given due recognition for their part in the provision of healthcare. In contrast, the proposed model focuses on providing an equitable healthcare, including access to traditional medicines. On the patient side, the proposed model requires out-of-pocket co-payments based on different income levels of the population. On the government side, the following subsection considers the benefits and the size of the financial commitment required to fund the IndiaHealth programme.

8.2.5 Benefits of the proposed model

The proposed healthcare model would provide significant benefits over the existing model for the patients, the industry, and the government. The current Indian healthcare model is limited to controlling the prices of drugs listed on the Schedule of the Drug Price Control Order (DPCO), and the number of drugs under price control is significantly small. The current model focuses on keeping the prices low on drugs that the DPCO considers necessary. There are no other provisions to ensure accessibility to medicines. Consequently, even at the controlled prices, drugs are unaffordable to the vast majority of the poor. The proposed model would ensure access to allopathic drugs as well as traditional medicines.

The current model provides limited access to public health institutions. There is no provision for facilitating access to private doctors or practitioners of traditional Indian healthcare systems. The proposed model would include access to public institutions, authorised doctors, and practitioners of traditional medicines.

The current policy restricts profits and discourages supply of controlled drugs. Manufacturers avoid using the controlled drugs and, where possible, substitute them with non-controlled drugs to maintain high profits. The proposed model would increase transparency enhancing certainty for investors and consumers. The guaranteed subsidy and the drug price under the proposed model would significantly enhance sales forecasts for the listed drugs. The sales would be boosted, because all Indians would have access to medicine. No social groups would be excluded from seeking healthcare due to affordability. The sales would significantly increase the size of the Indian pharmaceutical market as well as disease-specific sub-markets. These sub-markets are likely to attract new investments into research and development of drugs for tropical diseases that are more common in developing countries. Until now, sufferers of these diseases lacked the purchasing power and investors neglected these diseases, because the potential for high returns was unlikely.

The proposed model would provide several economic advantages to India. First, the increased access to medicine would improve health of India's labour force. This would effectively translate into increased productivity and higher economic growth, because good health is a significant contributor to the economy of a nation. Health assumes even greater significance in a poor country like India, where the only asset most people have is their bodies. Abegunde and Stanciole (2006) suggest that diseases reduce life expectancy and economic productivity depleting quality and quantity of the nation's labour force. Thus, broadening access to medicines would accelerate the Indian economy.

Second, India's provision of healthcare, would free resources currently occupied by segmented group insurances (employment and/or community based) and bring them all under one umbrella. For example, the dedicated health institutions, such as Railways Health Services, ESIS[14], or CGHS[15] hospitals and dispensaries currently serve specific population groups. These are public institutions, yet general public cannot access them. Only certain employee groups and their families have access to these institutions. Under the proposed model, all public institutions such as these would be streamlined and accessible to all Indians.

Finally, the consolidation of all the resources would provide a clear and complete picture to the planners and policy makers regarding the challenges ahead and the resources available.

8.2.6 Costing the IndiaHealth programme

In order to estimate the costs of the programme, thorough understanding of India's demographics is required. Currently, India is estimated to have 1.14 billion population (GOI 2007f). India has a young population relative to other countries. According to the latest census (2001), more than 55 per cent of Indians were younger than 24 in 2001 (GOI 2006b) and the share of the population over 65 years of age would increase significantly from 5 per cent in 2005 to more than 17 per cent in 2050 as the population begins to mature (United Nations 2005b).

The relevance of the demographics is that the utilisation of healthcare, including medicines, increases significantly in the old age relative to lower age groups. Expert estimates show that in Australia, the population over 65 years of age uses 4 times more healthcare than the younger population. This ratio is 6–9 times higher for the population over 80 years of age. If the entire population over 65 years of age (including those over 80 years of age) is pooled into a single group, the healthcare expenditure is around 4.5 times higher than the rest of the population (Australian Institute of Health and Welfare 2005). This is because the population over 80 years of age is significantly smaller than the 65–79 years age group. The same study suggests that children up to age of four years require significantly more healthcare than the children between 5 and 14 years of age. It is because children aged 0–4 years require health services, such as vaccination and nursing that the older children do not need. If the population between 5 and 64 is taken as one group, the healthcare expenditure of this group is only slightly higher than the expenditure level of the 0–4 age group. For costing of the proposed model, we consider that the population under four years and over 65 years of age would use 1.2 times and 4.5 times, respectively, more healthcare than the population in the 5–64 years age group.

Haub and Sharma (2006) provide estimates on India's population to 2050. They estimate India to reach 1.9 billion or even surpass 2 billion (high variant) by 2050 (see Figure 8.2). By medium and low variants, India is estimated to reach 1.6 billion and 1.3 billion, respectively.

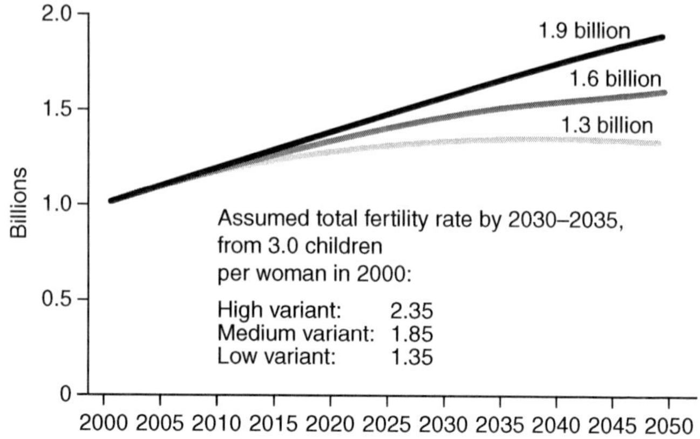

Figure 8.2 India's population projections (2000–50)
Source: Haub and Sharma (2006, p. 18).

The United Nations (2005a) provides estimates on India's population (2000–50) by age groups. We combine both foregoing studies on population projections to estimate the size of the aged group within the Indian population.

Taking the extreme case scenario of India reaching 2 billion population in 2050, the population of the over 65 year olds could reach 290 million, including around 60 million of those who would be over 80 years of age. If however India manages to restrict its population to 1.3 billion by the middle of the century, the number of those who would be more than 65 years of age is expected to be around 189 million, with an estimated population of 40 million of over 80 years of age. In either case, these projections foreshadow the need for significant additional resources to be spent on healthcare. When India's population begins to age, the share of children 0–4 years of age is expected to decline to less than half in 50 years from 2000. The share of the 5–14 years age group is also expected to decline significantly, while the shares of other three population groups are estimated to increase (see Figure 8.3).

With the population beginning to age, the share of the aged is expected to rise significantly over the next few decades. The aggregate share of the two age groups that consume proportionately higher share of healthcare (the 0–4 years and the 65+ years age group) would rise from 16.6 per cent of total population in 2000 to 21.4 per cent in 2050. Once again, this would require a significant increase in healthcare expenditure.

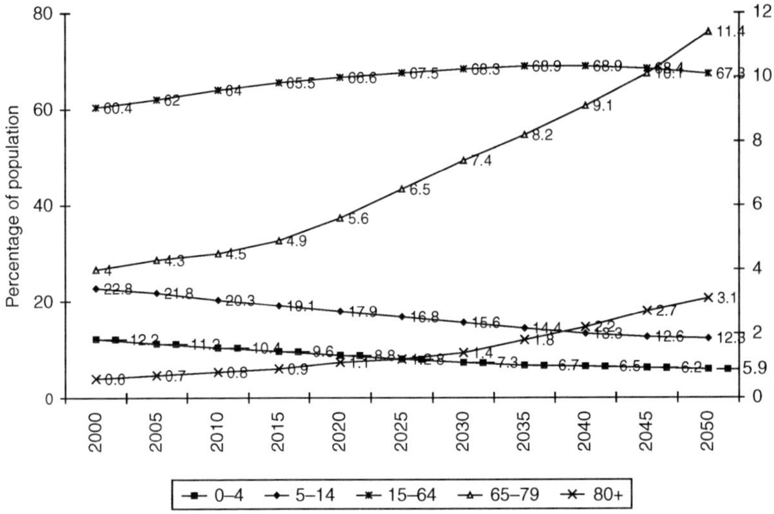

Figure 8.3 Projected population of India by age groups (2000–50) (share of total population)

Source: Author estimates based on Haub and Sharma (2006) (medium variant) and United Nations (2005a).

The IndiaHealth programme is an integrated programme that facilitates access to healthcare and access to subsidised medicines. In order to accurately assess the overall costs of the IndiaHealth programme, it would be imperative to estimate both, the costs of healthcare as well as the costs of medicines. After projecting the change in population shares, it is possible to estimate the out-of-pocket expenditure on medicines and on healthcare for the period 2006–15. First we estimate the out-of-pocket expenditure on medicines (see Table 8.4). Then we estimate the out-of-pocket health expenditure (see Table 8.5). These estimates are based on the assumption that the population in the 0–4 year age group and the 65+ year age group utilise 1.2 and 4.5 times, respectively, more medicines and healthcare than other age groups.

Table 8.5 provides estimates of household health expenditure, including medicines and other expenses such as doctors' fees, X-rays, and ultrasound, etc. Again these estimates are based on the assumption that the use of healthcare by the 0–4 years of age population and the 65+ year age group would be higher than the other age groups as shown in the Table. In the final column of Tables 8.4 and 8.5, the expenditure considers inflation and rises by 5 per cent per annum.

Table 8.4 Estimates of out-of-pocket *medicine* expenditure (Rs. million) and population groups (million)

Year	Total	0–4 (factor 1.2)		5–64 (factor 1)		65+ (factor 4.5)		Total OOP med. exp.	Total OOP med. exp. Incl. 5% CAGR
	Population	Population	Med. exp.	Population	Med. exp.	Population	Med. exp.		
1	2	3	4	5	6	7	8	9 (4 + 6 + 8)	10
2006	1140	126.5	57,635	956.5	363,164	57.0	97,388	518,187	518,187
2007	1160	127.6	58,137	973.8	369,732	58.6	100,122	527,991	554,390
2008	1181	127.5	58,091	993.2	377,098	60.2	102,855	538,045	593,194
2009	1201	127.3	58,000	1011.2	383,932	62.5	106,785	548,717	635,209
2010	1220	126.9	57,818	1028.5	390,501	64.7	110,544	558,862	679,301
2011	1237	126.2	57,499	1044.0	396,386	66.8	114,132	568,016	724,949
2012	1254	125.4	57,134	1059.6	402,309	69.0	117,891	577,334	773,683
2013	1271	124.6	56,770	1075.3	408,270	71.2	121,649	586,689	825,531
2014	1287	124.8	56,861	1088.8	413,396	73.4	125,408	595,665	880,068
2015	1303	125.1	56,998	1102.3	418,521	75.6	129,167	604,686	938,066

Note: CAGR = Compound annual growth rate.
Source: Author estimates based on United Nations (2005a); and GOI (2007c, 2007f).

Table 8.5 Estimates of total out-of-pocket *health* expenditure (Rs. million) and population groups (million)

Year	Total	0–4 (factor 1.2)		5–64 (factor 1)		65+ (factor 4.5)		Total OOP health exp.	Total OOP health exp. incl. 5% CAGR
	Population	Population	H/care exp.	Population	H/Care exp.	Population	H/Care exp.		
1	2	3	4	5	6	7	8	9 (4 + 6 + 8)	10
2006	1140	126.5	94,905	956.5	598,004	57.0	160,364	853,273	853,273
2007	1160	127.6	95,731	973.8	608,820	58.6	164,865	869,416	912,886
2008	1181	127.5	95,656	993.2	620,949	60.2	169,367	885,971	976,783
2009	1201	127.3	95,506	1011.2	632,202	62.5	175,838	903,545	1,045,967
2010	1220	126.9	95,205	1028.5	643,018	64.7	182,027	920,251	1,118,570
2011	1237	126.2	94,680	1044.0	652,709	66.8	187,935	935,324	1,193,737
2012	1254	125.4	94,080	1059.6	662,462	69.0	194,125	950,667	1,273,984
2013	1271	124.6	93,480	1075.3	672,278	71.2	200,314	966,072	1,359,360
2014	1287	124.8	93,630	1088.8	680,718	73.4	206,504	980,851	1,449,164
2015	1303	125.1	93,855	1102.3	689,158	75.6	212,693	995,706	1,544,667

Note: CAGR = Compound annual growth rate.
Source: Author estimates based on United Nations (2005a); and GOI (2007c, 200f).

Based on the total out-of-pocket health expenditure in the Table above, India's total health expenditure can be estimated. According to GOI (2005b), the total health expenditure in India comprises as follows:

Households (out-of-pocket)	72.0 per cent
Public expenditure on health (Central, state and local)	20.3 per cent
NGOs	0.1 per cent
Employment based	5.3 per cent
External support (e.g. donations to NGOs or governments)	2.3 per cent
Total	100 per cent

Taking the estimates of total out-of-pocket health expenditure as 72 per cent under the current situation, India's total health expenditure can be rebased as 100 per cent (see Table 8.6). Under the proposed model, the share of out-of-pocket health expenditure would decline from the current 72 per cent to around 33 per cent of total health expenditure. Correspondingly, public expenditure on healthcare would increase from around 20 per cent to around 67 per cent. The share of third party contributors, such as employers and private health insurers, is likely to fall significantly under the proposed model. This is based on the following assumptions. First, after the implementation of the IndiaHealth programme, the share of employers' contributions is likely to be limited to out-of-pocket co-payments towards the purchase of the medicine rather than the total cost of healthcare. This would reduce the employer contribution as share of the total health expenditure to around 1.7 per cent (around a third of the current level).

Second, the uptake and retention of private health insurance are likely to fall, because in the wake of IndiaHealth, the incentives to take up private health insurance would all but disappear. Third, the contribution of the NGOs is likely to be limited to national calamities and/or emergencies. Thus, the total contribution of the third parties is likely to be rendered negligible. Consequently, the public expenditure on health would also make up for the shortfall created by the reductions in contributions by the third parties. Should the share of the third parties not change as assumed, minor adjustments would need to be made to the share of public expenditure on health.

Table 8.6 shows that India would need to spend 1.62 per cent of the GDP to meet fully the share of public expenditure on health if the proposed model were implemented in 2010. These estimates consider the projected increase in India's population and take into account annual

Table 8.6 Projected distribution of total health expenditure (Rs. million) (2006–15)

Year	**Current situation**		**Proposed programme**			
	Total OOP health exp. incl. 5% CAGR (72%)	**Estimated total health exp. (THE) (100%)**	**Public exp on health. (PEH) at (67.33%)**	**Total OOP health exp. at (32.67%)**	**GDP estimates**	**PEH as % of GDP**
2006	853,273	1,185,101	797,897	387,204	39,743,850	2.01
2007	912,886	1,267,898	853,642	414,256	45,453,590	1.88
2008	976,783	1,356,643	913,392	443,251	50,916,870	1.79
2009	1,045,967	1,452,731	978,085	474,646	57,361,880	1.71
2010	1,118,570	1,553,570	1,045,977	507,593	64,612,270	1.62
2011	1,193,737	1,657,968	1,116,266	541,702	72,713,230	1.54
2012	1,273,984	1,769,422	1,191,305	578,117	81,814,440	1.46
2013	1,359,360	1,888,000	1,271,140	616,860	92,075,660	1.38
2014	1,449,164	2,012,728	1,355,116	657,612	103,585,118	1.31
2015	1,544,667	2,145,371	1,444,421	700,950	116,533,257	1.24

Note: CAGR = Compound annual growth rate.
Source: Author estimates based on GOI (2005b, 2007c); and IMF (2008).

inflation of 5 per cent. The estimates suggest that the level of public spending on health as a share of the GDP would progressively decline. Under the proposal, the level of public expenditure on health is estimated to be less than 1.3 per cent from 2014–15 onwards.

Sensitivities tests suggest that making changes to one variable in the model would affect the outcome for other variables. In case 1, co-payment for the lowest paying categories (B2 and A1) is raised from Rs. 10 to Rs. 15 per prescription. The Safety Net is also raised from Rs. 500 to Rs. 750. The payment schedule for the other categories remains unchanged. The test shows that the public contribution on health for 2010 declines from 1.62 per cent (base case) to 1.50 per cent (see Appendix C for details).

In case 2, co-payment schedule for the lowest paying categories remains unchanged. For the A2 and M1 categories, the co-payment is raised from Rs. 25 to Rs. 30 and the Safety Net is raised from Rs. 1125 to Rs. 1350. For the A3 and M2 categories, the co-payment is raised from Rs. 50 to Rs. 60 and the Safety Net is raised from Rs. 2000 to Rs. 2400. Consequently, the public contribution on health for 2010 declines from 1.62 per cent (base case) to 1.51 per cent (see Appendix D for details).

8.2.7 Funding the IndiaHealth programme

Subsequent to estimating the costs of the IndiaHealth programme, this sub-section considers the sources for funding the programme. According to the National Health Policy – 2002, India's public spending on health has declined from 1.3 per cent of the GDP in 1990 to 0.9 per cent of the GDP in 1999 (GOI 2002a) and the level of public health spending has remained at the latter rate ever since (Economic Research Foundation 2006; Mahal 2002; Raymus 2007). The Common Minimum Programme of the current United Progressive Alliance (UPA) government states that 'The UPA government will raise public spending on health to at least 2–3 per cent of GDP over the next five years' (GOI 2004, p. 7). If the government were to honour its commitment to raise the public spending on health, the entire IndiaHealth programme becomes easily affordable. This argument is based on the IMF estimates of India's current GDP and the forecasts for growth to 2013 (IMF 2008). The GDP estimates for 2014 and 2015 were based on the growth trends outlined in the IMF study. Figure 8.4 shows the public expenditure on health required under the proposed model as well as the level of expenditure on health committed by the government. The Figure also shows that India's total expenditure on health at around 3 per cent of the GDP in 2006 declining to below 2 per cent of the GDP from around 2014. The total expenditure

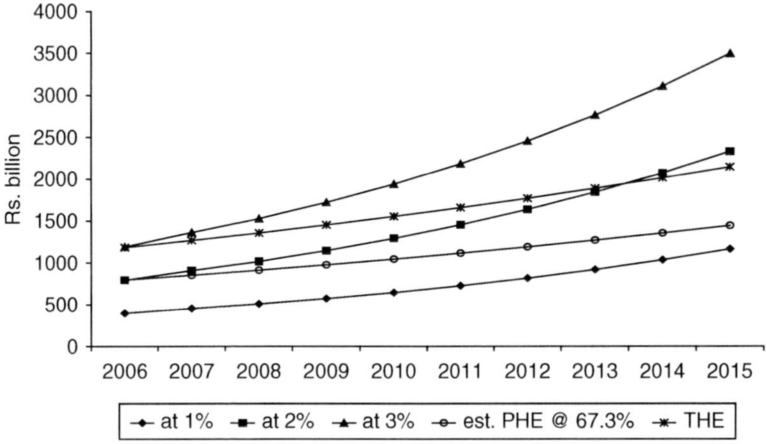

Figure 8.4 Variable levels of public expenditure on health relative to total health expenditure
Source: Author estimates based on IMF (2008); and GOI (2004).

on health includes the out-of-pocket private health expenditure as well as the public expenditure on health.

Figure 8.4 shows that by raising the public expenditure on health to 1.62 per cent of the GDP from 2010, the government could afford to fund the IndiaHealth programme. This level of public expenditure on health would not only be adequate to subsidise medicines, but also to fund other healthcare costs. It may be noted that this programme covers the entire population including those sections, which until now had no access to medicines. A subsequent rise in India's public expenditure on health to 3 per cent of the GDP over the next five years would provide additional resources for the programme. If the public expenditure on health as a share of the GDP were held constant over the coming years, the public health spending per capita would increase significantly. This is because the expected annual population increase is around 1.2 per cent compared with expected economic growth of 6–7 per cent in India. If the IndiaHealth programme were to be implemented in different stages, provision of subsidised medicines could form stage one of the programme.

The allocation of funds to finance the IndiaHealth programme would require re-prioritising of other government programmes meaning partial or complete withdrawal of funds to delay or cancel low priority programmes. Alternatively, IndiaHealth could be partially financed through budgetary deficits through issuing government bonds. The setting up of a programme of this magnitude would require significant additional infrastructure and human resources, who would be involved in issuing the IndiaHealth cards, awareness campaigns, validation, certification, and authorisation of doctors and pharmacists, and the preparation of formulary. Considering the difficulties associated with implementing a programme of such a magnitude, it would be envisaged that a 12–15 months' lead time be allowed for preparatory phase before the implementation.

In accordance with the proposed model, some structural changes would be required. Ministry of Health and Family Welfare would have two major functions; namely, the provision of healthcare undertaken by IndiaHealth, and provision of medicines undertaken by MedicineIndia. IndiaHealth would be sub-divided into allopathy and AYUSH (Ayurveda, Yoga & Naturopathy, Unani, Siddha, and Homoeopathy) that would be responsible for the development of access to their respective health systems (see Figure 8.5). MedicineIndia would be responsible for securing the supply of medicines to meet India's health needs, while IndiaHealth would be responsible for the distribution of the medicines. IndiaHealth would need to develop adequate infrastructure, and provide sufficient human resources to ensure the timely and equitable distribution of medicines to all sections of the population.

The proposed model would provide access to healthcare and medicines with progressive patient co-payments based on various income levels. The level of household contribution would decline substantially while the share of public expenditure on health would increase significantly under the proposal. The share of third party

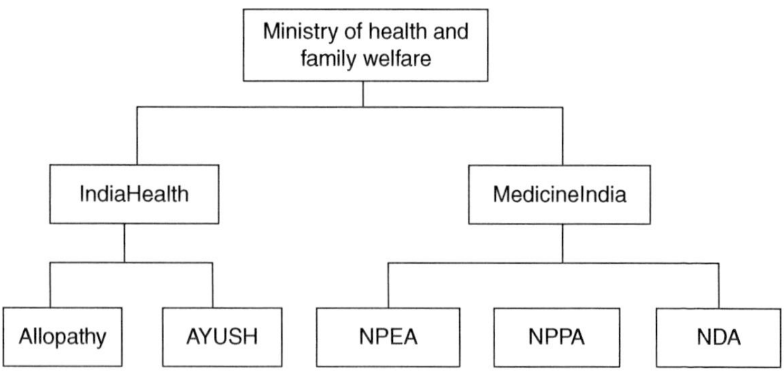

Figure 8.5 New structure under the proposed model
Source: Author.

contributors, such as employers and private health insurers, is likely to decline significantly. In the wake of the UPA government's commitment to raise the health expenditure to at least 2–3 per cent of the GDP, the proposed model would become affordable if the public expenditure on health was raised from the current level of 0.9 per cent to less than 2 per cent of the GDP.

8.3 Conclusions

At the current stage of economic development, India would need to introduce policies, which raise the health status of the poor. The population projections indicate that India's population could reach 2 billion by the middle of the century. With the people generally living longer, the share of the aged is expected to increase significantly, although India will enjoy a favourable age-structure of its population and will benefit from a rising share of working-age population (the so-called 'demographic dividend') over the next three decades. Eventually, however, demographic change would require a significant shift in the health policy and allocation of additional resources. The healthcare model presented in this chapter is financially affordable, implementable, and practical. This model could also be used as a guide to consider other policy options.

The proposed model does not claim to be the end goal for India, but would be a small step in the right direction to help India achieve its objective of *health for all*. This model would provide access to both the allopathic and the traditional healthcare providers. The IndiaHealth programme would provide access to medicines requiring patient co-payments based on patients' ability to pay. Our costing presented above suggests that the increase in the public expenditure on health required to fund the IndiaHealth programme is well within the level of commitment already given by the UPA government in its Common Minimum Programme. Our estimates indicate that by raising public expenditure on health from the current level of 0.9 per cent to 1.62 per cent of GDP by 2010, India would be able to overcome the barriers to access to medicines and provide affordable healthcare to all. Going forward, the ratio of public expenditure on health is expected to fall to 1.24 per cent of GDP by 2015. The implementation of this model, or another variation of it, should relieve India's households of significant health expenditure and help the country achieve better health outcomes.

Part III

Global Perspective

9
Is TRIPS Appropriate for Developing Countries?

9.1 Introduction

This chapter joins the global debate on the social and economic impact of raising the protection of IPRs in developing countries under the TRIPS agreement. More specifically, the purpose of this chapter is to examine the appropriateness of applying the harmonised regime of intellectual property rights under the TRIPS agreement. The focus of this discussion is only on the protection of pharmaceutical product patents, because this form of patent protection has the greatest impact on access to medicines.

The controversy about the appropriateness of TRIPS arises out of the conflict between the interests of the developing countries on the one hand and of the developed countries on the other. Until recently, the developing countries could 'free ride' the intellectual property created in the developed world without sharing the cost of its development. The TRIPS compliant regime disallows 'free riding' and raises both the standard of protection and the cost of medicines in the developing countries.

The large MNCs maintain that stringent IPRs are necessary to encourage innovation, industry development, and technology transfer. For example, Pfizer (2005) suggests that without stringent patent protection, large investments required to develop new drugs would not be possible. Similarly, Kevin W. Sharer, Chairman of the PhRMA, argues that 'a robust IP system is crucial to our success in developing innovative new medicines. Without it, our industry wouldn't exist and neither would our products' (cited in PhRMA 2007, p. 5).

The Indian experience, summarised in the earlier chapters, shows that a weak patent regime was crucial to the development of Indian pharmaceutical industry, and the advancement of innovation in the country. While the innovative activity was predominantly confined to reverse engineering, a limited number of new drugs were developed under the weak patent regime in India. The development of manufacturing processes made India a world leader in the production of generic drugs. Thus, India's experience contradicts the arguments advanced by Pfizer and PhRMA. These claims and counter claims lead into a worldwide debate on the desirability of stringent IPRs, considering their impact on the access to medicines in the developing countries. There is little doubt that the R&D in the pharmaceutical sector needs large investments. Whether these investments justify the level of protection advocated by the proponents of stringent IPRs is a question requiring further investigation. Against this backdrop, this chapter examines the appropriateness of TRIPS in the developing countries.

9.2 Patents in developed countries

The purpose of this section is to consider whether the TRIPS agreement has been prematurely imposed on the poor countries, depriving them of the same opportunities that the developed countries themselves had enjoyed at the early stages of economic development. Intellectual property has been a key economic driver in a large number of advanced economies. For example, intellectual property constitutes America's largest export (Posner 2002). Historically, many countries including the US benefited from copying technologies developed in advanced economies (UNDP 2005, p. 135). The US was copying British patents and copyrights in the nineteenth century. For example, the US permitted wholesale reprinting (piracy) of British authors' work causing British rights holders to suffer financial losses. The difference in price of imitated and that of the original product was huge. A locally produced copy of *A Christmas Carol* by Charles Dickens cost just six cents in 1843 compared with the British edition at $2.50 (Hesse 2002). Similar or more significant differences were noticeable between the prices of originator drugs and those of Indian generics (see Chapters 4–6 for details). According to the Human Development Report (2005), Japan, Korea, China, and Taiwan all upgraded their technological capabilities through 'reverse engineering', a technical term for copying someone else's work and developing innovative skills (UNDP 2005). If India, Brazil, and other developing countries are copying the patented products, they are doing so because it has been a part of the transitional process to eventually transform their economies to fully developed economies.

The US intellectual property regime not only permitted copying of elsewhere patented products, but also discriminated against foreign producers. The US provided incentives for domestic innovation and denied any protection for foreign technology (Hawthorne 2003). This provided the US producers access to foreign technology at a cost lower than other nations. This asymmetry between UK and US patent laws favoured inventors in the then developing economy of the US, rather than the UK, the more industrialised economy of the time (Jeremy 2004). In today's terms, the US patent law was a clear case of discrimination against foreign firms and imports in contrast to the doctrine of national treatment under the TRIPS agreement extended to all firms regardless of their origin.

9.2.1 Introduction of pharmaceutical product patents

The introduction of pharmaceutical product patents has generally been a two stage process. Stage one introduced only 'process' patents, encouraging participation in the drug development process. By design, Stage one may be called an *inclusive phase,* because it did not exclude anyone from making the product. Under stage two, introducing 'product' patents was phased in, after high level of innovative capabilities had been developed. This stage barred participation by others in any shape or form of the property and as such may be called an *exclusive phase.* A large number of developed countries, particularly in Europe, had delayed the introduction of pharmaceutical product patents until they had attained certain level of economic development. According to Basheer (2008), the delay was necessary, because learning and mastering to imitate are necessary steps to developing capabilities to innovate, a key to creating intellectual property (cited in Kumar 2008). In a memoir to the Reichstag[1], the German Association of Chemical Industry explicitly describes the rationale behind the patenting of 'process' versus 'product' as follows:

> ...the same chemical product can be obtained by different processes and methods and even starting from initially different materials and components. Hence, there is social value in patenting a new process, as it rewards the innovator without preventing further innovation. There is negative social value in patenting a specific product, as this would exclude all others from producing it, even through different processes.
>
> (Cited in Boldrin & Levine 2005, p. 3)

The Indian Patents Act 1970 was heavily criticised by the developed countries in the years preceding the implementation of TRIPS. The Patents Act 1970 was, in fact, based on the 'German system of allowing the patenting of methods or processes that led to drugs, but not allowing the patenting of the drugs themselves' (Drahos 2002b, p. 165).

During the development of the US pharmaceutical industry, foreign companies faced problems of high tariffs and discriminatory patent rules, as noted above. Unlike today, there were no pharmaceutical companies as such in nineteenth century in the US or in Europe. Pharmacists or druggists made and mixed their own compounds from ingredients mostly supplied by German companies. E. Merck & Co, one of the pioneers in pharmaceutical innovation, was based in Darmstadt (Germany). The company exported fine chemicals to the US in 1890 and noted that 'in light of *feeble* US drug regulations, problems developed – Merck labels were *illegally* placed on other companies' chemicals' resulting in significant losses of revenue (Hawthorne 2003, p. 21). Placing Merck labels on non-Merck products was illegal at German law but permissible in the US. Discriminatory treatment of foreign companies and high tariffs were eroding their market sales. Ultimately, these companies shifted to the US to manufacture locally.

Around the same time, other countries also had discriminatory rules against foreign companies and imports. For example, Switzerland had 'the [most] selective patent law ever enacted in modern times' (Schiff 1971, p. 93). The 1888 Swiss legislation discriminated against foreign companies and encouraged domestic imitators. The Swiss patent law did not include chemical compounds until 1907 when only process patents were introduced. Patents for pharmaceutical products were first introduced in Switzerland in 1977. Today, Switzerland is home to some of the most innovative companies in pharmaceutical industry including Novartis and Roche.

Similar to Switzerland, Italy also did not provide pharmaceutical product patents. The Italian industry consisted of a large number of small and medium sized independent pharmaceutical firms. In 1978, following a court ruling in favour of the MNCs, Italy had to introduce product patents. Scherer and Weisburst (1995) suggest that no significant increase in the discovery of innovative drugs was achieved after the Italian Supreme Court mandated the issue of pharmaceutical product patents. Another study suggests that the introduction of product patents in Italy did not only fail to translate the stringent protection into significant innovation progress, the domestic pharmaceutical industry in Italy was on the verge of collapse as a consequence of the regime change.

According to Boldrin and Levine (2005), 'the Italian pharmaceutical industry is, in fact, practically disappearing, together with the most valuable and patentable drugs it did not discover since 1978' (p. 9). Going by the Italian experience, the implementation of TRIPS in India is likely to put an end not only to imitation but also to innovation, suggest Boldrin and Levine.

In Argentina, pharmaceuticals were explicitly excluded from the patent legislation passed in 1864 (Rogers 1994). After copying drugs developed elsewhere for more than 130 years, the country introduced TRIPS compliant patent regime in 2000. The Patents and Designs Act 1911 had provided pharmaceutical product patents in India, but abolished under the Patents Act 1970. The UK first introduced product patents for pharmaceuticals in 1949, France in 1960, and Germany in 1968 (Chaudhuri 2005, p. 321).

Lanjouw (2002b) provides comparisons of stages of economic development measured by GDP per capita in selected countries at the time of their adoption of product patents in pharmaceuticals. It is clear from her study that all the developed countries had a five-digit GDP per capita at the time of adoption of pharmaceutical product patents. For example, Switzerland had GDP per capita of US$36,965 (1977), Norway US$30,389 (1992), and Japan US$24,043 (1976). This level of development compares with less than $500 GDP per capita in India and China at the adoption of product patents. The argument here is that a large number of developed countries did not introduce product patents in pharmaceuticals until certain level of economic development had been attained. The implementation of TRIPS and TRIPS-plus conditions in developing countries is denying the poor countries the same opportunities as enjoyed by the developed countries when they implemented product patents. Under the WTO obligations, the LDCs like Malawi with a GDP per capita of $156 are due to implement the TRIPS agreement in 2016. It is highly unlikely that the LDCs will be close to the level of development of say India or China, let alone reaching the level of developed countries examined in the Lanjouw study.

On the basis of the evidence presented, it can be concluded that the TRIPS agreement has been prematurely imposed on the poor countries depriving them of the same opportunities that the developed countries themselves had enjoyed at the early stages of economic development. The forced introduction of pharmaceutical product patents places the poor countries at a significant disadvantage on two accounts. First, the raised level of patent protection cuts short the process of learning and mastering of imitation harming the pace of industry development in the poor countries. Second, the patents-induced monopolies provide the MNCs' significant control over these markets with no or little competition from the local manufacturers restricting access to medicines. The TRIPS agreement fails to recognise and take into account the different levels of economic development across member states and the diversity in their needs. The TRIPS is simply a 'one size fits all' concept with significant disadvantages to the poor countries.

9.3 Costs and benefits of TRIPS

The aim of this section is to consider the costs and benefits of patents in general and the TRIPS agreement in particular. The significance of this section would be in the informed assessment of the implications of the TRIPS agreement. Because 'it is far more difficult to measure the positive effect of patents on innovation' (Lanjouw & Cockburn 2001, p. 266), discussions on the costs and benefits of patents generally tend to be restricted to emphasising the benefits. 'The costs of the patent system are usually ignored altogether or presented as trivial' (Macdonald 2002, p. 31). Yet, there are significant economic and social costs indeed.

The strengthening of the patent system has raised the costs of healthcare worldwide. These costs are more pronounced in the developing than in the developed countries. The introduction of TRIPS has delayed the entry of low-cost generics increasing the costs of healthcare in all countries, including the US. Drug prices fall by 60–70 per cent after generics enter the US market, where significant proportion of the population pays out-of-pocket for medicines. The absence of generics means that consumers would be forced to purchase the originator drugs at monopoly prices. Consequently, consumers would spend less elsewhere reducing social welfare. Prescription drugs in the developed countries, except the US, are significantly subsidised by universal health insurance programmes and the consumer spending is limited to co-payments. But the additional public expenditure on health, as a consequence of TRIPS, would be offset by delaying or cancelling other development programmes.

9.3.1 Costs and benefits to developing countries

In the developing countries, the effect is more far-reaching than the developed world for a number of reasons. First, medicines constitute around two-thirds of the total healthcare costs in developing countries compared with around 15–20 per cent in developed countries. Second, most of the drug expenditure is met by out-of-pocket household spending. Monopoly drug prices mean that the consumers are forced to make choices. The poor have to choose between seeking or not seeking treatment for a medical condition (World Bank 2002). The costs of treatment often results in cancelling a child's education, postponing a child's marriage, or running the family into deeper debt (GOI 2006d).

The main benefit to the developing countries of signing the TRIPS agreement was that it enabled them to access the markets of the developed countries. The poor countries have limited capability to export goods in the manufacturing or services sectors. Generally, the developing countries' economies are based on agricultural sector. Countries, such as India, China, and Brazil with substantial pharmaceutical and other manufacturing industries might be slightly better off than the rest of poor countries. The US and the European countries provide substantial subsidies to the agricultural sector, which they were to dismantle as a part of the deal to establish the WTO. So far, these countries have reneged on the undertaking to dismantle the subsidies. The position taken by the US and the EU has significantly reduced the scope of benefits of TRIPS to developing countries. The Nobel laureate economist Joseph Stiglitz (2002a) holds that the US and the Europe gained significantly from trade liberalisation and establishing of the WTO at the expense of poor countries. The Uruguay Round of negotiations opened the markets of the poor countries:

> ...to manufactured goods produced in the industrialised countries, but did not open up the markets of Europe and the US for agricultural products in which poor countries often have a comparative advantage...and...sub-Saharan Africa, the poorest region of the world, lost by about two per cent because of terms-of-trade effects.
>
> (Stiglitz 2002a, p. A20)

There is considerable cost to implement the WTO agreements. Finger and Schuler (2001) find that the implementation phase alone of the new responsibilities, including TRIPS, would cost each poor country around $150 million. This amount, accounting for the costs of acquiring and maintaining additional human and other resources, exceeds a year's development budget in many of the LDCs, suggest Finger and Schuler. The total economic costs of TRIPS and other agreements for developing countries are significantly higher but vary across countries.

A number of studies have examined the costs and benefits. For example, Finger (2002), studies the impact of TRIPS on different groups of countries. He uses a scale 0–9 to signify a net positive effect and a minus symbol to indicate a net negative effect of TRIPS. A score of 0 would equalise the costs and benefits. Finger concludes that while South Korea (−0.9) would be the *least* worse off and Brazil (−1.6) would be relatively *more* worse off than South Korea, and Mexico (−2.0) would be *most* worse off under TRIPS. This examination suggests that the costs of TRIPS outweigh the benefits in South Korea by 90 per cent, in Brazil by 160 per cent, and in Mexico 200 per cent. The US had the highest positive score (7.5), suggesting that the net gain to the US to be 750 per cent. It is not surprising that the US used all methods of persuasion, including coercion, to ensure intellectual property formed a part of the WTO ambit.

Oxfam (2002) estimates the annual costs of TRIPS in terms of high drugs prices at US$40 billion. The developed countries already had product patents for pharmaceuticals before the TRIPS agreements; thus, the additional costs primarily would come from developing countries, argues Oxfam. For example, the costs of pharmaceuticals are estimated to increase by US$425 million annually in Argentina alone, suggests Norgue (cited in Finger 2002, p. 13). Jack and Lanjouw (2005) suggest that because some countries have post-TRIPS higher drug prices, and nowhere are the prices lower, social welfare is certainly reduced. They further argue that 'because relatively poor countries have higher prices as a result of TRIPS, a welfare function with any aversion to inequality would suggest that welfare falls steeply' (p. 63).

Two studies compare the welfare costs of strengthening the IPRs in India to the society against the gains to the pharmaceutical companies. Dutta (2005) simulates the welfare effects of patents enforcement in India for a single drug still under patent in the US. India would incur over $1 million annually in net costs or a 7 per cent reduction in consumer welfare against a small profit to the global patent holder, concludes Dutta. Another study measures the impact of withdrawing four domestic pharmaceutical product groups in the fluoroquinolone sub-segment. Chaudhuri et al. (2003) find that in the absence of any price regulation and/or compulsory licensing, total annual welfare losses to the Indian economy would be around US$713 million. Of this, lost profits of domestic producers would constitute about US$50 million or 7 per cent of the total losses while the rest would be losses of consumer welfare. The financial benefits to MNCs would be about US$57 million.

These studies clearly suggest that costs of implementing TRIPS in developing countries, including India, are significantly higher than the benefits. Moreover, the costs are certain whereas the potential benefits are not certain and are a 'may be' at best. It is therefore not surprising that India, Brazil, and other developing countries vehemently opposed the inclusion of intellectual property in the Uruguay Round of negotiations. The threat of retaliatory sanctions by the US under the Special 301 provisions eventually forced the developing to sign the WTO agreements (Balasubramaniam 2002). Special 301 provisions remain the best example of a public law at the service of private industry in the US (Drahos 2002b).

9.3.2 Implications for developed countries

Healthcare costs in developed countries have also increased significantly because of strengthening of the patent regime in compliance with the TRIPS agreement. For example, the patent term in the US had to be extended from 17 years to 20 years under TRIPS. Applications filed on or after 8 June 1995 would be granted a 20-year term from the filing date (Patent Lens 2009). A study by Professor Schondelmeyer of University of Minnesota concludes that the cost of three-year extension of the patent term would exceed six billion dollars over the next 20 years. The annual savings lost by American consumers due to the delayed entry of less expensive generic drugs are likely to range from US$200 million to more than US$500 million, suggests the Schondelmeyer report (cited in Jorge 2004). A similar extension of three years of patent term in Canada on 25 products would cost Can$200 million annually in welfare losses, estimates Rhein (2001, p. 25). As this estimate represents only a fraction of the entire range of medicines, it can be safely assumed that the total size of the losses in Canada would be significantly higher.

As a part of the US–Australia FTA signed in 2004, Australia had to introduce a range of measures to strengthen patent protection, including the ever-greening of patents. Drahos et al. (2004) study the cost of these changes to Australia's regime and conclude that the cost of medicines under Australia's PBS would rise by at least a third. The Australia Institute concludes that the measures in the FTA are 'likely to delay the development of generic drugs in Australia by around three years' (cited in Drahos et al. 2004, p. 2). After examining the cost of five drugs for the period 2006–09, the Institute finds that the PBS would have to pay $1.1 billion more with the strengthened patent regime than without it. For the financial year 2005–06, the PBS contributed A$5.4 billion towards the costs of medicines. Against the findings of the Australia Institute measuring the impact on just five drugs, the estimates by Drahos et al. seem quite conservative. All three nations, namely the US, Canada, and Australia already had a stringent patent regime including pharmaceutical product patents. Therefore, deriving any additional benefits from extending the patent period in these countries would be highly unlikely. Yet, the increase in healthcare costs is significant. In the light of these studies, the Oxfam estimates for the developing countries (that is paying additional $40 billion to the developed countries) do not appear unreasonable.

9.3.3 Further implications for developing countries

Theoretically, the strengthening of patent regime may bring a range of benefits to India. The new regime may lead to increase in outsourcing, innovative activities, transfer of technology, and induce foreign investments in India. Some of these activities are, in fact, already taking place in India. Nonetheless, how much of these benefits can be attributed to TRIPS or globalisation remains questionable (see Chapters 4 and 5 for details). Most of these activities, in all likelihood, might have taken place in the absence of TRIPS. For example, MNCs save 50–60 per cent on costs by shifting some of their core functions to low-cost countries like India. Casting doubts over benefits of TRIPS to developing countries, Jorge (2004) suggests that not one new research and development or transfer of technology has taken place as a result of higher patents protection. Finger and Schuler (2001) conclude that the obligations 'imposed by the WTO agreements on customs,...intellectual property rights...can be characterized as the advanced countries saying to the others. Do it my way' (p. 23). The WTO agreements fail to consider the difference in the needs of the developing countries. Finger and Schuler suggest that these agreements including TRIPS are self-evident for inappropriate diagnosis and inappropriate remedy for developing countries. Pogge (2008) finds that the globalisation of pharmaceutical patents regime has imposed a very costly loss of freedom on the poor countries and cut off the poor patients' access to medicines. No illusions cast his judgement on costs and benefits, when he concludes that

> ...the TRIPS Agreement and its imposition are plainly unjust and will, in terms of the magnitude of harm caused, number among the largest human rights violations in history.
>
> (Pogge 2008, p. 76)

The problem stems from the flawed design of the TRIPS agreement. While TRIPS obliges developing nations to provide protection for drugs under patent, there is no obligation on MNCs to transfer technology or to invest into the developing nations. The absence of reciprocal obligations to commit both sides leads to an imbalance of costs and benefits. Moreover, as noted before, the costs are a certainty because member countries are committed to honour the agreement and the benefits remain a 'may be'. While it could be argued that it is too early to pass a judgement on the benefits, there could be no disagreement that the benefits would depend on the decisions made in the corporate offices of MNCs. A number of studies on multi-country theoretical models suggest that the incremental profits from extending stringent IPRs to poor countries may not stimulate significant additional R&D investments (see for example, Chin & Grossman 1990; Deardof 1992).

Three leading economists and Nobel Laureates have expressed serious concerns over the issues of globalisation, WTO, and TRIPS requirements forcing poor countries to adopt stringent patents regimes. Amartya Sen (2002) suggests that there are serious problems with the global institutional arrangements designed for a fair distribution of benefits including those for fair trade, medical initiatives, educational exchanges, facilities for technological dissemination. Sen believes that an overhaul of these arrangements is required for a number of reasons, not only for the 'inefficient and inequitable trade restrictions that repress exports from poor countries', but also for the 'patent laws that inhibit the use of lifesaving drugs for diseases like AIDS and that give inadequate incentive for medical research aimed at developing non-repeating medicines (such as vaccines)' (p. A6).

Jeffery Sachs (2000) argues that today's world is divided not by ideology but by technology. Countries and regions can be categorised in terms of their capabilities to innovate. North America, most of Europe, and Australia are *technological innovators*. These regions are the leaders in innovation. *Technological adopters* including Eastern Europe, parts of South America, South Africa, and India are the followers (imitators). The countries comprising most of Asia and Africa, as well as Central America, are the net users and termed as *technologically excluded*. Sachs suggests that there is an urgent need to address this great imbalance:

> ....At the government-to-government level, the international community should make a firm commitment to promote scientific and technological capacity in the poor countries. As part of this, rich countries should exercise restraint in the use of property rights. Rich countries are unilaterally asserting rights of private ownership over human and plant genetic sequences, or basic computer codes, or chemical compounds long in use in herbal medicines.

> These approaches are of dubious legitimacy and will worsen global inequities. A better balance needs to be struck between incentives for innovation on one hand, and the interests of the poorest on the other. (p. 8)

Joseph Stiglitz (2002a) argues that corporate advocates of protection of intellectual property rights have exaggerated its importance. The current structure of IPRs does not only not-serve its welfare purpose but has become harmful to the society, particularly to the developing countries. Stiglitz sees a need to review the structure and suggests that:

> .... Intellectual property rights, such as patents and trade marks, need to balance the interests of producers with those of users – not only users in developing countries, but researchers in developed countries. If we underprice the profitability of innovation to the inventor, we deter invention. If we overprice its cost to the research community and the end user, we retard its diffusion and beneficial effects on living standards. (p. A20)

There are a number of options for better balancing of the rights of innovators against those of the users of new drugs in poor countries. If the patents regime were to be totally abolished, new methods for providing incentives for innovative activities would need to be developed. Chaudhuri et al. (2003) suggest that 'patents may be a particularly inefficient way of encouraging discovery' (p. 7) and that a number of previously used alternatives, including direct subsidies for research, prizes and tournaments, and patent buyouts should be adopted. The advantage of direct subsidies is that the research can be directed to discover drugs of national interest. Groundbreaking innovations can be rewarded by cash-prizes in recognition for the contribution of the innovator. The downside of this approach may be insufficient stimulation to innovation if the recognition does not bring significant financial rewards. Alternatively, government could buyout a patent and place it in the public domain. This method should provide immediate access to the would-be manufacturers and increase market competition.

Frederic Scherer (2002), Professor Emeritus at Harvard University, has examined whether global welfare would be higher under a worldwide system of pharmaceutical product patents or under a framework that allows poor countries to free-ride on the new drugs developed in the industrialised countries. Scherer's study is based on Nordhaus (1969), which found a positive correlation between the number of new drugs developed annually and the R&D expenditure (cited in Scherer 2002). Scherer also examined how quasi-rents appropriated by innovators vary with the number of new drugs marketed. He considers three key variables in this examination: (1) the relative increase in producer's surplus that can be achieved through additional sales on patented drugs in poor countries; (2) the number of additional pharmaceutical products;[2] and (3) the average difference in the marginal utility of income for the third world relative to the first world. Accepting the notion that 'the richer a man becomes the less is the marginal utility of money to him' Scherer assigns 'greater weight to the benefits realised by poor nations than to those of rich nation inhabitants' (p. 4) and concludes that global welfare would be maximised by letting the poor countries free-ride on the patented drugs of the developed countries, at the expense of plausible discovery impairment. Scherer argues that during the debate over TRIPS someone like Kofi Annan should have said to the MNCs that:

> .... We will support your demand for strong patent rights throughout the world if you will commit 20 per cent of your research and development budgets to diseases specific to less-developed nations. (p. 9)

Scherer's argument is based on a trade-off struck between the pharmaceutical industry and the government in Canada. The industry persuaded the Canadian authorities to abandon its vigorously enforced compulsory licensing regime. In exchange, the industry agreed to establish in Canada R&D activities proportional to Canada's share of companies' drug sales. The TRIPS agreement commits member developing states to raise the protection of IPRs. But the agreement is silent on committing MNCs, the major beneficiaries of TRIPS, to undertake research for drugs specifically for tropical diseases. The industry, of its own initiative, has been reluctant to invest into discovering drugs for the poor countries.

Notwithstanding the above arguments, some experts warn against abolishing or weakening the patents regime. Their argument is based on the premise that drug prices always fall without patents and on patent expiry. Lower prices would mean a decline in profits, a fall in investment in R&D, leading in turn to a reduction in the number of new drugs discovered. For example, Lichtenberg (2006) estimates that if drug prices in certain cancer groups fell by 10 per cent, innovation would decline by 5–6 per cent in the long run. A steeper decline in prices would lead to more drastic reduction in innovation. Abbott and Vernon (2005) estimate that 40–50 per cent reduction in drug prices in the US would result in 30–60 per cent lesser innovative activities (cited in Lichtenberg 2006).

Hughes et al. (2002) suggest although accelerating generics entry would yield substantial gains in consumer surplus by providing greater access to the current stock of pharmaceuticals, the loss to future consumers would be significantly greater than the gains of today. In dollar value, society would lose three dollars in benefits of innovation for every dollar gained through easier access today, they argue.

Drug prices generally rise at a rate significantly higher than the CPI. Santerre and Vernon (2005) argue that if the drugs prices in the US had risen in line with the CPI between 1981 and 2000, the nation would have saved $319 billion, at a cost of 198 fewer new drugs brought into the market. They further conclude that at a cost of around $1.6 billion a drug, these costs are significantly lower than the welfare costs without the new drugs. The industry bodies representing innovator companies also vehemently oppose a review or weakening of TRIPS. For example, Harvey Bale, director-general of the International Federation of Pharmaceutical Manufacturers Association (IFPMA), warns that continuing debates on patents are hampering drug companies' decisions making on whether to enter into AIDS research (Bureau of National Affairs 2001).

The above studies suggest that while reduction in drug prices would benefit consumers in the short term, the decrease in future welfare would outweigh today's gains from lower drug prices. These studies implicitly advocate further strengthening of the patents regime, because they suggest the higher prices the society pays today, the more benefits the future consumers would get.

These studies overlook a number of factors, however. First, these studies fail to recognise the first-mover advantage in a fully competitive market. Being first is the most critical consideration in marketing pharmaceuticals. According to Gassmann et al. (2008):

> .... Time-to-market is extremely important in breakthrough pharmaceuticals. The first in the market captures between 40 per cent and 60 per cent of the market, and the second only around 15 per cent. Coming in third already means a negative business. (p. 16)

Hence, the market competition would propel companies to innovate for securing a competitive advantage. Second, the direction of innovation is determined by potential returns on investments and not by the number of patients or by the disease pattern. The future drugs are decided by the size of expected profits. The pharmaceutical R&D does not consider reducing the number of people suffering from specific diseases.

Third, many of the so-called innovations are minor modifications of existing compounds known as active pharmaceutical ingredients. Lleras-Muney and Lichtenberg (2002) suggest that 'there is a very large difference in the number of drugs and innovation: today are about 80,000 different drugs, but only about 2000 different active [pharmaceutical] ingredients' (p. 12). The APIs are the actual drugs with therapeutic value. The APIs are used in the manufacture of formulations in different strengths and forms such as injectibles, tablets, and so on. While the discovery of an API would be considered groundbreaking, developing new forms, strengths, and finding new uses of the same API would be minor modifications. The costs of discovering and developing a new API are significantly higher than minor modifications.

Several studies show that pharmaceutical R&D is driven by buying power of target market thereby ignoring the needs of poor nations. The R&D funds are invested more often into lifestyle and chronic diseases of wealthy nations for attractive returns. It is commonly argued that the high costs of drug development force the industry to charge higher prices for drugs. Scherer (2001) suggests that the relationship between the drug prices and the R&D costs is not seen in the right context and often misrepresented. He argues that in reality, it's the other way around: prices drive costs. The more a company can charge for a drug, the more it will spend on developing and marketing it. And that is perhaps why MNCs invest in innovations for drugs suitable for markets where the companies can charge the highest prices. The drugs developed specifically for poor countries would be low priced compared with those developed for the wealthy nations. It is not surprising therefore that the drug companies are less interested in developing drugs for tropical diseases. Even the innovative activities of the Indian pharmaceutical industry are focused on the lucrative markets of developed countries rather than developing drugs to fill the current vacuum of unmet needs of the domestic market.

Since the launch of Tagamet in 1976, the first blockbuster drug, the industry focus has been to search for the next blockbuster(s). Tagamet's huge financial success demonstrated that the introduction of just one blockbuster product could change the company fortunes and enable it to double or triple in size. This single event changed the mindset of pharmaceutical industry to what Nordmann (1997) calls 'blockbuster mentality' (p. 27). Recently, a spokesman for a MNC summed up the intentions of his company, which reflects the industry-wide view. He suggested that 'his company would rather find a cure for a bald American than a dying African' and that 'we have a financial commitment to our shareholders, therefore we have to focus on the $1.5 billion blockbuster drugs for the cardiovascular, metabolic and anti-infection market in the more developed countries' (cited in Chataway 2000, p. 21). Pfizer, the world's largest pharmaceutical company has earmarked $17 billion to scrutinise hundreds of drug and biotechnology companies over the next two years in search of the next blockbuster medicine (Pettypiece 2006). It is a pity that not even one-tenth or one-hundredth of that amount is reported to have been earmarked for the development of drugs relevant to poor countries. Blockbuster drugs are few and far between. Most of the new products are minor changes to existing drugs aimed at serving the rich nations. Less than 3 per cent of the global expenditure on pharmaceutical research is directed towards finding a cure for the so-called diseases of the poor nations. In the following quotation, Drahos (2002a) sums up nicely the dilemma the developing countries face with respect to access to medicines specific to their needs: 'If the poor want more patent-based R&D for malaria they will have to hope that it overtakes obesity and impotence as a problem in Western societies' (p. 6).

Kremer (2002) suggests that diarrhoeal diseases, malaria, measles, and tetanus collectively account for more than four million deaths annually in poor countries. Another half million deaths are caused by pertussis and syphilis. Yet, pharmaceutical companies have shown little interest in tropical diseases, such as malaria and tuberculosis simply because of lack of potential for hefty returns. Tuberculosis (TB) alone annually kills nearly 1.7 million worldwide (WHO 2002c). India accounts for one-third of the global TB burden and has the largest number of sufferers with active TB in the world (Misra et al. 2003). In many cases, the problem is not that there are no medicines for the disease. The problem is that parasites and bacteria develop resistance to drugs commonly used to treat malaria and tuberculosis rendering those drugs ineffective (WHO 2007). The second line drugs and then third line drugs need to be developed to stay ahead of parasites and bacteria. It is a process of continuous research and development to find effective treatment. Lehman (2003) suggests that traditional folks medicines are most likely to provide the key material of possible new drugs to address local and regional disease burdens. But such innovation has to be backed up by favourable government policies that is currently not the case in poor countries, argues Lehman.

Moran (2001) suggests that 1223 new drugs were developed between 1975 and 1996, of which, only 11 were for tropical diseases. Of these 11, 5 were spin-offs from veterinary research (humans share some diseases with dogs and horses). A handful came from US military research during the Vietnam War when tropical diseases were, briefly, an issue. Three came from pharmaceutical industry R&D, often accidentally while looking for cures for Western diseases (Moran 2001). A recent survey published in The Economist (2005a) indicates finds that of around 1500 drugs launched in the last three decades, less than 20 were tropical disease specific. This share amounts to around 0.01 per cent of the drug discovery output.

About three quarter of the global population lives in the developing and LDCs but consumes 14 per cent of the global drug supply (Torbet 1999). Based on *The Economist* study noted above, on average, 50 new drugs were discovered annually over the last 30 years. More recently, the annual average of new drugs introduced has been closer to 20. It would be too ambitious to expect that implementing TRIPS would greatly improve drug discovery for the diseases in the poor countries. Hypothetically, if just one drug was annually developed for the tropical diseases because of the poor countries agreeing to TRIPS, this would constitute 5 per cent of total R&D output of the more recent average. Undoubtedly, the development of just one new drug every year could save many lives in the developing world. But each new drug developed specifically for the diseases of the poor countries would come at a cost of $40 billion,[3] compared with the estimated costs[4] of $800 million for a new drug for the rest of the world. The poor countries would be paying 50 times more for a new drug than their wealthy counterparts. Although this hypothesis would seem like a rough deal for the poor countries, even this scenario would be highly unlikely despite TRIPS. The irony is that development of a new drug would make it available on the market, but not necessarily affordable to the poor. This situation would not significantly differ from today's reality where millions of poor remain without access to medicines. Khosla and Hunt (2008) in their report titled *Human Rights Guidelines for Pharmaceutical Companies in Relation to Access to Medicines* estimate that high prices deprive more than 2 billion people access to essential medicines in poor countries. They also suggest that improving access to medicines could annually save 10 million lives. So, what can be done to improve upon the current situation?

9.3.4 Recent investigations of protection of pharmaceutical patents

Of the recent literature available on the issue of intellectual property, especially on pharmaceutical patents, two reports are highly important. The first of these is a report of the Commission on Intellectual Property Rights (CIPR) (2002). The CIPR was established and based in London in 2001. The second report is the report of the European Commission's inquiry of the pharmaceutical sector (discussed later in the section). The terms of reference required the CIPR to particularly consider the interests of the developing countries. The CIPR was made up of experts from diverse backgrounds from a mix of developing and developed countries. The tasks assigned to the CIPR were to consider:

- how national IPR regimes could best be designed to benefit developing countries within the context of international agreements, including TRIPS;
- how the international framework of rules and agreements might be improved and developed – for instance in the area of traditional knowledge – and the relationship between IPR rules and regimes covering access to genetic resources; and
- the broader policy framework needed to complement intellectual property regimes including for instance controlling anti-competitive practices through competition policy and law.

The experts visited a range of countries, including Brazil, China, India, and South Africa. They also consulted senior government officials, the private sector as well as NGOs across Europe and the US. The CIPR commissioned 17 research papers and held 8 workshops in London. A large conference was also held in London in February 2002 with a view to identifying the issues and exploring the scope for moving the issues forward. The CIPR submitted its final report in September 2002.

The CIPR report recognises the diversity in the development stages and innovative capabilities among developing countries. For example, China, India, and some smaller developing countries have world class capacity in a number of science and technology sectors, such as space, nuclear technology, biotechnology, pharmaceuticals, software development, and aviation. By comparison, this capacity is relatively weak in countries in Sub-Saharan Africa (except South Africa). This diversity plays an important part in reaching the conclusions of the report.

The report considers the impact of IPRs in the developed as well as in the developing countries and is explicitly concerned that 'the costs of getting the IP system "wrong" in a developing country are likely to be far higher than in developed countries' (p. 4). This is because developed countries generally have adequate checks and balances in the competition regulations (e.g. Antitrust law) to prevent the IPRs inappropriately affecting public interest. This is not the case in most developing countries, making them considerably more vulnerable to inappropriate IP regimes. Thus, the report stresses that the 'standards of IP protection that may be suitable for developed countries may cause greater costs than benefits when applied in developing countries' (p. 5). To achieve an optimal balance in costs and benefits, the IPRs would vary depending on economic and social circumstances of each country. The report emphasises that IPRs should be considered as a tool to help society in the promotion of fulfilling human economic and social rights. The most fundamental human rights should not become subordinates to the requirement of IP protection under any circumstances. The IPRs are granted by governments for limited times whereas human rights are inalienable and universal.

The report is mindful that the granting of IPRs effectively provides benefits to those who have the knowledge and the inventive power, and increases the costs of access to those without. It is particularly apprehensive about industry interests overriding basic human rights in public policy formulation. It holds that:

> .... IP rights nowadays generally treated as economic and commercial rights, as is the case in TRIPS, and are more often held by companies rather than individual inventors. But describing them as 'rights' should not be allowed to conceal the very real dilemmas raised by their application in developing countries, where the extra costs they impose may be at the expense of the essential prerequisites of life for poor people.
>
> (Commission on Intellectual Property Rights 2002, p. 6)

The CIPR warns that IP policy in the developing countries is often formulated on the interests of the 'producer' and the end consumer is generally ignored. During IPR talks, negotiating teams from developed countries are mainly influenced by producer interests, because they see export opportunities. Developing countries, the consumers of IP, are often too weak to represent their own interests against those of the developed countries. The developing countries in this context are *second comers* in a world that has been shaped by the *first comers*. The report makes it very clear that IP regimes should be devised on the basis of a country's own needs and the level of economic development. It explicitly contends that:

> ... intellectual property systems may, if we are not careful, introduce distortions that are detrimental to the interests of developing countries. Very 'high' standards of protection may be in the public interest in developed countries with highly sophisticated scientific and technological infrastructures, but this does not mean the same standards are appropriate in all developing countries.
>
> (Commission on Intellectual Property Rights 2002, p. 8)

The main recommendations of the report are as follows:

- to ensure that global IP systems are designed to 'contribute to the development of developing countries by stimulating innovation and technology transfer relevant to them', while also providing them the 'products of technology at the most competitive prices possible'; and
- to ensure that 'the IP system facilitates, rather than hinders, the application of the rapid advances in science and technology for the benefit of developing countries' (p. 8).

With respect to pharmaceuticals, the report specifically recommends that developing countries should:

- limit the scope of subject matter that can be patented;
- apply standards such that only patents which meet strict requirements for patentability are granted and that the breadth of each patent is commensurate with the inventive contribution and the disclosure made;
- facilitate competition by restricting the ability of the patentees to prohibit others from building on or designing around patented inventions; and
- provide extensive safeguards to ensure that patent rights are not exploited inappropriately (p. 49).

The Indian Patents Act appears, to a certain extent, to have incorporated the recommendations of the report. Section 3(d) explicitly limits the scope of patentable subject matter, which has become a subject of international debate. It is designed to encourage genuine inventions of useful technologies but prevent granting rights to frivolous innovations. The application of the strict standards of Section 3(d) has been challenged by

MNCs (e.g. Novartis)[5] and the cases are before Indian courts. The third recommendation implicitly refers to prevent ever-greening and excessive patenting, which would block further innovation. The wide range of provisions for compulsory licensing in the Indian Act could be seen as a testimony to the final recommendation of the report.

The CIPR report also expresses concerns about the standards of patenting being lowered in the developed countries, particularly in the US, because too many patents are issued for inventions that are trivial and pressure exerted on patent examiners. Many of the patents would not prove valid if challenged in courts (p. 126). This concern is also shared by other experts. For example, Wyllie (2005) argues that the pharmaceutical industry should consider itself fortunate that 'definitions of novelty and innovation by the USA and the European patent offices are seldom rigorously applied' (p. 1359).

Following the CIPR report, two separate enquiries were undertaken in the US. First, the Federal Trade Commission (along with the Department of Justice) investigated a wide range of issues related to patenting. The FTC report titled *To Promote Innovation: The Proper Balance of Competition and Patent Law and Policy* was published in 2003. This report considers that:

> ....Competition can stimulate innovation. Competition among firms can spur the invention of new or better products or more efficient processes. Firms may race to be the first to market an innovative technology. Companies may invent lower cost manufacturing processes, thereby increasing their profits and enhancing their ability to compete. Competition can prompt firms to identify consumers' unmet needs and develop new products or services to satisfy them.
>
> (Federal Trade Commission 2003, pp. 1–2)

But patents also can stimulate innovation. The FTC report emphasises that the US Constitution authorises Congress 'to promote the progress of science and useful arts, by securing for limited times to... inventors the exclusive right to their respective...discoveries' (p. 2). There is a need to find a balance between IPRs and competition. While granting patents on obvious invention can harm competition, overzealous Antitrust enforcement can undermine the innovation that patents promote. Similar to the CIPR report, the FTC report also warns against excessive and frivolous patenting. Because one firm's questionable patent may lead its competitors to abandon further research in the areas that the patent improperly covers. The FTC report is explicitly concerned that:

> ...More patents in more industries and with greater breadth are not always the best ways to maximize consumer welfare. A questionable patent can raise costs and prevent competition and innovation that otherwise would benefit consumers. (p. 18)

The FTC report makes a particular reference to the biotech industry in which firms refrain from entering or continuing research projects in order to avoid infringing questionable patents. In *Bonito Boats v. Thunder Craft Boats*, (1989), the Supreme Court held that 'free competition is the base line on which the patent system's incentive to creative effort depends' (p. 3).

Some of the recommendations of the FTC report are as follows.

> *Publication of all patent applications 18 months after filing.*
>
> Until recently, patents were only published when granted. Early publication would avoid other firms investing (between the filing date and issuance of patent) in innovative activities that might infringe the patent to be issued. India already publishes filed patent applications, which provide the basis for pre-grant opposition.
>
> *Consider possible harm to competition – along with other possible benefits and costs – before extending the scope of patentable subject matter.*
>
> The FTC warns that over the last two decades, patentable subject matter has expanded at the expense of market competition creating an imbalance in favour of patentees. The pendulum needs to swing back to centre to rebalance. The current Indian Patents Act appears to be specific about what can be patented. So far the Indian courts have applied the law in the right spirit favouring the consumer and the Indian industry.
>
> *Challenges to the validity of a patent to be determined based on a 'Preponderance of the Evidence'.*
>
> At present, an issued patent is viewed valid in the US. The onus is on the challenger 'to prove its invalidity by clear and convincing evidence' (p. 8). The FTC finds this requirement unjustified. An overly strong presumption of a patent's validity is inappropriate. The

FTC suggests that courts should require only a 'preponderance of the evidence' to rebut the presumption of validity.

Allow post-grant review of and opposition to patents.

An administrative procedure is recommended for post-grant review and opposition to allow for meaningful challenges to patent validity short of federal court litigation. In India, application opposing a patent can be filed within 12 months from the date of grant.

The FTC report is mindful of patent litigations in US courts and the large funds required to fight them. The US would reduce patent litigations if it introduced pre-grant opposition similar to India. This would not jeopardise the innovative activities of competitors and save in litigation costs. This report highlights the lax practices adopted in issuing patents. While competition and patents both induce innovation, non-genuine (invalid) patents unnecessarily block competitors' innovative activities, finds the report.

The second enquiry in the US was undertaken by the National Academies Board on Science Technology and Economic Policy. The report *A Patent System for the 21st Century* was published in 2004. This report considers that the patent system has worked well for 200 years with a high level of innovation. While this report agrees, to a great extent, that a significant number of patents granted are sub-standard, it does not see a need for fundamental changes. This report also recommends a review after issuance of a patent (post-grant opposition). It also recommends limited protection from patent infringement liability be afforded to academic research. In 2002, Federal Court ruled that even non-commercial scientific research was not exempt and refused to provide to relief to university research. Both enquiries in the US have highlighted the problem areas within the current system of patents. The current system appears to allow exploitation that results in blocking rather than inducing innovation. This raises the cost of innovation as well as delaying further progress.

In the UK, the House of Commons appointed a Health Committee to examine the expenditure, administration, and policy of the Department of Health and its associated bodies. The report *The Influence of the Pharmaceutical Industry* was published in 2005. While the investigation does not explicitly focus on patents, it finds the current direction of pharmaceutical R&D less than satisfactory. The report had no doubt in industry's ability 'to produce excellent science and important drugs' but questioned 'its ability to put the health of the nation consistently before the needs and expectations of its shareholders' (House of Commons Health Committee 2005, p. 97). It expresses concerns that in recent years, large pharmaceutical companies have become ever more focused on a marketing-based approach. The focus of new drugs should be on increasing real therapeutic benefits for sufferers and not just raising revenues. Sir Richard Sykes'[6] remarks in the report succinctly describe the situation pharmaceutical industry finds itself today:

> .... Today the industry has got a very bad name. That is very unfortunate for an industry that we should look up to and believe in, and that we should be supporting. I think there have to be some big changes.
>
> (House of Commons Health Committee 2005, p. 101)

The report acknowledges that in a free market society, 'pharmaceutical companies will inevitably continue to be the dominant influence in deciding what research is undertaken' (p. 5). This cannot however continue unchallenged because 'we need an industry, which is led by the values of its scientists not those of its marketing force', concludes the report (p. 6). The recommendations focus on improving and making the regulatory process transparent currently dominated by secrecy. While no patent specific issues were investigated, the general conduct of the industry does not appear to have the spirit the industry reaps the rewards for. The report finds that on numerous occasions, the industry withheld critical test data to obtain marketing approvals. The industry influenced the decisions of the authorities and pressurised them to accelerate the approval leading to authorities compromising on efficacy and safety issues. In recent years, a number of drugs, such as Vioxx have been withdrawn from markets for safety reasons.

9.3.4.1 European Commission inquiry

In January 2008, the European Commission launched an investigation into the pharmaceutical sector. There were several reasons for this enquiry. First, the Commission had received information suggesting that competition in the sector may be restricted or distorted. Second, the number of innovative novel medicines reaching the market had declined. Third, introduction of generics had been delayed, as compared with what might be generally expected. The scope of this inquiry was limited to prescription drugs and to the period 2000–07. A preliminary report was presented in Brussels on 28 November 2008 to coincide with the public consultations.

The inquiry considered among other things certain blockbusters with patent expiry falling in the period of investigation and reports on certain patent settlements. A range of pharmaceutical companies, most of them originators but also some generic companies, were selected and unannounced inspections were conducted at these companies. These inspections resulted in more than 20,000 pages being copied, bringing to light 'documents that could not have been gathered otherwise' (e.g. through information requests) (European Commission 2008, p. 24). Subsequently, the inquiry met with other stakeholders, including industry associations representing originator as well as generic companies, consumer groups, insurance companies, doctors, and pharmacists. More than 200 questionnaires were sent out to largest originator and generic companies. In total, more than 6000 submissions were received making it 'one of the most thorough investigations of the European pharmaceutical sector ever' (European Commission 2008, p. 25).

The report emphasises the importance of patents in the sector to allow originator companies to recoup their substantial investments and reward their innovative efforts. However, the preliminary findings also suggest that originator companies develop and practise defensive patenting strategies primarily to block the development of new competing products. The following findings of the report provide a strategic view of the industry behaviour with regard to exploiting the patents system:

> .... Originator companies have designed and implemented strategies (a 'tool-box' of instruments) aimed at ensuring continued revenue streams for their medicines..... the successful implementation of these strategies include filing for up to 1300 patents EUwide in relation to a single medicine (so-called 'patent clusters'), engaging in disputes with generic companies leading to nearly 700 cases of reported patent litigation, concluding settlement agreements with generic companies which may delay generic entry and intervening in national procedures for the approval of generic medicines. The additional costs caused by delays to generic entry can be very significant for the public health budgets and ultimately the consumer.
>
> (European Commission 2008, p. 401)

The concerns raised by the above reports highlight a significant shift from and within the concept of patenting. It appears that the scope of patents has been significantly widened in recent years. Notwithstanding the patent system needs to keep pace with the development of new technologies, granting patents for frivolous innovations has lowered the quality of patents. Companies employ considerable resources on blocking introduction of competitor products through unnecessary and excessive patenting, which is counterproductive to the spirit of patents. On the one hand, these practices raise the costs of R&D for competing research companies (e.g. for royalties). On the other hand, the introduction of new products is delayed. In both cases, the consumer pays higher costs.

9.4 Conclusions

This chapter set out to examine whether the TRIPS agreement was appropriate for the developing countries. A large number of developed countries did not introduce pharmaceutical product patents until they had achieved certain stage of economic development. The TRIPS agreement disregards this reality and forces all member states to adopt stringent patent protection, including pharmaceutical product patents, irrespective of their stage of development. The TRIPS is a 'one size fits all' regime creating numerous problems for the poor in developing countries. Copying technologies developed in the advance economies is a necessary step to developing innovative capabilities. While most of the developed countries, including the US, benefited from copying discoveries and inventions of others, TRIPS denies developing countries the same opportunity.

Costs of TRIPS are considerable and certain, while benefits remain a 'may be' at best. Healthcare costs to all countries, including the US, have increased significantly as a consequence of TRIPS. But the developing countries are the biggest losers under the new regime. Large pharmaceutical companies based in the developed countries are the biggest winners.

A number of inquiries into the pharmaceutical industry in general and into the patenting issues in particular were conducted in recent years. The reports are explicit about costs being greater than benefits of raising standards of IPRs in developing countries to the same level as that of developed countries. An unambiguous concern was that the number of patents per product filed particularly in the pharmaceutical industry was very high. In addition, the research priorities in the pharmaceutical industry were determined by its marketing force and not by the value of its scientists.

10
Which Way Ahead?

10.1 Introduction

The primary aim of this chapter is to consider alternatives to improve access to medicines in poor countries. This chapter seeks to add to the current debate on TRIPS and its appropriateness for the pharmaceutical industry. On the one hand, leading economists suggest significant changes to the TRIPS agreement labelled as too stringent and denying access to medicines in developing countries. Equally, there are calls from the *big pharma*[1] not to dismantle or weaken the TRIPS patent regime in any way. Because doing so would be counter-productive, argues the industry. Considering the dichotomy of the views, the level of controversy TRIPS has raised is not surprising. The wide coverage in the literature is a testimony to the significance of the controversy. Of all the intellectual property within TRIPS, the issue of pharmaceutical product patents has been the most controversial one (Alsegård 2004). However, the TRIPS agreement is a set of rules on which all WTO members agreed. It may not suit the circumstances and interests of every member state; nevertheless, it is an agreed set of rules.

10.2 Alternative models

This section considers a range of measures to improve upon the current system of patents. These measures could be viewed as a form of compromises in the bigger scheme of things. The models considered below are not exhaustive but selected on their significance relative to their role in the possible development of new drugs.

10.2.1 Differential pricing

Differential pricing refers to a practice under which products are sold at a high price in high-income countries and at low prices in poor countries. It should be clear from the outset that differential pricing would apply to patented products, because other firms are barred from competing. Advocates of this strategy suggest that charging differential prices in different markets is a better way to provide medicine at affordable prices than a global price. For example, Danzon (2001) argues that low drug prices in poor countries would contribute to increasing access to medicines, while prices in high-income countries would help companies recoup R&D investments. This pricing method is a way to balance between providing medicine to the needy and charging a higher price to those who can afford to pay for it. Different price regimes in different markets allow firms to continue to invest in the R&D activities as the returns from the rich nations make up for the low prices in the poor nations.

The concept of differential pricing sounds fair to consumers in both groups of nations. If drug prices were adjusted to buyer's ability to pay, there could be a range of prices for the same products across countries with different income levels. A recent World Bank study provides a guide, which could be considered for designing the pricing structure. According to the World Bank (2003), countries with less than $745 GDP per capita are classified as low-income countries. Countries with higher than $745 GDP per capita have a range of classifications: namely, $745–$2975 (lower middle income), $2976–$9206 (upper middle income), and more than $9206 (high income).

Companies would need to further adjust the pricing levels because upper and lower gap in second and third income groups is far too large. While the income structure in the World Bank report provides a guide, it does not reflect the reality on the ground. For example, India's rising GDP per capita might place the country in the lower middle income bracket and raise the prices above the lowest mark. This would be counter-productive because more than 800 million Indians do not have access to medicines (WHO 2004b) and India arguably has the world's lowest drug prices.

There are two issues with the concept of differential pricing. First, companies run the risk of parallel trade, that is unauthorised export of drugs from low price countries into high price countries, because 'arbitrage is a natural reaction to price differences' (Barton 2001, p. 11). This problem was recently highlighted when GSK's low priced HIV/AIDS drugs destined for Africa were found being sold in Belgium, Germany, and the Netherlands (Darbourne 2003). Similarly, differential pricing has been the centre of a recent dispute within the EU. The MNCs had supplied products to Portuguese pharmacies at a lower rate than their counterparts in northern European countries. The products intended for sale in Portugal were found selling in France and other higher priced markets. Second, as suggested by Kremer (2002), differential pricing could unleash political backlash from consumer groups in high-income countries once they find out significant price differences pressing for lower prices at home. For example, the case of importing ARVs into South Africa in 2001, to a great extent, exposed the significant difference in price of the same drug manufactured by different companies. If the ARVs cost just a few hundred dollars in Brazil, the US AIDS activists might object to paying $10,000 per year (Kremer 2002).

10.2.2 Differential patenting

Under differential patenting, the world would be divided in two broad categories: namely, the rich and the poor countries. Pharmaceutical firms will have to choose between developed (assumed rich) and developing (assumed poor) when applying for patent protection for drugs for global diseases. Products developed for global diseases, such as cancer or cardiovascular, would be patented in the rich countries (e.g. US), but patents would not be enforced in poor countries. This would allow generics to enter the poor markets forcing down the prices in the poor countries. Should the patentee sue the generics manufacturer for patent infringement in poor countries, its patent in the rich market would be deemed invalid, suggests Lanjouw (2002a), the pioneering advocate of this approach. She suggests that the basis of the proposed framework already exists in the US. Under the current US law, inventors must apply first for a US patent for an invention made in the US. The law in the UK also has similar requirements. Patent applications in other countries must not be filed within six months of the filing date in the US (or within six weeks in the UK). For subsequent applications in other countries, the inventor must obtain a 'foreign filing licence' from the US patent and trademark office (PTO). Under the proposed mechanism for a cancer drug for example, the applicant would need to make a declaration to the US PTO similar to the following:

> ....I, the undersigned, request a license to make foreign patent filings covering the invention described in US patent application No. X, with the understanding that this permission will not be used to

> restrict the sale or manufacture of drugs for Cancer in India by suing for patent infringement in India.
>
> (Lanjouw 2002a, p. 8)

Lanjouw argues that originators would recoup their investments in the rich markets where they would have monopoly pricing. For the fear of jeopardising the patent in a rich market, originators would not object to generics entering the poor markets. This would extend access to medicines in the poor countries. Drugs for tropical diseases have almost no sale potential in rich countries, and as such would be patented in poor countries. The problem with this approach is that enforcing patents in poor countries would push up the prices but not create purchasing power. In the absence of purchasing power, a reality in poor countries, how are the returns on investments going to be generated? Kremer (2002) also points out, Lanjouw's 'proposal is robust to errors in the list of global diseases ... [because] ... incentives for R&D on diseases of developing countries are inadequate' (pp. 77–8). New ways to provide incentives for investors or finance the R&D would still be required. International assistance programmes as well as public policies in poor countries could incorporate funding the essential medicines.

10.2.3 Donating drugs

Under this proposal, the industry simply donates the needed drugs to the poor countries. Advocates of this approach suggest that there is no need to take out patents or adopt differential pricing strategies, because there is always a chance of these strategies backfiring (e.g. parallel trade). For example, Kremer (2002) argues that pharmaceutical firms in wealthy countries could benefit from donating drugs to poor countries. Because this 'could bolster firms' reputations, rather than posing a public relations challenge in maintaining prices in developed nations' (p. 78). He suggests that government in developed nations provide enhanced tax deductions to pharmaceutical firms that make donations of approved drugs to developing nations. The current provision by the US government is based on the product's manufacturing cost, which is often very low. Kremer therefore suggests that developed nations provide a tax relief based on either on a given percentage of the US price (or in that country) of the drug to be donated or on estimate of social benefits or measured in dollars per Disability Adjusted Life Years (DALY) saved.

A number of issues in Kremer's proposal need to be considered. First, Barton (2001) finds the concept of donating drugs 'wonderful and ... extremely helpful' but questions the long-term sustainability of the concept (p. 16). In 2000, Boehringer Ingelheim announced to supply Nevirapine free for five years to prevent mother-to-child transmission of HIV. Merck has also been donating Ivermectin to treat river blindness for a long time. However, a commitment to supplying drugs at marginal cost may be a better option in the long run, argues Barton. Under the strategy adopted by UNAIDS, Boehringer Ingelheim, Bristol-Myers Squibb (BMS), GSK, and Merck have agreed to supply Rwanda, Senegal, and Uganda drugs at concessional rates, which is more sustainable than simply donating drugs (Barton 2001).

Second, the concept of donating drugs is based on voluntary offer. Thus, an element of risk is there that firms may not continue to donate if such donation did not suit their political or commercial interests. And that is why, when producers wanted to donate ARVs to African countries, the 'activists insisted on countries paying for the drugs at low prices' (Kremer 2002, p. 78). Third, the quality of donated drugs is often questionable. Past experiences of the WHO in Albania and Macedonia suggest that many gifts of unusable drugs were donated (cited in Saunders 1999). A number of other countries, where disasters aid was provided, have had the same experience. Armenian earth quake, Mitch and George hurricanes in Central America, the civil war in Rwanda, Sierra Leone, Bosnia, Croatia, and many countries of the former Soviet Union had all accumulated large amounts of unusable donated drugs. According to a Tanzanian nun, in-charge of drug supply at a remote mission hospital, 'only 10 per cent [of the donated drugs] were useful and the rest ended up on the hospital bonfire' (cited in Saunders 1999, p. 7).

10.2.4 Orphan Drug Act as a model

Under the US law, 'orphan drug' is described as a drug for a disease or medical condition affecting less than 200,000 persons in the US (Government of the United States 2008). This number of patients is far too small to generate sufficient returns on investments for a new drug. Recognising this, the US Congress passed the Orphan Drug Act in 1983 providing incentives to invest into developing drugs for diseases in this category. This Act offered economic incentives, including R&D tax credits, clinical research grants programmes, accelerated approval process at the FDA, and a guaranteed seven-year market exclusivity from the date of marketing approval (Grabowski 2002). This exclusivity was independent of any patent protection afforded by the PTO. While less than 10 drugs for orphan diseases were discovered in ten years preceding the Orphan Drug Act, more than 200 drugs and biologicals were developed between 1983 and 1999 (Government of the United States 2008; Grabowski 2002).

Grabowski (2002, 2005) argues that the lack of potential returns places tropical diseases in a condition similar to the orphan diseases in the US. He suggests an Act similar to the Orphan Drug Act at the international level to provide exclusive rights. He further suggests that funding for developing these drugs could come from governments, NGOs, or public–private partnerships.

The Orphan Drug Act works well in the US because of purchasing power of the population. The added exclusivity extends the number of years, in which the innovator can recoup its investments compensating for the small patient population. In contrast, the poor in developing countries do not have the same purchasing power. Not only the funding for the development of the drug has to be arranged, but also the purchase of drug has to be funded publicly or through international aid. An Act at the international level similar to the Orphan Drug Act could work in conjunction with the TRIPS agreement.

10.2.5 Incremental value based rewards

This concept refers to variable rewards based on the level of innovation. A groundbreaking innovation would warrant a full 20-year protection, while an incremental innovation (minor improvement) would be judged for its contribution and rewarded accordingly. This type of system of rewarding would be ideal for pharmaceutical industry, where new inventions are rare and minor improvements are quite common. Hollis (2005) suggests that pharmaceutical markets do not function effectively enough to stimulate drug research and development. This is because on the one hand, significant proportions of research are focused on drugs with relatively little incremental therapeutic value. On the other hand, inadequate incentives are provided to innovate in areas of great therapeutic value. Hollis suggests a system to reward innovators based on incremental therapeutic value of their innovation. The more therapeutic value over existing drugs a new drug would offer, the more benefits the innovators would receive. This would align innovators' incentives with the social objectives and possibly lead to a better way to allocating R&D investment. Hollis further suggests that the rewards would be paid directly to innovators and patents compulsorily licensed to enable competitive pricing, which, to a certain extent, would solve the problem of access to essential drugs.

In theory, rewarding innovators on incremental value would be a fair system. The implementation might become complex, however.

Assessing the incremental value requires an unbiased approach by the authorities that is acceptable to innovators. Failure to get agreements would only lead to litigations unnecessarily wasting valuable human and other resources. Furthermore, this concept does not treat all inventions equally, and as such, would contravene the TRIPS agreement.

10.2.6 Advance purchase commitments

Advance purchase commitments (APCs) refer to one or more sponsors (e.g. governments) committing to a minimum price and volume for an eligible product. The APCs are considered suitable for developing vaccines for immunising large populations in poor countries. If no suitable product were developed, no payments would be made (Berndt et al. 2005). This model is based on the experience of the UK. In 1994, the UK government committed in advance to purchase the treatment for brain swelling (Foroohar 2006). Developing countries have about 90 per cent of the global disease burden, yet only 3 per cent of the R&D expenditure of the pharmaceutical industry is directed to address the needs of these countries. The current gap in R&D required and R&D available highlights the enormity of the problem. Numerous promising drug projects, particularly for the disease of the poor are dropped for the lack of funding (Berry 2005). The APCs guarantee minimum sales helping investors calculate the level of risk they can take.

Kremer and Glennerster (2004) suggest that under the APC model, developer of malaria or HIV vaccine could receive around $3 billion. This figure is based immunising 200 million people at $15 to $20 each in developed countries. In developing countries, the price could be dropped to $1-a-shot. Miguel and Kremer (2002) suggest that school-based mass treatment of intestinal worm infections would cost as little as $7 per DALY saved and such treatments could reduce the disease burden by more than 70 per cent (cited in Kremer 2002). A major advantage of this model is that no public monies are committed if no positive results shown. As Light (2005) points out, a major drawback of this model is that it is more suitable to 'big pharma' strategy than small innovators. Only large pharmaceutical companies could invest hundreds of millions of dollars in a gamble of no certainty of success. Lofgren (2005) concludes that an effective response to the neglected disease calamity requires more than what the APC model offers.

10.2.7 Public–Private Partnerships (PPPs)

In recent years, another model has emerged to address the 'neglected disease' dilemma. Under this model, the risk is shared by sponsors/governments providing part of the R&D funding. In contrast, the APC model requires the developer to fund its own R&D with only successful products providing guaranteed sales. Unlike the APC model, the PPP model is suitable for all small and large innovators. In 2004, a plethora of 92 PPP collaborative projects were in progress with promising results. The list of sponsors included the Medicines for Malaria Venture, the TB Alliance, the Institute for OneWorld Health, and the Drugs for Neglected Diseases Initiative. According to Moran (2005), 63 of these projects were for neglected diseases, with 2 drugs close to registration. A further 18 drugs were at advance stages of clinical trials and 8–9 new drugs were expected by 2010.

Around 80 per cent of the funding for PPP projects has come from private philanthropists, such as the Bill and Melinda Gates (BMG) Foundation (Moran 2005). The BMG Foundation contributed $450 million, Wellcome Trust (the UK) $27.1 million, and the Canadian Institutes of Health Research $4.5 million. The 'Grand Challenges in Global Health' provides a good example of how funding is distributed under the PPP model. According to Scrip News (2005d), $436 million have been allocated to scientific institutes under the collaborated Public–Private Partnerships worldwide.

Most of the projects involve developing new delivery methods for vaccines using latest (e.g nano, needle-free) technologies. The new methods of delivery would offer significant advantages over conventional methods. First, the new methods would eliminate the need for administering vaccines by qualified medical personnel. Second, administering new vaccines would not require any equipment such as syringes. New vaccines are expected to be developed in form of powder or a spray. Third, these methods would significantly increase immunisation at the village level. Other projects involving vaccines for malaria, TB, HIV, and vector would be expected to save many lives in the developing world if successful.

10.2.8 Open access

This model refers to open (unrestricted) access to data, ideas, and insight for researchers in science and technology (Barton 2003). The rationale behind this model is that a research scientist or engineer with access to the work of predecessors is more effective than without it. And his/her contribution to scientific/technological progress will be greater if others have access to his/her work. In recent years, 'open access' model has gained significant attention for two main reasons.

First, the current framework in the US limits licensing of publicly funded research to domestic firms (Maskus & Reichman 2004). Second, the EU has also introduced similar framework; thus, both the US and the EU placing companies/researchers from foreign countries at significant disadvantage. These are protectionist measures, which raise the cost of research and erect unnecessary barriers to advances in research.

Without open access model, firms based in developed countries are not disadvantaged to the extent as the firms in the developing countries are. Because of public funding rules noted above, firms based in the EU gain against the losses in the US. But firms from developing countries get locked out from participating in research in advance technologies. The quality of research in the poor countries could be as good as that of those firms based in the US or the EU, but they lack the resources to advancements. Consequently, developing countries remain unable to develop capabilities to match those in the developed world. This raises the cost of acquisition of new technologies and slows the pace of development in low- and middle-income countries.

Experts such as Barton and Maskus (2004) suggest a multilateral agreement under the WTO to ensure global 'open access'. They provide the following reasons in their justification for such an agreement:

- the recent 'significant policy shift toward making knowledge a private commodity, despite its inherent character as a public good, raising fundamental questions for science, education, and the diffusion of information';
- despite the promise held that stronger technology protection under TRIPS 'would expand flows of knowledge to poor countries, very little gains have emerged in this regard';
- the exclusive rights under TRIPS have 'the potential for limiting access of developing countries to even publicly generated basic research that might otherwise enable greater competition and local innovation'; and
- 'the economics of knowledge creation and the non-rival nature of information imply that global investments in basic science and technology are underfunded in comparison with a global optimum. Knowledge is a prime example of a global public good that can be more effectively provided by cooperative multilateral actions' (p. 370).

The 'open access' model could provide an impetus into innovation, reducing the cost of information on previous studies. However, if no agreement is reached at the international level, it could place the providers of 'open access' at a disadvantage. Large MNCs could access the research results under 'open access' and build on them placing the follow-up innovation under patent. The Central Drug Research Institute (CDRI), India's leading research institute, is currently trialling a number of projects under the PPP collaborative arrangements with 'open access' model.

10.2.9 Health Impact Fund

The Health Impact Fund (HIF), primarily financed by governments, would be set up to complement the current patent system. A large number of experts including Aidan Hollis, Michael Ravvin, Thomas Faunce, and Devi Sridhar have discussed the concept of HIF. Pogge (2008), also a discussant, provides an overview of the model. Under this model, companies could opt to patent the new drug in the usual manner or forego monopoly pricing in exchange for a reward (a form of compensation) from the HIF. If a company registers the drug with HIF, the company agrees to market the drug globally at no higher than the cost price. The HIF provides the company, for an agreed number of years, rewards based on the global health impact of the new drug. The company may choose to patent the drug anywhere, but cannot apply monopoly pricing during the agreed term. After the reward term, the company would provide zero-priced licences of essential technology for the manufacture and sale of the drug. Pogge believes that 'with the HIF, traditionally neglected diseases such as tuberculosis, malaria and tropical diseases would rise to afford some of the most lucrative research opportunities' (p. 77).

While the overall HIF ideology sounds promising, the following would need to be considered. First, rewards based on global health impact would be difficult to determine and open to manipulation. The health impact of a drug for a tropical disease prevalent in poor countries could be low relative to a drug developed for an orphan disease in a wealthy country, despite the fact that the former would treat larger number of patients than the latter drug. Second, in absolute terms, the contribution of poor countries to the HIF would be negligible relative to that of their wealthy counterparts. On the one hand, the natural question is that why would the wealthy countries contribute to reward companies to develop drugs for the diseases that hardly affect the health of their citizens but are prevalent in the poor countries? On the other hand, the contribution of the poor nations alone would not be sufficiently great to attract the attention of investors in pharmaceutical research. Therefore, the question that begs to be asked is how much weight would be allocated to each country's capacity to contribute to finance the HIF in order to ensure an equitable reward system that is fair to investors as well as consumers in all participating countries? The concept of HIF is also not clear on what happens in cases of non-contributory (presumed poor to extremely poor) countries.

10.2.10 Minimum patenting

In addition to the proposals noted above, we suggest additionally that the option of *minimum patenting* (explained below) should also be considered. The *minimum patenting* model would apply exclusively to drugs and pharmaceuticals. Unlike other industries, the drugs and pharmaceutical industry has a direct impact on human health. Thus, the industry needs to be treated with special care. Health is also an inalienable and universal right. Similarly, the Right to Life is enshrined under the Constitution of India. Under the proposed *minimum patenting* model, while pharmaceutical product patents would continue to be granted, process patents would be limited to a single process that is actually used in the manufacture of the patented product. The TRIPS agreement obliges member countries to provide patents for both *products and processes in all fields of technology* (Article 27), but members are under no obligation to provide for *excessive*[2] patenting. The Agreement provides that *members may... adopt measures necessary to protect public health* (Article 8). And limiting patents to product and a single process would be a necessary measure for protecting public health in poor countries. Companies manufacture a product using a process and deserve to be granted patent protection for what they have produced and how they have produced it. However, granting more patents than that for the same product is not rewarding innovation, but hindering it. Once a product is patented, no matter how many processes are developed by the firm's competitors, the same product cannot be marketed until the patent expires on the originator product. The practice of excessive patenting contravenes the spirit in which patents are granted, delays technological progress, raises health costs, and in the case of pharmaceuticals, literally denies access to medicines.

All the models discussed above are thought-out strategies by different experts. The experts may differ in their approach to addressing the issues they see in TRIPS. But they are unanimous in their dissatisfaction with the TRIPS agreement. Their main concern is the restrictive nature of TRIPS with respect to access to medicines in poor countries. The underlying assumption in the models presented above is that if the medicine is made available, half the battle is won. It may be partly true too. However, affordability is the real battle for the poor, which is not addressed under any of the models.

10.3 Conclusions

A large number of experts find the TRIPS regime unsatisfactory and suggest alternatives to improve upon the current situation. These models offer a variety of compromises, but also highlight the manifold shortcomings of the current patent regime. However, the alternatives also offer only partial solutions to the problem of providing affordable healthcare in poor countries. The proposed models fail to understand the enormity of the crisis the poor face in paying for medicines.

Another important factor overlooked in the current regime as well as in most of the alternative models is the basic premise for patents, which is to granting patents to reward inventors and spur innovation in order to improve human life. The spirit of patents is to accelerate the process of scientific and technical progress. The recent report of the EU Commission reveals the extent of manipulation of the system by firms, some of which were found to have filed for up to 1300 patents EU wide for a single drug. As noted in earlier chapters, a few hundred patents for a single drug are not uncommon in the US. This type of industry conduct is purely driven by greed contravening the basic premise of patents. The level of excessive patenting permitted under the current regime undermines the spirit of patenting. Policy makers need to seriously review the whole concept of patents and revisit the reasons for granting patents.

These alternative models might induce investments into developing new drugs for tropical diseases. But the fundamental problem of affordability of drugs in poor countries remains unresolved under these models. This is why developing countries, like India, need to consider alternative approaches for providing equitable access to healthcare, including access to medicines to all sections of the society.

Such a model – IndiaHealth – has been proposed in Chapter 8 for addressing the problem of access to healthcare and medicines in India. It must be noted that the IndiaHealth model is not an alternative to the current model of TRIPS, but represents a kind of broader strategy that must be developed in India in the wake of the implementation of the TRIPS agreement to ensure better access to medicines. Otherwise medicines will become even more inaccessible than they are now due to the eventual (but certain) rise in drug prices. The IndiaHealth model provides a guide for other developing countries to develop similar strategies in order to broaden access to medicines.

11
Final Conclusions

11.1 Introduction

Based on the discussion in the previous chapters, the main conclusions of this book are brought together in this chapter. As has been stated, the book deals with the impact of the TRIPS agreement on the pharmaceutical industry and the access to medicines in India, acknowledging that the introduction of the TRIPS compliant regime from 1 January 2005 marked a major shift in India's public policy on the protection of intellectual property rights (IPRs) and will have important repercussions for several industries and sectors. However, the focus of this book is only on the pharmaceutical industry and healthcare in India.

In order to fully explore the issues arising in the pharmaceutical industry and healthcare, it became essential to gain a good understanding of how the global pharmaceutical industry operates, what is involved in bringing new medicinal drugs onto the market, and what role is played by the regulatory frameworks both at the WTO and the government in India? As a result, Chapters 2 and 3 were devoted to covering these topics before the key questions highlighted in Chapter 1 were addressed.

It was noted in Chapter 2 that the WTO has become one of the most powerful multilateral institutions today. The WTO is an intergovernmental organisation with an enforcement mechanism to ensure implementation of its decisions. Having incorporated the General Agreement on Tariffs and Trade (GATT), the jurisdiction of the WTO also includes the agreement on Trade-Related Aspects of Intellectual Property Rights (TRIPS). The TRIPS agreement stipulates minimum standards for protection of intellectual property. The Agreement has considerably raised the level of protection in the developing countries, a large number of which did not previously provide product patents for pharmaceuticals. All WTO member countries, except the least developed countries (LDCs), are obliged under the TRIPS Agreement to provide product as well as process patents for 20 years. The least developed countries have until 2016 to implement the same provisions.

The Doha Declaration on TRIPS and Public Health reaffirms the rights of member states to protect public health and emphasises the benefits of certain flexibilities, such as compulsory licensing and parallel imports, that are built into the TRIPS agreement for use by member countries, should the need arise. The LDCs, which have insufficient capacity to manufacture pharmaceuticals to meet their own public health needs, can import low-cost generics during the protection period.

In recent years, the US and the EU countries have negotiated with developing countries bilateral and regional agreements on free trade, investment, and other issues. These agreements have forced developing countries to forfeit their right to use flexibilities provided under TRIPS raising the protection standards to TRIPS-plus level. Thanks to such constraints, not only the poor countries, but also countries like Singapore and Australia are unable to make full use of the flexibilities provided under TRIPS.

The structure and the role of global pharmaceutical industry in developing new drugs were discussed in Chapter 3, where it was noted that this industry is dominated by large MNCs that are principally based in the EU, Japan, and the US and hold most of the pharmaceutical patents worldwide. Through mergers and acquisitions, the MNCs are progressively getting larger and typically have much larger new product pipelines than ever before. In particular, the US dominates global pharmaceutical industry in its capacity as being both the largest single manufacturer and the largest single consumer of pharmaceuticals. In recent years, there has been a shift of R&D from the European countries, who until recently were the leaders in pharmaceutical innovation, to the US, which has further intensified this trend.

The global pharmaceutical industry has enjoyed consistently high rates of growth in sales revenues for many years. Global pharmaceutical sales increased from US$356 billion in 2000 to US$643 billion in 2006. In 2004, the global pharmaceutical sales crossed the half a trillion dollar mark for the first time. The world market growth recorded annually around 9.5 per cent in 2001 and 2002, peaked at 16.4 per cent in 2003, and declined to 12.5 per cent in 2004. The growth has slowed down to less than 8 per cent per annum since then.

The development strategy of the large pharmaceutical MNCs has also shifted in recent years towards developing the so-called 'blockbuster' drugs. These blockbuster drugs have become the backbone of the large MNCs for recouping their R&D investments. The increasing concentration of the large companies on blockbuster drugs has the worrying implications that the industry may be guilty of ignoring the development of those drugs that are badly needed by the populations of the developing countries, simply because the sales revenues from these drugs are not as high as from selling the blockbusters.

11.2 Answering specific questions

11.2.1 How does the regime change impact on India's pharmaceutical exports, particularly exports of the low-cost imitations of patented drugs to the poor countries?

The discussion in Chapter 4 described in some detail how India's pharmaceutical industry developed initially under the protection of the anti-competitive government policies introduced in the 1970s, but has continued its rapid growth in subsequent years even after the introduction of industrial de-licensing as a part of the economic reforms in 1991. Today, the Indian pharmaceutical industry has grown into a globally competitive indigenous industry that is increasingly integrating into the global industry through not only imports and exports, but also via FDI, outsourcing, and contracting arrangements with overseas partners.

A net importer of pharmaceuticals until the late 1980s, India is now a net exporter of pharmaceuticals. The economic liberalisation and the reforms to industrial policies introduced since 1991 provided a boost to India's exports of pharmaceuticals. The highly regulated markets, including the US, are the top 10 destinations for India's pharmaceutical exports. India's pharmaceutical industry has also contributed significantly to increasing access to medicines in the importing countries by supplying less expensive medicines.

While overseas MNCs once dominated the Indian pharmaceutical market, they now account for less than a quarter of the domestic market. Leading domestic firms generate significant share of their revenues in overseas markets. But the industry has a large number of small manufacturing firms that account for around half of the domestic supply by volume.

The likely impact of TRIPS on India's pharmaceutical exports is also considered in Chapter 4. Based on the data examined, we have concluded that in terms of value of exports, this impact is likely to be quite small – only around 1 per cent of India's pharmaceutical exports may be in jeopardy due to TRIPS. However, the overall impact may be greater if the number of patients who benefit from India's low-priced exports of drugs is considered, especially in the area of HIV/AIDS. Moreover, the implementation of the new patent regime would close all future opportunities to develop new processes for providing cheaper generic drugs. This loss would adversely affect access to medicines for the poor not only in India, but also in the other developing countries. Thus, the overall impact of TRIPS on potential exports and patient welfare is likely to be considerably greater than simply the value of exports lost.

After addressing the issue of how India's exports might increase access to medicines, we conclude that the Indian pharmaceutical industry has contributed, and continues to contribute, significantly to lowering drugs prices in the importing countries. Leading Indian firms, including Ranbaxy, DRL, Cipla, Sun Pharma, Torrent, Wockhardt, Nicholas Piramal, Lupin, and Zydus Cadila earn significant proportions of their sales revenues from overseas markets. With its exports selling at low prices, India's pharmaceutical industry is contributing to extend access to medicines in the importing countries.

11.2.2 What is the effect of TRIPS on foreign direct investment (FDI) into the Indian pharmaceutical industry?

After examining the likely impact of the implementation of TRIPS on the flows of FDI into India's pharmaceuticals industry in Chapter 4, we reached the conclusion that this impact is likely to be insignificant. Indeed, the empirical evidence challenges the assumption, often implicit in the patent advocacy literature such as PhRMA, that FDI inflows are positively correlated with more stringent patent protection regimes. We note that in India, the level of FDI into the pharmaceutical sector rose after product patents were abolished, fell to its lowest levels between 1980 and 1990, but started to rise again following the economic reforms in 1991. Today, the pharmaceutical sector in India is one of the top ten sectors to attract FDI. Globally, India ranks second behind China, but ahead of the US and the UK, in respect of investor confidence. The FDI into the pharmaceutical industry is not affected only by the protection of IPRs. Other factors, including R&D and manufacturing costs, availability and costs of skilled labour, exports potential, and compliance certification for quality also play a significant role in investment decisions of overseas firms.

11.2.3 How is the business model of domestic firms changing after TRIPS?

In the wake of the recent changes to the industrial landscape, Indian pharmaceutical firms have adopted a mixture of new business models. Leading Indian pharmaceutical companies are expanding through overseas acquisitions and exports now constitute a significant share of their annual sales revenue. Other firms are opting for alliances and contract manufacturing roles. There are indications that some Indian firms may relocate their manufacturing operations to the LDCs to take advantage of the delayed implementation of TRIPS in those countries. The survival of small manufacturers could be jeopardised by the changing dynamics in the market, which would be counterproductive from the access to medicines perspective. With the abolition of highly protective measures that once favoured the Indian pharmaceutical industry, the new industrial landscape foreshadows significant challenges for the indigenous players.

11.2.4 What impact does the regime change have on the innovative activities within the Indian pharmaceutical industry?

In Chapter 5, we also examined the innovative activities originating in India. These activities were measured in terms of patent filings in the US and in India. While these activities related to the entire industrial sector, the Indian institutional activity within the pharmaceutical industry shows a significant increase in recent years, particularly with its patent filings in the US. The US filings by Indian pharmaceutical institutions increased more than 25 times in the ten years to 2002. By contrast, the increase in the US filings by India-based foreign enterprises was negligible during the same period.

The patent filings at the Indian Patent Office also show a similar trend. The level of increase in the filings by Indian institutions within the pharmaceutical industry is relatively lower than the rate of change in their filings in the US over the study periods. In fact, the patent filings in India by foreign enterprises declined during the same period. This examination shows that in anticipation of TRIPS being implemented in India, Indian institutions began investing heavily in pharmaceutical innovation. The same is not found in the case of foreign enterprises.

Although innovative activities in India have increased substantially over the last decade and India is increasingly becoming a significant player in filing patent applications in the US, innovative activity is heavily concentrated in India's public institutes under the ambit of the CSIR.

Only a small number of pharmaceutical companies other than public institutes are engaged in patent filings in the US. This suggests that in terms of innovative activities only a limited number of Indian firms are globally competitive. This fact poses a challenge for the Indian government to develop more effective incentive mechanisms for better outcomes.

11.2.5 How effective have the price controls in India been in providing access to medicines until now and what form of price controls is India likely to have in future?

The effectiveness of India's price controls on drug prices is discussed in Chapter 6. After their introduction in the 1960s, price controls became most rigid in the 1970s, but have been progressively amended and gradually relaxed since the 1980s, reducing, in turn, the number of drugs under price control. India's price controls have had limited success in lowering drug prices, which are admittedly low relative to many other countries, but not sufficiently low relative to household incomes and other relevant factors affecting affordability of healthcare. Only one-in-three Indians are considered to be able to afford to buy medicines in India.

Our examination of India's price controls on medical drugs reveals that the price controls do not help in making affordable even those medicines that are considered by the government-appointed experts to be essential medicines. In the lead up to the implementation of the TRIPS agreement in 2005, there were apprehensions among citizen groups and other stakeholders that after 2005 drug prices would rise substantially in India, which would further erode the drug affordability. Our analysis of post-2005 price changes on 405 drugs confirms those fears.

The findings of our examination of the so-called voluntary price reductions announced by several pharmaceutical firms in 2006 are reported in Chapter 6. During negotiations with the government regarding the scope of drug price controls, 11 firms announced that prices of a total of 886 formulations would be voluntarily reduced from 1 October 2006. After undertaking an item by item examination of that list, we found that the list of 886 items also included items such as a pregnancy test card, 7 Ayurvedic medicines, at least 31 forms of iron, vitamins, or other nutritional supplements, and had only 134 drugs that were listed in the CIMS, Drug Today and other reference books. Furthermore, out of these 134 items, 103 items had a price higher than the agreed price while 16 items had a lower price. Consequently, this price reduction agreement would have minimum impact on the sales revenue of the companies involved. The implications for the consumer are that despite the widely publicised price reductions, most of these drugs continue to be sold at higher prices and benefits of the claimed price reductions to the consumer would be limited.

11.2.6 How can India extend access to medicines to its entire population?

The issues related to the access to medicines are a central concern in this book and are discussed in Chapter 8. First, the factors that deny access to medicines are explored and secondly a new model is developed for providing better access to healthcare and to medicines for the entire population of India. While the number of the poor in India living below the poverty line has declined over the last three decades, poverty remains the largest impediment to access to medicine in India. In the past, government policies have focused mainly on controlling drug prices rather than providing healthcare. There is no doubt that the share of India's population with access to medicines has increased since the 1980s. However, around two-thirds of the population still remains without access to medicines.

India's public expenditure on health is significantly low even by the standards of the developing countries. Correspondingly, the share of private health expenditure is very high, as most of the healthcare costs are met by out-of-pocket household expenditure and the coverage of health insurance is almost nonexistent. Without a comprehensive programme to pay for these medicines through additional public health expenditure, India's policy on controlling drug prices will remain incapable of providing affordable healthcare.

It was concluded that in terms of India's provision of healthcare, implications of both the low public spending on health and the high share of drugs relative to the total health care costs have contributed significantly to high private health expenditure. Both these issues need to be addressed together. India's past experience showed that controlling drug prices alone was not sufficient to provide an affordable healthcare to all. Indian policy makers could learn from other countries and consider the options discussed earlier to develop a strategy or set of strategies to negotiate and maintain low drug prices. There is a need to streamline the hierarchical nature of the regulatory structure, recognise drug pricing and affordability as inseparable and interdependent in providing healthcare. Any future policy would need to be developed in full recognition of this reality.

At the current stage of economic development, India needs to introduce policies, which raise the health status of the poor. The population projections indicate that India's population could reach two billion by the middle of the century. With the people generally living longer, the share of the aged is expected to increase significantly, although India will enjoy a favourable age-structure of its population and will benefit from a rising share of working-age population (the so-called 'demographic dividend') over the next three decades. Eventually, however, demographic change would require a significant shift in the health policy and allocation of additional resources. India would need to raise significantly its public expenditure on health from the current level of 0.9 per cent of GDP.

We have developed a model – IndiaHealth – which has been presented in Chapter 8 for addressing the problem of access to health care and medicines in India. It must be noted that the introduction of the IndiaHealth proposal is not an alternative to the current model of TRIPS, but represents the kind of broader strategy that must be developed in India in the wake of the implementation of TRIPS to ensure better access to medicines. Otherwise medicines will become even more inaccessible than they are now due to the eventual (but certain) rise in drug prices. The fact is that other developing countries will also need to develop similar strategies to deal with their specific situations. This fact further enhances the potential contribution of this book, as it can show the right way for countries other than India.

The IndiaHealth model considers demographic characteristics and income levels. The demographics provide a basis for the estimates of healthcare requirements (e.g. elderly population tend to be more frequent user of healthcare than the younger people). Data on the income levels are used to determine patient co-payments ensuring affordability of prescribed drugs. For example, the BPL population of less than $1-a-day would make no co-payments towards the cost of medicines. These costs are covered by the public expenditure on health. Based on the income levels of the Indian population, there is a three-tier co-payment schedule. After reaching the SafetyNet threshold in a calendar year, the patient co-payments are reduced for the remainder of the year. This model would provide access to both the allopathic and the traditional healthcare providers. An important feature of the model is that it includes the assumption that practitioners of traditional Indian medicines would be authorised to prescribe medicines in the same way as doctors and dispensers of the allopathic medicine. Because these practitioners of traditional Indian medicines are easily accessible at the village level, their inclusion in the overall healthcare programme would play a significant role in extending access to medicines to India's entire population.

The proposed model does not claim to be the ultimate goal for India, but would be a helpful step in the right direction for achieving the objective of *health for all*. Our costing suggests that the increase in the public expenditure on health required to fund the IndiaHealth programme is well within the level of commitment already given by the UPA government in its Common Minimum Programme. Our estimates indicate that by raising public expenditure on healthcare to 1.62 per cent of GDP by 2010, India should be able to overcome the barriers to affordability of medicines. Going forward, the ratio of public expenditure on health is expected to fall to 1.24 per cent of GDP by 2015. The implementation of this model, or another variation of it, should relieve India's households of significant health expenditure and help the country to achieve better health outcomes. Sensitivity analysis for further variations in certain parameters of the model is presented in Appendix D and E.

11.2.7 Is the TRIPS Agreement fair to developing countries?

Finally, we return to the fundamental issue about the fairness of the TRIPS regime from the standpoint of the developing countries. Although the stated objectives of IPRs under the TRIPS agreement include *mutual advantage of producers and users* and *to a balance of rights and obligations*, the TRIPS Agreement clearly favours the drug producers. The Agreement obliges members to provide for criminal proceedings with penalties of imprisonment and/or fines for commercial infringers of copyrights and other intellectual property rights. The Agreement calls for punishing (small) firms/individuals inflicting a monetary damage to the right holder. The Agreement would indeed be balancing the *rights and obligations of producers and users* if it also called for the same kind of treatment for companies for excessive patenting (such as filing up to 1300 patents on a single medicine). This level of patenting of 'anything and everything' denies access to medicines and has a realistic potential for loss of life. This issue needs to be addressed in the next review of TRIPS. Independent of TRIPS, developing countries need to consider amending their regimes to introduce provisions similar to those of Article 61 of TRIPS and fill this gap.

It is noted at the outset of this discussion that a large number of the developed countries did not introduce pharmaceutical product patents until they had achieved certain stage of economic development. The TRIPS agreement disregards this reality and forces all member states to adopt stringent patent protection, including pharmaceutical product patents, irrespective of their stage of development. The TRIPS agreement is a 'one size fits all' regime creating numerous problems for the poor in developing countries. Copying technologies developed in the advance economies is a necessary step to developing innovative capabilities. While most of the developed countries, including the US, benefited from copying discoveries and inventions of others, TRIPS denies developing countries the same opportunity.

The critics of TRIPS also question the underlying rationale behind the TRIPS agreement by pointing out, for example, that while pharmaceutical firms may be justified in asking for patent protection to recover their developmental costs, as pharmaceutical research is expensive and involves a process spanning over several years, the industry's claims regarding R&D costs and the time required for developing new drugs appear to be exaggerated. The methodology used in the studies on which these claims have been widely criticised for inflating costs. The industry has also attracted criticism for spending significantly more on marketing than it does on R&D, and for indulging in unethical practices, such as providing perks to physicians in return for prescribing their medicines. Some critics have asserted that if ethical standards were effectively enforced, the methods employed by pharmaceutical firms to promote new and expensive drugs would breach these standards in most countries.

Thus, while the costs of TRIPS are certain, its benefits remain a potential 'may be' at best. Healthcare costs to all countries, including the US, have increased significantly as a consequence of TRIPS. But the developing countries are the biggest losers under the new regime. Large pharmaceutical companies based in the developed countries are the big winners.

A large number of experts find the TRIPS regime unsatisfactory and suggest alternatives to improve upon the current situation. Suggested models include donating drugs, differential patenting, differential pricing, replicating the Orphan Drug Act at the global level, Advance Purchase Commitments, Public–Private Partnerships, Health Impact Fund, and the open access model. These models offer a variety of compromises, but also highlight the multiple deficiencies of the current patent protection regime. Each of these proposals provides a partial solution to the problems generated by the current regime. But each potential solution suffers from some drawbacks.

These alternative models might induce investments into developing new drugs for tropical diseases. But the fundamental problem of affordability of drugs in poor countries remains unresolved under these models. This is why developing countries, like India, need to consider alternative approaches for providing equitable access to healthcare, including access to medicines to all sections of the society.

In addition to discussing these alternatives, we have also suggested in Chapter 9 our own option of *minimum patenting* for further consideration. The *minimum patenting* model would apply exclusively to drugs and pharmaceuticals. Under the proposed *minimum patenting* model, while pharmaceutical product patents would continue to be granted, process patents would be limited to a single process that is actually used in the manufacture of the patented product. While the TRIPS agreement obliges member countries to provide patents for both *products and processes in all fields of technology* (Article 27), members are under no obligation to provide for *excessive* patenting. The Agreement provides that *members may ... adopt measures necessary to protect public health* (Article 8). And limiting patents to product and a single process would be a necessary measure for protecting public health in poor countries. Companies manufacture a product using a process and deserve to be granted patent protection for what they have produced and how they have produced it. However, granting more patents than that for the same product is not rewarding innovation, but hindering it. Once a product is patented, no matter how many processes are developed by the firm's competitors, the same product cannot be marketed until the patent expires on the originator product. The practice of excessive patenting contravenes the spirit in which patents are granted, delays technological progress, raises health costs, and in the case of pharmaceuticals, literally denies access to medicines.

Appendix A

Examination of drug prices the domestic firms agreed to reduce

Table A.1 Voluntary price reduction – market prices versus claimed prices

CIMS	DT	IDR	Original	Name of the formulation and strength	Therapeutic category/ Composition		Pack Size	Claimed prices					Market prices			
Page/reference			S. No.					Old price (Rs.)	New price (Rs.)	Reduction %age	Old price per unit	New price per unit	CIMS	DT	IDR	Status
	305	187	13	Bacipen 250	Antibacterial	Cap	10	30.80	28.50	7.47%	3.08	2.85		2.88	2.88	H
	305	187	14	Bacipen 500	Antibacterial	Cap	10	57.60	53.00	7.99%	5.76	5.30		5.38	5.38	H
		191	15	Odinol 25 mg	Cardiovascular	Tab	14	11.50	8.50	26.09%	0.82	0.61			0.71	H
		191	16	Odinol 50 mg	Cardiovascular	Tab	14	19.00	16.00	15.79%	1.36	1.14			1.25	H
		204	17	Alcephin 250	Antibacterial	Cap	10	62.00	51.00	17.74%	6.20	5.10			6.20	H
		204	18	Alcephin 500	Antibacterial	Cap	10	110.00	95.50	13.18%	11.00	9.55			11.00	H
		204	19	Alcephin	Antibacterial	Dry syrup	30 ml	23.85	21.00	11.95%	0.80/ml	0.70/ml			0.70/ml	E
		204	20	Alcephin Kid	Antibacterial	Tab	10	29.95	21.00	29.88%	3.00	2.10			3.00	H
295	696	312	50	Alsigra 50	Antifungals	Tab	4	72.00	51.00	29.17%	7.20	5.10	7.20	7.20	7.20	H
268		273	72	Forminal 1000	Antidiabetics	Tab	10	16.05	12.50	22.12%	1.61	1.25	1.50		1.50	H
270	966	297	75	Piolem 15	Antidiabetics drug	Tab	10	18.00	16.00	11.11%	1.80	1.60	1.80	1.80	1.80	H

270	966	297	76	Piolem 30	Antidiabetics drug	Tab	10	35.00	32.00	8.57%	3.50	3.20	3.50	3.50	3.50	H
	1,051		101	Folinal plus	Iron & Vitamins supplements	Syrup	300 ml	72.00	63.50	11.81%	0.24/ml	0.21/ml		0.37/ml		H
	312	180	111	Amoxil	Amoxycillin	Dry syrup	30 ml	25.68	22.47	12.50%	1.00/ml	0.86/ml		0.47/ml	0.49/ml	L
	312	180	114	Amoxil 250 mg	Amoxilcillin 250 mg	Cap	20 × 10	802.50	748.32	6.75%	4.01	3.74		3.10	3.58	L
	312	180	115	Amoxil 500 mg	Amoxilcillin	Cap	20 × 10	1510.84	1337.41	11.48%	7.55	6.69		5.90	5.50	L
	528		164	Cadflo 20 mg	Fluoxetine	Cap	30 × 10 C	898.80	791.80	11.90%	3.00	2.64		2.35		L
	418		173	Cadithro 50 mg	Roxythromycin	Tab	20 × 10 T	1005.80	963.00	4.26%	5.03	4.82		4.70		L
	418		174	Cadithro 150 mg	Roxythromycin	Tab	20 × 10T	1647.80	1498.00	9.09%	8.24	7.49		11.13		H
476	825	212	176	Ceticad 10 mg	Cetrizine HCl	Tab	50 × 10 T	1281.86	805.71	37.15%	2.56	1.61	2.60	2.60	2.60	H
188	548	236	178	Domcolic 10 mg ×	Domperidone	Tab	50 × 10 T	1352.48	1070.00	20.89%	2.70	2.14	2.53	2.53	2.53	H
373	479		184	Flumed 150 mg	Fluconazole	Tab	20 × 1	684.80	577.80	15.63%	34.20	28.85	30.00	26.00		M
73	629	264	190	Lanzofast 30 mg	Lansoprazole as enteric-coated granules	Cap	20 × 10 C	1070.00	856.00	20.00%	5.35	4.14	4.93	4.90	4.93	H
	250		198	Nimdus-P	Nimesulide 100 mg + Paracetamol 500 mg	Tab	20 × 10T	620.60	513.60	17.24%	3.10	2.57		2.90		H

Table A.1 (Continued)

CIMS	DT	IDR	Original	Name of the formulation and strength	Therapeutic category/ Composition			Claimed prices					Market prices			
Page/reference			S. No.				Pack Size	Old price (Rs.)	New price (Rs.)	Reduction %age	Old price per unit	New price per unit	CIMS	DT	IDR	Status
	250		199	Nimdus-Plus	Nimesulide 100 mg + Paracetamol 500 mg	Tab	50 × 10	1551.50	1086.05	30.00%	3.10	2.17		2.90		H
	354		201	Oriphex 125 DT	Cephalexin	Tab	20 × 10T	628.95	588.50	6.43%	3.14	2.94		3.25		H
318		204	203	Oriphex 250 mg	Cephalexin	Cap	20 × 10C	1305.40	1177.00	9.84%	6.53	5.89	6.50		6.50	H
318		204	204	Oriphex 500 mg	Cephalexin	Cap	10 × 10C	1150.25	1016.50	11.63%	11.50	10.17	12.10		12.10	H
308	306	187	210	Zycillin 250 mg	Ampicillin Trihydrate	Cap	20 × 10C	642.00	535.00	16.67%	3.21	2.68	3.00	3.00	3.00	H
308	306	187	211	Zycillin 500 mg	Ampicillin Trihydrate	Cap	20 × 10C	1241.20	1070.00	13.79%	6.21	5.35	5.80	5.80	5.80	H
380	510	173	330	Zelbend 400 mg,	Albendazole I.P. excipient qs	Tab	20 × 10	2675.00	2247.00	16.00%	13.38	11.23	10.00	10.00	10.00	L
	409		404	Cadimycetin 500 mg	Chloramphenicol	Cap	10 × 10 C	730.28	642.00	12.09%	7.30	6.42		6.83		H
	409		405	Cadimycetin 250 mg	Chloramphenicol	Cap	20 × 10C	770.40	663.40	13.89%	3.85	3.31		3.60		H

	1094		419	Cadpro 250 gm GB	Protein	Granules	250 gm	149.75	136.96	8.54%	0.60/gm	0.55/gm		0.50/gm		L
155	148	239	425	Canvas 5 mg	Enalapril	Tab	30 × 10	635.58	535.00	15.82%	2.12	1.78	0.07	0.07	0.07	L
	318		495	Zox LB 250	Amoxycillin 250 mg + Lacto Bacillus	Cap	10 × 10C	406.60	321.00	21.05%	4.07	3.21		3.80		H
	318		496	Zox LB 500	Amoxycillin 500 mg + Lacto Bacillus	Cap	10 × 10C	757.56	695.50	8.19%	7.58	6.96		7.08		H
380	508	173	501	Alzad Suspension	Albendazole 5 ml-IP-200 mg	Liquid	10 ml Bot	21.61	17.41	19.43%	2.16/ml	1.74/ml	1.83/ml	1.83/ml	1.83/ml	H
380	508	173	502	Alzad	Albendazole IP –400 mg	Tab	1	14.80	11.87	19.81%	14.80	11.87	12.00	2.56	12.00	H
112		240	532	Enpril 10 mg	Enalapril	Tab	10	54.86	49.37	10.00%	5.49	4.94	2.18		2.18	L
112		240	533	Enpril 5 mg	Enalapril	Tab	10	30.60	27.54	10.00%	3.06	2.75	1.20		1.20	L
118	154	269	544	Lozitan 50 mg	Losarten	Tab	10	46.42	32.49	30.00%	4.64	3.25	3.90	3.90	3.90	H
332		209	559	Nosocef 250 mg	Ceftriaxone	Inj	1 vial	47.48	37.98	20.00%	47.48	37.98	48.80		48.80	H
322	344	205	565	O-Powercef 100 mg	Cefixime DT	Tab	10	137.15	109.72	20.00%	13.72	10.97	27.00	27.00	27.00	H
322		205	566	O-Powercef 200 mg	Cefixime	Tab	4	100.23	80.18	20.00%	25.06	20.05	49.00		49.00	H
322		205	567	O-Powercef DS	Cefixime 50 mg/5 ml	Liquid	30 ml	63.30	50.64	20.00%	2.11/ml	1.69/ml	3.27/ml		3.27/ml	H
207	209	292	573	Pyrexon 650 mg	Paracetamol-IP-DT	Tab	6	9.59	8.63	10.00%	1.60	1.44	1.35	1.35	1.35	L

Table A.1 (Continued)

CIMS	DT	IDR	Original	Name of the formulation and strength	Therapeutic category/ Composition			Claimed prices					Market prices			
Page/reference			S. No.				Pack Size	Old price (Rs.)	New price (Rs.)	Reduction %age	Old price per unit	New price per unit	CIMS	DT	IDR	Status
74	621	288	574	RESEC	Omeprazole – IP	Cap	10	46.95	37.56	20.00%	4.70	3.76	3.98	3.95	3.98	H
		195	602	Beclasone – C 15 gm	Topical Steroids	Cream	15 gm	22.90	14.80	35.37%	1.53/gm	0.99/gm			1.53/gm	H
		195	603	Beclasone – C 5 gm	Topical Steroids	Cream	5 gm	11.75	8.60	26.81%	2.35/gm	1.72/gm			2.35/gm	H
		195	604	BECLASONE – GM 15 gm	Topical Steroids	Cream	15 gm	24.90	16.90	32.13%	1.66/gm	1.13/gm			1.66/gm	H
		195	605	Beclasone – GM 5 gm	Topical Steroids	Cream	5 gm	13.90	9.60	30.94%	2.78/gm	1.92/gm			2.78/gm	H
		219	608	Ciprobiotic – 250	Anti-Bacterial	Tab	10	30.66	11.60	62.17%	3.07	1.16			2.88	H
		219	609	Ciprobiotic – 500	Anti-Bacterial	Tab	10	59.42	20.40	65.67%	5.94	2.04			5.87	H
		220	610	Ciprobiotic – TN – 250	Anti-Bacterial	Tab	10	34.64	22.20	35.91%	3.46	2.22			2.99	H
		220	611	Ciprobiotic – TN – 500	Anti-Bacterial	Tab	10	67.94	39.10	42.45%	6.79	3.91			5.99	H
297		181	671	Ranoxyl Caps 250 mg	Amoxicillin	Cap	10	42.00	37.80	10.00%	4.20	3.78	3.00		3.00	L

297		181	672	Ranoxyl Caps 500 mg	Amoxicillin	Cap	10	67.20	60.48	10.00%	6.72	6.05	5.30		5.30	L
297		181	675	Ranoxyl Syrup 60 ml.	Amoxicillin 125 mg/5 ml	Dry syrup	60 ml	29.40	26.46	10.00%	0.49/ml	0.44/ml	0.42/ml		0.42/ml	L
155	149	240	688	Invoril 5mg	Enalapril 5 mg	Tab	10	23.73	18.98	20.02%	2.38	1.90	1.88	1.88	1.88	L
380		173	702	Lupibend 400	Anthelmintics	Tab	50 × 1	626.76	575.00	8.26%	12.54	11.50	12.00		12.00	H
382		270	703	Lupimeb	Anthelmintics	Tab	20 × 6	240.26	219.20	8.76%	2.00	1.10	1.92		1.92	H
76		288	710	Lupome-D	Antipeptic Ulcerants	Cap	20 × 10	940.14	835.60	11.12%	4.70	4.18	4.18		4.18	E
134		178	711	Defidin 5 mg	Antihypertensives	Tab	5 × 6 × 10	678.99	600.60	11.55%	2.26	2.00	2.17		2.17	H
380		173	716	Lupibend 10 ml	Anthelmintics	Syrup	10 ml	21.94	18.80	14.30%	2.19/ml	1.88/ml	2.10		2.10/ml	H
354		285	723	Eufox 200	Antibiotics	Tab	10 × 10	887.91	731.20	17.65%	8.88	7.31	7.31		7.31	E
356		286	725	Eufox-Tz	Antibiotics	Tab	10 × 10	1044.60	835.60	20.01%	10.45	8.36	8.36		8.36	E
509		275	742	Lupigyl Gel	Anthelmintics	Gel	30 gm	28.20	20.35	27.85%	0.94/gm	0.68/gm	1.35/gm		1.35/gm	H
232		281	748	Lupisulide Gel	Pain Management	Gel	30 gm	25.07	16.70	33.39%	0.84/gm	0.56/gm	1.20/gm		1.20/gm	H
232		281	753	Lupisulide	Pain Management	Tab	5 × 5 × 10	626.76	391.75	37.50%	2.50	1.56	2.40		2.40	H
76		291	762	Lupipan 40	Antipeptic Ulcerants	Tab	10 × 10	626.76	313.40	50.00%	6.27	3.13	6.00		6.00	H
320	354	204	768	Rofex 500 mg Caps	Anhydrous Cephalaxin	Cap	10 × 10	118.18	105.00	11.15%	1.18	1.05	10.57	11.82	10.57	H
320	354	204	771	Cephalaxin	Cephalaxin	Cap	20 × 10	62.66	60.00	4.25%	0.31	0.30	5.94	6.27	5.94	H
		281	786	Nicip	Analgesics/ Antipyretics/ Anti-inflammatory	Tab	10's	25.00	21.00	16.00%	2.50	2.10			2.50	H
		212	787	Cetcip	Antiallergic	Tab	10's	33.65	25.00	25.71%	3.37	2.50			2.75	H

Table A.1 (Continued)

CIMS	DT	IDR	Original	Name of the formulation and strength	Therapeutic category/ Composition			Claimed prices					Market prices			
Page/reference			S. No.				Pack Size	Old price (Rs.)	New price (Rs.)	Reduction %age	Old price per unit	New price per unit	CIMS	DT	IDR	Status
		287	788	Omecip 10	Antacid	Cap	10's	24.00	19.50	18.75%	2.40	1.95			2.40	H
		287	789	Omecip 20	Antacid	Cap	15's	58.50	46.00	21.37%	3.90	3.07			3.90	H
		281	790	Nodard	Analgesics/ Antipyretics/ Anti-inflammatory	Tab	10's	25.00	21.00	16.00%	2.50	2.10			2.50	H
232		282	792	Niciflex-T	Analgesics/ Antipyretics/ Anti-inflammatory	Tab	10's	55.00	40.00	27.27%	5.50	4.00	5.50		5.50	H
189		236	793	Vomistop 10 DT	Antiemetics/ Antinauseants	Tab	10's	24.00	16.00	33.33%	2.40	1.60	2.40		2.40	H
408		330	794	Bromex	Anti Cough & Cold Preparations	Liquid	100 ml	27.00	22.00	18.52%	0.27/ml	0.22/ml	0.27/ml		0.27/ml	H
308		187	796	Megasyn 250	Antibiotics	Cap	10's	30.00	24.00	20.00%	3.00	2.40	3.00		3.00	H
241		230	798	Verub	Pain relieving ointment	Gel	30 gm	37.00	30.00	18.92%	1.23/gm	1.00/gm	1.23/gm		1.23/gm	H
		313	799	Burnheal	Antiseptic	Powder	10 gm	21.00	16.00	23.81%	2.10/gm	1.60/gm			2.10/gm	H

	293	800	Paracod	Analgesics/ Antipyretics/ Anti-inflammatory	Tab	10's	31.00	25.00	19.35%	3.10	2.50		3.10	H
382	264	801	Levomol 50	Anthelmintics	Tab	1's	7.75	6.00	22.58%	7.75	6.00	7.75	7.75	H
382	264	802	Levomol 150	Anthelmintics	Tab	1's	15.70	13.50	14.01%	15.70	13.50	15.70	15.70	H
	238	803	Vominate	Antiemetics/ Antinauseants	Tab	10's	19.50	15.00	23.08%	1.95	1.50		1.95	H
344		804	Q-Gat 200	Antibiotics & Antibacterials	Tab	5's	40.00	33.00	17.50%	8.00	6.60	8.00		H
242	383	806	Powergel	Pain relieving ointment	Gel	30 gm	37.00	30.00	18.92%	1.23/gm	1.00/gm	1.23/gm	1.23/gm	H
196	296	807	Phenotone 30	Antiepileptic drugs	Tab	10's	7.40	6.00	18.92%	0.74	0.60	0.74	0.74	H
196	296	808	Phenotone 60	Antiepileptic drugs	Tab	10's	10.20	9.00	11.76%	1.02	0.90	1.02	1.02	H
	346	809	Fericip	Vitamins Supplements	Cap	10's	73.34	55.00	25.01%	7.33	5.50		4.50	H
	173	810	Alfarich 0.25	Vitamins Supplements	Cap	10's	65.00	50.00	23.08%	6.50	5.00		5.00	E
518	195	811	Becderm	Topical preparations	Cream	15 gm	18.00	15.00	16.67%	1.20/gm	1.00/gm	1.20/gm	1.20/gm	H
408	330	813	Bromex	Anti Cough & Cold Preparations	Cream	10's	12.00	9.00	25.00%	1.20	0.90	1.20	1.20	H
519		814	Cloderm	Antifungal cream	Cream	15 gm	28.00	24.00	14.29%	1.87	1.60	2.13/gm		H
409	331	815	Cofdex Forte	Anti Cough & Cold Preparations	Liquid	100 ml	35.00	29.00	17.14%	0.35/ml	0.29/ml	0.35/ml	0.35/ml	H

Table A.1 (Continued)

CIMS	DT	IDR	Original	Name of the formulation and strength	Therapeutic category/ Composition			Claimed prices					Market prices			
Page/reference			S. No.				Pack Size	Old price (Rs.)	New price (Rs.)	Reduction %age	Old price per unit	New price per unit	CIMS	DT	IDR	Status
		335	816	Ridcof	Anti Cough & Cold Preparations	Liquid	60 ml	20.00	17.00	15.00%	0.33/ml	0.28/ml			0.33/ml	H
409		331	817	Cofdex Plus	Anti Cough & Cold Preparations	Liquid	60 ml	27.00	23.00	14.81%	0.27/ml	0.23/ml	0.27/ml		0.27/ml	H
		332	818	Dexcof	Anti Cough & Cold Preparations	Liquid	100 ml	30.00	27.00	10.00%	0.30/ml	0.27/ml			0.30/ml	H
236		299	819	Dolocip DT	Analgesics/ Antipyretics/ Anti-inflammatory	Tab	10's	44.50	25.00	43.82%	4.45	2.50	3.00		3.00	H
73		255	823	Helipac Kit	Antacid	Tab	6's Kit	25.20	20.00	20.63%	4.20	3.33	4.20		4.20	H
228		254	824	Osteocip	Analgesics/ Antipyretics/ Anti-inflammatory	Tab	10's	150.00	100.00	33.33%	15.00	10.00	15.00		15.00	h
411		333	825	Lexcof	Anti Cough & Cold Preparations	Liquid	50 ml	26.00	23.00	11.54%	0.52/ml	0.46/ml	0.52/ml		0.52/ml	H

428		349	827	Maxiferon soft	Vitamins/ Nutritional Supplements	Cap	10's	27.00	23.00	14.81%	2.70	2.30	2.70		2.70	H
73		278	828	Mosapid 5	Antacid	Tab	10's	27.00	20.00	25.93%	2.70	2.00	2.70		2.70	H
		318	831	Toscof	Anti Cough & Cold Preparations	Liquid	100 ml	30.00	24.00	20.00%	0.30/ml	0.24/ml			0.30/ml	H
82		371	832	Urisoda	Systemic Alkalizer	Granules	4 gm	8.50	6.00	29.41%	2.13/gm	1.50/gm	2.13/gm		2.13/gm	H
		275	833	Vominorm	Antiemetics/ Antinauseants	Inj	2 ml	6.00	4.00	33.33%	3.00	2.00			3.00	H
178		229	834	Zepose	Antidepressant	Inj	2 ml	12.00	6.00	50.00%	6.00/ml	3.00/ml	6.00/ml		6.00/ml	H
302	326	184	835	Clavam 375 mg	Amoxicillin + Clavulanate Potassium	Tab	10's	296.40	197.08	33.51%	29.64	19.91	28.50	28.50	28.50	H
302	326	184	836	Clavam 625 mg	Amoxicillin + Clavulanate Potassium	Tab	10's	379.60	207.48	45.34%	37.96	20.75	19.95	36.50	19.95	H
302	326	184	837	Clavam	Amoxicillin And Clavulanate	Dry syrup	30 ml	72.80	48.78	33.00%	2.43/ml	1.63/ml	2.50/ml	2.33/ml	2.50/ml	H
302	326	184	839	Clavam 1000 mg	Amoxicillin + Clavulanate Potassium	Tab	10's	483.60	311.48	35.59%	48.36	31.15	29.95	46.50	29.95	H
302		184	840	Clavam DT	Amoxicillin + Clavulanate Potassium	Tab	10's	132.60	82.68	37.65%	13.26	8.27	12.75		12.75	H
	1127		845	Gemfos	Risedronate Sodium	Tab	4's	208.00	124.80	40.00%	52.00	31.20		50.00		H
330	351	209	847	Tazid 250 mg	Ceftazidime	Inj	Vial	86.32	78.00	9.64%	86.32	78.00	85.00	75.00	85.00	H

Table A.1 (Continued)

CIMS	DT	IDR	Original	Name of the formulation and strength	Therapeutic category/ Composition			Claimed prices					Market prices			
Page/reference			S. No.				Pack Size	Old price (Rs.)	New price (Rs.)	Reduction %age	Old price per unit	New price per unit	CIMS	DT	IDR	Status
330	351	209	848	Tazid 500 mg	Ceftazidime	Inj	Vial	161.20	145.60	9.68%	161.20	145.60	140.00	162.00	140.00	M
330	351	209	849	Tazid 1000 mg	Ceftazidime	Inj	Vial	280.80	192.40	31.48%	280.80	192.40	270.00	185.00	270.00	H
	382		850	Zocef 250 mg	Cefuroxime Sodium	Inj	Vial	58.76	46.80	20.35%	58.76	46.80		56.50		H
336	382	211	851	Zocef 750 mg	Cefuroxime Sodium	Inj	Vial	118.56	99.84	15.79%	118.56	99.84	99.84	114.00	99.84	M
	382		852	Zocef 1.5 gm	Cefuroxime Sodium	Inj	Vial	225.68	187.20	17.05%	225.68	187.20		217.00		H
	382		853	Zocef 125 mg	Cefuroxime Axetil	Tab	10's	161.20	135.20	16.13%	16.12	13.52		15.50		H
	382		854	Zocef 250 mg	Cefuroxime Axetil	Tab	10's	338.00	206.96	38.77%	33.80	20.70		32.50		H
	382		855	Zocef 500 mg	Cefuroxime Axetil	Tab	10's	676.00	395.20	41.54%	67.60	39.52		65.00		H
	367	209	859	Cefxo 1 gm	Ceftriaxone	Inj	Vial	98.00	82.00	16.32%	98.00	82.00		75.00	75.00	L
	367	209	860	Cefxo 250 mg	Ceftriaxone Inj	Inj	Vial	43.00	35.80	16.74%	43.00	35.80		30.00	30.00	L

	367	209	861	Cefxo 500 mg	Ceftriaxone Inj	Inj	Vial	58.00	48.30	16.72%	58.00	48.30		50.00	50.00	H
476		212	864	Oncet	Cetirizine Dihydrochloride	Tab	10's	25.00	15.00	40.00%	2.50	1.50	1.00		1.00	L
382	507	270	876	Helmintol 100 mg	Mebendazole	Tab	6's	6.95	5.80	16.55%	1.16	0.97	0.99	1.16	0.99	H
	245	281	878	Nimsaid	Nimesulide	Tab	10's	24.00	20.00	16.67%	2.40	2.00		1.87	1.87	L
	697	313	882	Vigreks 100 mg	Sildenafil Citrate	Tab	4's	108.00	90.00	16.67%	27.00	22.50		25.00	25.00	H
	697	313	883	Vigreks 50 mg	Sildenafil Citrate	Tab	4's	72.00	60.00	16.67%	18.00	15.00		14.90	14.90	L

Note: CIMS, DT (Drug Today), and IDR are considered to reflect the market prices.
The letter in the last column represents the status of the market price relative to the claimed price reduction.
H = the market price is higher than the claimed price;
L = the market price is lower than the claimed price;
E = the market price is equal to the claimed price; and
M = the market price is mixed, which means at least in one of the reference books the price is higher while in the other books the price is lower than the claimed price.
Source: Author calculations based on Government of India (2006h), CIMS (2007), Drug Today (2007), and IDR (2008).

Appendix B

Examination of changes to drug prices

Table B.1 Price changes to drugs for cardiovascular diseases

Category	DPCO	NL EM	Brand	Form	Strength	Qty	Therapeutic group	Company	Price change %	
Drug name/ Year	1995	2003							1994–2004	2005–2008
Carboprost Tromethamine			Prostodin	Inj	250 mcg/ml	1 ml	Uterine stimulants	Astra Zeneca	−2.74	24.31
Carboprost Tromethamine			Deviprost	Inj	250 mcg/ml	1 ml	Uterine stimulants	DRL		12.97
Sildenafil Citrate			Alsigra	Tab	25 mg	4	Uterine stimulants	Alembic		0.00
Sildenafil Citrate			Alsigra	Tab	50 mg	4	Uterine stimulants	Alembic		0.00
Bisoprolol			Concor	Tab	5 mg	10	Anti-anginals	Merck	−5.55	9.34
Atenolol + Nifedipine		yes	Cardules Plus 10 mg	Tab	50 mg + 10 mg	10	Anti-anginals	Nicholas Piramal	3.74	40.00
Atenolol + Nifedipine		yes	Cardules Plus 20 mg	Tab	50 mg + 20 mg	10	Anti-anginals	Nicholas Piramal		37.59
Nifedapine		yes	Cadules	Cap	10 mg	10	Anti-anginals	Nicholas Piramal		43.18
Nifedapine		yes	Cadules	Cap	10 mg (Retard)	10	Anti-anginals	Nicholas Piramal		62.80
Nifedapine		yes	Cadules	Cap	20 mg (Retard)	10	Anti-anginals	Nicholas Piramal		35.48
Nifedipine		yes	Depin	Cap	5 mg	50 × 3	Anti-anginals	Zydus Cadila	6.24	0.00
Nifedipine		yes	Depin	Cap	10 mg	4 × 30	Anti-anginals	Zydus Cadila		0.00
Nifedipine		yes	Depin	Cap	20 mg (Retard)	30	Anti-anginals	Zydus Cadila		0.00

Table B.1 (Continued)

Category	DPCO	NL EM	Brand	Form	Strength	Qty	Therapeutic group	Company	Price change %	
Drug name/ Year	**1995**	**2003**							**1994–2004**	**2005–2008**
Indapamide			Lorvas	Tab	2.5 mg	10	Anti-hypotensives	Torrent	6.78	0.00
Metoprolol + Hydrochlorothiazide			Selopres	Tab	100 mg + 12.5 mg	10	Anti-Hypertensives	Astra Zeneca	0.00	0.00
Chlonidine + Hydrochlorothiazide		yes	Arkamin-H	Tab	100 mcg + 20 mg	10	Anti-Hypertensives	Unisearch	2.05	17.85
Chlonidine		yes	Arkamin	Tab	100 mcg	10	Anti-Hypertensives	Unisearch		18.46
Enalapril maleate		yes	Enace	Tab	2.5 mg	10	Anti-Hypertensives	Nicholas Piramal	4.52	18.80
Enalapril maleate		yes	Enace	Tab	5 mg	10	Anti-Hypertensives	Nicholas Piramal		20.23
Enalapril maleate		yes	Enace	Tab	10 mg	10	Anti-Hypertensives	Nicholas Piramal		6.90
Enalapril maleate + Hydrochlorothiazide		yes	Enace-D	Tab	10 mg + 25 mg	10	Anti-Hypertensives	Nicholas Piramal	5.87	15.64
Reserpine + Dihydrallazine + Hydrochlorothiazide			Adelphane-Esidrex	Tab	0.1 mg + 10 mg + 10 mg	10	Anti-Hypertensives	Novartis	7.00	10.14
Reserpine + Dihydrallazine			Adelphane	Tab	0.1 mg + 10 mg	10	Anti-Hypertensives	Novartis		10.14
Ramipril			Cardace	Tab	1.25 mg	10	Cardiac Disorders	Sanofi-Aventis	2.13	0.00
Ramipril			Cardace	Tab	2.5 mg	10	Cardiac Disorders	Sanofi-Aventis		1.43
Ramipril			Cardace	Tab	5 mg	10	Cardiac Disorders	Sanofi-Aventis		5.00
Ramipril			Cardace	Tab	10 mg	10	Cardiac Disorders	Sanofi-Aventis		0.00

Ramipril + Hydrochlorothiazide		Cardace – H	Tab	2.5 mg + 12.5 mg	10	Cardiac Disorders	Sanofi-Aventis		4.76
Digoxin	yes	Cardioxin	Tab	0.25 mg	10	Cardiac Disorders	Novartis	11.28	0.00
Digoxin	yes	Lanoxin	Tab	0.25 mg	10	Cardiac Disorders	GSK	16.64	17.63
Atenolol + Nifedipine	yes	Tenofed	Cap	50 mg + 20 mg	10	Peripheral Vasodilators	IPCA	–0.35	6.89
Atenolol		Tenolol	Tab	25 mg	14	Peripheral Vasodilators	IPCA	7.51	7.84
Atenolol	yes	Tenolol	Tab	50 mg	14	Peripheral Vasodilators	IPCA		8.73
Atenolol	yes	Tenolol	Tab	100 mg	14	Peripheral Vasodilators	IPCA		0.00

Source: For 1994–2004 MIMS India, as cited in Sakthivel 2006, for 2005–08, Drug Today, various issues, CIMS India, 2007 July–October, and IDR Pharmacy Tripple Compendium, 2008, November 07–January 08.

Table B.2 Price changes to drugs for central nervous system disorders

Category	DPCO	NL EM	Brand	Form	Strength	Qty	Therapeutic group	Company	Price change %	
Drug name/ Year	**1995**	**2003**							**1994–2004**	**2005–2008**
Paracetamol + Caffeine + Cadeine		yes	Zimalgin	Cap	500 mg + 15 mg + 5 mg	10	Mast cell stablizer	Shreya	7.48	0.08
Aspirin + Calcarborae + Anhydrous citric acid	yes		Disprin	Tab	350 mg + 105 mg + 35 mg	12 × 10	Analgesics and Antipyretics	Reckitt Benckiser	−0.26	0.00
Carbamazepine	yes	yes	Mazetol	Tab	100 mg	10	Analgesics and Antipyretics	Nicholas Piramal	−1.36	1.93
Carbamazepine	yes	yes	Mazetol	Tab	200 mg	10	Analgesics and Antipyretics	Nicholas Piramal		1.87
Carbamazepine	yes		Mazetol	Tab	400 mg	10	Analgesics and Antipyretics	Nicholas Piramal		6.83
Carbamazepine	yes	yes	Mazetol – SR	Tab	200 mg	10	Analgesics and Antipyretics	Nicholas Piramal		2.43
Carbamazepine	yes		Mazetol – SR	Tab	400 mg	10	Analgesics and Antipyretics	Nicholas Piramal		2.25
Metoclopromide		yes	Reglan	Tab	10 mg	10	Antiemetics and Antinauseants	CFL Pharma	3.57	31.23
Metoclopromide		yes	Reglan	Syrup	5 mg/5 ml	30 ml	Antiemetics and Antinauseants	CFL Pharma		29.82

Metoclopromide			Reglan	Inj	10 mg/ml	2 ml	Antiemetics and Antinauseants	CFL Pharma		33.33
Metoclopromide			Reglan	Inj	10 mg/ml	10 ml	Antiemetics and Antinauseants	CFL Pharma		29.63
Metoclopromide		yes	Reglan	Tab	10 mg	10	Intestinal motility/Alimentary system	CFL Pharma		0.00
Metoclopromide		yes	Reglan	Syrup	5 mg/5 ml	30 ml	Intestinal motility/Alimentary system	CFL Pharma		0.00
Metoclopromide			Reglan	Inj	10 mg/ml	2 ml	Intestinal motility/Alimentary system	CFL Pharma		0.00
Metoclopromide			Reglan	Inj	10 mg/ml	10 ml	Intestinal motility/Alimentary system	CFL Pharma		0.00
Imipramine		yes	Antidep	Tab	25 mg	10	Antidepressants	Torrent	2.12	0.00
Imipramine		yes	Antidep	Tab	75 mg	10	Antidepressants	Torrent		0.00
Lithium Carbonate			Licab/XL	Tab	300 mg	10	Antidepressants	Torrent	−1.04	0.00
Lithium Carbonate			Licab	Tab	400 mg	10	Antidepressants	Torrent		0.00
Lorazepam			Larpose	Tab	1 mg	10	Sedatives and Tranquilisers	Cipla	−0.42	13.33
Lorazepam			Larpose	Tab	2 mg	10	Sedatives and Tranquilisers	Cipla		13.90
Trifluoperazine + Trihexyphenidyl		yes	Trinicalm Plus	Tab	5 mg + 2 mg	10	Sedatives and Tranquilisers	Torrent	−0.13	0.00
Trifluoperazine + Trihexyphenidyl + Chlorpromazine	yes	yes	Trinicalm Forte	Tab	5 mg + 2 mg + 50 mg	10	Sedatives and Tranquilisers	Torrent		0.00
Trifluoperazine		yes	Trinicalm	Tab	5 mg	10	Antiemetics and Antinauseants	Torrent		0.00
Clozapine			Sizopin	Tab	25 mg	10	Sedatives and Tranquilisers	Sun Pharma	0.00	8.57

Table B.2 (Continued)

Category	DPCO	NL EM	Brand	Form	Strength	Qty	Therapeutic group	Company	Price change %	
Drug name/ Year	**1995**	**2003**							**1994–2004**	**2005–2008**
Clozapine			Sizopin	Tab	100 mg	10	Sedatives and Tranquilisers	Sun Pharma		3.24
Haloperidol		yes	Serenace	Tab	1.5 mg	10	Sedatives and Tranquilisers	RPG Pharma	0.00	23.77
Haloperidol		yes	Serenace	Tab	5 mg	10	Sedatives and Tranquilisers	RPG Pharma		23.53
Haloperidol		yes	Serenace	Tab	10 mg	10	Sedatives and Tranquilisers	RPG Pharma		23.77
Haloperidol			Serenace	Tab	20 mg	10	Sedatives and Tranquilisers	RPG Pharma		10.21
Haloperidol			Serenace	Liquid	2 mg/1 ml	15 ml	Sedatives and Tranquilisers	RPG Pharma		50.38
Haloperidol		yes	Serenace	Inj	5 mg/ml	5 × 1 ml	Sedatives and Tranquilisers	RPG Pharma		42.72
Clozapine			Lozapin	Tab	25 mg	10	Antiemetics and Antinauseants	Torrent	1.76	0.00
Clozapine			Lozapin	Tab	100 mg	10	Antiemetics and Antinauseants	Torrent		0.00
Diazepam		yes	Paxum	Tab	5 mg	10	Sedatives and Tranquilisers	East India	2.40	37.44
Diazepam		yes	Paxum	Inj	5 mg/ml	2 ml	Sedatives and Tranquilisers	East India		38.54
Diazepam			Elcion CR	Cap	10 mg	10	Sedatives and Tranquilisers	Ranbaxy	4.13	0.00

Lorazepam		Ativan	Tab	1 mg	10	Sedatives and Tranquilisers	Wyeth	5.66	0.00
Lorazepam		Ativan	Tab	2 mg	10	Sedatives and Tranquilisers	Wyeth		0.00
Fluphenazine		Anatensol Inj.	Inj	25 mg/ml	1 ml vial	Sedatives and Tranquilisers	Nicholas Piramal	12.99	0.00
Fluphenazine		Anatensol Inj.	Tab	1 mg	10	Sedatives and Tranquilisers	Nicholas Piramal		0.00
Phenobarbitone	yes	Gardenal	Tab	30 mg	10	Hypnotics	Nicholas Piramal	0.00	40.17
Phenobarbitone	yes	Gardenal	Tab	60 mg	10	Hypnotics	Nicholas Piramal		38.40
Phenobarbitone		Gardenal	Syrup	20 mg/5 ml	60 ml	Hypnotics	Nicholas Piramal		23.37
Phenytoin + Phenobarbitone	yes	Garoin	Tab	100 mg + 50 mg	10	Anticonvulsants	Nicholas Piramal	7.00	31.54
Phenytoin Sodium		Dilantin	Kapseals	100 mg	100	Anticonvulsants	Pfizer	0.00	24.04
Phenytoin Sodium		Dilantin	Kapseals	25 mg	100	Anticonvulsants	Pfizer		26.01
Phenytoin Sodium	yes	Dilantin	Syrup	25 mg/ml	100 ml	Anticonvulsants	Pfizer		21.28
Phenytoin Sodium + Ethanol	yes	Dilantin	Inj	50 mg + 9.5% v/v	2 ml	Anticonvulsants	Pfizer		21.43
Phenytoin + Phenobarbitone		Dilantin – P	Kapseals	100 mg + 32 mg	100	Anticonvulsants	Pfizer		0.00
Phenytoin Sodium	yes	Epsolin	Tab	100 mg	100	Anticonvulsants	Cadila	4.21	0.00
Phenytoin Sodium	yes	Epsolin	Inj	50 mg/ml	50 × 2 ml	Anticonvulsants	Cadila		0.00
Phenytoin Sodium	yes	Eptoin	Tab	50 mg	50	Anticonvulsants	Abbott	8.32	0.00
Phenytoin Sodium	yes	Eptoin	Tab	100 mg	100	Anticonvulsants	Abbott		0.00
Phenytoin Sodium		Eptoin	Syrup	30 mg/5 ml	200 ml	Anticonvulsants	Abbott		0.00
Trihexyphenidyl	yes	Pacitane	Tab	2 mg	10	Neurodegenerative Disease	Wyeth	6.70	0.00

Source: For 1994–2004 MIMS India, as cited in Sakthivel 2006, for 2005–08, Drug Today, various issues, CIMS India, 2007 July–October, and IDR Pharmacy Tripple Compendium, 2008, November 07–January 08.

Table B.3 Price changes to drugs for infections and infestations

Category	DPCO	NL EM	Brand	Form	Strength	Qty	Therapeutic group	Company	Price change %	
Drug name/ Year	1995	2003							1994–2004	2005–2008
Ceftriaxone sodium			Monocef	Inj	125 mg	Vial	Antibiotics	Aristo	–2.58	1.82
Ceftriaxone sodium		yes	Monocef	Inj	250 mg	Vial	Antibiotics	Aristo		6.76
Ceftriaxone sodium			Monocef	Inj	500 mg	Vial	Antibiotics	Aristo		5.24
Ceftriaxone sodium		yes	Monocef	Inj	1 gm	Vial	Antibiotics	Aristo		2.93
Ceftriaxone sodium			Monocef	Inj	2 gm	Vial	Antibiotics	Aristo		2.94
Cefpodoxime proxetil			Monocef – O	Tab	100 mg	6	Antibiotics	Aristo		–0.60
Cefpodoxime proxetil			Monocef – O	Tab	200 mg	6	Antibiotics	Aristo		–0.60
Cefpodoxime proxetil			Monocef – O	Dry syrup	50 mg/5 ml	30 ml	Antibiotics	Aristo		–1.81
Cefpodoxime proxetil			Monocef – O	Dry syrup	100 mg/5 ml	30 ml	Antibiotics	Aristo		–1.76
Ceftriaxone sodium		yes	Oframax	Inj	250 mg	Vial	Antibiotics	Ranbaxy	–0.17	0.00
Ceftriaxone sodium			Oframax	Inj	500 mg	Vial	Antibiotics	Ranbaxy		0.00
Ceftriaxone sodium		yes	Oframax	Inj	1 gm	Vial	Antibiotics	Ranbaxy		0.00
Penicillin-G pot	yes		Pentids – 200	Tab	200,000 i.u	6	Antibiotics	Nicholas Piramal	–0.05	6.06
Penicillin-G pot	yes		Pentids – 400	Tab	400,000 i.u	6	Antibiotics	Nicholas Piramal		6.25

Penicillin-G pot	yes	yes	Pentids – 600	Tab	600,000 i.u	4	Antibiotics	Nicholas Piramal		6.35
Benzathine Penicillin-G	yes	yes	Pencom	Inj	600,000 i.u	5 vials	Antibiotics	Alembic	0.58	−1.27
Benzathine Penicillin-G	yes	yes	Pencom	Inj	1,200,000i.u	5 vials	Antibiotics	Alembic		−1.21
Benzathine Penicillin-G	yes	yes	Penidure LA6	Inj	600,000 i.u	Vial	Antibiotics	Wyeth		0.00
Benzathine Penicillin-G	yes	yes	Penidure LA12	Inj	1,200,000 i.u	Vial	Antibiotics	Wyeth		0.00
Benzathine Penicillin-G	yes	yes	Penidure LA24	Inj	2,400,000 i.u	Vial	Antibiotics	Wyeth		0.00
Erythromycin	yes	yes	Erythrocin	Tab	250 mg	10	Antibiotics	Pfizer	8.57	−33.62
Erythromycin	yes	yes	Erythrocin	Tab	500 mg	10	Antibiotics	Pfizer		−34.26
Erythromycin	yes	yes	Eltocin	Tab	250 mg	10	Antibiotics	IPCA	3.03	−36.08
Erythromycin	yes	yes	Eltocin	Tab	500 mg	10	Antibiotics	IPCA		−58.39
Erythromycin	yes	yes	Eltocin	Dry syrup	125 mg/5 ml	30 ml	Antibiotics	IPCA		−34.32
Cefotaxime	yes	yes	Claforan	Inj	250 mg	Vial	Antibiotics	Sanofi-Aventis	2.22	0.00
Cefotaxime	yes	yes	Claforan	Inj	500 mg	Vial	Antibiotics	Sanofi-Aventis		0.00
Cefotaxime	yes		Claforan	Inj	1 gm	Vial	Antibiotics	Sanofi-Aventis		0.00
Chloramphenicol		yes	Reclor	Cap	250 mg	10	Antibiotics	Nicholas Piramal	0.00	15.63
Chloramphenicol		yes	Reclor	Cap	500 mg	6	Antibiotics	Nicholas Piramal		14.86
Chloramphenicol		yes	Chloromycetin	Cap	500 mg	6	Antibiotics	Pfizer	5.73	24.14
Chloramphenicol		yes	Chloromycetin	Palmitate susp	125 mg/5 ml	60 ml	Antibiotics	Pfizer		0.00
Chloramphenicol			Chloromycetin	Kapseal	250 mg	10	Antibiotics	Pfizer		24.25
Amoxicillin + Cloxacillin	yes	yes	Novaclox	Caps	250 mg + 250 mg	9	Antibiotics	Cipla	7.19	−52.65
Amoxicillin + Cloxacillin	yes		Novaclox	P-Tab	125 mg + 125 mg	15	Antibiotics	Cipla		−51.70
Amoxicillin + Cloxacillin	yes		Novaclox 250	Inj	125 mg + 125 mg	Vial	Antibiotics	Cipla		0.00

Table B.3 (Continued)

Category	DPCO	NL EM	Brand	Form	Strength	Qty	Therapeutic group	Company	Price change %	
Drug name/ Year	**1995**	**2003**							**1994–2004**	**2005–2008**
Amoxicillin + Cloxacillin	yes	yes	Novaclox 500	Inj	250 mg + 250 mg	Vial	Antibiotics	Cipla		−1.54
Amoxicillin + Cloxacillin	yes	yes	Novaclox 1000	Inj	500 mg + 500 mg	Vial	Antibiotics	Cipla		−1.58
Amoxicillin + Cloxacillin	yes		Novaclox Neonate	Inj	50 mg + 25 mg	2 ml vial	Antibiotics	Cipla		0.00
Amoxicillin + Cloxacillin + Lactic Acid Bacillus	yes	yes	Novaclox – LB	Cap	250 mg + 250 mg + 60 million cells	6	Antibiotics	Cipla		−1.58
Amoxicillin	yes	yes	Novamox	Cap	250 mg	15	Antibiotics	Cipla	8.67	0.00
Amoxicillin	yes	yes	Novamox	Cap	500 mg	6	Antibiotics	Cipla		0.00
Amoxicillin	yes	yes	Novamox	Dry syrup	125 mg/5 ml	30 ml	Antibiotics	Cipla		0.00
Amoxicillin	yes	yes	Novamox	Dry syrup	125 mg/5 ml	60 ml	Antibiotics	Cipla		0.00
Amoxicillin	yes		Novamox (DT)	Tab	125 mg	15	Antibiotics	Cipla		0.00
Amoxicillin	yes	yes	Novamox (DT)	Tab	250 mg	15	Antibiotics	Cipla		0.00
Ampicillin	yes	yes	Campicilin	Cap	250 mg	10	Antibiotics	Cadila	10.90	24.32
Ampicillin	yes	yes	Campicilin	Cap	500 mg	10	Antibiotics	Cadila		−25.22
Ampicillin	yes	yes	Campicilin	Dry syrup	125 mg/5 ml	40 ml	Antibiotics	Cadila		0.00
Ampicillin	yes	yes	Campicilin	Dry syrup	125 mg/5 ml	60 ml	Antibiotics	Cadila		7.42
Ampicillin	yes		Campicilin	P-Drops	100 mg/ml	10 ml	Antibiotics	Cadila		0.00
Ampicillin	yes		Campicilin	Inj	250 mg	Vial	Antibiotics	Cadila		0.00
Ampicillin	yes	yes	Campicilin	Inj	500 mg	Vial	Antibiotics	Cadila		0.00
Ampicillin	yes	yes	Bacipen	Cap	250 mg	4	Antibiotics	Alembic		0.00
Ampicillin	yes	yes	Bacipen	Cap	500 mg	4	Antibiotics	Alembic		0.00

Ampicillin	yes	yes	Bacipen	Inj	500 mg	Vial	Antibiotics	Alembic		0.00
Amoxicillin + Cloxacillin	yes	yes	Suprimox	Cap	250 mg + 250 mg	15	Antibiotics	Rexcel/Ranbaxy	3.89	−56.36
Amoxicillin + Cloxacillin	yes		Suprimox	P-Tab	125 mg + 125 mg	10	Antibiotics	Rexcel/Ranbaxy		−51.48
Amphotericin B		yes	Fungizone Intravenous	Inj	50 mg	Vial	Antifungals	Nicholas Piramal	7.50	0.00
Clofazimine		yes	Hansepran	Cap	50 mg	10	Antileprotics	Nicholas Piramal	7.85	0.00
Clofazimine		yes	Hansepran	Cap	100 mg	10	Antileprotics	Nicholas Piramal		0.00
Mebendazole		yes	Mebex	Tab	100 mg	6	Anthelmintics and other anti-infestive drugs	Cipla		4.91
Mebendazole		yes	Mebex	Susp	100 mg/5 ml	30 ml	Anthelmintics and other anti-infestive drugs	Cipla		6.66
Mebendazole			Mebex	Grannules	200 mg/5 mg	5 gm Sachets	Anthelmintics and other anti-infestive drugs	Cipla		7.20
Mebendazole + Pyrantel Pamoate	yes		Mebex Plus	Tab	150 mg + 100 mg	2	Anthelmintics and other anti-infestive drugs	Cipla	0.00	−1.66
Metronidazole	yes	yes	Flagyl	Tab	200 mg	10	Anti-amoebics, anti-giardiasis	Nicholas Piramal	2.52	−1.92
Metronidazole	yes	yes	Flagyl	Tab	400 mg	10	Anti-amoebics, anti-giardiasis	Nicholas Piramal		−1.74

Table B.3 (Continued)

Category	DPCO	NL EM	Brand	Form	Strength	Qty	Therapeutic group	Company	Price change %	
Drug name/ Year	**1995**	**2003**							**1994–2004**	**2005–2008**
Metronidazole	yes		Flagyl	Susp	200 mg/5 ml	30 ml	Anti-amoebics, anti-giardiasis	Nicholas Piramal		−5.13
Metronidazole	yes		Flagyl	Susp	200 mg/5 ml	60 ml	Anti-amoebics, anti-giardiasis	Nicholas Piramal		−4.56
Metronidazole + Furazolidone	yes	yes	Flagyl – F	Tab	400 mg + 100 mg	10	Anti-diarrhoreals	Nicholas Piramal		3.55
Metronidazole + Furazolidone	yes	yes	Flagyl – F	Susp	100 mg + 30 mg/5 ml	60 ml	Anti-diarrhoreals	Nicholas Piramal		7.40
Metronidazole + Diloxanide Furoate	yes	yes	Flagyl – DF	Tab	400 mg + 500 mg	15	Anti-diarrhoreals	Nicholas Piramal		−0.09
Metronidazole	yes	yes	Aristogyl	Tab	200 mg	10	Anti-amoebics, anti-giardiasis	Aristo	4.74	−1.09
Metronidazole	yes	yes	Aristogyl	Tab	400 mg	10	Anti-amoebics, anti-giardiasis	Aristo		−1.27
Metronidazole	yes		Aristogyl	Susp	100 mg/5 ml	60 ml	Anti-amoebics, anti-giardiasis	Aristo		−1.17
Metronidazole + Furazolidone + Simethicone	yes	yes	Aristogyl – F	Tab	400 mg + 100 mg + 50 mg	10	Anti-amoebics, anti-giardiasis	Aristo		0.00
Metronidazole + Furazolidone	yes		Aristogyl – F	Susp	100 mg + 30 mg/5 ml	60 ml	Anti-amoebics, anti-giardiasis	Aristo		−1.32
Metronidazole + Diloxanide Furoate + Simethicone	yes	yes	Aristogyl Plus	Tab	400 mg + 500 mg + 100 mg	10	Anti-amoebics, anti-giardiasis	Aristo		−1.17
Ciprofloxacin	yes	yes	Ciprowin	Tab	250 mg	10	Quinolones	Alembic	0.00	0.00

Ciprofloxacin	yes	yes	Ciprowin	Tab	500 mg	10	Quinolones	Alembic		0.00
Ciprofloxacin	yes		Ciprowin	Tab	750 mg	10	Quinolones	Alembic		0.00
Ciprofloxacin	yes		Ciprowin	Infusion	100 mg/50 ml	100 ml	Quinolones	Alembic		0.00
Ciprofloxacin + Trinidazole	yes	yes	Ciprowin – TZ – 250	Tab	250 mg + 300 mg	10	Anti-diarrhoreals	Alembic		0.00
Ciprofloxacin + Trinidazole	yes		Ciprowin – TZ – 500	Tab	500 mg + 600 mg	10	Anti-diarrhoreals	Alembic		0.00
Ciprofloxacin + Benzalkonium chloride	yes	yes	Ciprowin E/E Drops	Drops	3 mg + 0.012% v/v/ml	5 ml	Anti-infective prep	Alembic		0.00
Ciprofloxacin	yes		Ciplox	Tab	100 mg	10	Sulphonamides and other Bact.	Cipla	3.38	–0.83
Ciprofloxacin	yes	yes	Ciplox	Tab	250 mg	10	Sulphonamides and other Bact.	Cipla		–0.80
Ciprofloxacin	yes	yes	Ciplox	Tab	500 mg	10	Sulphonamides and other Bact.	Cipla		–0.80
Ciprofloxacin	yes		Ciplox	Tab	750 mg	10	Sulphonamides and other Bact.	Cipla		–0.80
Ciprofloxacin	yes		Ciplox Infusion	Infusion	100 mg/50 ml	100 ml	Sulphonamides and other Bact.	Cipla		0.00
Ciprofloxacin	yes	yes	Ciplox – OD	Tab	500 mg	5	Sulphonamides and other Bact.	Cipla		0.00
Ciprofloxacin	yes		Ciplox	Tab	100 mg	5	Sulphonamides and other Bact.	Cipla		0.00

Source: For 1994–2004 MIMS India, as cited in Sakthivel 2006, for 2005–08, Drug Today, various issues, CIMS India, 2007 July–October, and IDR Pharmacy Tripple Compendium, 2008, November 07–January 08.

Table B.4 Price changes to drugs for malaria

Category	DPCO	NL EM	Brand	Form	Strength	Qty	Therapeutic group	Company	Price change %	
Drug name/ Year	**1995**	**2003**							**1994–2004**	**2005–2008**
Chloroquine	yes		Emquin	Tab	250 mg	10	Antimalarials	Merck	7.29	−16.14
Chloroquine	yes		Emquin	Tab	250 mg	1000	Antimalarials	Merck		0.00
Chloroquine	yes		Emquin	D.S.	500 mg	20 × 5	Antimalarials	Merck		−3.07
Chloroquine	yes		Emquin	Susp	160 mg/ 10 ml	60 ml	Antimalarials	Merck		1.97
Chloroquine	yes		Emquin	Inj	64.5 mg/ml	15 × 30 ml	Antimalarials	Merck		9.19
Chloroquine	yes		Melubrin	Tab	250 mg	10	Antimalarials	Ranbaxy	−2.58	0.00
Chloroquine	yes		Nivaquine	Tab	250 mg	10	Antimalarials	Nicholas Piramal		−16.13
Chloroquine	yes		Nivaquine	Susp	80.65 mg/ 5 ml	60 ml	Antimalarials	Nicholas Piramal		−7.29
Chloroquine	yes	yes	Nivaquine	Inj	40 mg/ml	2 ml amp	Antimalarials	Nicholas Piramal		20.33
Chloroquine	yes	yes	Nivaquine	Inj	40 mg/ml	5 ml amp	Antimalarials	Nicholas Piramal		5.88
Chloroquine	yes	yes	Nivaquine	Inj	40 mg/ml	30 ml	Antimalarials	Nicholas Piramal		5.41
Mefloquine			Mefliam	Tab	250 mg	6	Antimalarials	Cipla		0.00
Mefloquine			Facital	Tab	250 mg	6	Antimalarials	Cadila		0.00
Quinine sulphate		yes	Kunen	Tab	300 mg	10	Antimalarials	Merrind		0.00
Quinine sulphate			Kunen	Tab	600 mg	10	Antimalarials	Merrind		0.00

Source: For 1994–2004 MIMS India, as cited in Sakthivel 2006, for 2005–08, Drug Today, various issues, CIMS India, 2007 July–October, and IDR Pharmacy Tripple Compendium, 2008, November 07–January 08.

Table B.5 Price changes to drugs for HIV/AIDS

Category	DPCO	NL EM	Brand	Form	Strength	Qty	Therapeutic group	Company	Price change %	
Drug name/ Year	**1995**	**2003**							**1994–2004**	**2005–2008**
Zidovudine		yes	Zidovir	Cap	100 mg	10	Antiretorvirals	Cipla	−7.67	0.00
Zidovudine		yes	Zidovir	Cap	100 mg	100	Antiretorvirals	Cipla		0.00
Zidovudine		yes	Zidovir	Cap	300 mg	10	Antiretorvirals	Cipla		0.00
Zidovudine		yes	Zidovir	Cap	300 mg	60	Antiretorvirals	Cipla		0.00
Zidovudine			Zidovir	Syrup	50 mg/ml	100 ml	Antiretorvirals	Cipla		−33.33
Zidovudine			Zidomax	Cap	100 mg	10	Antiretorvirals	Alkem		0.00
Zidovudine		yes	Zidomax	Tab	300 mg	10	Antiretorvirals	Alkem		0.00
Zidovudine			Zydowin	Cap	100 mg	10	Antiretorvirals	Zydus Vaccicare		0.00
Zidovudine		yes	Zydowin	Tab	300 mg	10	Antiretorvirals	Zydus Vaccicare		0.00
Stavudine		yes	Stavir	Cap	30 mg	10	Antiretorvirals	Cipla		0.00
Stavudine		yes	Stavir	Tab	40 mg	10	Antiretorvirals	Cipla		0.00
Lamivudine + Zidovudine		yes	Combivir	Tab	150 mg + 300 mg	10	Antiretorvirals	GSK		0.00
Lamivudine + Zidovudine		yes	Duovir	Tab	150 mg + 300 mg	60	Antiretorvirals	Cipla		0.00
Lamivudine + Zidovudine		yes	Lamuzid	Tab	150 mg + 300 mg	10	Antiretorvirals	Zydus Vaccicare		0.00
Lamivudine + Zidovudine		yes	Zidolam	Tab	150 mg + 300 mg	10	Antiretorvirals	Genix		−23.64

Source: For 1994–2004 MIMS India, as cited in Sakthivel 2006, for 2005–08, Drug Today, various issues, CIMS India, 2007 July–October, and IDR Pharmacy Tripple Compendium, 2008, November 07–January 08.

Table B.6 Price changes to drugs for Tuberculosis

Category	DPCO	NL EM	Brand	Form	Strength	Qty	Therapeutic group	Company	Price change %	
Drug name/ Year	**1995**	**2003**							**1994–2004**	**2005–2008**
Rifampicin + Isoniazid	yes	yes	Rimpazid	Tab	450 mg + 300 mg	10	Antituberculosis	Cadila Health	12.39	0.00
Rifampicin + Isoniazid	yes	yes	Rimactazid 450/300	Tab	450 mg + 300 mg	20 × 4	Antituberculosis	Novartis		−12.17
Rifampicin + Isoniazid	yes	yes	Rimactazid	Dis ped	100 mg + 50 mg	10	Antituberculosis	Novartis		−12.19
Rifampicin + Isoniazid	yes	yes	Rimactazid Plus	Tab	600 mg + 300 mg	25 × 4	Antituberculosis	Novartis		−12.13
Rifampicin	yes	yes	Rimactane	Cap	300 mg	4	Antituberculosis	Novartis	2.90	0.00
Rifampicin	yes	yes	Rimactane	Tab	450 mg	20 × 4	Antituberculosis	Novartis		−11.07
Ethambutol + INH		yes	Myconex 800	Tab	800 mg + 300 mg	10	Antituberculosis	Le Sante	0.00	4.17
Ethambutol + INH		yes	Inabutol Forte	Tab	800 mg + 300 mg	10	Antituberculosis	Themis Chemicals	9.96	0.00
Ethambutol + INH		yes	Combunex	Tab	800 mg + 300 mg	10	Antituberculosis	Lupin	13.45	0.00
Pyrazinamide		yes	P-Zide	Tab	500 mg	10	Antituberculosis	Le Sante	0.00	0.00
Pyrazinamide		yes	P-Zide	Tab	750 mg	11	Antituberculosis	Le Sante	0.00	0.00
Pyrazinamide		yes	P-Zide	Tab	1000 mg	12	Antituberculosis	Le Sante	0.00	0.00
Pyrazinamide		yes	PZA-Ciba	Tab	500 mg	10	Antituberculosis	Novartis	7.56	0.00
Pyrazinamide		yes	PZA-Ciba	Tab	750 mg	10	Antituberculosis	Novartis		0.00
Pyrazinamide		yes	PZA-Ciba	Tab	1000 mg	10	Antituberculosis	Novartis		0.00
Pyrazinamide			PZA-Ciba	Susp	5%	100 ml	Antituberculosis	Novartis		0.00
Streptomycin	yes	yes	Ambistryn-S	Inj	0.75 gm	vial	Antituberculosis	Nicholas Piramal	8.96	−7.31
Streptomycin	yes	yes	Ambistryn-S	Inj	1.00 gm	vial	Antituberculosis	Nicholas Piramal		−8.15

Source: For 1994–2004 MIMS India, as cited in Sakthivel 2006, for 2005–08, Drug Today, various issues, CIMS India, 2007 July–October, and IDR Pharmacy Tripple Compendium, 2008, November 07–January 08.

Table B.7 Price changes to drugs for alimentary, musculo-skeletal disorders, hormones, and genito-urinary system

Category	DPCO	NL EM	Brand	Form	Strength	Qty	Therapeutic group	Company	Price change %	
Drug name/ Year	1995	2003							1994–2004	2005–2008
Nalidixic Acid	yes	yes	Gramoneg	Tab	500 mg	8	Antidiarrhoeals	Rextar	–0.41	0.00
Nalidixic Acid	yes		Gramoneg	Syrup	300 mg/ 5 ml	30 ml	Antidiarrhoeals	Rextar		0.00
Nalidixic Acid + Metronida-zole	yes		Gramoneg – M	Syrup	150 mg + 100 mg/5 ml	30 ml	Antidiarrhoeals	Ranbaxy		0.00
Nalidixic Acid + Metronida-zole	yes	yes	Gramoneg – M	Tab	300 mg + 200 mg	8	Antidiarrhoeals	Ranbaxy		0.00
Norfloxacin + Tinidazole	yes	yes	Gramoneg – TN	Tab	400 mg + 600 mg	10	Antidiarrhoeals	Ranbaxy		0.00
Nalidixic Acid	yes		Negadix	Tab	Kid 125 mg	10	Urinary anti-infectives	CFL Pharma	–0.38	0.00
Nalidixic Acid + Metronida-zole	yes	yes	Negadix – M	Tab	300 mg + 200 mg	6	Urinary anti-infectives	CFL Pharma		0.00
Nalidixic Acid + Metronida-zole	yes		Negadix – M	Susp	150 mg + 100 mg	60 ml	Urinary anti-infectives	CFL Pharma		0.00
Oxytocin		yes	Pitocin	Inj	10 i.u.	1 amp	Drugs acting on uterus	Pfizer	0.77	20.51
Glibenclamide		yes	Euglucon	Tab	5 mg	10	Hyper and hypoglycaemics	Nicholas Piramal	8.35	33.33
Glibenclamide		yes	Daonil	Tab	5 mg	10	Hyper and hypoglycaemics	Sanofi-Aventis	6.81	0.00

Table B.7 (Continued)

Category	DPCO	NL EM	Brand	Form	Strength	Qty	Therapeutic group	Company	Price change %	
Drug name/ Year	**1995**	**2003**							**1994–2004**	**2005–2008**
Frusemide	yes	yes	Frusenex	Tab	40 mg	10	Diuretics and Antidiuretics	Geno	−1.03	0.00
Frusemide	yes		Frusenex	Tab	100 mg	10	Diuretics and Antidiuretics	Geno		0.00
Frusemide	yes	yes	Lasix	Tab	40 mg	10	Diuretics and Antidiuretics	Sanofi-Aventis		−1.66
Frusemide	yes		Lasix	Tab	High dose	10	Diuretics and Antidiuretics	Sanofi-Aventis		0.00
Frusemide	yes	yes	Lasix	Inj	10 mg/2 ml	2 ml Amp	Diuretics and Antidiuretics	Sanofi-Aventis		1.41
Frusemide	yes	yes	Lasix	Inj	High dose 10 mg	5 × 25 ml	Diuretics and Antidiuretics	Sanofi-Aventis		0.00
Frusemide + Amiloride	yes		Frumil	Tab	40 mg + 5 mg	10	Diuretics and Antidiuretics	Geno	8.24	0.00
Spironolactone	yes	yes	Aldactone	Tab	25 mg	10	Diuretics and Antidiuretics	RPG	4.34	−6.04
Spironolactone	yes		Aldactone	Tab	100 mg	10	Diuretics and Antidiuretics	RPG		−8.17
Spironolactone + Hydroflume-thiazide	yes	yes	Aldactide	Tab	25 mg + 25 mg	10	Diuretics and Antidiuretics	RPG		0.00
Ibuprofen	yes	yes	Brufen	Tab	200 mg	10	Non-Steroid anti-inlm. Drugs	Abbott	4.66	0.00
Ibuprofen	yes	yes	Brufen	Tab	400 mg	10	Non-Steroid anti-inlm. Drugs	Abbott		0.00

Ibuprofen	yes		Brufen	Tab	600 mg	10	Non-Steroid anti-inlm. Drugs	Abbott		0.00
Ibuprofen + Paracetamol	yes	yes	Combiflam	Tab	400 mg + 325 mg	10	Non-Steroid anti-inlm. Drugs	Sanofi-Aventis	7.16	−1.67
Ibuprofen + Paracetamol	yes		Combiflam	Susp	100 mg + 162.5 mg/5 ml	60 ml	Non-Steroid anti-inlm. Drugs	Sanofi-Aventis		−1.62
Insulin NPH	yes	yes	Actrapid	Inj	40 i.u.	10 ml	Hyper and hypoglycaemics	Abbott	3.99	0.00
Insulin NPH	yes	yes	Actrapid MC	Inj	40 i.u.	10 ml	Hyper and hypoglycaemics	Abbott		0.00
Insulin NPH	yes	yes	Lentard	Inj	40 i.u./ml	10 ml	Throid and antithroid drugs	Abbott	1.24	0.00
Insulin NPH	yes	yes	Iletin – L	Inj	40 i.u./ml	10 ml	Throid and antithroid drugs	Eli Lilly		0.00
Insulin NPH	yes	yes	Iletin – NPH	Inj	40 i.u./ml	10 ml	Throid and antithroid drugs	Eli Lilly		0.00
Insulin NPH	yes	yes	Iletin – R	Inj	40 i.u./ml	10 ml	Throid and antithroid drugs	Eli Lilly		0.00
Prednisolone	yes	yes	Wysolone	Tab	5 mg	10	Corticosteroids and related drugs	Wyeth	−5.10	0.00
Prednisolone	yes	yes	Wysolone	Tab	10 mg	10	Corticosteroids and related drugs	Wyeth		0.00
Prednisolone	yes		Wysolone	Tab	20 mg	10	Corticosteroids and related drugs	Wyeth		0.00
Prednisolone	yes		Wysolone	Tab	30 mg	10	Corticosteroids and related drugs	Wyeth		0.00
Prednisolone	yes		Wysolone	Tab	40 mg	10	Corticosteroids and related drugs	Wyeth		0.00

Table B.7 (Continued)

Category	DPCO	NL EM	Brand	Form	Strength	Qty	Therapeutic group	Company	Price change %	
Drug name/ Year	**1995**	**2003**							**1994–2004**	**2005–2008**
Magnesium +		yes	Pepticaine	Liquid	Combination	120 ml	Gastro-intestinal sedatives and Ulcer drugs	Pfizer	3.44	0.00
Magnesium +		yes	Solacid	Tab	Combination	10	Gastro-intestinal sedatives and Ulcer drugs	Dey's Pharma	10.60	25.00
Magnesium +		yes	Solacid	Syrup	Combination	170 ml	Gastro-intestinal sedatives and Ulcer drugs	Dey's Pharma		19.40
Magnesium +		yes	Solacid	Syrup	Combination	340 ml	Gastro-intestinal sedatives and Ulcer drugs	Dey's Pharma		18.42
Magnesium +		yes	Solacid – O	Susp	Combination	170 ml	Gastro-intestinal sedatives and Ulcer drugs	Dey's Pharma		14.28

Note: The + symbol at the end of a drug name denotes formulations made from more than three drugs. While all the drugs were considered for the analysis, it was considered appropriate to limit the listing to three drugs for this study.

Source: For 1994–2004 MIMS India, as cited in Sakthivel 2006, for 2005–08, Drug Today, various issues, CIMS India, 2007 July–October, and IDR Pharmacy Tripple Compendium, 2008, November 07–January 08.

Table B.8 Price changes to drugs for nutrition and respiratory system

Category	DPCO	NL EM	Brand	Form	Strength	Qty	Therapeutic group	Company	Price change %	
Drug name/ Year	**1995**	**2003**							**1994–2004**	**2005–2008**
Vitamin A	yes	yes	Rovigon	Tab	Vitamin A 10,000 i.u + Vitamin E 25 mg	10	Vitamins	Nicholas Piramal	0.44	0.00
Salmeterol			Serobid	Inhaler	25 mcg/ metered dose	200 mdi	Bronchospasm	Cipla	3.40	0.00
Salmeterol			Serobid	Rotahaler		30	Bronchospasm	Cipla		0.00
Salmeterol			Serobid	Rotacap	50 mcg	30	Bronchospasm	Cipla		0.00
Salmeterol			Salmeter	Inhaler	25 mcg/ metered dose		Bronchospasm	DRL	−0.67	0.00
Ephedrine + Theophylline + phenobarbitone	yes	yes	Asmapax Depot	Tab	50 mg + 65 mg + 30 mg	10	Bronchospasm	Nicholas Piramal	−0.34	−1.63
Ephedrine + Theophylline + phenobarbitone	yes	yes	Alergin	Tab	20 mg + 100 mg + 15 mg	10	Bronchospasm	Cipla	7.36	0.00
Iron + (Salts/complex)	yes		Anemidox	Cap	Combination	3 × 10	Anaemia; Neutropenia	Merck	14.18	−1.32
Iron + (Salts/complex)			Imferon	Liquid	Combination	200 ml	Anaemia; Neutropenia	Shreya	4.36	7.35
Iron + (Salts/complex)			Imferon	Cap	Combination	15	Anaemia; Neutropenia	Shreya		64.47

Table B.8 (Continued)

Category	DPCO	NL EM	Brand	Form	Strength	Qty	Therapeutic group	Company	Price change %	
Drug name/ Year	**1995**	**2003**							**1994–2004**	**2005–2008**
Iron dextran + Vitamin B-12 + Folic acid		yes	Imferon	Inj	50 mg of elemental iron + 12,500 mcg + 2.5 mg/ml	2 ml	Anaemia; Neutropenia	Shreya		−6.43
Iron dextran + Vitamin B-12 + Folic acid		yes	Imferon	Inj	50 mg of elemental iron + 12,500 mcg + 2.5 mg/ml	10 ml	Anaemia; Neutropenia	Shreya		−0.80
Iron dextran + Vitamin B-12		yes	Imferon B – 12	Inj	50 mg of elemental iron + 500 mcg/ml	2 ml	Anaemia; Neutropenia	Shreya		0.00
Iron dextran + Vitamin B-12 + Folic acid		yes	Imferon F – 12	Inj	50 mg of elemental iron + 500 mcg + 2.5 mg/ml	20 × 2 ml	Anaemia; Neutropenia	Shreya		12.40
Budesonide			Pulmicort	Inhaler	100 mcg	100 doses	Bronchospasm relaxants	Astra Zeneca	8.93	38.51
Budesonide			Pulmicort	Inhaler	100 mcg	400 doses	Bronchospasm relaxants	Astra Zeneca		0.00
Salbutamol	yes	yes	Salmaplon	Tab	2 mg	10	Bronchospasm relaxants	Khandelwal	4.06	−68.00

Salbutamol	yes	yes	Salmaplon	Tab	4 mg	10	Bronchospasm relaxants	Khandelwal		−70.40
Salbutamol	yes	yes	Salbetol	Tab	2 mg	10	Bronchospasm relaxants	FDC	2.57	0.00
Salbutamol	yes	yes	Salbetol	Tab	4 mg	10	Bronchospasm relaxants	FDC		0.00
Carbohydrate+	yes		Ferradol Food	Powder	Combination	200 gms	Tonics; appetite stimulants	Pfizer	−2.06	0.00
Carbohydrate+	yes		Ferradol Food	Powder	Combination	450 gms	Tonics; appetite stimulants	Pfizer		0.00
Amino acid + Glycine + Sorbitol			Astymin – 3	Infusion	81.2 mg + 10 mg + 50 mg/ml	200 ml	Tonics; appetite stimulants	Tablet India		11.75
Amino acid + Glycine + Sorbitol			Astymin – 3	Amp	81.2 mg + 10 mg + 50 mg/ml	20 ml	Tonics; appetite stimulants	Tablet India		8.31
L-isoleucine+			Astymin – SN	Infusion	Combination	200 ml	Tonics; appetite stimulants	Tablet India		10.27
L-isoleucine+	yes		Astymin	Syrup	Combination	110 ml	Tonics; appetite stimulants	Tablet India		21.37
L-isoleucine+	yes		Astymin	Syrup	Combination	200 ml	Tonics; appetite stimulants	Tablet India		22.99
Vitamin A+	yes	yes	Astymin Forte	Cap	Combination	10 × 2	Tonics; appetite stimulants	Tablet India	2.05	13.52
Vitamin C+	yes		Astymin – C	Drops	Combination	15 ml	Tonics; appetite stimulants	Tablet India		19.89
Magnesium+			Astymin-M Forte	Cap	Combination	10	Tonics; appetite stimulants	Tablet India		16.98
Dextrose+			Leclyte	Powder	Combination	30 gms	Mineral and parenteral nutritional suppl.	Albert David	0.00	0.00
Dextrose+			Leclyte – G	Inj	Combination	500 ml	Plasma expanders	Albert David		−39.20

Table B.8 (Continued)

Category	DPCO	NL EM	Brand	Form	Strength	Qty	Therapeutic group	Company	Price change %	
Drug name/ Year	**1995**	**2003**							**1994–2004**	**2005–2008**
Dextrose+			Leclyte – M	Inj	Combination	500 ml	Plasma expanders	Albert David		−39.20
Dextrose+			Leclyte – P	Inj	Combination	500 ml	Plasma expanders	Albert David		−39.20
Dextrose+			Leclyte – R	Inj	Combination	500 ml	Plasma expanders	Albert David		0.00
Dextrose+			Leclyte – W	Powder	Combination	27.5 gms	Mineral and parenteral nutritional suppl.	Albert David		0.00
Calcium Carbonate + Vitamin D3			Ossivite	Tab	0.625 g+100 i.u.	10	Mineral and parenteral nutritional suppl.	Wyeth	5.62	0.00
Calcium Carbonate + Vitamin D3			Ossivite	Tab	1.25 g+200 i.u.	10	Mineral and parenteral nutritional suppl.	Wyeth		0.00
Vitamin A+	yes	yes	Filibon	Cap	Combination	50	Mineral and parenteral nutritional suppl.	Wyeth	2.90	0.00
Dextromethrophan+			Grilinctus	Syrup	Combination	100 ml	Expectorants, Cough Suppr., Decongestants	Franco Indian	4.67	53.66
Dextromethrophan+			Grilinctus	Syrup	Combination	450 ml	Expectorants, Cough Suppr., Decongestants	Franco Indian		25.00
Terbutaline + Bromhexcine			Grilinctus BM	Syrup	2.5 mg + 8 mg/5 ml	100 ml	Expectorants, Cough Suppr., Decongestants	Franco Indian		25.00
Terbutaline + Bromhexcine			Grilinctus BM	Pead syrup	1.5 mg + 4 mg/5 ml	30 ml	Expectorants, Cough Suppr., Decongestants	Franco Indian		16.86

Terbutaline + Bromhexcine	yes	Grilinctus BM	Tab	2.5 mg + 8 mg/5 ml	10	Expectorants, Cough Suppr., Decongestants	Franco Indian		43.40
Terbutaline+		Bro-Zedex	Syrup	Combination	100 ml	Expectorants, Cough Suppr., Decongestants	Wockhardt	5.69	0.00
Terbutaline+		Bro-Zedex	Liquicap	Combination	6	Expectorants, Cough Suppr., Decongestants	Wockhardt		0.00
Chlorpheniramine + Ammonium chloride + Sodium citrate		Piriton Expectorant	Liquid	2.5 mg + 125 mg + 55 mg/5 ml	120 ml	Expectorants, cough suppressants, mucolytics and decongestants	GSK	5.42	0.00
Chlorpheniramine + Ammonium chloride + Sodium citrate		Piriton Expectorant	Liquid	2.5 mg + 125 mg + 55 mg/5 ml	460 ml	Expectorants, cough suppressants, mucolytics and decongestants	GSK		3.00
Chlorpheniramine + Codeine		Corex	Syrup	4 mg + 10 mg/5 ml	50 ml	Expectorants, cough suppressants, mucolytics and decongestants	Pfizer	−0.24	24.27
Chlorpheniramine + Codeine		Corex	Syrup	4 mg + 10 mg/5 ml	100 ml	Expectorants, cough suppressants, mucolytics and decongestants	Pfizer		24.00
Dextromethorphan + Chlorpheniramine + Menthol		Corex – DX	Syrup	10 mg + 4 mg + 0.1 mg/5 ml	50 ml	Expectorants, cough suppressants, mucolytics and decongestants	Pfizer		30.23
Dextromethorphan + Chlorpheniramine + Menthol		Corex – DX	Syrup	10 mg + 4 mg + 0.1 mg/5 ml	100 ml	Expectorants, cough suppressants, mucolytics and decongestants	Pfizer		30.50

Note: The + symbol at the end of a drug name denotes formulations made from more than three drugs. While all the drugs were considered for the analysis, it was considered appropriate to limit the listing to three drugs for this study.

Source: For 1994–2004 MIMS India, as cited in Sakthivel 2006, for 2005–08, Drug Today, various issues, CIMS India, 2007 July–October, and IDR Pharmacy Tripple Compendium, 2008, November 07–January 08.

Table B.9 Price changes to drugs for ENT, skin, and surgical anaesthetics

Category	DPCO	NL EM	Brand	Form	Strength	Qty	Therapeutic group	Company	Price change %	
Drug name/ Year	**1995**	**2003**							**1994–2004**	**2005–2008**
Lignocaine+		yes	Xylocaine c Adrenaline	Inj	Combination	30 ml	Anaesthetics	Astra Zeneca	6.44	43.95
Lignocaine + Methyl paraben		yes	Xylocaine c Adrenaline	Topical 4%	42.7 mg/ml + 1 mg/ml	30 ml	Anaesthetics	Astra Zeneca		51.42
Lignocaine + Methyl paraben + Sodium chloride		yes	Xylocaine 1%	Inj	10.7 mg + 1 mg + 6 mg/ml	30 ml	Anaesthetics	Astra Zeneca		47.51
Lignocaine + Methyl paraben		yes	Xylocaine 1%	Inj	21.3 mg + 1 mg + 6 mg/ml	30 ml	Anaesthetics	Astra Zeneca		35.40
Lignocaine + Methyl paraben + Propyl paraben			Xlyocaine Jelly 2%	Gel	21.3 mg + 0.61 mg + 0.27 mg/ml	30 gms	Anaesthetics	Astra Zeneca		35.90
Lignocaine + Propylene glycol		yes	Xylocaine Oint 5%	Ointment	5%w/w + 25%w/w	20 gms	Anaesthetics	Astra Zeneca		43.95
Lignocaine + Ethanol			Xylocaine Spray	Spray	100 mg + 28.29% v/v per ml	500 md	Anaesthetics	Astra Zeneca		0.00
Lignocaine + Methyl paraben			Xylocaine	Spray	100 mg + 28.29% v/v per ml	800 md	Anaesthetics	Astra Zeneca		0.00
Lignocaine + Methyl paraben + Propyl paraben		yes	Viscous 2%	Viscous	21.3 mg + 0.61 mg + 0.27 mg/ml	100 ml	Anaesthetics	Astra Zeneca		50.99
Lignocaine + Sodium chloride		yes	Xylocard	Vial	21.3 mg + 6 mg/ml	50 ml	Ventricular arrhythmias	Astra Zeneca		50.96

Lignocaine + Dextrose		yes	Xylocaine Heavy 5%	Inj	53.5 mg + 75 mg	25 × 2 ml	Spinal anaesthesia	Astra Zeneca		0.00
Lignocaine + Glucose		yes	Gesicain Heavy 5%	Inj	5% + 7.5%	25 × 2 ml	Spinal anaesthesia	Nicholas Piramal		5.51
Lignocaine		yes	Gesicain c Adrenaline 2%	Inj	2%	30 ml	Anaesthetics	Nicholas Piramal	9.99	0.00
Lignocaine		yes	Gesicain	Inj	2%	30 ml	Anaesthetics	Nicholas Piramal		0.00
Lignocain + Carboxy-methylcellulose			Gesicain Jelly 2%	Gel	2% + 3.5%	30 ml	Anaesthetics	Nicholas Piramal		0.00
Ligocaine		yes	Gesicain Oint 5%	Ointment	5%	10 gm	Anaesthetics	Nicholas Piramal		5.49
Ligocaine		yes	Gesicain Topical 4% SOLN	Soln	4%	30 ml	Anaesthetics	Nicholas Piramal		5.49
Ketamine		yes	Ketmin	Inj	10 mg/ml	10 ml	Anaesthetics	Themis Medicare	−3.58	0.00
Ketamine		yes	Ketmin	Inj	50 mg/ml	2 ml	Anaesthetics	Themis Medicare		0.00
Ketamine		yes	Ketalar	Inj	10 mg	20 ml	Anaesthetics	Pfizer	0.00	0.00
Ketamine		yes	Ketalar	Inj	50 mg	2 ml	Anaesthetics	Pfizer		0.00
Ketamine		yes	Ketalar	Inj	50 mg	10 ml	Anaesthetics	Pfizer		0.00
Lignocaine+	yes		Otek-AC+	Drops	Combination	5 ml	Anti-infective prep.	FDC	7.88	28.42
Chloramphenicol			Chloromycetin Aplicaps	Aplicaps (eye)	250mg	50	Anti-infective prep	Pfizer		27.48
Chloramphenicol + Benzocaine			Chloromycetin	Drops (eye)	5% w/v + 1% w/v	5 ml	Anti-infective prep	Pfizer		0.00
Chloramphenicol + Benzocaine + Propylene glycol			Chloromycetin	Drops (ear)	5% w/v + 1% w/v + q.s	5 ml	Aural Preparations	Pfizer		24.49
Gentamycin + Benzalkonium	yes	yes	Genticyn Eye/Ear	Drops	Gentamycin 0.3%	5 ml	Aural Preparations	Nicholas Piramal		0.27

Table B.9 (Continued)

Category	DPCO	NL EM	Brand	Form	Strength	Qty	Therapeutic group	Company	Price change %	
Drug name/ Year	**1995**	**2003**							**1994–2004**	**2005–2008**
Gentamycin + Benzalkonium	yes	yes	Genticyn E/E	Drops	0.3% + 0.04%	5 ml	Anti-infective prep	Allergan	3.26	0.00
Gentamycin+	yes	yes	Genticyn B Eye/Ear	Drops	Combination	5 ml	Anti-inflamatory/ Anti-allergic	Nicholas Piramal		0.00
Gentamycin+	yes	yes	Genticyn HC	Drops	Combination	5 ml	Anti-inflamatory/ Anti-allergic	Nicholas Piramal		0.00
Fluticasone			Zoflut	Cream	0.05%	5 gm	Topical steroid Prep	Cipla	1.22	0.00
Fluticasone			Zoflut	Cream	0.05%	10 gm	Topical steroid Prep	Cipla		0.00
Fluticasone			Zoflut	Lotion	0.05%	10 ml	Topical steroid Prep	Cipla		0.00
Fluticasone			Zoflut	Ointment	0.05%	10 gm	Topical steroid Prep	Cipla		0.00
Nitrofurazone			Furacin-S	Cream	0.02%	20 gms	Topical steroid Prep	GSK	0.00	−28.87
Nitrofurazone			Furacin-S	Cream	0.02%	500 gms	Topical steroid Prep	GSK		−4.28
Crotamiton + Hydrocortisone			Crotorax-HC	Cream	10% + 0.25%	10 gms	Topical steroid Prep	Nicholas Piramal	0.18	0.00
Crotamiton			Crotorax	Cream	10%	20 gms	Topical steroid Prep	Nicholas Piramal		0.00
Crotamiton			Crotorax	Lotion	10%	60 ml	Topical steroid Prep	Nicholas Piramal		0.00
Heparin + Benzyl nicotinate			Beparine	Cream	50.i.u + 3 mg/g	15 gm	Misc. skin prep.	Biological E	8.45	0.20
Sodium diatrizoate + Meglumine antimonate		yes	Urografin 60%/76%	Inj	1600 + 10400 mg	20 ml	Diagnostic Agents	German Remedies	18.19	0.00
Sodium diatrizoate + Meglumine antimonate		yes	Urografin 60%/76%	Inj	2000 + 13200 mg	20 ml	Diagnostic Agents	German Remedies		0.00

Bupivacaine	yes	Marcaine	Inj	0.50%	20 ml	Surgical antibacterials	Nicholas Piramal	2.38	0.00
Bupivacaine		Marcaine Hyperbaric	Inj	1%	2 ml	Surgical antibacterials	Nicholas Piramal		0.00
Bupivacaine + Sodium Chloride + Methyal paraben	yes	Sensorcaine	Inj 0.25%	2.64 + 8 + 1 mg/ml	20 ml	Surgical antibacterials	Astra Zeneca	8.44	64.98
Bupivacaine + Sodium Chloride + Methyl paraben	yes	Sensorcaine	Inj 0.25%	5.28 + 8 + 1 mg/ml	20 ml	Surgical antibacterials	Astra Zeneca		0.00
Bupivacaine + Dextrose monohydrate	yes	Sensorcaine Heavy	Inj	5 + 80 mg/ml	5 × 4 ml	Surgical antibacterials	Astra Zeneca		0.00
Bupivacaine +	yes	Sensorcaine 0.5% with Adrenaline	Inj	Combination	20 ml	Surgical antibacterials	Astra Zeneca		0.00
Beclomethasone dipropionate		Beclate – 200	Inhaler	200 mg	200 md	Local reactants on the nose	Cipla	1.97	0.00
Beclomethasone dipropionate	yes	Beclate Inhaler	Inhaler	50 mcg	200 doses	Local reactants on the nose	Cipla		0.00
Beclomethasone dipropionate		Beclate Inhaler	Inhaler	100 mcg	200 doses	Local reactants on the nose	Cipla		0.00
Beclomethasone dipropionate		Beclate Rotacaps	Inhaler	100 mcg	3 × 10	Local reactants on the nose	Cipla		0.00
Beclomethasone dipropionate		Beclate Rotacaps	Inhaler	200 mcg	30	Local reactants on the nose	Cipla		0.00
Beclomethasone dipropionate + Chinoform		Beclate Rotacaps	Inhaler	400 mcg	30	Local reactants on the nose	Cipla		0.00

Table B.9 (Continued)

Category	DPCO	NL EM	Brand	Form	Strength	Qty	Therapeutic group	Company	Price change %	
Drug name/ Year	**1995**	**2003**							**1994–2004**	**2005–2008**
Beclomethasone dipropionate			Beclate-C	Cream	0.025% w/w + 3%	15 gm	Topical steroid Prep	Cipla		0.00
Beclomethasone dipropionate + Neomycin			Beclate-N	Cream	0.025% + 0.5%	15 gm	Topical steroid Prep	Cipla		0.00
Beclomethasone dipropionate + Salicyclic acid		yes	Beclate-S	Ointment	0.1% + 3%	15 gm	Topical steroid Prep	Cipla		0.00
Atropine + Prednisolon + Chlorobutanol		yes	Atrisolon	Drops	1% + 0.25% + 0.5%	5 ml	Anti-inflammatory and anti-allergic prep.	Intas	2.31	0.00

Note: The + symbol at the end of a drug name denotes formulations made from more than three drugs. While all the drugs were considered for the analysis, it was considered appropriate to limit the listing to three drugs for this study.
Source: For 1994–2004 MIMS India, as cited in Sakthivel 2006, for 2005–08, Drug Today, various issues, CIMS India, 2007 July–October, and IDR Pharmacy Tripple Compendium, 2008, November 07–January 08.

Table B.10 Price changes to drugs for cancer and other related treatments

Category	DPCO	NL EM	Brand	Form	Strength	Qty	Therapeutic group	Company	Price change %	
Drug name/ Year	**1995**	**2003**							**1994–2004**	**2005–2008**
Allopurinol		yes	Zyloric	Tab	100 mg	10	Gout	GSK	4.80	13.64
Allopurinol			Zyloric	Tab	300 mg	10	Gout	GSK		0.00
Bleomycin		yes	Bleocin	Inj	15 mg	Vial	Carcino-chemotherapeutic Drugs	Khandelwal	0.85	−9.62
Chlorambucil			Leukeran	Tab	2 mg	25	Carcino-chemotherapeutic Drugs	GSK	8.87	0.00
Chlorambucil			Leukeran	Tab	5 mg	25	Carcino-chemotherapeutic Drugs	GSK		0.00
Cyclophosphamide		yes	Endoxan-Asta	Tab	50 mg	10	Carcino-chemotherapeutic Drugs	German Remedies	3.64	0.00
Cyclophosphamide		yes	Endoxan-Asta	Inj	200 mg	Vial	Carcino-chemotherapeutic Drugs	German Remedies		0.00
Cyclophosphamide		yes	Endoxan-Asta	Inj	500 mg	Vial	Carcino-chemotherapeutic Drugs	German Remedies		0.00
Cyclophosphamide			Endoxan-Asta	Inj	1 gm	Vial	Carcino-chemotherapeutic Drugs	German Remedies		0.00
Doxorubicin		yes	Doxorubicin-Meijin	Inj	10 mg	Vial	Carcino-chemotherapeutic Drugs	Khandelwal	1.10	0.00

Table B.10 (Continued)

Category	DPCO	NL EM	Brand	Form	Strength	Qty	Therapeutic group	Company	Price change %	
Drug name/ Year	**1995**	**2003**							**1994–2004**	**2005–2008**
Doxorubicin		yes	Doxorubicin-Meijin	Inj	50 mg	Vial	Carcino-chemotherapeutic Drugs	Khandelwal		0.00
Etopside + Benzyl alcohol + Ethyl alcohol		yes	Etosid	Inj	100 mg + 150 mg + 30%/5 ml	5 ml	Carcino-chemotherapeutic Drugs	Cipla	−0.91	0.00
Etopside + Benzyl alcohol + Ethyl alcohol		yes	Etosid	Cap	100 mg + 150 mg + 30%/5 ml	4	Carcino-chemotherapeutic Drugs	Cipla		0.00
Fluorouracil			Fluracil	Cap	250 mg	10	Carcino-chemotherapeutic Drugs	Biochem	0.71	0.00
Fluorouracil			Fluracil	Inj	500 mg	10 ml/2 × 5 ml	Carcino-chemotherapeutic Drugs	Biochem		107.40
Heparin + Benzyl nicotinate			Thrombophop	Oint	5000 i.u + 0.2/100 g	20 gm	Carcino-chemotherapeutic Drugs	German Remedies	0.00	0.00
Heparin			Thrombophop	Gel	20,000 i.u/ 100 g	20 gm	Carcino-chemotherapeutic Drugs	German Remedies		0.00

Methotrexate	yes	Neotrexate	Tab	2.5 mg	10	Carcino-chemotherapeutic Drugs	GSK	0.00	6.20
Methotrexate	yes	Biotrexate	Tab	2.5 mg	10	Carcino-chemotherapeutic Drugs	Biochem	1.04	−6.08
Methotrexate	yes	Biotrexate	Inj	50 mg	2 ml	Carcino-chemotherapeutic Drugs	Biochem		0.00
Tamoxifen	yes	Mamofen	Tab	10 mg	10	Carcino-chemotherapeutic Drugs	Khandelwal	0.00	4.62
Tamoxifen	yes	Nolvadex	Tab	10 mg	50	Carcino-chemotherapeutic Drugs	Astra Zenecca	2.84	0.00
Vincristine+	yes	Cytocristin	Inj	Combination	1 ml	Carcino-chemotherapeutic Drugs	Cipla	1.08	6.67

Note: The + symbol at the end of a drug name denotes formulations made from more than three drugs. While all the drugs were considered for the analysis, it was considered appropriate to limit the listing to three drugs for this study.

Source: For 1994–2004 MIMS India, as cited in Sakthivel 2006, for 2005–08, Drug Today, various issues, CIMS India, 2007 July–October, and IDR Pharmacy Tripple Compendium, 2008, November 07–January 08.

Appendix C

Sensitivity test: Case 1

Payment schedule for the lowest income category remains unchanged. For the other categories, the co-payments are raised from Rs. 25 to Rs. 30 and from Rs. 50 to Rs. 60. The Safety Net threshold is also raised from Rs. 1125 to Rs. 1350 and from Rs. 2000 to Rs. 2400.

Table C.1 Entitlements of IndiaHealth cards at a glance

S. No	Income p.a. (Rs.)	Category	Colour	Co-payment per prescription (Rs.)	SafetyNet Threshold (Rs.)	Co-payment (post SafetyNet) per prescription (Rs.)
1	None	S-Card	Brown	Nil	N. A.	Nil
2	<15,000	B1-Card	Red	Nil	N. A	Nil
3	15,001–40,000	B2-Card	Yellow	10	500	Nil
4	15,001–40,000	A1-Card	White/Yellow	10	500	Nil
5	40,001–100,000	A2-Card	White/Purple	30	1350	10
6	40,001–100,000	M1-Card	Purple	30	1350	10
7	>100,000	A3-Card	White/Green	60	2400	30
8	>100,000	M2-Card	Green	60	2400	30

Note: The threshold would kick in at 40 prescriptions for B2 and A1 Categories, at 45 prescriptions for M1 and A2 categories, and at 50 prescriptions for M2 and A3 categories.
Source: Author.

Table C.2 Calculating health and medicine expenditure (Rs.)

Category	Population	Health (monthly)		Medicine (monthly)	
	(Million.)	Per capita (Rs.)	Total Rs. (Million.)	Per capita (Rs.)	Total Rs. (Million.)
Rural	798	44	35,112	28.16	22,471.68
Urban	342	71	24,282	39.76	13,597.92
Total (India)	1140		59,394		36,069.6
Based on the above Table		**Health (yearly)**		**Medicine (yearly)**	
Rural			421,344		269,660.2
Urban			291,384		163,175
Total (India)			712,728		432,835.2
Per person		625.2		379.68	
Per family		3126		1898.4	

Source: Author estimates based on GOI (2007c, 2007f).

Table C.3 Annual expenditure on medicines under current and proposed models

S. No.	Category	Estimated population (million)	Estimated no. of cards (million)	Total drug expenditure – India (Rs. million)	Total out-of-pocket co-payments (Rs. million)	Government contribution (Rs. million)	Average OOP med. exp per family (Rs.)	Average out-of-pocket drug expenditure per family (Rs.)
				(current)	(proposed)	(proposed)	(proposed)	(current)
1	2	3	4	5	6	7 = (5 – 6)	8	9
1	S-Card	40	40.00	15,187.2	0	15,187.2	0	1898.4
2	B1-Card	350	86.50	132,888	0	132,888	0	1898.4
3	B2-Card	450	85.50	170,856	42,750	128,106	500	1898.4
4	A1-Card	5	2.50	1,898.4	1,250	648.4	500	1898.4
5	A2-Card	5	2.50	1,898.4	3,712.5	0	1485	1898.4
6	M1-Card	190	38.00	72,139.2	56,430	15,709.2	1485	1898.4
7	A3-Card	5	2.50	1,898.4	6,600	0	2640	1898.4
8	M2-Card	95	19.00	36,069.6	50,160	0	2640	1898.4
	Total	1140	276.50	432,835	160,903	271,933	582	1898.4
				100%	37.17	62.83		

Note: At 5 per cent, 17.5 million elderly population would be issued with 8.75 million B1-Cards. At 5 members per family, 332.5 million population would be issued with 66.5 million B1-Cards (Aged). At 5 per cent of 450 million of B2- population, 22.5 million elderly population would be issued with 11.25 million B1-Cards (Aged) Thus, the number of cards issued in B1 category would be higher and in B2 would be lower than straight forward dividing the total population by 5 in those categories.
Source: Author estimates based on GOI (2007c, 2007f).

Table C.4 Estimates of total out-of-pocket *medicine* expenditure (Rs. million) and population groups (million)

Year	Total	0–4 (factor 1.2)		5–64 (factor 1)		65+ (factor 4.5)		Total OOP med. exp	Total OOP med exp Incl. 5% CAGR
	Population	Population	Med. Exp.	Population	Med. Exp.	Population	Med. Exp.		
1	2	3	4	5	6	7	8	9 (4 + 6 + 8)	10
2006	1140	126.5	57,635	956.5	363,164	57.0	97,388	518,187	518,187.3
2007	1160	127.6	58,137	973.8	369,732	58.6	100,122	527,991	554,390.1
2008	1181	127.5	58,091	993.2	377,098	60.2	102,855	538,045	593,194.1
2009	1201	127.3	58,000	1011.2	383,932	62.5	106,785	548,717	635,208.9
2010	1220	126.9	57,818	1028.5	390,501	64.7	110,544	558,862	679,300.7
2011	1237	126.2	57,499	1044.0	396,386	66.8	114,132	568,016	724,948.9
2012	1254	125.4	57,134	1059.6	402,309	69.0	117,891	577,334	773,682.5
2013	1271	124.6	56,770	1075.3	408,270	71.2	121,649	586,689	825,530.5
2014	1287	124.8	56,861	1088.8	413,396	73.4	125,408	595,665	880,068.1
2015	1303	125.1	56,998	1102.3	418,521	75.6	129,167	604,686	938,066.4

Source: Author estimates based on United Nations (2005a); and GOI (2007c, 2007f).

Table C.5 Estimates of total out-of-pocket *health* expenditure (Rs. million) and population groups (million)

Year	Total	0–4 (factor 1.2)		5–64 (factor 1)		65 + (factor 4.5)		Total OOP health exp.	Total OOP health exp. incl. 5% CAGR
	Population	Population	Health exp.	Population	Health exp.	Population	Health exp.		
1	2	3	4	5	6	7	8	9 (4 + 6 + 8)	10
2006	1140	126.5	94,905	956.5	598,004	57	160,364	853,273	853,273
2007	1160	127.6	95,731	973.8	608,820	58.6	164,865	869,416	912,886
2008	1181	127.5	95,656	993.2	620,949	60.2	169,367	885,971	976,783
2009	1201	127.3	95,506	1011.2	632,202	62.5	175,838	903,545	1,045,967
2010	1220	126.9	95,205	1028.5	643,018	64.7	182,027	920,251	1,118,570
2011	1237	126.2	94,680	1,044	652,709	66.8	187,935	935,324	1,193,737
2012	1254	125.4	94,080	1059.6	662,462	69	194,125	950,667	1,273,984
2013	1271	124.6	93,480	1075.3	672,278	71.2	200,314	966,072	1,359,360
2014	1287	124.8	93,630	1088.8	680,718	73.4	206,504	980,851	1,449,164
2015	1303	125.1	93,855	1102.3	689,158	75.6	212,693	995,706	1,544,667

Source: Author estimates based on United Nations (2005a); and GOI (2007c, 2007f).

Table C.6 Projected distribution of total health expenditure (Rs. million)

Year	Current situation		Proposed programme			
	Total OOP health exp. incl. 5% CAGR	**Estimated total health exp. (THE)**	**Public health exp. (PHE)**	**Total OOP health exp.**	**GDP estimates**	**PHE as % of GDP**
	−72%	**−100%**	**62.83%**	**37.17%**		
2006	853,273	1,185,101	744,551	440,551	39,743,850	1.87
2007	912,886	1,267,898	796,568	471,329	45,453,590	1.75
2008	976,783	1,356,643	852,323	504,320	50,916,870	1.67
2009	1,045,967	1,452,731	9,126,92	540,040	57,361,880	1.59
2010	1,118,570	1,553,570	9,760,45	577,525	64,612,270	1.51
2011	1,193,737	1,657,968	1,041,634	616,334	72,713,230	1.43
2012	1,273,984	1,769,422	1,111,656	657,767	81,814,440	1.36
2013	1,359,360	1,888,000	1,186,153	701,846	92,075,660	1.29
2014	1,449,164	2,012,728	1,264,515	748,213	103,585,118	1.22
2015	1,544,667	2,145,371	1,347,849	797,522	116,533,257	1.16

Source: Author estimates based on GOI (2005b, 2007c); and IMF (2008).

Appendix D

Sensitivity test: Case 2

Co-payment for the lowest income category is raised to Rs. 15 and Safety Net threshold raised to Rs. 750. The payment schedule for the other categories remains unchanged.

Table D.1 Entitlements of IndiaHealth cards at a glance

S. No	Income p.a. (Rs.)	Category	Colour	Co-payment per prescription (Rs.)	SafetyNet Threshold (Rs.)	Co-payment (post SafetyNet) per prescription (Rs.)
1	None	S-Card	Brown	Nil	N.A.	Nil
2	<15,000	B1-Card	Red	Nil	N.A	Nil
3	15,001–40,000	B2-Card	Yellow	15	750	Nil
4	15,001–40,000	A1-Card	White/Yellow	15	750	Nil
5	40,001–100,000	A2-Card	White/Purple	25	1125	15
6	40,001–100,000	M1-Card	Purple	25	1125	15
7	>100,000	A3-Card	White/Green	50	2000	25
8	>100,000	M2-Card	Green	50	2000	25

Note: The threshold would kick in at 40 prescriptions for B2 and A1 Categories, at 45 prescriptions for M1 and A2 categories, and at 50 prescriptions for M2 and A3 categories.
Source: Author.

Table D.2 Calculating health and medicine expenditure (Rs.)

Category	Population (Million)	Health (monthly)		Medicine (monthly)	
India	**1140**	**Per capita (Rs.)**	**Total Rs. (Million.)**	**Per capita (Rs.)**	**Total Rs. (Million.)**
Rural	798	44	35,112	28.16	22,471.68
Urban	342	71	24,282	39.76	13,597.92
Total (India)			59,394		36,069.6
Based on the above Table		**Health (yearly)**		**Medicine (yearly)**	
Rural			421,344		269,660.2
Urban			291,384		163,175
Total (India)			712,728		432,835.2
Per person		625.2		379.68	
Per family		3126		1898.4	

Source: Author estimates based on GOI (2007c, 2007f).

Table D.3 Annual expenditure on medicines under current and proposed models

S. No.	Category	Estimated population (million)	Estimated no. of cards (million)	Total drug expenditure – India (Rs. million)	Total out-of-pocket co-payments (Rs. million)	Government contribution (Rs. million)	Average out-of-pocket co-payments per family (Rs.)	Average out-of-pocket drug expenditure per family (Rs.)
				(current)	(proposed)	(proposed)	(proposed)	(current)
1	2	3	4	5	6	7 = (5 – 6)	8	9
1	S-Card	40	40.00	15,187.2	0	15,187.2	0	1898.4
2	B1-Card	350	86.50	132,888	0	132,888	0	1898.4
3	B2-Card	450	85.50	170,856	64,125	106,731	750	1898.4
4	A1-Card	5	2.50	1,898.4	1,875	23.4	750	1898.4
5	A2-Card	5	2.50	1,898.4	3093.75	0	1238	1898.4
6	M1-Card	190	38.00	72,139.2	47,025	25,114.2	1238	1898.4
7	A3-Card	5	2.50	1,898.4	5,500	0	2200	1898.4
8	M2-Card	95	19.00	36,069.6	41,800	0	2200	1898.4
	Total	1100	236.50	432,835	163,419	269,416	691	1898.4
				100%	37.76	62.24		

Note: At 5 per cent, 17.5 million elderly population would be issued with 8.75 million B1-Cards (Aged). At 5 members per family, 332.5 million population would be issued with 66.5 million B1-Cards. At 5 per cent of 450 million of B2-population, 22.5 million elderly population would be issued with 11.25 million B1-Cards (Aged). Thus, the number of cards issued in B1 category would be higher and in B2 would be lower than straightforward dividing the total population by 5 in those categories.

Source: Author based on GOI (2007c, 2007f).

Table D.4 Estimates of total out-of-pocket *medicine* expenditure (Rs. million) and population groups (million)

Year	Total population	0–4 (factor 1.2)		5–64 (factor 1)		65 + (factor 4.5)		Total OOP med. exp.	Total OOP med. exp. Incl. 5% CAGR
		Population	Med. Exp.	Population	Med. Exp.	Population	Med. Exp.		
1	2	3	4	5	6	7	8	9 (4+6+8)	10
2006	1140	126.5	57,635	956.5	363,164	57.0	97,388	518,187	518,187
2007	1160	127.6	58,137	973.8	369,732	58.6	100,122	527,991	554,390
2008	1181	127.5	58,091	993.2	377,098	60.2	102,855	538,045	593,194
2009	1201	127.3	58,000	1011.2	383,932	62.5	106,785	548,717	635,209
2010	1220	126.9	57,818	1028.5	390,501	64.7	110,544	558,862	679,301
2011	1237	126.2	57,499	1044.0	396,386	66.8	114,132	568,016	724,949
2012	1254	125.4	57,134	1059.6	402,309	69.0	117,891	577,334	773,683
2013	1271	124.6	56,770	1075.3	408,270	71.2	121,649	586,689	825,531
2014	1287	124.8	56,861	1088.8	413,396	73.4	125,408	595,665	880,068
2015	1303	125.1	56,998	1102.3	418,521	75.6	129,167	604,686	938,066

Source: Author estimates based on United Nations (2005a); and GOI (2007c, 2007f).

Table D.5 Estimates of total out-of-pocket *health* expenditure (Rs. million) and population groups (million)

Year	Total population	0–4 (factor 1.2)		5–64 (factor 1)		65 + (factor 4.5)		Total OOP health exp	Total OOP health exp Incl. 5% CAGR
		Population	H/care exp	Population	H/C exp	Population	H/C exp		
1	2	3	4	5	6	7	8	9 (4+6+8)	10
2006	1140	126.5	94,905	956.5	598,004	57.0	160,364	853,273	853,273
2007	1160	127.6	95,731	973.8	608,820	58.6	164,865	869,416	912,886
2008	1181	127.5	95,656	993.2	620,949	60.2	169,367	885,971	976,783
2009	1201	127.3	95,506	1011.2	632,202	62.5	175,838	903,545	1,045,967
2010	1220	126.9	95,205	1028.5	643,018	64.7	182,027	920,251	1,118,570
2011	1237	126.2	94,680	1044.0	652,709	66.8	187,935	935,324	1,193,737
2012	1254	125.4	94,080	1059.6	662,462	69.0	194,125	950,667	1,273,984
2013	1271	124.6	93,480	1075.3	672,278	71.2	200,314	966,072	1,359,360
2014	1287	124.8	93,630	1088.8	680,718	73.4	206,504	980,851	1,449,164
2015	1303	125.1	93,855	1102.3	689,158	75.6	212,693	995,706	1,544,667

Source: Author estimates based on United Nations (2005a); and GOI (2007c, 2007f).

Table D.6 Projected distribution of total health expenditure (Rs. million) (2006–2015)

Year	Current situation		Proposed programme			
	Total OOP health exp incl. 5% CAGR	Estimated total health exp (THE)	Public health exp (PHE)	Total OOP health exp	GDP estimates	PHE as % of GDP
	–72%	**–100%**	**62.24%**	**37.76%**		
2006	853,273	1,185,101	737,661	447,440	39,743,850	1.86
2007	912,886	1,267,898	789,198	478,700	45,453,590	1.74
2008	976,783	1,356,643	844,437	512,206	50,916,870	1.66
2009	1,045,967	1,452,731	904,247	548,485	57,361,880	1.58
2010	1,118,570	1,553,570	967,013	586,557	64,612,270	1.50
2011	1,193,737	1,657,968	1,031,995	625,973	72,713,230	1.42
2012	1,273,984	1,769,422	1,101,370	668,053	81,814,440	1.35
2013	1,359,360	1,888,000	1,175,177	712,822	92,075,660	1.28
2014	1,449,164	2,012,728	1,252,814	759,914	103,585,118	1.21
2015	1,544,667	2,145,371	1,335,377	809,994	116,533,257	1.15

Source: Author estimates based on GOI (2005b, 2007c); and IMF (2008).

Notes

2 The WTO and the TRIPS Agreement

1. Pharmaceutical sector inquiry: Preliminary report submitted on 28 November 2008 found up to 1300 patents filed EU-wide on a single medicine. We have termed this act as *excessive patenting*.

3 The Global Pharmaceutical Industry and Developing New Drugs

1. Product with annual sales of more than a billion dollars.
2. According to Pammolli and Riccaboni (2007), the off-shoring of manufacture by the US pharmaceutical firms increased five times between 1996 and 2004.

4 Development of India's Pharmaceutical Industry

1. Certain drugs are reserved for manufacture by the SSI, for which to qualify, the total outlay must not exceed Rs. 10 million ($222,000). This limit is currently in the process of being increased to Rs. 50 million ($1.15 million).
2. The actual drug or salt used in the formulation (e.g. the drug Paracetamol used in Panadol).
3. Filed to obtain approvals for bulk drugs.
4. Filed to obtain approvals for generic versions of formulations.
5. No breakdown of the export value of each drug was available separately. The value of the whole item was used in calculation.
6. Item no. 211 had four drugs, of which patents on all but paclitaxel had expired. Paclitaxel is a natural molecule, thus a product patent would not be applicable to it *per se*. However, considering that a patent on its 'method of working' exists in South Africa till 2013, the whole item was included in the examination, as its export may be affected by the new patent regime in India.
7. Foreign Exchange Regulation Act (FERA).
8. The significance of this period is that it covers the period of restrictive measures of the 1970s as well as the period following economic reforms in 1991.
9. For the years obtained from the IMF database and average for each period derived.
10. The FDI confidence index was not available for 2006.

5 TRIPS and the Indian Patents Regime

1. The High Court is the highest court in a state/province. The Supreme Court is the apex court of India.

2. Defined as mastering the ability to read patents 'in such a way that you can bypass someone's invention', and 'to write patents in such a way that nobody can bypass you' (Mashelkar 2003).
3. Indian Network for People Living with HIV/AIDS, the Manipur Network of Positive People, and the Lawyers Collective.
4. (Chapter XVI, Section 84(1)).
5. As noted earlier, Roche has a patent on Taraceva in India.

6 Price Controls and Drug Affordability in India: Policy Options

1. Author calculations based on *CIMS* (2007).
2. List of drugs under price control.
3. Under Section (2) of the Essential Commodities Act, medicines are considered essential commodities.
4. As listed in Schedule – I appended to the DPCO – 1970.
5. Transfer pricing refers to companies charging their subsidiary significantly at a higher price for a product than otherwise available.
6. The All India Drug Action Network (AIDAN), the Medico Friends Circle (MFC), the Low Cost Standard Therapeutics (LOCOST), and the Jan Swasthya Sahyog.
7. The 354 drugs on the NLEM list minus the 15 drugs currently under price control.
8. Dispensed as received, that is without breaking the packs or taking out small quantities from bottles and so on.
9. CIMS, Drug Today, and IDR are the reference books used by medical practitioners to prescribe medicines.
10. Uttar Pradesh is the most populous state in India.
11. Emails to Sakthivel were not replied. (on record with the author).
12. Email from the TGA on record with the author.

7 Health Insurance in India

1. The Union Government contributes 75 per cent and the states 25 per cent.
2. Organisation for Economic Co-operation and Development.
3. Denotes holders of a Pensioner Concession Card; Australian Seniors Health Card; Health Care Card; or DVA White, Gold, or Orange Card. (http://www.pbs.gov.au/html/consumer/pbs/about). These cards are means tested, which means that people with assets above the government threshold would be ineligible.

8 Broadening Access to Medicines and Healthcare in India

1. While the official estimates suggest 233 million population lives below the poverty line in India, experts such as Patnaik (2010) find considerable discrepancies and inconsistencies in the methodology used in the estimates and

claim the actual figure to be significantly higher. Our estimate of 350 million for the BPL population may be closer to reality.
2. The expression used in drug evaluation literature.
3. The yoga practitioners would be excluded for two reasons. First, under yogic therapies, no medicine is dispensed. The main focus is on physical exercises and body postures. Two, there is no framework in place for validation of the yogic claims or for qualifications.
4. Includes the Department of Veterans Affairs-issued Pensioner Concession Cards and Commonwealth Seniors Health Cards. The Department of Human Services through Centrelink also issues a range of Health Care Cards and other types of concession cards, such as Disability Support Pension Card.
5. Consumer Price Index.
6. Wholesale Price Index used in India.
7. Over the age of 65 years.
8. Adjusted up from 1991 figures of 38.8 million for disabled in Government of India (2003b, p. 98).
9. Under the proposal, the year would mean Indian accounting year (April–March) because it would be easier for budgetary planning and accounting purposes.
10. Medicines specifically listed under the 20-day Rule (e.g. for chronic diseases such as HIV/AIDS).
11. Based on Government of India (2007f).
12. Total out-of-pocket payments/total number of IndiaHealthcards.
13. Rs. 141,419/150 (sum of all cards except S and B1 categories).
14. Employees' State Insurance Scheme (ESIS).
15. Central Government Health Scheme (CGHS).

9 Is TRIPS Appropriate for Developing Countries?

1. The German Parliament until 1945.
2. It is assumed that each product would have identical demand functions.
3. Oxfam (2002) estimates, the poor countries would contribute $40 billion annually in TRIPS-inflicted additional costs.
4. Deliberate use of this figure rather than the recent estimates of $1.3 billion, because the *actual* outlay is less than half of the new estimates and the developing countries would be *actually* paying additional costs.
5. See Chapter 5 for more details.
6. Rector, Imperial College, London.

10 Which Way Ahead?

1. Around 100 world's largest pharmaceutical companies based in the US, EU, and Japan.
2. Such as 1300 patents on a single drug noted earlier in the chapter.

References

A T Kearney 2004, 'FDI Confidence Index', Global Business Policy Council, vol. 7, October.

———2005, 'FDI Confidence Index', Global Business Policy Council, vol. 8, December.

———2007, *New Concerns in an Uncertain World: The 2007 A.T. Kearney Foreign Direct Investment confidence index*, Global Business Policy Council, Vienna, VA.

Abbott, FM 1998, 'The enduring enigma of TRIPS: A challenge for the world economic system', *Journal of International Economic Law*, vol. 1, no. 4, pp. 497–521.

———2003, *The Competition Provisions in the TRIPS Agreement: Implications for Technology Transfer*, Paper presented to WIPO–WTO Joint Workshop: Intellectual Property Rights and Transfer of Technology, Geneva, 17 November.

———2005, 'The WTO medicines decision: World pharmaceutical trade and the protection of pubic health', *American Journal of International Law*, vol. 99, no. 2, pp. 317–58.

Abegunde, D & Stanciole, A 2006, 'An estimation of the economic impact of chronic noncommunicable diseases in selected countries', Working paper, World Health Organization, Geneva, 30 May, viewed 23 January 2009, http://www.who.int/chp/working_paper_growth%20model29may.pdf.

Acharya, A & Ranson, MK 2005, 'Health care financing for the poor: Community-based health insurance schemes in Gujarat', *Economic and Political Weekly*, vol. 40, no. 38, pp. 4141–50.

Aderibigbe, MR 1990, 'The Nigerian patent system and the new industrial policy', *World Patent Information*, vol. 12, no. 2, pp. 95–9.

Adikibi, OT 1988, 'The multinational corporation and monopoly of patents in Nigeria', *World Development*, vol. 16, no. 4, pp. 511–26.

Aggarwal, A 2004, 'Strategic approach to strengthening the international competitiveness in the knowledge based industries: The Indian pharmaceutical industry', Discussion paper RIS-DP # 80/2004, Research and Information System for the Non-Aligned and Other Developing Countries, New Delhi.

Ahuja, R & Narang, A 2005, 'Emerging trends in health insurance for low-income groups', *Economic and Political Weekly*, vol. 40, no. 38, pp. 4151–7.

Aiyer, S 2006, 'Indian MNCs: Indian companies hunt for assets abroad to acquire global scale', *India Today*, vol. 31, no. 44, pp. 38–48.

Alexander, J 2007, 'ICMR launches medical innovation fund to support novel initiative in drug research', *Pharmabiz*, 20 February.

Alsegård, E 2004, 'Global pharmaceutical patents after the Doha Declaration: What lies in the future?', *SCRIPT-ed*, vol. 1, no. 1, 23 February.

Angell, M 2004, *The Truth About the Drug Companies: How They Deceive Us and What To Do About It*, Random House, New York.

Ashton, TS 1964, *The Industrial Revolution: 1760–1830*, Oxford University Press, London, UK.

Australian Bureau of Statistics 2006, 'Population projections, Australia, 2004 to 2101', viewed 23 June 2008, http://www.abs.gov.au/ausstats/abs@.nsf/ProductsbyCatalogue/5A9C0859C5F50C30CA25718C0015182F?OpenDocument.

Australian Institute of Health and Welfare 2005, *Health system expenditure on disease and injury in Australia, 2000–01*, Health and Welfare expenditure series no. 21, 2nd edn, Canberra.

Austrom, D & Howard, P 1994, 'Speeding drugs to market: Strategies for re-engineering', *Scrip Magazine*, October, pp. 50–2.

Babu, G 2007, 'Cadila Pharma to launch SEZ in the third quarter of 2008', *Pharmabiz*, 11 May.

Baker, BK 2008, 'Ending drug registration apartheid: Taming data exclusivity and patent/registration Linkage', *American Journal of Law & Medicine*, vol. 34, no. 2/3, pp. 303–44.

Balasubramaniam, K 2002, 'Access to medicines: Patents, prices and public policy – consumer perspectives', in P Drahos & R Mayne (eds), *Global Intellectual Property Rights: Knowledge, Access and Development*, Palgrave Macmillan, New York, pp. 90–107.

Ballance, R, Pogány, J & Forstner, H 1992, *The World's Pharmaceutical Industries: An International Perspective on Innovation, Competition and Policy*, United Nations Industrial Development Organization and Edward Elgar Publishing, Aldershot, England.

Barry, M 2003, 'Presidential address: Diseases without borders – Globalization's challenge to the American society of tropical medicine and hygiene: A call for public advocacy and activism', *The American Journal of Tropical Medicine and Hygiene*, vol. 69, no. 1, pp. 3–7.

Barton, J 2001, 'Differentiated pricing of patented products', rev. edn, Working paper no. 63, Indian Council for Research on International Economic Relations, New Delhi, November.

———2003, *Preserving the Global Scientific and Technological Commons*, Paper presented to Science and Technology Diplomacy Initiative and the ICTSD-UNCTAD Project on IPRs and Sustainable Development Policy Dialogue on a Proposal for an International Science and Technology Treaty, Room 25, Palais des Nations, Geneva, 11 April, viewed 23 February 2006, http://stdev.unctad.org/capacity/Barton.doc.

Barton, JH & Maskus, KE 2004, 'Economic perspectives on a multilateral agreement on open access to basic science and technology', *SCRIPT-ed*, vol. 1, no. 3, pp. 367–87.

Berndt, ER, Glennerster, R, Kremer, MR, Lee, J, Levine, R & Weizsäcker, G 2005, 'Advanced purchase commitments for a malaria vaccine: Estimating costs and effectiveness', Discussion paper no. PEPP/2, Suntory and Toyota International Centres for Economics and Related Disciplines, London School of Economics and Political Science, London, April, viewed 14 March 2006, http://sticerd.lse.ac.uk/dps/pepp/pepp02.pdf.

Berry, A 2005, 'Third-world medicine: A new way of developing drugs for neglected diseases of the poor world', *The Economist*, 14 April.

Bhagat, M 1982, *Aspects of Drug Industry in India*, Centre for Education and Documentation, Bombay.

Bidwai, P 2007, 'Novartis patents case far from dead', Transnational Institute, viewed 3 December 2008, http://www.tni.org/detail_page.phtml?act_id=17188.

Bisserbe, N 2006, 'It's jungle out there', *Economic Times*, 15 October.

Blech, J 2006, *Inventing Disease and Pushing Pills: Pharmaceutical Companies and the Medicalisation of Normal Life*, Routledge, London and New York.

Blendon, RJ, Schoen, C, DesRoches, CM, Osborn, R, Scoles, KL & Zapert, K 2002, 'Inequities in health', *Health Affairs*, vol. 21, no. 3, pp. 182–91.

Bloomberg 2006, 'Pfizer investors to suffer from halting of Lipitor replacement: Big M&A to come?', *Seeking Alpha*, no. 4, December, viewed 27 January 2009, http://seekingalpha.com/article/21659-pfizer-investors-to-suffer-from-halting-of-lipitor-replacement-big-m-a-to-come.

Boldrin, M & Levine, D 2005, *The Pharmaceutical Industry*, University of California, viewed 23 February 2006, http://levine.sscnet.ucla.edu/papers/ip.ch.9.m1004.pdf.

Bower, DJ & Sulej, JC 2007, 'The Indian challenge: The evolution of a successful new global strategy in the pharmaceutical industry', *Technology Analysis & Strategic Management*, vol. 19, no. 5, pp. 611–24.

Braee, R 2001, *New Zealand Pharmaceutical Pricing and Reimbursement Policies*, European Commission, Brussels.

Brown, P 2004, 'Fiddling with prices', *Scrip Magazine*, June, pp. 3–4.

Bureau of National Affairs 2001, 'Rewriting TRIPS could hurt research: Pharmaceutical industry strongly warns WTO', *WTO Reporter*, 20 September.

Cai, Q & Salmon, JW 2005, 'What role may pharmaeconomics play in pharmaceutical pricing and reimbursement in China?', *Journal of Pharmaceutical Finance, Economics & Policy*, vol. 14, no. 1, pp. 51–75.

Caplow, T, Hicks, L & Wattenberg, B 2006, *The First Measured Century*, Public Broadcasting Services, Arlington, VA, viewed November 2006, http://www.pbs.org/fmc/book/2work4.htm.

Central Drug Research Institute (CDRI) 2008, *New Drugs*, Central Drug Research Institute, Lucknow, viewed 12 April 2008, http://www.cdriindia.org/newdrugs.htm.

Chadha, A 2006, 'Destination India for the pharmaceutical industry', *The Delhi Business Review*, vol. 7, no. 1, pp. 1–8.

Chataway, J, Tait, J & Wield, D 2007, 'Frameworks for pharmaceutical innovation in developing countries: The case of Indian pharma', *Technology Analysis & Strategic Management*, vol. 19, no. 5, pp. 697–708.

Chataway, M 2000, 'A radical idea for how pharma can help the developing world', *Scrip Magazine*, October, pp. 21–5.

Chaturvedi, K 2005, 'Policy and technology co-evolution in the Indian pharmaceutical industry', DPP Working paper no. 50, Development Policy and Practice, Faculty of Technology, The Open University, Walton Hall, Milton Keynes, December.

Chaudhuri, S 2005, *The WTO and India's Pharmaceutical Industry: Patent Protection, TRIPS and Developing Countries*, Oxford University Press, New Delhi.

Chaudhuri, S, Goldberg, P & Jia, P 2003, 'The effects of extending intellectual property rights protection to developing countries: A case study of the Indian pharmaceutical market', Working paper no. 10159, National Bureau of Economic Research, Cambridge, MA, December.

Chin, J & Grossman, G 1990, 'Intellectual property rights and north-south trade', in RW Jones & AO Krueger (eds), *The Political Economy of International Trade: Essays in Honor of Robert E. Baldwin*, Basil-Blackwell, Cambridge, MA, pp. 90–107.

CIMS 2007, *CIMS*, vol. 98, no. 3, Bio Gard Publishers, Bangalore, July–October.

Cipla 2005, *Annual Report 2004–05*, Cipla Pharmaceuticals, Mumbai.

———2008, *Annual Report 2007–08*, Cipla Pharmaceuticals, Mumbai.

Clements, PJ 2007–08, 'The Hatch-Waxman Act and the conflict between antitrust law and patent law', *IDEA: The Intellectual Property Law Review*, vol. 48, no. 3, pp. 381–407.

Clift, C 2007, 'Data protection and data exclusivity in pharmaceuticals and agrochemicals', in A Krattiger, RT Mahoney, L Nelsen, JA Thomson, AB Bennett, K Satyanarayana, GD Graff, C Fernandez and SP Kowalski (eds), *Intellectual Property Management in Health and Agricultural Innovation: A Handbook of Best Practices*, MIHR, Oxford, UK and PIPRA, Davis, USA, vol. 2.

Cole, JH 2001, 'Patents and copyrights: Do the benefits exceed the costs?', *Journal of Libertarian Studies*, vol. 15, no. 4, pp. 79–105.

Collier, R 2009, 'Drug development cost estimates hard to swallow', *Canadian Medical Association Journal*, vol. 180, no. 3, 3 February.

Commission on Intellectual Property Rights 2002, 'Integrating intellectual property rights and development policy', London, September, viewed 5 June 2005, http://www.iprcommission.org/papers/pdfs/final_report/CIPRfullfinal.pdf.

Commission on Intellectual Property Rights Innovation and Public Health 2006, *Public Health: Innovation and Intellectual Property Rights*, World Health Organization, Geneva.

Commission on Macroeconomics and Health 2001, *Macroeconomics and Health: Investing in Health for Economic Development*, World Health Organization, Geneva.

Congressional Budget Office (CBO) 1998, *Pricing and Competition in the Pharmaceutical Market: How Increased Competition from Generic Drugs Has Affected Prices and Returns in the Pharmaceutical Industry*, Congressional Budget Office, Government of the United States, Washington, DC.

Cornish, WR 1989, *Intellectual Property: Patents, Copyrights, Trademarks and Allied Rights*, Sweet and Maxwell, London.

Correa, CM 2002a, 'Pro-competitive measures under TRIPS to promote technology diffusion in developing countries', in P Drahos and R Mayne (eds), *Global Intellectual Property Rights: Knowledge, Access and Development*, Palgrave Macmillan, New York, pp. 40–60.

———2002b, 'Unfair competition under the TRIPS agreement: Protection of data submitted for the registration of pharmaceuticals', *Chicago Journal of International Law*, vol. 3, no. 1, pp. 69–86.

———2006, 'Implications of bilateral free trade agreements on access to medicines', *Bulletin of the World Health Organization*, vol. 84, no. 5, pp. 399–404.

Cruddas, J & Gannon, Z 2009, A bitter pill to swallow: Drugs for people not just for profit, *Compass*, London, 26 August.

Cutler, DM 2007, 'The demise of the blockbuster?', *The New England Journal of Medicine*, vol. 356, no. 13, pp. 1292–3.

Cygnus 2005, *Industry Insight: Indian Pharmaceuticals*, Cygnus Business Consulting & Research, Hyderabad.

——2007, *Quarterly Performance Analysis of Companies (October–December 2006): Indian Pharmaceutical Industry*, Cygnus Business Consulting & Research, Hyderabad.

Danzon, P 2001, *Differential Pricing: Reconciling R&D, IP and Access*, paper presented to WHO/WTO Workshop on Differential Pricing and Financing of Essential Drugs, Hosbjor, Norway, 8–11 April, viewed 14 October 2004, http://www.wto.org/english/tratop_e/trips_e/hosbjor_presentations_e/12danzon_e.pdf.

Danzon, PM, Epstein, A & Nicholson, S 2007, 'Mergers and acquisitions in the pharmaceutical and biotech industries', *Managerial and Decision Economics*, vol. 28, no. 4–5, pp. 307–28.

Darbourne, A 2003, 'Access to medicines: Worlds apart', *Scrip Magazine*, February, pp. 36–8.

Das, SC, Mandal, M & Mandal, SC 2007, 'A critical study on availability and price variation between different brands: Impact on access to medicines', *Indian Journal of Pharmaceutical Sciences*, vol. 69, no. 1, pp. 160–3.

David, P 1993, 'Intellectual property institutions and the panda's thumb: Patents, copyrights, and trade secrets in economic theory and history', in M Wallerstein, M Mogee and R Schoen (eds), *Global Dimensions of Intellectual Property Rights in Science and Technology*, National Academy Press, Washington, DC, pp. 19–61.

Davis, M 1994, 'Patents in healthcare: Subsidy and victimisation?', *Scrip Magazine*, December, pp. 6–8.

Deardof, A 1992, 'Welfare effects of global patent protection', *Economica*, vol. 59, no. 233, pp. 35–51.

Deloitte Recap 2009, 'Biotech database', Deloitte Recap LLC, viewed 28 January 2009, http://www.deloitte.com/.

DeNavas-Walt, C, Proctor, BD & Smith, J 2007, *Income, Poverty, and Health Insurance Coverage in the United States: 2006*, US Census Bureau, U.S Department of Commerce, Economics and Statistics Administration.

Department of Health 2005, 'Reimbursement of "standard" branded generic medicines: A further consultation', viewed 17 July 2007, http://www.dh.gov.uk/en/Consultations/Closedconsultations/DH_4121799.

DiMasi, JA 1991, *The Cost of Innovation in the Pharmaceutical Industry: New Drug R&D Cost Estimates*, Pharmaceutical Manufacturers Association, Washington, DC.

——2001, 'New drug development in the United States from 1963 to 1999', *Clinical Pharmacology & Therapeutics*, vol. 69, no. 5, May, pp. 286–96.

DiMasi, JA & Grabowski, HG 2007, 'The cost of biopharmaceutical R&D: Is biotech different?', *Managerial and Decision Economics*, vol. 28, no. 4–5, pp. 469–79.

DiMasi, JA, Hansen, RW & Grabowski, HG 2003, 'The price of innovation: New estimates of drug development costs', *Journal of Health Economics*, vol. 22, no. 2, pp. 151–85.

Dongre, RCK 1982, *Shrimad Bhagwad-Rahasya [The Secret of God]*, Maanas Prakashan, New Delhi.

Dr Reddy's 2004, 'Address by Dr. K Anji Reddy', Pharmacophore 2004, International Symposium, Innovating Drugs: Emerging Perspectives, Hyderabad, 16–17 January, viewed 10 January 2006, http://www.drreddys.com/coverview/pdf/speeches/Pharmacophore2004_address.pdf.

———2005, *Annual Report 2004–2005*, Dr Reddy's Labs, viewed 15 September 2005, http://www.drreddys.com/investors/pdf/annualreport2005.pdf.
———2008, 'API-product list', viewed 18 September 2008, http://www.drreddys.com/gchemicals/api_productlist.htm.
Drahos, P 2002a, 'Introduction', in P Drahos & R Mayne (eds), *Global Intellectual Property Rights: Knowledge, Access and Development*, Palgrave Macmillan, New York, pp. 1–12.
———2002b, 'Negotiating intellectual property rights: Between coercion and dialogue', in P Drahos & R Mayne (eds), *Global Intellectual Property Rights: Knowledge, Access and Development*, Palgrave Macmillan, New York, pp. 161–82.
Drahos, P & Braithwaite, J 2002, 'Intellectual property, corporate strategy, globalisation: TRIPS in context', *Wisconsin International Law Journal*, vol. 20, no. 3, pp. 451–80.
Drahos, P, Faunce, T, Goddard, M & Henry, D 2004, 'The FTA and the PBS: A Submission to the Senate Select Committee on the US-Australia Free Trade Agreement', Government of Australia, Canberra.
Drahos, P 2008, '"Trust me": Patent offices in developing countries', *American Journal of Law & Medicine*, vol. 34, no. 2, pp. 151–74.
Drohan, M 1996, 'Canada can take heart from earlier WTO ruling: Backgrounder for countries in danger of being pushed around by large neighbours, decision backing Venezuela over U.S. was special', *The Globe and Mail*, 13 March, p. A12.
Drug Today 2005, *Drug Today*, vol. 12, no. 3, January–March.
———2007, *Drug Today*, vol. 15, no. 2, October–December.
Duckett, SJ 2004, 'Drug policy down under: Australia's Pharmaceutical Benefits Scheme', *Health Care Financing Review*, vol. 25, no. 3, pp. 55–67.
Dukes, G 2006, *The Law and the Ethics of the Pharmaceutical Industry*, Elsevier, Amsterdam.
Dunkley, G 2001, *The Free Trade Adventure: The Uruguay Round and Globalism – A Critique*, Melbourne University Press, Melbourne.
Dutta, A 2005, 'Free entry in the market for drugs in India: Implications for social welfare', MIT, viewed 22 February 2006, http://econ-www.mit.edu/graduate/candidates/download_res.php?id=254.
Economic Research Foundation 2006, 'Government health expenditure in India: A benchmark study undertaken for the MacArthur Foundation', viewed 1 July 2008, http://www.macroscan.org/anl/oct06/pdf/Health_Expenditure.pdf.
EFPIA 2006, *The Pharmaceutical Industry in Figures*, European Federation of Pharmaceutical Industries and Associations, Brussels, viewed 22 November 2006, http://www.efpia.org/6_publ/infigures2006.pdf.
———2008, *The Pharmaceutical Industry in Figures*, European Federation of Pharmaceutical Industries and Associations, Brussels, viewed 3 August 2008, http://www.efpia.eu/Content/Default.asp?PageID=559&DocID=4883.
Elliott, R 2008, *Delivery Past Due: Agreement Between Rwanda and Canadian Generic Pharmaceutical Company Represents Historic First Use of WTO Rules on Compulsory Licensing For Export, But Could Be Last*, Paper presented to XVII International AIDS Conference, Mexico City, 3–8 August, viewed 2 January 2008, http://www.aids2008.org/Pag/Abstracts.aspx?SID=290&AID=15940.
Ellis, RP, Alam, M & Gupta, I 2000, 'Health insurance in India: Prognosis and prospectus', *Economic and Political Weekly*, vol. 35, no. 4, pp. 207–17.

Embassy of the United States 2008, 'IPR toolkit India: Patents', viewed 28 October 2008, http://newdelhi.usembassy.gov/iprpatents.html.

Essentialdrugs 2004, 'India-drug: Total number of drug units in India', *Essential Drugs*, viewed 5 October 2004, http://www.essentialdrugs.org/indiadrug/archive/200401/msg00032.php.

EurActiv 2005, 'Review of EU pharmaceutical legislation', 11 February, viewed 12 December 2008, http://www.euractiv.com/en/health/new-medicines-legislation/article-117531.

European Commission 2008, *Pharmaceutical Sector Inquiry: Preliminary Report*, European Commission, Brussels, 28 November, viewed 10 December 2008, http://ec.europa.eu/comm/competition/sectors/pharmaceuticals/inquiry/preliminary_report.pdf.

European Generic Medicines Association 2007, 'Generic market shares across Europe in 2006', viewed 5 July 2007, http://www.egagenerics.com/doc/fac-GxMktEur_2006.pdf.

European Parliament 2007, 'Written declaration', 0022/2007, 26 February, viewed 13 January 2009, http://www.europarl.europa.eu/sides/getDoc.do?pubRef=-//EP//NONSGML+WDECL+P6-DCL-2007-0022+0+DOC+PDF+V0//EN&language=EN.

Federal Trade Commission 2003, 'To Promote Innovation: The Proper Balance of Competition and Patent Law and Policy', Washington, DC, 28 October, viewed 15 October 2008, http://www.ftc.gov/opa/2003/10/cpreport.shtm.

Ferreiro, A 2000, 'Private health insurance in India: Would its implementation affect the poor?', in D Peters, GNV Ramana & KS Rao (eds), *Private Health Insurance and Public Health Goals in India: Report on a National Seminar*, World Bank, New Delhi, pp. 79–83.

FICCI 2005, Competitiveness of the Indian Pharmaceutical Industry in the New Product Patent Regime: FICCI Report for National Manufacturing Competitiveness Council (NMCC), Federation of Indian Chambers of Commerce and Industry, New Delhi.

——2007, 'Govt to Frame India Innovation Act to Spur Research and Innovation: Kapil Sibal', Federation of Indian Chambers of Commerce and Industry, New Delhi.

FierceBiotech 2006, 'Dr. Reddy's to buy betapharm in $570M deal', viewed 3 February 2007, http://www.fiercebiotech.com/story/dr-reddy-s-to-buy-betapharm-in-570m-deal/2006-02-16.

Finger, JM 2002, 'Implementing the Uruguay Round Agreements', in P Lloyd & C Milner (eds), *The World Economy: Global Trade Policy 2001*, Blackwell Publishing, Oxford, UK, pp. 7–18.

Finger, JM & Schuler, P 2001, 'Implementation of Uruguay round commitments: The development challenge', World Bank Policy Research Working paper no. 2215, World Bank, Washington DC, viewed 23 June 2003, http://econ.worldbank.org/external/default/main?ImgPagePK=64202990&entityID=000094946_01013005324822&pagePK=64210502&theSitePK=544849&piPK=64210520.

Flink, JJ 1990, 'Henry Ford and the triumph of the automobile', in W Caroll & J Pursell (eds), *Technology in America: A History of Individuals and Ideas*, MIT Press, Cambridge, MA.

Food and Drug Administration (FDA) 2008, *Electronic Orange Book: Approved Drug Products with Therapeutic Equivalence Evaluations*, Food and Drug Administration, Government of the United States of America, viewed 2 December 2008, http://www.fda.gov/cder/ob/docs/querytn.htm.

Foroohar, R 2006, 'A new drug deal', *Newsweek*, December 2005–February 2006, p. 78.

Frank, R & Hensley, S 2002, 'Pfizer to buy Pharmacia for $60 billion in stock', *The Wall Street Journal*, 15 July, p. 1.

Galpalli, N 2004, 'GATT agreement: Effect on drug prices in India', Pharmainfo.net, viewed 18 February 2005, http://pharmainfo.net/subjects-viewpage-pageid-82.html.

Gambardella, A 1995, *Science and Innovation: The US Pharmaceutical Industry During the 1980s*, Cambridge University Press, New York.

Gambardella, A, Orsenigo, L & Pammolli, F 2000, Global Competitiveness in Pharmaceuticals: A European Perspective, Report Prepared for the Directorate General Enterprise of the European Commission, Brussels.

Garg, CC 2000, 'Implications of current experiences of health insurance in India', in D Peters, GNV Ramana & KS Rao (eds), *Private Health Insurance and Public Health Goals in India: Report on a National Seminar*, World Bank, New Delhi, pp. 3–42.

Gassmann, O, Reepmeyer, G & von Zedtwitz, M 2004, *Leading Pharmaceutical Innovation: Trends and Drivers for Growth in the Pharmaceutical Industry*, Springer-Verlag, Berlin.

———2008, *Leading Pharmaceutical Innovation: Trends and Drivers for Growth in the Pharmaceutical Industry*, 2nd edn, Springer-Verlag, Berlin.Gehl Sampath, P 2006, 'India's product patent protection regime: Less or more of "Pills for the Poor"?', *The Journal of World Intellectual Property*, vol. 9, no. 6, pp. 694–726.

Genepharm 2005, *Annual Report*, Genepharm Australasia, Melbourne.

General Insurance Corporation of India 2008, 'History in brief', viewed 9 July 2008, http://gicofindia.in/en/.

Generic Handbook 2007, *Generic Handbook*, 2nd edn, VOI Consulting, New Orleans.

Global-Challenges 2008, 'AIDS: Third world: 1999–2008: Global issues of the twenty-first century and United Nations challenges', viewed 20 September 2008, http://www.global-challenges.org/30aids-thirdworld.html.

Global Forum for Health Research 1999, 'The 10/90 report on health research', Global Forum for Health Research, Geneva, viewed 4 January 2009, http://www.globalforumhealth.org/filesupld/1090_report_99/99ex_summary.PDF.

———2004, *The 10/90 Gap in Health Research*, Global Forum for Health Research, Geneva, viewed 4 January 2009, http://www.globalforumhealth.org/filesupld/1090_report_03_04/109004_chap_5.pdf.

Goddard, M, Hauck, K, Preker, A & Smith, PC 2006, 'Priority setting in health: A political economy perspective', *Health Economics, Policy and Law*, vol. 1, no. 1, pp. 79–90.

Goozner, M 2004, *The $800 Million Pill: The Truth Behind the Cost of New Drugs*, University of California, Berkeley and Los Angeles, CA.

Government of Australia 2006, *Expenditure and Prescriptions Twelve Months to 30 June 2006*, Department of Health and Ageing, Canberra, Australia.

———2007a, *Australian Regulation of Prescription Medical Products*, Therapeutic Goods Administration, Department of Health and Ageing, Canberra.

———2007b, *Pharmaceutical Benefits Scheme (PBS) Reform*, Therapeutic Goods Administration, Department of Health and Ageing, Canberra.

———2008, 'What is intellectual property? an introduction to intellectual property', viewed 10 December 2008, http://www.ipaustralia.gov.au/ip/introduction.shtml.

———2010, *Overview of the PBS Safety Net?*, Medicare Australia, Canberra, viewed 27 January 2010, http://www.medicareaustralia.gov.au/public/services/scripts/pbs.jsp.

Government of Canada 2008, *How Does the PMPRB Review the Pricing Information For All Patented Medicines Sold in Canada?*, Patented Medicine Prices Review Board, Ottawa, viewed 27 August 2008, http://www.pmprb-cepmb.gc.ca/english/view.asp?x=272#16.

Government of India (GOI) 1952, *First Five-Year Plan (1952–57)*, Planning Commission of India, New Delhi.

———1957, *Second Five-Year Plan (1957–1962)*, Planning Commission of India, New Delhi.

———1972, *The Patent Act 1970*, Office of the Controller General of Patents, Designs and Trade Marks, Kolkata.

———1977, *Drug Policy – 1977*, Department of Chemicals and Petrochemicals, Ministry of Chemicals and Fertilizers, New Delhi.

———1980, *Sixth Five-Year Plan (1980–85)*, Planning Commission of India, New Delhi.

———1986, Drug Policy – 1986, Department of Chemicals and Petrochemicals, Ministry of Chemicals and Fertilizers, New Delhi.

———1994, Drug Policy – 1994, Department of Chemicals and Petrochemicals, Ministry of Chemicals and Fertilizers, New Delhi.

———1995, *Drugs (Price Control) Order 1995*, Department of Chemicals and Petrochemicals, Ministry of Chemicals and Fertilizers, Government of India, New Delhi.

———1999, *The Patents (Amendment) Act, 1999*, no. 17 of 1999, 26 March 1999, http://ipindia.nic.in/ipr/patent/patact_99.PDF.

———2002a, *National Health Policy – 2002*, Ministry of Health and Family Welfare, Government of India, New Delhi.

———2002b, *The Patents (Amendment) Act, 2002*, no. 38 of 2002, 25 June 2002, http://ipindia.nic.in/ipr/patent/patentg.pdf.

———2002c, *Pharmaceutical Policy – 2002*, Press Information Bureau, Government of India, viewed 16 January 2003, http://pib.nic.in/archive/lreleng/lyr2002/rfeb2002/15022002/r1502200212.html.

———2002d, *Pharmaceutical Policy – 2002*, Department of Chemicals and Petrochemicals, Ministry of Chemicals and Fertilizers, New Delhi.

———2003a, *Functions of NPPA*, National Pharmaceutical Pricing Authority, Government of India, New Delhi.

———2003b, *Health Information of India 2000 & 2001*, Central Bureau of Health Intelligence, Directorate General of Health Services, Ministry of Health & Family Welfare, New Delhi.

———2003c, *Statistical Pocket Book – India 2002*, Central Statistical Organisation, Ministry of Statistics and Programme Implementation, New Delhi.

———2004, *National Common Minimum Programme of the Government of India*, Government of India, New Delhi.

———2005a, *Draft – National Pharmaceuticals Policy: 2006*, Department of Chemicals and Petrochemicals, Ministry of Chemicals and Fertilizers viewed 12 February 2006, http://chemicals.nic.in/npp_circulation_latest.pdf.

———2005b, *National Health Accounts 2001–02*, National Health Accounts Cell, Ministry of Health and Family Welfare, New Delhi.

———2005c, *The Patents (Amendment) Act, 2005*, no. 15 of 2005, 5 April 2005, viewed 16 November 2005, http://patentoffice.nic.in/ipr/patent/patent_2005.pdf.

———2005d, *Pharmaceuticals*, Department of Chemicals and Petrochemicals, viewed 12 December 2005, http://chemicals.nic.in/pharma1.htm.

———2005e, *Report of the National Commission on Macroeconomics and Health*, National Commission on Macroeconomics and Health, Ministry of Health and Family Welfare, New Delhi.

———2005f, *Seventh Report on Availability and Price Management of Drugs and Pharmaceuticals*, Standing Committee on Chemicals and Fertilizers (2005–06), Department of Chemicals and Petrochemicals, Ministry of Chemicals and Fertilizers, New Delhi.

———2006a, *Annual Report 2005–2006*, Department of Chemicals and Petrochemicals, Ministry of Chemicals and Fertilizers, New Delhi.

———2006b, *Census of India 2001: Population Projections for India and States 2001–2026*, Technical Group on Population Projections, Office of the Registrar General, New Delhi.

———2006c, *(Draft) Towards Faster and More Inclusive Growth: An Approach to the 11th Five-Year Plan*, Planning Commission, New Delhi.

———2006d, *Household Assets Holding, Indebtedness, Current Borrowings and Repayments of Social Groups in India: All-India Debt and Investment Survey, NSS 59th Round*, no. 503 (59/18.2/4), National Sample Survey Organisation, Ministry of Statistics & Programme Implementation, New Delhi.

———2006e, *Morbidity, Health Care and the Condition of the Aged, NSS 60th Round*, 507 (60/25.0/1), National Sample Survey Organisation, Ministry of Statistics and Programme Implementation, New Delhi.

———2006f, *National Health Profile 2006*, Central Bureau of Health Intelligence, Directorate General of Health Services, Ministry of Health and Family Welfare, New Delhi.

———2006g, 'Notice for termination of exclusive marketing right EMR/1/2002', *The Patent Office Journal*, no. 7, 17 February.

———2006h, *Reduction in Prices of Certain Categories of Medicines (Promised)*, Department of Chemicals and Petro-Chemicals, Ministry of Chemicals and Fertilizers, New Delhi, viewed 23 September 2008, http://chemicals.nic.in/ReductionList112006.pdf.

———2006i, *Sectors Attracting Highest FDI Inflows*, Department of Industrial Policy and Promotion, Ministry of Commerce & Industry, Government of India, New Delhi.

———2006j, *Selected Socio-economic Statistics India*, Central Statistical Organisation, Ministry of Statistics and Programme, New Delhi.

———2007a, 'Actual reduction in prices of medicines as on 14 May 2007', Department of Chemicals and Petrochemicals, Ministry of Chemicals and Fertilizers, New Delhi.

———2007b, *Drugs and Pharmaceutical Exports (Commodity-wise)*, Directorate General Commercial Intelligence and Statistics (DGCIS), Kolkata.

———2007c, *National Family Health Survey 2005–06 (NFHS-3)*, Ministry of Health and Family Welfare, New Delhi.

———2007d, *Report of the Special Subject Group: Unshackling Indian Industry*, Prime Minister's Council on Trade and Industry, New Delhi.

———2007e, *Report of the Working Group on Drugs and Pharmaceuticals for the 11th Five-Year Plan (2007–2012)*, Planning Commission of India, New Delhi.

———2007f, *Statistical Pocket Book India, Combined Issue 2006 & 2007*, 45th edn, Central Statistical Organisation, Ministry of Statistics and Programme Implementation, New Delhi.

———2008a, *Annual Report*, Department of Scientific & Industrial Research, Ministry of Science and Technology, New Delhi.

———2008b, 'Mainstreaming of ISM&H practitioners and bare-foot doctors', viewed 23 June 2008, http://populationcommission.nic.in/ISM&H.htm.

———2009, 'Annual Report', Department of Pharmaceuticals, Ministry of Chemicals and Fertilizers, New Delhi.

———2010, 'List of Drugs Approved for Marketing in India', Central Drugs Standard Control Organisation, Directorate General of Health Services, Ministry of Health and Family Welfare, New Delhi.

Government of the United States 2008, *The Orphan Drug Act (as Amended)*, SEC. 526 [360bb](a)(2), U.S. Food and Drug Administration, Washington, DC, viewed 24 August 2008, http://www.fda.gov/orphan/oda.htm.

Grabowski, H 2002, 'Patents, innovation and access to new pharmaceuticals', *Journal of International Economic Law*, vol. 5, no. 4, pp. 849–60.

———2005, 'Increasing R&D incentives for neglected diseases: Lessons from the Orphan Drug Act', in KE Maskus & JH Reichman (eds), *International Public Goods and Transfer of Technology under a Globalized Intellectual Property Regime*, Cambridge University Press, New York, pp. 457–80.

Graf von der Schulenburg, JM 2007, *Valuing Pharmaceutical Innovation in the European Union: The German Perspective*, Leibniz University, Hannover, Germany, Presentation, viewed 7 May 2008, http://www.lse.ac.uk/collections/LSEHealth/eventsAndSeminars/MerckSeminar2007/Workshopagendas andpresentations/ByMatthiasGrafvonderSchulenburg.pdf.

Gray, A & Matsebula, T 2003, 'Drug pricing in South Africa- policy and praxis', *Journal of Pharmaceutical Finance, Economics & Policy*, vol. 12, no. 2, pp. 95–121.

Gupta, AS 2004, 'Misplaced initiatives in the health sector', *People's Democracy*, vol. 28, no. 52.

Gupta, I & Trivedi, M 2005, 'Social health insurance redefined: Health for all through coverage for all', *Economic and Political Weekly*, vol. 40, no. 38, pp. 4132–40.

Hansen, R 1979, 'The pharmaceutical development process: Estimates of development costs and times and the effects of proposed regulatory changes', in RI Chien (ed.), *Issues in Pharmaceutical Economics*, Lexington Books, D C Heath & Co, Lexington, MA.

Harten, C & Ballantyne, P 2004, 'The impact of cost sharing within Canadian provincial drug benefit programs: A review', *Journal of Pharmaceutical Finance, Economics & Policy*, vol. 13, no. 1, pp. 35–53.

Harvey, K, Faunce, TA, Lokuge, B & Drahos, P 2004, 'Will the Australia–United States Free Trade Agreement undermine the Pharmaceutical Benefits Scheme?', *The Medical Journal of Australia*, vol. 181, no. 5, pp. 256–9.

Harvey, KJ 2005, 'The Pharmaceutical Benefits Scheme 2003–2004', *Australia and New Zealand Health Policy*, vol. 2, no. 2.

Haub, C & Sharma, OP 2006, 'India's population reality: Reconciling change and tradition', *Population Bulletin*, vol. 61, no. 3.

Hawthorne, F 2003, *The Merck Druggernaut: The Inside Story of a Pharmaceutical Giant*, John Wiley & Sons, Hoboken, New Jersey.

Hayek, FA 1988, *The Fatal Conceit*, University of Chicago Press, Chicago.

Heinen, C & Perry, R 2006, 'Big pharma's Indian renaissance', *Scrip Magazine*, February, p. 33.

Henry, D, Lopert, R & Lang, D 2001, *Levelling the Playing Field: Using Evidence to Determine 'Fair' Drug Prices*, Paper presented to WHO/WTO Workshop on Differential Pricing and Financing of Essential Drugs, Hosbjor, Norway, 8–11 April, viewed 7 September 2005, http://www.wto.org/english/tratop_e/trips_e/hosbjor_presentations_e/37henry_e.pdf.

Hertz, AZ 1997, 'Shaping the trident: Intellectual property under NAFTA, investment protection agreements and at the World Trade Organization', *Canada-United States Law Journal*, vol. 23, pp. 261–326.

Hesse, C 2002, 'The rise of intellectual property, 700 B.C.–A.D. 2000: An idea in the balance', *Daedalus*, vol. 131, no. 2, pp. 26–45.

Hiddleston, S 2007, 'No need to patent small changes', *Frontline*, vol. 24, no. 5.

Hoekman, B 2002, 'The WTO: Functions and basic principles', in B Hoekman, A Mattoo & P English (eds), *Development, Trade, and the WTO: A Handbook*, The International Bank for Reconstruction and Development/The World Bank, Washington, DC.

Hofstede, G 2001, *Culture's Consequences: Comparing Values, Behaviors, Institutions and Organizations Across Nations*, Sage Publications, Thousand Oaks, Calif.

Hollis, A 2005, *An Efficient Reward System for Pharmaceutical Innovation*, Institute of Health Economics, Department of Economics, University of Calgary, Calgary.

Hope, J 2003, 'Biotechnology project', Open source, Research School of Social Sciences, Australian National University, Canberra, viewed 17 November 2006, http://rsss.anu.edu.au/~janeth/Law.html.

House of Commons Health Committee 2005, *The Influence of the Pharmaceutical Industry*, Government of the United Kingdom, London.

Hughes, JW, Moore, MJ & Snyder, EA 2002, '"Napsterizing" pharmaceuticals: Access, innovation and consumer welfare', Working paper no. 9229, National Bureau of Economic Research, Cambridge, MA, October.

Humer, FB 2005, 'Innovation in the pharmaceutical industry: Future prospects', Talk to the Zuericher Volkswirtschaftliche Gesellschaft, Roche Pharmaceuticals, Zurich, 16 March.

Ibrahim, MIM & Bahri, S 2003, 'Drug policies and pricing mechanism: The Malaysian perspective', *Journal of Pharmaceutical Finance, Economics & Policy*, vol. 12, no. 1, pp. 77–94.

IDR 2008, *IDR Pharmacy Triple Compendium*, Indian Drug Review, vol. 13, November 2007–January 2008.

IFPMA 2004, 'Encouragement of New Clinical Drug Development: The Role of Data Exclusivity', International Federation of Pharmaceutical Manufacturers Associations, Geneva.

IMF 2008, 'Report for selected countries and subjects', *World Economic Outlook Database*, International Monetary Fund, Washington, DC, viewed 15 July 2008, http://www.imf.org/external/pubs/ft/weo/2008/01/weodata/weorept.aspx?sy=2006&ey=2013&scsm=1&ssd=1&sort=country&ds=.&br=1&c=534&s=NGDP_R%2CNGDP_RPCH%2CNGDP%2CNGDPD%2CNGDPPC%2CNGDPDPC%2CPPPGDP%2CPPPPC&grp=0&a=&pr.x=67&pr.y=2.

IMS Health 2004, *IMS Lifecycle Incorporating R&D Focus, New Product Focus, and Patent Focus*, CD, London, November.

INHATA 2008, 'IQWiG – Institut für Qualität und Wirtschaftlichkeit im Gesundheitswesen', *Global Networking for Effective Healthcare*, viewed 30 September 2008, http://www.inahta.org/Members/IQWiG/.

Insurance Regulatory and Development Authority (IRDA) 2007, *Annual Report 2005–06*, Hyderabad.

———2008, *Annual Report 2006–07*, Hyderabad.

Inter-Ministerial Consultative Committee (IMCC) 2007, *Report on Steps to be Taken by Government of India in the Context of Data Protection Provisions of Article 39.3 of TRIPS Agreement*, Department of Chemicals and Petrochemicals, Ministry of Chemicals and Fertilizers, Government of India, New Delhi.

IP-Watch 2006, 'Pretest submitted to first patent filing of HIV/AIDS drug in India', Intellectual Property Watch, Geneva, viewed 28 October 2008, http://www.ip-watch.org/weblog/index.php?p=254&print=1.

Jack, W & Lanjouw, JO 2005, 'Financing pharmaceutical innovation: How much should poor countries contribute?', *The World Bank Economic Review*, vol. 19, no. 1, January, pp. 45–67.

Jatania, P 2004, 'In search of the sugar-coating: The new product patents regime will decide the future of hundreds of leukaemia patients', *Indian Express*, 19 December.

Jeremy, D 2004, 'Patents and Technology Transfer Between Nations: 1790–1851: Help, Hindrance or Irrelevance: Lessons from History', paper presented to Intellectual Property Rights, Economic Development, and Social Welfare: What does History tell us?, Ironbridge Gorge Museum, Coalbrookdale, 26 April.

Jorge, MF 2004, 'TRIPS-plus provisions in trade agreements and their potential adverse effects on public health', *Journal of Generic Medicines*, vol. 1, no. 3, pp. 199–211.

Jyothi-Datta, PT 2006, 'Roche gets product patent on Hepatitis C', *The Hindu Business Line*, 3 March.

Kamath, G 2004, 'Is the pharma dream run over?', *Business World India*, 1 November.

———2007, 'Beyond generics: Indian pharma companies are hiving off R&D units into separate companies in their quest for new drugs', *Business World*, 28 December.

Kamath, G & Krishnan, GS 2004, 'Generics market: Creeping acquisition', *Business World*, 2 August, p. 8.

Kassirer, JP 2005, *On the Take: How Medicine's Complicity with Big Business can Endanger your Health*, Oxford University Press, New York.

Kaul, S 2004, 'In better health than ever: Zydus Cadila prepares itself for the challenges of the post WTO era', *Business India*, 26 April–9 May, pp. 61–5.

Keayla, BK 1996, 'New patent regime: Implications for domestic industry, research and development and consumers', National Working Group on Patent Laws, Centre for Study on GATT Laws, New Delhi.

Khan, BZ 2002, 'Intellectual property and economic development: Lessons from American and European history', Study paper 1a, Commission on Intellectual Property Rights, viewed 24 October 2008, http:www.iprcommission.org/papers/word/study_papers/sp1a_khan_study.doc.

Khosla, R & Hunt, P 2008, *Human Rights Guidelines for Pharmaceutical Companies in Relation to Access to Medicines*, Human Rights Centre, University of Essex, viewed 1 February 2010, http://www.essex.ac.uk/human_rights_centre/research/rth/docs/Final_pharma_for_website.pdf.

Klein, N 2003, 'Bush's AIDS test', *The Nation*, 27 October, p. 12.

Knowledge at Wharton 2008, 'An increasingly affluent Middle India is harder to ignore', *India Knowledge@Wharton*, viewed 12 July 2008, http://knowledge.wharton.upenn.edu/india/articlepdf/4303.pdf?CFID=74092837&CFTOKEN=85340977&jsessionid=9a3095fb819e56262155.

Koshy, S 1995, 'The effects of TRIPS on Indian Patent Law: A pharmaceutical perspective', *Boston University Journal of Science & Technology Law*, vol. 1, no. 4, pp. 123–49.

KPMG 2006a, *The Indian Pharmaceutical Industry: Collaboration for Growth*, KPMG International, Mumbai.

KPMG 2006b, *India Pharma Inc Competing Globally*, KPMG International, Mumbai.

Kremer, M 2002, 'Pharmaceuticals and the developing world', *Journal of Economic Perspectives*, vol. 16, no. 4, pp. 67–90.

Kremer, M & Glennerster, R 2004, *Strong Medicine: Creating Incentives for Pharmaceutical Research on Neglected Diseases*, Princeton University Press, Princeton.

Kumar, R 2008, 'Encourage innovation with holistic approach: Basheer', *The Hindu Business Online*, 13 October, viewed 31 October 2008, http://www.hindu.com/biz/2008/10/13/stories/2008101350051600.htm.

Labonte, R & Schrecker, T 2006, *Globalization and Social Determinants of Health: Analytic and Strategic Review Paper*, Institute of Population Health, University of Ottawa, 11 March, viewed 11 November 2008, http://www.who.int/social_determinants/resources/globalization.pdf.

Lacetera, N 2001, 'Corporate governance and the governance of innovation: The case of the pharmaceutical industry', *Journal of Management and Governance*, vol. 5, no. 1, pp. 29–59.

Lalitha, N 2002, 'Indian pharmaceutical industry in WTO regime', *Economic and Political Weekly*, vol. 37, no. 34, 24–30 August.

Lall, S 1974, 'The international pharmaceutical industry and less-developed countries, with special reference to India', *Oxford Bulletin of Economics and Statistics*, vol. 36, no. 3, pp. 143–72.

Lanjouw, J 1998, 'The Introduction of pharmaceutical product patents in India: Heartless exploitation of the poor and suffering?', Working paper no. 6366, National Bureau of Economic Research, Cambridge, MA, January.

———2002a, 'A new global patents regime for diseases: U.S, and international legal issues', *Harvard Journal of Law & Technology*, vol. 16, no. 1, Fall, pp. 1–40.

———2002b, 'Intellectual property and the availability of pharmaceuticals in poor countries', CGD Working paper no. 5, Centre for Global Development, April, viewed 24 May 2004, http://www.cgdev.org/content/publications/detail/2785.

Lanjouw, JO & Cockburn, IM 2001, 'New pills for poor people? Empirical evidence after GATT', *World Development*, vol. 29, no. 2, pp. 265–89.

Lehman, B 2003, *The Pharmaceutical Industry and the Patent System*, Earth Institute, Columbia University, viewed 12 June 2007, http://www.earthinstitute.columbia.edu/cgsd/documents/lehman.pdf.

Lewis, G, Class, S & Edery, E 2005, 'Growth in moderation', *Scrip Magazine*, February, pp. 28–33.

Lichtenberg, FR 2006, 'Importation and innovation', Working paper no. 12539, National Bureau of Economic Research, Cambridge, MA, September.

Light, DW 2005, 'Making practical markets for vaccines', *PLoS Medicine*, vol. 2, no. 10, p. 271.

Lippoldt, D 2006, 'Intellectual property rights, pharmaceuticals and foreign direct investment', Policy brief, Groupe d'Economie Mondiale de Sciences Po., Paris, November, viewed 27 April 2008, http://gem.sciences-po.fr/content/publications/pdf/lippoldt_IPRs_Pharma_FDI1106.pdf.

Lleras-Muney, A & Lichtenberg, FR 2002, 'The effect of education on medical technology adoption: Are the more educated more likely to use new drugs?', Working paper, no. 9185, National Bureau of Economic Research, Cambridge, MA, September.

Lloyd, I 2002, 'R&D revolution remains just around the corner', *Scrip Magazine*, February, pp. 72–3.

Lofgren, H 2005, 'Purchase commitments: Big business bias or solution to the 'Neglected Disease' dilemma?', *Australian Review of Public Affairs*, 31 October, viewed 12 December 2005, http://www.australianreview.net/digest/2005/10/lofgren.html.

———2007, 'Reshaping Australian drug policy: The dilemmas of generic medicines policy', *Australia and New Zealand Health Policy*, vol. 4, no. 11, pp. 1–4.

Macdonald, S 2002, 'Exploring the hidden costs of patents', in P Drahos & R Mayne (eds), *Global Intellectual Property Rights: Knowledge, Access and Development*, Palgrave Macmillan, New York, pp. 13–39.

Machlup, F 1958, *An Economic Review of the Patent System: Study of the Subcommittee on Patents, Trademarks, and Copyrights of the Committee on the Judiciary*, Presented to Eighty Fifth Congress, Study no. 15, United States Senate, Government of the United States, Washington, DC.

Machlup, F & Penrose, E 1950, 'The patent controversy in the nineteenth century', *The Journal of Economic History*, vol. 10, no. 1, pp. 1–29.

Madanmohan, TR & Krishnan, RT 2003, 'Adaptive strategies in the Indian pharmaceutical industry', *International Journal of Technology and Management*, vol. 25, no. 3–4, pp. 227–46.

Mahal, A 2000, 'Private entry into health insurance in India: An assessment', in D Peters, GNV Ramana & KS Rao (eds), *Private Health Insurance and Public*

Health Goals in India, Report on a National Seminar, World Bank, New Delhi, pp. 46–76.
———2002, 'Health policy challenges for India: Private health insurance and lessons from the international experience', in TN Srinivasan (ed.), *Trade, Finance and Investment in South Asia*, Social Science, New Delhi, pp. 395–463.
Malhotra, P 2008, 'The impact of TRIPS on innovation and exports: A case study of the pharmaceutical industry in India', *Indian Journal of Medical Ethics*, vol. 5, no. 2, pp. 61–5.
Malhotra, P & Grewal, B 2008, 'TRIPS-plus: Free trade agreements jeopardising public health in developing nations', in TV Hoa & C Harvie (eds), *Regional Trade Agreements in Asia*, Edward Elgar, Cheltenham, UK, pp. 216–39.
Managing Intellectual Property 2007, 'AIDS patent first in India', *Weekly News*, 19 December.
Mansfield, E 1986, 'Patents and innovation: An empirical study', *Management Science*, vol. 32, no. 2, pp. 173–81.
———1995, 'Intellectual property protection, direct investment, technology transfer: Germany, Japan and the United States', Discussion paper no. 27, International Finance Corporation, The World Bank, Washington, DC, September.
Mashelkar, RA 2003, 'Whither India with the international patents regime?', *Chemical Business*, April–June, pp. 77–92.
Maskus, K 2000a, 'Intellectual Property Rights and Foreign Direct Investment', Centre for International Economic Studies, University of Adelaide, Adelaide, Australia, May.
———2000b, 'Regulatory standards in the WTO', Working paper 00-1, Institute for International Economics, Washington, January, viewed 16 November 2004, http://www.iie.com/publications/wp/wp.cfm?ResearchID=121.
Maskus, KE & Reichman, JH 2004, 'The globalization of private knowledge goods and the privatization of global public goods', *Journal of International Economic Law*, vol. 7, no. 2, pp. 279–320.
Mathew, J 2006, 'Ranbaxy eyes stake in marketing allies', *Economics Times*, 12 July, viewed 19 July 2006, http://economictimes.indiatimes.com/articleshow/1733416.cms.
———2008, 'Cipla unveils Roche's generic version of anti-infection drug', *Business Standard*, 24 September.
Mathew, T & Torreblanca, M 2005, 'India steps up to the plate', *Scrip Magazine*, November, pp. 47–9.
Mathieu, MP (ed.) 2007, *Parexel's Bio/Pharmaceutical R&D Statistical Sourcebook 2007/2008*, Parexel International Coroporation, Waltham, MA, USA.
May, C & Sell, S 2006, *Intellectual Property Rights: A Critical History*, Lynne Rienner, Boulder, Colorado.
Mayne, R 2002, 'The global campaign on patents and access to medicines: An Oxfam perspective', in P Drahos & R Mayne (eds), *Global Intellectual Property Rights: Knowledge, Access and Development*, Palgrave Macmillan, New York, pp. 244–58.
———2005, 'Regionalism, bilateralism, and 'TRIPS Plus' agreements: The threat to developing countries', United Nations Development Program, Occasional Paper no. 2005/18, viewed 6 September 2005, http://hdr.undp.org/docs/publications/background_papers/2005/HDR2005_Mayne_Ruth_18.pdf.

Mazumdar-Shaw, K 2007, 'Biotechnology Partnering Opportunities with India', paper presented to BioBreakfast, Melbourne Town Hall, 16 March.

McEwan, JG 2005, 'Is the cure worse than the disease? An overview of the Patent Reform Act of 2005', *The John Marshall Review of Intellectual Property Law*, vol. 5, no. 1, pp. 55–77.

McLachlan, AJ, Ramzan, I & Milne, RW 2007, 'Frequently asked questions about generic medicines', *Australian Prescriber*, vol. 30, no. 2, pp. 41–3.

Medicines Australia 2008, 'Global pharmaceutical industry: Facts at a glance', Canberra, March, viewed 17 November 2008, http://www.medicinesaustralia.com.au/pages/images/Global%20-%20facts%20at%20a%20glance.pdf.

Medico Friends Circle 2006, 'Submission to the Government of India: A balanced pharmaceutical policy', Pune, 10 July, viewed 17 October 2008, http://www.mfcindia.org/PMdrugpricing.html.

MedIndia 2007, 'Patents: Appellate board becomes functional', MedIndia.com, Chennai, 10 April, viewed 28 May 2007, http://www.medindia.net/news/view_news_main.asp?x=19886.

Melethil, S 2005, 'Patent issues in drug development: Perspectives of a pharmaceutical scientist-attorney', *The American Association of Pharmaceutical Scientists (AAPS) Journal*, vol. 7, no. 3, pp. E723–28.

Minwalla, S 2003, 'Drug promotion in India', *Healthy Skepticism International News*, vol. 21, no. 9, viewed 10 June 2008, http://www.healthyskepticism.org/publications/editions/2003/9.htm.

Misra, R, Chatterjee, R & Rao, S 2003, *India Health Report*, Oxford University Press, New Delhi.

Mokyr, J 1990, *The Lever of Riches: Technological Creativity and Economic Progress*, Oxford University Press, London.

Morag-Sela, T, Cohn, I, Kowalski, TJ, Jarecki-Black, J & Clyde-Watson, Z 2004, 'Intellectual property law in Israel, and US and European objections: Market exclusivity vs. data exclusivity', *Nature Biotechnology*, vol. 22, no. 12, pp. 1591–2.

Moran, M 2001, 'Bitter medicine: Why the developing world can't get drugs', *On Line Opinion*, 15 April, viewed 25 January 2006 http://www.onlineopinion.com.au/view.asp?article=1971.

———2005, 'A breakthrough in R&D for neglected diseases: New ways to get the drugs we need', *PLOS*, vol. 2, no. 9, viewed 12 December 2005, http://medicine.plosjournals.org/perlserv/?request=get-document&doi=10.1371/journal.pmed.0020302.

MSF 2008, 'Pre-grant opposition victory in India', *Campaign for Access to Essential Medicines*, viewed 28 October 2008, http://www.msfaccess.org/main/access-patents/pre-grant-opposition-victory-in-india/.

Mueller, JM 2007a, 'Taking TRIPS to India: Novartis, patent law, access to medicines', *The New England Journal of Medicine*, vol. 356, no. 6, pp. 541–3.

———2007b, 'The tiger awakens: The tumultuous transformation of India's patent system and the rise of Indian pharmaceutical innovation', *University of Pittsburgh Law Review*, vol. 68, no. 3, pp. 491–641, viewed 24 April 2007, http://lawreview.law.pitt.edu/issues/68/68.3/Mueller.pdf.

Mukherjee, S 2005, 'Pharmaceutical research and development in India – Looking up?', *Business Briefing: Pharma Outsourcing*, 11 March, pp. 98–103.

Mukreja, DN 2004, 'Against all sceptics', *Business World*, 16 August, pp. 29–34.

Murray, CJL & Lopez, AD (eds) 1996, *The Global Burden of Disease: A Comprehensive Assessment of Mortality and Disability from Diseases, Injuries, and Risk Factors in 1990 and Projected to 2020*, Global Burden of Disease and Injury Series, Volume I, The Harvard School of Public Health on behalf of the World Health Organization and the World Bank, Cambridge, MA.

mX 2006, 'Record deal ends tax row', *mX*, 12 September, p. 11.

Nagendranath, A & Chari, P 2002, *Health Insurance in India: The Emerging Paradigms*, Paper presented to Insurance '02: A Seminar on the Emerging Issues in the Indian Insurance Sector, IIFT-School of International Business Management, New Delhi, 6 September.

Nanda, N 2006, *Options for Using Competition Law/Policy Tools in Dealing with Anti-Competitive Practices in the Pharmaceutical Industry and the Heath Delivery System*, Report Prepared for World Health Organization & Ministry of Health and Family Welfare, Government of India, CUTS Centre for Competition, Investment and Economic Regulation (CUTS C-CIER), CUTS International, Jaipur.

Nanda, N & Khan, A 2005, 'Competition policy for the pharmaceuticals sector in India', in P Mehta (ed.), *Towards a Functional Competition Policy for India*, Academic Foundation, New Delhi.

Nard, CA & Morriss, AP 2006, 'Constitutionalizing patents: From Venice to Philadelphia', *Review of Law & Economics*, vol. 2, no. 2, pp. 223–321.

Narrain, S 2004, 'A life-saving order', *Frontline*, vol. 21, no. 15.

———2005, 'A costly prescription', *Frontline*, vol. 22, no. 4.

Narula, R 2004, 'A recipe for litigation', *Scrip Magazine*, June, p. 39.

NIPER 2006, *Impact of TRIPS on Pharmaceutical Prices, with Specific Focus on Generics in India*, National Institute of Pharmaceutical Education and Research, Department of Chemicals and Petrochemicals, Ministry of Chemicals and Fertilizers, Government of India, Mohali.

NISTADS 2005, *Indian Patenting Activity in International and Domestic Patent System: Contemporary Scenario*, National Institute of Science Technology and Development Studies, Office of the Principal Scientific Advisor to the Government of India, New Delhi.

Nordmann, RM 1997, 'A quarter century of monumental change', *Scrip Magazine*, April, pp. 28–9.

North, DC 1968, 'Source of productivity change in ocean shipping 1600–1850', *Journal of Political Economy*, vol. 76, no. 5, September/October, pp. 953–70.

Novartis 2004, 'Novartis India Analyst Meeting', Novartis India, 16 July 2004.

Nunnenkamp, P & Spatz, J 2003, 'Intellectual property rights and foreign direct investment: The role of industry and host-country characteristics', Kiel Working Paper no. 1167, Kiel Institute for World Economics, Kiel, Germany, June.

OECD 2001, *Report on Competition and Regulation Issues in the Pharmaceutical Industry*, Organisation for Economic Co-operation and Development, Paris.

———2008, *Pharmaceutical Pricing Policies in a Global Market*, Directorate for Employment, Labour and Social Affairs, Organisation for Economic Co-operation and Development, Paris.

OneIndia 2007, 'Rs 750 Crore Rashtriya Swasthya Bima Yojana Launched', viewed 17 June 2008, http://news.oneindia.mobi/2007/10/03/451757.html.

OPPI 2003, 'Pharmaceutical Industry in India: Fact Sheet – 2003', Organisation of Pharmaceutical Producers of India, Mumbai, viewed 9 August 2005. http://www.indiaoppi.com/keystat.htm.

———2006, 'Indian pharmaceutical industry: Fact sheet – 2004', Organisation of Pharmaceutical Producers of India, viewed 12 February 2006, http://www.indiaoppi.com/keystat.htm.

Outterson, K 2008, 'Should access to medicines and TRIPS flexibilities be limited to specific diseases?', *American Journal of Law & Medicine*, vol. 34, no. 2, pp. 317–38.

Oxfam 2002, *Rigged Rules and Double Standards: Trade, Globalisation, and the Fight Against Poverty*, Oxfam International, London.

Palit, A & Nawani, S 2007, 'Technological capability as a determinant of FDI inflows: Evidence from developing Asia and India' Working paper no. 193, Indian Council for Research on International Economic Relations, New Delhi, April, viewed 23 September 2008, http://www.icrier.org/pdf/Working_Paper_193.pdf.

Pammolli, F & Riccaboni, M 2007, *Innovation and Industrial Leadership: Lessons from Pharmaceuticals*, Center for Transatlantic Relations, The Johns Hopkins University, Washington, DC.

Patent Lens 2009, 'Initiative for open innovation', Canberra, viewed 9 January 2009, http://www.patentlens.net/daisy/patentlens/2973.html.

Patnaik, U 2010, 'Trends in Urban Poverty Under Economic Reforms: 1993–94 to 2004–05', *Economic and Political Weekly*, vol. 45, no. 4, pp. 42–54.

Perlitz, U 2008, *India's Pharmaceutical Industry on Course for Globalisation*, Deutsche Bank Research, Frankfurt, 9 April, viewed 11 August 2008, http://www.dbresearch.com/PROD/DBR_INTERNET_EN-PROD/PROD0000000000224095.pdf.

Pettypiece, S 2006, 'Pfizer shops for drugs, profits', *Detroit Free Press*, 1 July, viewed 3 July 2006, http://www.freep.com/apps/pbcs.dll/article?AID=20060701/BUSIENESS06/607010363/1019/BUSINESS.

Pfizer 2005, *Hatch-Waxman Economics: Balanced Incentives are the Key*, Pfizer Inc, New York.

———2007, *Annual Review*, Pfizer Inc. New York.

Phadke, A 2000, 'End of drug control?', *India-Seminar*, viewed 25 September 2008, http://www.india-seminar.com/2000/489/489%20phadke.htm.

Pharmaceutical & Drug Manufacturers 2005a, 'Indian pharmaceutical industry: An overview', viewed 12 June 2005, http://www.pharmaceutical-drug-manufacturers.com/pharmaceutical-industry/.

———2005b, 'Number of units, pharma industry statistics', viewed 3 November 2005, http://www.pharmaceutical-drug-manufacturers.com/pharma-industry-statistics/.

PhRMA 2002, *Annual Report*, Pharmaceutical Research and Manufacturers of America, Washington, DC.

———2004, *Industry Profile*, Pharmaceutical Research and Manufacturers of America, Washington.

———2007, *Annual Report*, Pharmaceutical Research and Manufacturers of America, Washington, DC.

———2008a, *Annual Report*, Pharmaceutical Research and Manufacturers of America, Washington, DC.

——2008b, *Pharmaceutical Industry Profile 2008*, Pharmaceutical Research and Manufacturers of America, Washington, DC.

Pogge, T 2008, 'Access to medicines', *Public Health Ethics*, vol. 1, no. 2, pp. 73–82.

Posner, RA 2002, 'The law and economics of intellectual property', *Daedalus*, vol. 131, no. 2, pp. 5–12.

Pradhan, S 1983, *International Pharmaceutical Marketing*, Quorum Books, Westport, CT.

Prahalad, CK 2005, *The Fortune at the Bottom of the Pyramid: Eradicating Poverty Through Profits*, Wharton School Publishing, Upper Saddle River, NJ.

Public Citizen 2001, *Rx R&D myths: The Case Against the Drug Industry's Scare Card*, Public Citizen Congress Watch, Washington, DC, July, viewed 9 September 2003, http://www.citizen.org/documents/ACFDC.PDF.

Pugatch, MP 2004, *Intellectual Property and Pharmaceutical Data Exclusivity in the Context of Innovation and Market Access*, paper presented to Dialogue on Ensuring Policy Options for Affordable Access to Essential Medicines, Bellagio, Italy, 12–16 October.

Ram, P 2006, 'India's new TRIPS-Compliant patent regime: Between drug patents and the right to health', *Chicago-Kent Journal of Intellectual Property*, vol. 5, no. 2, Spring, pp. 195–206.

Rangnekar, D 2005, 'No pills for poor people? Understanding the disembowelment of India's patent regime', *Economic and Political Weekly*, vol. 41, no. 5, pp. 409–17.

Raymus, P 2007, *Review of Healthcare in India*, Centre for Enquiry into Health and Allied Themes, New Delhi, January, viewed 1 July 2008, http://www.cehat.org/infocentre/r51tables1.pdf#page=373.

Reichman, JH 2000, 'The TRIPS Agreement comes of age: Conflict of cooperation with the developing countries?', *Case Western Reserve Journal of International Law*, vol. 32, no. 3, pp. 441–70.

Reichmann, JH 1998, 'Securing compliance with the TRIPS agreement after US v India', *Journal of International Economic Law*, vol. 1, no. 4, pp. 586–601.

Reserve Bank of India (RBI) 2005, *Exchange Control Manual: Foreign/FERA Companies and Foreign Nationals*, Reserve Bank of India, Government of India, 31 May, viewed 21 February 2007, http://www.rbi.org.in/upload/ECM/pdfs/Chapter11.pdf.

——2007, *State Finances: A Study of Budgets of 2006–07*, Reserve Bank of India, Government of India, New Delhi.

——2008, *Annual Report 2007–08*, Reserve Bank of India, Government of India, New Delhi.

Rhein, R 2001, 'Canada keeps costs in check', *Scrip Magazine*, February, pp. 24–5.

Rogers, A 1994, 'Patents in Argentina: Problems and paradoxes', *Scrip Magazine*, December, pp. 10–1.

Roumeliotis, G 2006, 'India set to overtake Italy in API production', viewed 28 August 2006, http://www.in-pharmatechnologist.com/Materials-Formulation/India-set-to-overtake-Italy-in-API-production.

Roy, N & Madhiwala, N 2003, *Surviving the Indian Pharmatical Jungle*, Forum for Medical Ethics, Mumbai.

Ruston, G 1955, 'On the origin of trademarks', *The Trade-Mark Reporter*, vol. 45, no. 2, pp. 127–44.

Sachs, JD 2000, 'A new map of the world', *The Economist*, 22 June.

Sager, A & Socolar, D 2006, 'Massachusetts health spending soars to $62.1 billion in 2006: Spending here is world's highest – 33% per person above USA average, an unprecedented excess', Boston University School of Public Health, Health Reform Program, Boston, 28 June, viewed 17 July 2007, http://dccwww.bumc.bu.edu/hs/Mass%20Health%20Spending%20Soars%20to%20$62%201%20Billion%20in%202006%20FINAL%2028June.pdf.

Sakthivel, S 2005, 'Access to essential drugs and medicine', *Financing and Delivery of Health Care Services in India*, Commission on Macroeconomic and Health, and Ministry of Health and Family Welfare, New Delhi, pp. 185–212.

Santerre, RE & Vernon, JA 2005, 'Assessing consumer gains from a drug price control policy in the U.S.', Working paper no. 11139, National Bureau of Economic Research, Cambridge, MA, February.

———2006, 'Assessing consumer gains from a drug price control policy in the United States', *Southern Economic Journal*, vol. 73, no. 1, pp. 233–45.

Sauer, C & Sauer, RM 2007, 'Is it possible to have cheaper drugs and preserve the incentive to innovate? The benefits of privatizing the drug approval process', *Journal of Technology Transfer*, vol. 32, no. 5, pp. 509–24.

Saunders, P 1999, 'It's time to call a halt to poor drug donation practice', *Scrip Magazine*, September, pp. 7–9.

Scherer, FM 2000, 'The pharmaceutical industry', in JP Newhouse (ed.), *Handbook of Health Economics*, Volume. I, Elsevier, Amsterdam, pp. 1297–336.

———2001, 'The link between gross profitability and pharmaceutical R&D spending', *Health Affairs*, vol. 20, no. 5, September/October, pp. 216–20.

———2002, 'A Note on Global Welfare in Pharmaceutical Patenting', Federal Reserve Bank of Philadelphia, Philadelphia, November, Working paper no. 03–11, viewed 11 May 2007, <http://ssrn.com/abstract=570565>.

———2007, 'Uncertainty and choice: The challenges of pharmaceutical efficacy, safety and cost', *Managerial and Decision Economics*, vol. 28, no. 4–5, pp. 267–83.

Scherer, FM & Watal, J 2001, *The Economics of Parallel Trade in Pharmaceutical Products*, Paper presented to WHO/WTO Workshop on Differential Pricing and Financing of Essential Drugs, Hosbjor, Norway, 8–11 April, viewed 5 January 2004, http://www.wto.org/english/tratop_e/trips_e/hosbjor_presentations_e/hosbjor_presentations_e.htm.

Scherer, FM & Weisburst, S 1995, 'Economic effects of strengthening pharmaceutical patent protection in Italy', *International Review of Industrial Property and Copyright Law*, vol. 138, no. 26, pp. 1009–24.

Schiff, E 1971, *Industrialisation Without National Patents: The Netherlands, 1869–1912; Switzerland, 1850–1907*, Princeton University Press, Princeton, NJ.

Schneider, F & Frey, BS 1985, 'Economic and political determinants of foreign direct investment', *World Development*, vol. 13, no. 2, pp. 161–75.

Schreyoegg, J & Busse, R 2005, 'Physician-drug budgets in Germany and effects on prescription behaviour', *Journal of Pharmaceutical Finance, Economics & Policy*, vol. 14, no. 3, pp. 77–95.

Schweitzer, SO 1997, *Pharmaceutical Economics and Policy*, Oxford University Press, New York.

Scott, A 2006, 'Blockbuster drug numbers increase', *Chemical Week*, vol. 168, no. 12, p. 31.

Scrip 2006, 'Company partnerships', *Scrip 100*, Informa Plc, London, p. 25.

Scrip News 2005a, 'Canadian industry can expel firms for marketing offences', *Scrip News*, no. 3114, 9 December.
———2005b, Indian proposal for generic prescribing opposed, *Scrip News*, vol. 3072, 15 July, p. 18.
———2005c, 'US payers stand to benefit from targeted medicine', *Scrip News*, vol. 3117, p. 13.
———2005d, 'World's scientists get $436 million to tackle diseases', *Scrip News*, vol. 3069, p. 15.
Sen, A 2002, 'How to judge globalism: Global links have spread knowledge and raised average living standards, but the present version of globalism needlessly harms the world's poorest', *The American Prospect*, vol. 13, no. 1, pp. A2–6.
Seyoum, B 1996, 'The impact of intellectual property rights on foreign direct investment', *Columbia Journal of World Business*, vol. 31, no. 1, pp. 50–9.
Shadlen, K 2009, 'Reforming and reinforcing the revolution: The post-TRIPS politics of patents in Latin America', Working paper no. 09–02, Global development and Environment Institute, Tufts University, April.
Shah, D 2003, *Experience of India*, Paper presented to The Role of Generics and Local Industry in Attaining the MDGs in Pharmaceuticals and Vaccines, World Bank, Washington, DC, 24–25 June, viewed 4 July 2007, wbln0018.worldbank.org/HDNet/hddocs.nsf/9b2b70eeb6c333fb852568aa0073e2a1/dc5eece4d602253685256d4a004c41ce.
Shiva, V 2004, 'TRIPS, human rights and the public domain', *The Journal of World Intellectual Property*, vol. 7, no. 5, pp. 665–73.
Singh, K 2008, 'NGO to seek compulsory licensing of cancer drugs', *Economic Times*, 31 March.
Singleton, A 2006, 'Can pharmaceuticals be developed without patents?', Samizdata.net, London, 9 January, viewed 23 February 2006, http://www.samizdata.net/blog/archives/008450.html.
Sketris, I, Bowles, S & Manuel, R 2003, 'Canadian public policies and practices related to drug prices, utilization and expenditures', *Journal of Pharmaceutical Finance, Economics & Policy*, vol. 12, no. 1, pp. 23–54.
Smith, SE 2000, *Opening Up to the World: India's Pharmaceutical Companies Prepare for 2005*, Asia/Pacific Research Center, Institute for International Studies, Stanford University, Stanford.
So, AD 2004, 'A fair deal for the future: Flexibilities under TRIPS', *Bulletin of the World Health Organization*, vol. 82, no. 11, pp. 813–4.
Solow, RM 1957, 'Technical change and the aggregate production', *The Review of Economics and Statistics*, vol. 39, no. 3, August, pp. 312–20.
Srinivasan, S 2008, 'How TRIPS benefits Indian industry and how it may not benefit the Indian people', *Indian Journal of Medical Ethics*, vol. V, no. 2, pp. 66–9.
Stiglitz, JE 2002a, 'Globalism's discontents: Integration with the global economy works just fine when sovereign countries define the terms, it works disastrously when terms are dictated', *The American Prospect*, vol. 13, no. 1, pp. A16–21.
———2002b, *Globalization and its Discontents*, W.W. Norton & Company, New York.
———2006, *Making Globalization Work*, W.W. Norton and Company, New York.

Stoate, N 2001/2002, 'EU enlargement, the Bolar exemption and parallel imports: The consequences for market exclusivity', *Bio Science Law Review*, vol. 5, no. 5, pp. 161–82.

Swain, N, Mishra, C, Jayasimha, K & Vijayalakshmi, S 2002, 'Indian pharmaceutical industry: An analysis', *The Icfaian Journal of Management Research*, vol. 1, no. 6, pp. 5–28.

Sweeny, K 2002, *The Technological Revolution*, Paper presented to Pharmaceuticals in Australia: Access, Costs and Industry Development, Melbourne, 16 September.

———2008, 'Accounting for growth in the pharmaceutical benefits scheme', PhD Book, Victoria University, Melbourne, Australia, April.

Tamilnadu Pharmaceutical Sciences Welfare Trust 2008, 'Drugs approved by the Drugs Controller General (India) during January 1988 to August 2006', viewed 12 December 2008, http://www.pictrust.com/links/newdrugs.phtml.

Taylor, P 2005, 'Sun pharma buys hungarian plant', *In-Pharmatechnologist*, viewed 9 September 2005, http://www.in-pharmatechnologist.com/news/news-ng.asp?id=61850-sun-generic-india-hungary.

The Economist 2005a, 'Alternative medicine: Neglected diseases are fighting for attention', *The Economist*, 16 June, pp. 8–9.

———2005b, 'Health at a glance: OECD indicators', *The Economist*, 16 June.

The Expert Committee 2003, *Report of the Expert Committee on a Comprehensive Examination of Drug Regulatory Issues, Including the Problem of Spurious Drugs*, Ministry of Health and Family Welfare, Government of India, New Delhi.

The Sen Committee 2005, *Report: Task Force to Explore Options Other Than Price Control for Achieving the Objective of Making Available Life-Saving Drugs at Reasonable Prices*, Department of Chemicals and Petrochemicals, Government of India, New Delhi.

The Seth Committee 2004, *National List of Essential Medicines 2003*, Directorate General of Health Services, Ministry of Health and Family Welfare, Government of India, New Delhi.

The Tribune 2004, 'Government to cut prices of drugs', *The Tribune*, 22 December.

The Wharton School 2008, *Eli Lilly's Rajiv Gulati on Pharma's Prospects in India and China*, The Wharton School, The University of Pennsylvania, 16 October, viewed 18 October 2008, http://knowledge.wharton.upenn.edu/india/articlepdf/4325.pdf?CFID=75279634&CFTOKEN=29111060&jsessionid=a83096d931ea33394241.

Timmermans, K 2007, 'Monopolizing clinical trial data: Implications and trends', *PLoS Medicine*, vol. 4, no. 2, pp. 206–10.

Torbet, J 1999, 'Globalisation and its impact on access to medicines', *Scrip Magazine*, May, pp. 8–10.

UNCTAD 2005, *World Investment Report: Transnational Corporations and the Internationalization of R&D*, United Nations Conference on Trade and Development, New York.

———2007, *World Investment Report: Transnational Corporations, Extractive Industries and Development*, United Nations Conference on Trade and Development, New York.

UNCTC 1993, *World Investment Report: Transnational Corporations and Integrated International Production*, The United Nations Centre on Transnational Corporations, New York.

UNDP 2003, *Making Global Trade Work for People*, Earthscan Publications, London.
———2005, *Human Development Report*, United Nations Development Programme, Geneva.
United Nations 2005a, *India Demographic Profile 2000–2050*, United Nations Population Division, Department of Economic and Social Affairs, New York, viewed 12 August 2008, http://esa.un.org/unpp/p2k0data.asp.
———2005b, *World Population Prospects: The 2004 Revision*, Department of Economic and Social Affairs, Population Division, New York.
Verband der Forschender Arzeneimittelhersteller 2007, *Heath Care Reform 2007*, German Association of Research-based Pharmaceutical Companies, 27 March, viewed 23 July 2007, http://www.vfa.de/en/articles/art_2007-03_010.html.
Verheugen, G 2005, 'Commission push on pharma innovation', viewed 1 June 2007, http://www.euractive.com/Article?tcmuri=tcm:29-140360-16&type=News.
Vernon, JA & Manning, RL 2007, 'Editorial', *Managerial and Decision Economics*, vol. 28, no. 4–5, p. 229.
Weissman, R 2007, 'Big pharma and AIDS: Act II patents and the price of second-line treatment', *Multinational Monitor*, vol. 28, no. 2.
WHO 2002a, 'Promoting rational use of medicines: Core components', *WHO Policy Perspectives on Medicines, no. 5,* World Health Organization, Geneva.
———2002b, 'The selection of essential medicines', *WHO Policy Perspectives on Medicine, no. 4,* World Health Organization, Geneva.
———2002c, *The World Health Report 2002: Reducing Risks, Promoting Healthy Life*, World Health Organization, Geneva.
———2003a, 'Effective medicines regulation: Ensuring safety, efficacy and quality', *WHO Policy Perspectives on Medicine, no. 7,* World Health Organization, Geneva.
———2003b, 'How to develop and implement a national drug policy', *WHO Policy Perspectives on Medicine, no. 6*, World Health Organization, Geneva.
———2004a, 'Equitable access to essential medicines: A framework for collective action', *WHO Policy Perspective on Medicines, no. 8*, World Health Organization, Geneva.
———2004b, *The World Medicines Situation*, World Health Organization, Geneva.
———2006a, 'Elements of a global strategy and plan of action, A/PHI/IGWG/1/4', Intergovernmental Working Group on Public Health, Innovation and Intellectual Property, World Health Organization, Geneva.
———2006b, *The World Health Report 2006: Working Together for Health*, World Health Organization, Geneva.
———2007, *World Health Report 2007: A Safer Future – Global Public Health Security in the 21st Century*, World Health Organization, Geneva, Switzerland.
WHO/WTO 2001, 'Report of the workshop on differential pricing and financing of essential drugs', *Hosbjor*, Norway, 8–11 April.
Wikipedia 2008, 'Cipla and the fight against HIV/AIDS in the developing world', viewed 21 September 2008, http://en.wikipedia.org/wiki/Cipla.
Wilding, I 2002, 'Injecting innovation into the drug development process', *Scrip Magazine*, October, pp. 15–6.
World Bank 2002, *India: Raising the Sights – Better Health Systems for India's Poor – Findings, Analysis and Options*, World Bank, Washington, DC.

———2003, *The Little Data Book*, The World Bank, Washington, DC.

———2006, *World Development Report: Equity and Development*, The World Bank, Washington, DC.

WTO 1994, *Agreement on Trade-Related Aspects of Intellectual Property Rights (TRIPS)*, The World Trade Organization, Geneva, 15 April, viewed 12 February 2003, http://www.wto.org/english/docs_e/legal_e/27-trips_01_e.htm.

———2000, *Canada: Patent Protection of Pharmaceutical Products*, WT/DS114/R, World Trade Organization, Geneva, 17 March, viewed 17 February 2007, http://www.wto.org/english/tratop_e/dispu_e/7428d.pdf.

———2006a, *10 Common Misunderstandings About the WTO*, World Trade Organization, Geneva.

———2006b, *Compulsory Licensing of Pharmaceuticals and TRIPS*, World Trade Organization, Geneva, viewed 28 May 2007, http://www.wto.org/english/tratop_e/trips_e/public_health_faq_e.htm.

———2010, *Understanding the WTO: The Agreements*, World Trade Organization, Geneva, viewed 16 March 2010, http://www.wto.org/english/thewto_e/whatis_e/tif_e/agrm1_e.htm.

Wyllie, MG 2005, 'Evergreening: There's life in the old drug yet', *British Journal of Urology*, vol. 95, no. 9, 12 May, pp. 1359–60.

Yusuf, A & Moncayo von Hase, A 1992, 'Intellectual property protection and international trade-exhaustion of rights revisited', *World Competition*, vol. 16, no. 1, pp. 115–31.

Zutshi, BK 1998, 'Bring TRIPS into the multilateral trading system', in J Bhagwati & M Hirsch (eds), *The Uruguay Round and Beyond: Essays in Honour of Arthur Dunkel*, Springer, Berlin, pp. 37–49.

Index